H.D.
A BIBLIOGRAPHY
1905–1990

H. D.
A BIBLIOGRAPHY

1905–1990

Michael Boughn

Published for the Bibliographical Society of
the University of Virginia
by the University Press of Virginia
Charlottesville and London

for H.D.
1886–1961
and
E.A.B.
1926–1986

A Linton R. Massey Descriptive Bibliography

THE UNIVERSITY PRESS OF VIRGINIA
Copyright © 1993 by the Rector and Visitors
of the University of Virginia

All material by H.D. copyright © 1993 by Perdita Schaffner. Used by permission of New Directions Publishing Corporation, Agents.
All material by Richard Aldington copyright © 1993 by Alister Kershaw, literary executor for the Estate of Richard Aldington. Used with his permission.
All material from the Grove Press Archives copyright © 1993 by Grove Press. Used with permission of Grove-Wiedenfield and the Grove Press Records, George Arents Research Library for Special Collections at Syracuse University.
Correspondence by H.D. and Richard Aldington reprinted with permission of the Yale Collection of American Literature, Beinecke Rare Book and Manuscript Library, Yale University; Department of Special Collections, University Research Library, University of California at Los Angeles; and The Poetry/Rare Books Collection, University Libraries, State University of New York at Buffalo.

First published 1993

Frontispiece: H.D. and her daughter Perdita. (Courtesy of the Yale Collection of American Literature, Beinecke Rare Book and Manuscript Library, Yale University)

Library of Congress Cataloging-in-Publication Data
Boughn, Michael.
  H.D. : a bibliography, 1905–1990 / Michael Boughn.
    p. cm.
  "A Linton R. Massey descriptive bibliography"—T.p. verso.
  Includes index.
  ISBN 0-8139-1412-4
  1. H. D. (Hilda Doolittle), 1886–1961—Bibliography.   I. Title.
Z8237.4.B68   1993
[PS3507.O726]
016.811'52—dc20   92-28953
                                                                CIP

Printed in the United States of America

Contents

	Acknowledgments	vi
	Bibliographical Method	vii
	Abbreviations	x

Part 1   Work by H.D.

A	Books, Pamphlets, and Broadsides	3
B	Contributions to Books and Pamphlets	83
C	Contributions to Periodicals	95
D	Translations	109
E	Miscellanea	115

Part 2   Work on H.D.

F	Reviews	121
G	Articles in Periodicals	147
H	Books and Parts of Books	165
I	Dissertations and Theses	183
J	Miscellanea	187

	Index of Titles by H.D.	191
	General Index of Titles and Names	197

Acknowledgments

The production of any work such as this necessarily depends on the spiritual, technical, and financial assistance of numerous people. While it is impossible to name them all, I would like to indicate those to whom I am most deeply indebted. The community of spiritual support includes Elizabeth Brown, Betty Cohen, Peter Murphy, Jack and Cass Clarke, and Kay Clark, all of whom continued, at various times, to believe in the importance of this work when I wavered. Without them, the work truly could not have been completed.

To name all the library staff on whom this work was dependent would be impossible, but I am particularly indebted to staff at the Poetry/Rare Books Collection at SUNY Buffalo, including the curator, Robert Bertholf, for allowing me free access to the collection, and especially Michael Basinski and Mark Thackeray for the numerous items they provided. Similarly, Louis Silverstein, the cataloguer of the H.D. collection at the Beinecke Library at Yale, went out of his way to assist me in collecting material. The patience and energy of the interlibrary loan staff at SUNY Buffalo's Lockwood Library was invaluable. Without the dedicated help of Fran Abosch, Ann Hohl, and Anne Clifford, I could not even have begun this project. I also owe thanks to the staff at the Beinecke Library at Yale University.

The initial bibliographical work done by Jackson Bryer and Pamela Robler in their checklist of H.D. published in *Contemporary Literature* 10 (1969) has been essential as a starting point for much of this work. I also received invaluable help from Diana Collecott and from Helmut Salzinger in tracking down some English and German citations. The staff of New Directions guided me through their files and provided invaluable support. I would also like to thank the GRAD Council of the Graduate Student Association of SUNY Buffalo for generously providing me with funding to do some of the necessary research.

Joan Crane, Curator of the Clifton Waller Barrett Library of American Literature at the University of Virginia Library, kindly and generously read the manuscript with great attention to detail. Her copious criticism transformed an earnest but amateur venture into what I hope will be a useful bibliography. My debt to her is incalculable. I would also like to express my gratitude to Kendon Stubbs and Kathryn Morgan of the Bibliographical Society of the University of Virginia who have patiently guided me through the difficult and trying process of publication. Finally, I would like to thank Robin Blaser. In 1968 he lent me his personal copies of the Oxford University Press editions of the war trilogy, then long out of print, thus initiating the interest and devotion on which this work is founded. Twenty years later, he read this manuscript with his usual impeccable intelligence and care.

Bibliographical Method

Every bibliography is unique, its form dependent on the nature of the author's work and the uses to which the bibliographer sees his or her work being put. In general, I have tried to follow the examples of Donald Gallup, Emily Wallace, and Leon Edelstein and to incorporate the most useful features developed in their work. Joan Crane's criticism has also played a decisive role in the final shape of this work.

Format and methods:

Section A lists in chronological order all independently published writings by H.D. including books and pamphlets other than proof copies, which have not been included. The descriptive method is based on that developed by Fredson Bowers in *Principles of Bibliographical Description* and modified by the work of G. Thomas Tanselle. Following Tanselle, I have identified colors using the ISCC-NBS Centroid Color Chart. I have not used, however, the full color names as they appear in the chart. Aesthetically, it becomes very unpleasant and awkward having to read long, ungainly descriptions (i.e., "very deep grayish reddish brown"), unnecessarily complicating already difficult reading. Since most identifications will take place without the benefit of the Centroid Color Chart, a simple visual identification (i.e., light brown, dark brown, or red brown) is much more useful to someone with a book in hand they are trying to identify. For those who feel the need for more detailed identification, the Centroid Color Chart numbers will refer them to an actual color chip corresponding as closely as possible to the color.

In the same spirit, I have avoided unnecessary use of the color chart. Most papers, for example, are identified simply as "cream" or "white." It seems unlikely this will lead to any more confusion than the gratuitous use of color chart numbers and names which, finally, are rarely more than approximations anyway. Similarly, since "black" is black, identification is unnecessary. The same holds true with "gold" or "gilt," "silver," and "white."

Unless otherwise noted, all printing is in black, and all type is roman. Color descriptions in brackets hold true until canceled by a new notation. Punctuation inside quotation marks is part of the description; punctuation outside quotation marks is not. All edges are assumed to be plain and trimmed unless otherwise noted. "Perfect binding" refers to the method of binding in which all pages are cut and held together at the back by adhesive.

As a general principle, I have tried to be as inclusive as possible without overly cluttering the text. Information on copyright pages is transcribed when it is deemed either necessary or useful for identification purposes, or simply interesting. Otherwise it is identified by the number of lines. Whenever possible I have included full descriptions of dust jackets, considering them an important part of the book as produced for sale. In the case of the second impression of H.D.'s *Collected Poems*, for instance, the only indication of a new impression is the dust jacket, which states "Second Edition" on the spine, and the unannounced correction of two typographical errors in the text.

Section B lists the first appearances of work by H.D. in first editions of books. I have not included brief fragments of letters and poems quoted in books and articles or bookseller's and auction catalogs which have printed letters or parts of manuscripts and books. The descriptions are somewhat abbreviated relative to Section A.

Section C includes first periodical appearances of work by H.D. listed chronologically with periodicals covering longer periods coming before those covering shorter ones. If two periodicals have the same date, they are listed alphabetically by title. I have not included complete poems quoted in book reviews, with one or two exceptions which are noted.

Section D lists alphabetically by language translations of H.D.'s work into other languages. Within each language, items are listed chronologically under the headings "Books," "Anthologies," and "Periodicals." I have listed all translations about which I have definite information, but there are undoubtedly others which I have not seen.

Section E lists chronologically miscellaneous appearances of H.D.'s work including musical settings, recordings, certain catalogs and programs, and broadsides and postcards.

Section F lists all reviews of H.D.'s work under the titles of the books which are organized chronologically according to date of publication. Reviews of books which have been reissued are included under the initial publication. Some of the items are incomplete since I was working from clipping files which did not include all the necessary bibliographical information, frequently omitting page numbers, and sometimes the date. Items of this nature which I have been unable to locate for one reason or another are marked with an asterisk (*). Reviews of work relevant to H.D. which include discussions of her are included at the end of this section under the heading "Miscellanea."

Section G lists chronologically all periodical articles and parts of articles which include significant references to H.D.'s life and work. I have not included contextual references, i.e., references which merely mention H.D. as part of a context without otherwise noting or discussing her work.

Section H lists chronologically all books and parts of books devoted to H.D. Where the dates are the same, the books have been organized alphabetically. Again, mere contextual references have not been included.

Section I lists chronologically all dissertations and theses which deal significantly with H.D.

Section J includes a chronological listing of miscellaneous material about H.D. including newspaper articles, published letters, catalogs, programs, photographs, postcards, and obituaries.

The listings, especially in Part 2, are complete only through the end of 1989, although when possible later items have been included.

In compiling the bibliographical entries I have tried to adhere as closely as possible to the rules set forth in the 1985 *MLA Style Manual*, even though this has resulted in some apparent inconsistencies. The revisions in the 1985 edition of *The MLA Style Manual* aim, among other things, at reducing the amount of information in any entry to the absolute minimum needed to locate the given text. Thus a periodical which appears monthly or bimonthly requires less notational information than one which appears irregularly (see sections 4.7.1–4.7.6 in *The MLA Style Manual*). This explains the apparent inconsistency in entries such as **C119** and **C122**. The first describes *Life and Letters Today* using both a volume and issue number, whereas the second identifies the same magazine only by date. This is because *Life and Letters Today* began as a quarterly journal that used only issue numbers and had separate pagination for each issue (*The MLA Style Manual* 4.7.2) and then later switched format to become a regular monthly (*The MLA Style Manual* 4.7.5).

I have used these conventions rather than some other for two reasons. First, this bibliography is directed primarily toward the scholarly constituency which uses *The MLA Style Manual*. Second, the revisions in the latest edition of *The MLA Style Manual* are geared toward the eventual digitalization of all this information in one data base, and I hoped to make this work consistent with and useful to that larger project.

Abbreviations

CaOTU	University of Toronto
CtY	Yale University
CU-Riv	University of California at Riverside
CU-SC	University of California at Santa Cruz
NBu	Buffalo and Erie County Library
NBuU	State University of New York at Buffalo
NDP	New Directions Publishing Corporation
NNC	Columbia University
PPT	Temple University
PU	University of Pennsylvania
CP (1925)	*Collected Poems* (**A6**)
CP (1983)	*Collected Poems* (**A38**)
SP (1957)	*Selected Poems* (**A25**)

Part 1

Work by H.D.

A

Books, Pamphlets, and Broadsides

A1 *Choruses from Iphigeneia in Aulis*

a First edition, 1916

[cover title] The Poet's Translation Series. No. 3. 6d. net. | CHORUSES FROM IPHIGENEIA | IN AULIS | TRANSLATED BY H.D. | [twenty-two-line introduction to the translation]

[A][10]; pp. 1–18 [19–20]. Cream wove paper, 16 × 12.3 cm. A single stapled gathering.

P. 1: cover title; pp. 2–19: text; at foot of p. 19: 'BALLANTYNE PRESS, LONDON'; p. 20: advertisement for the Poet's Translation Series (six titles, twenty-three lines).

Contains *Choruses from Iphigeneia in Aulis*. Reprinted in *CP* (1925) and *CP* (1983).

CtY (3 copies); PPT; CaOTU.

b First American edition, 1916

Choruses from | Iphigeneia in Aulis | Translated from the Greek of | Euripides | *By* H.D. | [device depicting a Greek ship] | Cleveland | The Clerk's Press | 1916

[1][20]; pp. [i–ii] [1–5] 6 [7] 8–35 [36–38]. Cream hand-made paper with horizontal chain lines watermarked 'TUSCANY ITALY [device],' 12.7 × 10 cm. Fore and bottom edges uncut. First and last leaf pastedown endpapers. Cover of heavy medium gray (C265) wove paper pasted over cardboard, 14.1 × 10.9 cm. Front cover: 'THE CHORUSES FROM | IPHIGENEIA IN AULIS'.

Pp. i–ii: blank; p. 1: half title, 'Choruses from | Iphigeneia in Aulis'; p. 2: colophon, 'This edition consists of forty copies only, | printed upon Tuscany hand-made paper. | This is Number [number supplied in pencil]'; p. 3: title page; p. 4: blank; pp. 5–6: introduction; pp. 7–33: text; p. 34: printer's note, 'The publisher of the original English edi-|tion of 'Choruses from Iphigeneia in Aulis,' | Richard Aldington, has kindly given me | permission to make this limited reprint for | some of those friends who are interested in | collecting the publications of The Clerk's | Press. Of the translation it is sufficient to | say that it was made by a poet who has in-|terpreted the spirit of the original. It has | been highly praised in England, especially | by Professor J.W. Mackail, a translator | himself of recognized ability. | [¶] If by means of this booklet an apprecia-|tion of the work of the 'Poets' Translation | Series' is extended in Cleveland the pleasure | derived from setting the type and printing | will be the Clerk's sufficient reward.'; p. 35: printer's impress, 'Typography and Presswork by Charles C. | Bubb, Clerk in Holy Orders [dot] August 12 [dot] | CLEVELAND : PRINTED AT THE | [device: double cross with heart on shield] | CLERK'S PRIVATE PRESS MCMXVI'; pp. 36–38: blank.

40 copies published 12 August 1916.

In a letter to Charles C. Bubb dated 19 June 1916, Richard Aldington wrote: "Do you wish to reprint the first six pamphlets or the second six [i.e., *The Egoist* Poets' Translation Series pamphlets]? Suppose, as an experiment, you try number 3, the choruses number 3, the choruses from Iphigeneia, which has been very highly praised here, among others by Professor J.W. Mackail, whose fine translations must be known to you. If you printed fifty copies privately, reserving the author's copyright, I think there would be no objection." In a letter to Bubb dated 9 Sept. 1916, H.D. wrote: "I am answering for myself and for my husband as well. We were both very happy indeed to see the 'Choruses' done so beautifully. It will be an inspiration to us to go on with our work."

Contains *Choruses from Iphigeneia in Aulis*.

CtY (2 copies); NN.

   c   Second English edition, 1919

THE POETS' TRANSLATION SERIES | Second Set: No. 3 | [double rules] | CHORUSES FROM THE | IPHIGENEIA IN AULIS | AND THE HIPPOLYTUS | OF EURIPIDES | TRANSLATED BY H.D. | [double rules] | LONDON: THE EGOIST LTD. | 23 Adelphi Terrace House, Robert Street, W.C. 2 | 1919

[A]⁴ B–E⁴; pp. [1–2] 3–23 [24] 25–37 [38–40]. Cream wove paper, 18.3 × 12.1 cm. Endpapers of the same cream wove paper. Covers of pale yellow (C73) laid paper with horizontal chain lines pasted over stiff cardboard. Front cover: '[dark blue (C183)] THE POETS TRANSLATION SERIES | Second Set No. 3 | [double rules] | CHORUSES FROM THE | IPHIGENEIA IN AULIS | AND THE HIPPOLYTUS | OF EURIPIDES | TRANSLATED BY H.D. | [device depicting a satyr within a dark blue oval] | [double rules] | LONDON: THE EGOIST LTD. | 23 Adelphi Terrace House, Robert Street, W.C. 2 | Price 2/6 net'.

P. 1: title page; p. 2: blank; pp. 3–23: text of Iphigeneia; p. 24: blank; pp. 25–37: text of Hippolytus; pp. 38–39: advertisements; p. 40: printer's imprint, '[within an ornamental rule frame] *At the* PELICAN PRESS | [Pelican Press device] | 2 CARMELITE ST. | FLEET ST., LONDON | E.C.'. An errata slip has been inserted between pp. 2 and 3. It reads: '[double rules] | ERRATA | [rule] | P.3, line 13, for *Menelaos* read *Menelaus* | P.5, line 12, for *Odysseos* read *Odysseus* | [double rules] | *Choruses from Iphigeneia*'.

Contains "Choruses from the Iphigeneia in Aulis," "Choruses from the Hippolytus of Euripides." Reprinted in *CP* (1925) and *CP* (1983).

NBuU; CtY; PPT; PU; NNC.

A2   *Sea Garden*

a.i First edition, 1916

SEA GARDEN | BY | H.D. | LONDON | CONSTABLE AND COMPANY LTD. | 1916

A⁴ B–D⁸; pp. [π1–2] [i–iv] v [vi] 1–47 [48]. Cream wove paper, 19.4 × 14.1 cm. Uncut bottom and fore edges. Endpapers of slightly heavier cream wove paper. Covers of red (C15) paper glued over stiff cardboard, 19.4 × 14.3 cm. Front cover: 'H.D. | SEA GARDEN | [leaf ornament] | [at left] THE NEW | POETRY | SERIES [at right] LONDON: | CONSTABLE | & CO. LTD.' Spine, from tail to head: 'H.D.: SEA GARDEN'. PPT, CtY copy 5, and NN have alternate binding of gray green (C122) laid paper over boards. Stamped at top of front cover in olive green (C128): 'SEA GARDEN | [black] [leaf ornament]'.

Pp. π1–2: blank; p. i: half title, 'SEA GARDEN | [leaf ornament]'; p. ii: acknowledgment, 'The editors and publishers concerned have | kindly given me permission to reprint some of | the poems in this book which appeared origin-|ally in "Poetry" (Chicago), "The Egoist" | (London), "The Little Review" (Chicago), | "Greenwich Village" (New York), the first | Imagist anthology (New York: A. and C. Boni. | London: Poetry Bookshop), the second Imagist | anthology ("Some Imagist Poets," London: | Constable and Co. Boston: Houghton Mifflin | Co.).'; p. iii: title page; p. iv; 'PRINTED IN GREAT BRITAIN. | CHISWICK PRESS: CHARLES WITTINGHAM AND CO. | TOOKS COURT, CHANCERY LANE, LONDON.'; p. v: contents; p. vi: blank; pp. 1–47: text; p. 48: printer's imprint, '[Chiswick lion and anchor device] | CHISWICK PRESS: CHARLES WHITTINGHAM AND CO. | TOOKS COURT, CHANCERY LANE, LONDON.'

Published at 2s.

Contains "Sea Rose," "The Helmsman," "The Shrine," "Mid-Day," "Pursuit," "The Contest," "Sea Lily," "The Wind Sleepers," "The Gift," "Evening," "Sheltered Garden," "Sea Poppies," "Loss," "Huntress," "Garden," "Sea Violet," "The Cliff Temple," "Orchard," "Sea Gods," "Acon," "Night," "Prisoners," "Storm," "Sea Iris," "Hermes of the Ways," "Pear Tree," "Cities," "The City Is Peopled." Reprinted in *CP* (1925) and *CP* (1983).

NBuU; CU-Riv; CtY (5 copies); PPT; NN (2 copies); NNC.

a.ii First American edition (English sheets), 1916

SEA GARDEN | BY | H.D. | BOSTON AND NEW YORK | HOUGHTON MIFFLIN COMPANY | 1916

Collation, contents, and text contents as in **A2a.i**. The English sheets with reset (supplied) American title page. Trimmed edges, 19.5 × 14.2 cm. Yellowish cardboard cover, 19.4 × 14.2 cm, with dark green (C126) cloth shelfback, over which a dark olive green (C128) wove paper dust jacket, 20.1 × 14.2 cm, has been pasted at the spine. Front cover: 'Sea Garden : Imagist Poems | By "H.D." | THE NEW POETRY SERIES | [Houghton device] | HOUGHTON MIFFLIN COMPANY | BOSTON AND NEW YORK | [leaf ornament]'.

NBuU; NBu; CU-SC; CtY (copy 4 contains corrections in H.D.'s hand); PPT.

a.iii First edition, second impression (photo-offset from **A2a.ii**), 1975

Poetry Reprint Series | SEA GARDEN | by H.D. | St. James Press | St. Martin's Press | London New York

[1–4]⁸; pp. [π1–4] [i–iv] v [vi] 1–47 [48–54]. White wove paper, 19.6 × 14.3 cm. Endpapers of slightly stiffer white wove paper. Covers of deep purplish blue (C201) textured paper over boards, 20.3 × 14.9 cm. Spine, from head to tail, gilt: 'H.D. SEA GARDEN St. James/St. Martin's'. Constable title page reproduced on p. iii.

P. π1: title page; p. π2: copyright, 'Copyright 1916 by Constable and Company | Reprinted 1975 by St. James Press | All rights reserved. For information write: | St. James Press Ltd., 1a Montagu Mews North, London W1H 1AJ | or | St. Martin's Press, Inc., 175 Fifth Ave., New York, N.Y. 10010 | Printed in the U.S.A. | ISBN 0 900997 21 5 | Library of Congress Catalog Card Number: 75-10006 | This reprint first published in the U.K. and U.S.A. in 1975'; p. π3: '[within a decorative rule frame] SEA GARDEN was first published in | 1916. The cover was of cardboard with | a light red dust jacket. This reprint is | photographed from the copy in the Uni-|versity of London Library. | [below the decorative rule frame] Poetry Reprint Series: Set One | Robert Graves: Over the Brazier | H.D.: Sea Garden | Wallace Stevens: Harmonium | John Betjeman: Mount Zion | Conrad Aiken: Earth Triumphant'; p. π4: blank; pp. i–iv, 1–48: as in **A2a.i** pp. 49–54: blank.

James Laughlin, at New Directions, wrote to Richard Martin 16 April 1974, stating that St. James planned to market 1,000 copies in England and 2,000 copies through St. Martin's Press in this country, but that the American copies would be an import from their printing in England.

Text contents as in **A2a.i**.

Personal copy.

A3   *The Tribute and Circe*

a   First edition, 1917

[three red orange (C34) fleurs-de-lis] | [large red orange initial letter *T* extending four lines on the left] [in faux civilité letterpress] The Tribute and Circe, | Two Poems by H.D. | Printed at The Clerk's | Private Press, Cleveland, | Ohio, in the Year [triangle of three dots] mdcccxvii | [three red orange fleurs-de-lis]

[1–2]¹⁰; pp. [1–6] 7–39 [40]. Cream laid paper with horizontal chain lines, watermarked 'TUSCANY ITALY [device]', approximately 13 × 10 cm. Uncut fore and bottom edges. Endpapers of same cream laid paper. Covers of pink gray (C10) beveled laid paper with horizontal chain lines pasted over cardboard, 14.2 × 10.6 cm, watermarked 'FABRIANO ITALY'. The cardboard is 12.7 × 10 cm. Front cover, in faux civilité: 'The Tribute and Circe | Two Poems by | H.D.' The preliminary initial *S* on p. 7 is elaborately hand-supplied in blue ink with foliated border extending down the inner margin; the letter is gilt. The text is decorated throughout with reddish orange fleurs-de-lis. The text is printed in faux civilité. Bubb supplied the preliminary initial by hand, varying the decoration in each copy.

P. 1: half title, '[three red orange fleurs-de-lis] | The Tribute and Circe, Two | Poems by H.D. | [three red orange fleurs-de-lis]; p. 2: colophon and acknowledgments, 'Fifty copies only of this edition | have been printed of which this is | Number [supplied in pencil] | These poems were originally pub-|lished in 'The Egoist' and are now | reprinted by permission of the Author'; p. 3: title page; p. 4: blank; p. 5: dedication, '[three red orange fleurs-de-lis] | To | Richard Aldington | A Little Offering from | The Author and the Printer | [line of three red orange fleurs-de-lis]'; p. 6: blank; pp. 7–39: text; p. 40: printer's imprint, 'Typography and Presswork done by | Charles Clinch Bubb, Clerk in | Holy Orders at his Press in | [device: woodcut double cross surmounting letter *B* in a heart on an ornamental shield] | Cleveland, Ohio, February mcmxvii'.

Published 9 February 1917 in an edition of 50 copies.

In a letter to Bubb in the research library at the University of California at Los Angeles, undated but probably written in late 1916, H.D. said: "I am enclosing Tribute. I should like to see it in one of your booklets sometime, as my husband says he wants it printed! I think the usual clear Roman type you use as a rule would suit this particular poem better than the script, as this is so essentially classical (or pseudo classical) in feeling! For another kind of poem, I think the type you refer to would be charming!— Do not worry about this poem. It is a purely personal affair—an attempt to express for Richard what I felt his part in this soldiering to be!—Will you print as dedication on title page 'To Richard Aldington!'" In a letter dated 24 March [1917] she wrote: "The Tribute, he thought perfect and thanked you for your 'offering.'"

Contains "The Tribute," "Circe." "Circe" reprinted in *Hymen*, *CP* (1925), *CP* (1983). "The Tribute" reprinted in *CP* (1925), *CP* (1983).

NBuU; CtY (2 copies); PPT; NN.

A4   *Hymen*

a.i   First edition, 1921

[all within a box of double rules] [first two lines in hollow letters] HYMEN | BY H.D. | [below] LONDON | THE EGOIST PRESS | *2 Robert Street, Adelphi, W.C.* | 1921

A-C⁸; pp. [1–6] 7–46 [47–48]. Cream wove paper, 21.5 × 13.7 cm. End-papers of same cream wove paper. Covers of paper pasted over cardboard, 21.8 × 13.9 cm, printed in gray blue (C186) to resemble woven fabric. Cream paper title label at top of front cover, 4.8 × 10.3 cm, printed in deep blue (C179): within a box of an ornamental rule, in hollow letters, 'HYMEN | By H.D. | London: The Egoist Press. Price 3/'. Variant binding at CtY of stiff cardboard covered by an alternating pattern of black and red orange (C36); inside the front cover is H.D.'s bookplate.

P. 1: title page; p. 2: dedication, 'FOR BRYHER AND PERDITA'; p. 3: poem of three six-line strophes in italics beginning 'They said:'; p. 4: acknowledgments, 'Acknowledgements are due to the editors of | the following periodicals in which certain | of these poems have appeared: *Poetry* (Chicago), | *The Dial, Contact,* and the *Bookman* (New | York), *The Nation, The Sphere, The Anglo-|French Review* and *The Egoist* (London).'; p. 5: contents; p. 6: blank; pp. 7–47: text; at foot of p. 47: '*Printed in England at the Pelican Press, 2 Carmelite Street, London E.C.*'; p. 48: blank.

CtY copy 2 is inscribed 'H.D. | Kusnacht | May 1954' and contains penciled corrections in H.D.'s hand and the note, 'Selections:— | see Contents'.

Contains "Hymen," "Demeter," "Simaetha," "Thetis," "Circe," "Leda," "Hippolytus Temporizes," "Cuckoo Song," "The Islands," "At Baia," "Sea Heroes," "Not Honey," "Evadne," "Song," "Why Have You Sought," "The Whole White World," "Phaedra," "She Contrasts Herself with Hippolyta," "She Rebukes Hippolyta," "Egypt," "Prayer," "Helios." Reprinted in *CP* (1925), *CP* (1983).

NBuU; CU-Riv; CtY (4 copies); PPT; NNC.

a.ii First American edition (English sheets), 1921

HYMEN | By | H.D. | NEW YORK | HENRY HOLT AND COMPANY | 1921

Collation, contents, and text contents as in **A4a.i**. Cream wove paper, 22 × 15 cm; fore and bottom edges uncut. Gatherings quadruple stitched. Endpapers of heavier, smooth cream wove paper. The cover is a single quarto fold of light green (C122) heavy laid paper with vertical chain lines, watermarked with an oval containing the she-wolf suckling Romulus and Remus; beneath, 'ROMA'. Beveled edges. Front cover lettered in green (C126), all within double gilt rule frame: 'HYMEN | *BY* H.D.' At foot of p. 47: '*Printed in England at the Pelican Press, 2 Carmelite Street, London, E.C.*' On title page of CtY copy 2, hand-stamped in purple ink below the date: 'Made in U.S.A.'

CtY (2 copies); PU; PPT; NNC; NBu.

A5 *Heliodora*

a.i First edition, 1924

Heliodora | *And Other Poems* | *by* H.D. | [publisher's device] | Jonathan Cape | Eleven Gower Street, London

[A]⁸ B-H⁸; pp. [1–4] 5 [6] 7 [8] 9–11 [12] 13–127 [128]. Cream laid paper with vertical chain lines. Bottom and fore edges uncut, 19 × 12.5 cm. Endpapers of smooth cream wove paper. Covers of various decorative papers over boards, 19.3 × 13.2 cm: alternating square patterns in orange (C72) and brown (C49). Purple (C257) cloth shelfback. White paper title label on spine, 3.1 × 1.8 cm, printed in brown (C49): '[decorative rule] | HELIO-|DORA | & *other poems* | *by* | H.D. | [decorative rule]'. Variant binding at CtY, CaOTU, NN, and NNC: decorative paper over boards, diamond pattern in dark brown (C44) with beige (C79) and tan (C91) cloth shelfbacks.

Dust jacket of cream wove paper printed in brown. Front cover: 'HELIO-DORA | AND OTHER POEMS BY | H.D.' Beneath the title is an ornament of an elaborately knotted line in the form of an inverse isosceles triangle. Spine: 'HELIO-|DORA | & | *other poems* | *by* | H.D. | [below] [publisher's device] | JONATHAN | CAPE | LTD.' The front inner flap has a seventeen-line statement on H.D. in deep brown by Louis Untermeyer under the heading 'HELIODORA'. At foot of flap: '*Heliodora 5s. net.*'

P. 1: half title, 'Heliodora | *And Other Poems*'; p. 2: blank; p. 3: title page; p. 4: copyright, 'FIRST PUBLISHED 1924 | ALL RIGHTS RESERVED | PRINTED IN GREAT BRITAIN BY BUTLER AND TANNER LTD., FROME AND LONDON'; p. 5: acknowledgments, 'Acknowledgements for permission to re-|print certain poems is due to: *Nation, Sphere,* | *Egoist* (London); *Bookman, Poetry, Double* | *Dealer* (New York, Chicago, New Orleans); *Transatlantic, Gargoyle* (Paris); *The Imagist* | *Anthologies* and the *Miscellany of American* | *Poetry* (1922).'; p. 6: blank; p. 7: note (twelve lines); p. 8: blank; pp. 9–10: contents; p. 11: poem in twenty-seven lines of italic, 'Wash of cold river'; p. 12: blank; pp. 13–127: text; p. 128: blank.

Published in the summer of 1924 at 5s. According to Michael Bott, the Keeper of the Archives and Manuscripts at the University of Reading Library where the Jonathan Cape archives are deposited, there is no production ledger containing the relevant information. Reprinted in *CP* (1925) and *CP* (1983) where "Oread," "The Pool," "Moonrise," "Sitalkis," "Hermonax," and "Orion Dead" are moved into a section titled "The God," a collection never published separately.

Contains "Wash of Cold River," "Holy Satyr," "Lais," "Heliodora," "Helen," "Nossis," "Centaur Song," "Oread," "The Pool," "Thetis," "At Ithaca," "We Two," "Fragment Thirty-six," "Flute Song," "After Troy," "Cassandra," "Epigrams," "Fragment Forty," "Toward the Piraeus," "Moonrise," "At Eleusis," "Fragment Forty-one," "Telesila," "Fragment Sixty-eight," "Lethe," "Sitalkis," "Hermonax," "Orion Dead," "Charioteer," "The Look-Out," "Odyssey," "Hyacinth," "Ion."

NBuU; CU-Riv; CtY (4 copies); PPT; CaOTU; NN.

a.ii First American edition (English sheets), 1924

Heliodora | *And Other Poems* | *by* H.D. | Boston and New York | Houghton Mifflin & Company | MADE AND PRINTED IN GREAT BRITAIN.

Cancellans title page tipped in on a stub.

Collation and text contents as in **A5a.i**. Paper as in **A5a.i** with fore and bottom edges rough cut, 18.8 × 12.5 cm. Endpapers of heavier smooth wove paper. Covers of blue (C182) paper over boards with grayish yellow (C90) cloth back. Publisher's device blind-stamped on front cover. White paper title label at top of spine, 4 × 1.7 cm, printed: '[ornamental rule] | HELIO-|DORA | *and* | other | *Poems* | By | H.D. | [ornamental rule]'.

Dust jacket of pale orange yellow (C73) stock printed in deep yellow brown (C75). Front cover, within a decorative frame: '[engraving of a Greek pastoral scene] | HELIODORA | AND OTHER POEMS BY | H.D. | [fourteen-line blurb] | HOUGHTON MIFFLIN COMPANY'. Spine: '[thick-thin rule] | HELIO-|DORA | *&* | *Other* | *Poems* | by | H.D. | [publisher's device] | Houghton | Mifflin | Company | [thin-thick rule]'. Back cover: advertisements for eleven Houghton Mifflin titles. Front inner flap: '[at top] $1.50 | [below price, an advertisement for Amy Lowell's *Fir-Flower Tablets*]'. Back inner flap: advertisement for Amy Lowell's *Legends*.

Contents as in **A5a.i** with altered copyright (p. 4): 'MADE AND PRINTED IN GREAT BRITAIN BY | BUTLER AND TANNER LTD., FROME AND LONDON'.

Published 1 August 1924 in an edition of 520 copies at $1.50.

CtY; PPT; NBu.

A6 *Collected Poems*

a.i First edition, 1925

Collected Poems | *of* | *H.D.* | [deep orange (C51): publisher's device] | [black] *Published in New York by* | *BONI AND LIVERIGHT* | *1925*

[1–19]⁸ [20]⁶; pp. [π1–2] [i–iv] v–viii [1–2] 3–62 [63–64] 65–101 [102–104] 105–143 [144–146] 147–212 [213–214] 215–306. Cream wove paper, 18.8 × 12.9 cm, watermarked 'WARREN'S OLDE STYLE'. Bottom and fore edges rough cut. Endpapers of a heavier yellowish wove paper. Covers green (C147) cloth, 19.5 × 13.8 cm. Front cover, within five gilt-stamped border rules, gilt: 'COLLECTED | POEMS *of* | H.D.' Gilt lettering on spine: 'Collected | Poems *of* | H.D.' Below: 'BONI & | LIVERIGHT'. Alternate binding at CWB of greenish blue (±C173) cloth.

Dust jacket of light yellow (C90) laid paper with horizontal chain lines. Front cover, within a green (C132) ornamental rule frame: '[three-line quote from Louis Untermeyer] | [three-line quote from Conrad Aiken] | [rule] | [between two vertical rules] COLLECTED | POEMS OF | H.D. | [rule] | [seven-line quote from the *Times Literary Supplement*]'. Spine: 'COLLECTED | POEMS | OF | *H.D.* | [in green (C132): publisher's device] | Boni & | Liveright'. Back cover: '*Amy Lowell on* | *H.D.*' above a fifteen-line statement, the first letter a green drop initial. Front inner flap: '*COLLECTED POEMS OF* | *H.D.*' above a twenty-seven-line blurb, the first letter a green drop initial. At foot: '$2.50'. Back inner flap has an advertisement for three verse anthologies.

Pp. π1–2: blank; p. i: half title, '*Collected Poems | H.D.*'; p. ii: blank; p. iii: title page; p. iv: copyright, 'COPYRIGHT, 1925, BY | BONI AND LIVERIGHT, INC. | [short rule] | *All Rights Reserved* | PRINTED IN THE UNITED STATES OF AMERICA'; pp. v–viii: contents; p. 1: section title, '*SEA GARDEN*'; p. 2: blank; pp. 3–62: text; p. 63: section title, '*THE GOD*'; p. 64: blank; pp. 65–101: text; p. 102: blank; p. 103: section title, '*CHORUSES FROM THE | IPHIGENEIA IN AULIS AND THE | HIPPOLYTUS OF EURIPIDES | TRANSLATED BY H.D. | [ornament]*'; p. 104: blank; pp. 105–143: text; p. 144: blank; p. 145: section title, '*HYMEN*'; p. 146: untitled poem in italics of three six-line stanzas beginning 'They said:'; pp. 147–212: text; p. 213: section title, '*HELIODORA | AND OTHER POEMS*'; p. 214: ten lines under the heading 'NOTE'; pp. 215–306: text.

Published 1 May 1925.

CtY copy 1 inscribed 'H.D. Aldington | *Am Strand* | Kusnacht | bie Zurich' and pasted inside front cover is a photo taken from the Parthenon. Corrections in H.D.'s hand on p. 30 (line 9, life/lift), p. 191 (epigraph, tea/Bee) and p. [214] (line 7 foul/four). The changes on pp. 191 and 214 are corrected in the second printing.

Contains Sea Garden (section title for the following twenty-seven poems): "Sea Rose," "The Helmsman," "The Shrine," "Mid-Day," "Pursuit," "The Contest," "Sea Lily," "The Wind Sleepers," "The Gift," "Evening," "Sheltered Garden," "Sea Poppies," "Loss," "Huntress," "Garden," "Sea Violet," "The Cliff Temple," "Orchard," "Sea Gods," "Acon," "Night," "Prisoners," "Storm," "Sea Iris," "Hermes of the Ways," "Pear Tree," "Cities"; The God (section title for the following eleven poems): "The God," "Adonis," "Pygmalion," "Eurydice," "Oread," "The Pool," "Moonrise," "Orion Dead," "Hermonax," "Sitalkis," "The Tribute"; Choruses (section title for the following three poems): "1. From Iphigeneia," "2. From Hippolytus," "3. From Odyssey"; Hymen (section title for the following twenty-two poems): "Hymen," "Demeter," "Simaetha," "Thetis," "Circe," "Leda," "Hippolytus Temporizes," "Cuckoo Song," "The Islands," "At Baia," "Sea Heroes," "Fragment 113," "Evadne," "Song," "Why Have You Sought?" "White World," "Phaedra," "She Contrasts Herself with Hippolyta," "She Rebukes Hippolyta," "Egypt," "Prayer," "Helios"; Heliodora (section title for the following twenty-six poems): "Wash of Cold River," "Holy Satyr," "Lais," "Heliodora," "Helen," "Nossis," "Centaur Song," "Thetis," "At Ithaca," "We Two," "Fragment Thirty-six," "Flute Song," "After Troy," "Cassandra," "Epigrams," "Fragment Forty," "Toward the Piraeus," "At Eleusis," "Fragment Forty-one," "Telesila," "Fragment Sixty-eight," "Lethe," "Charioteer," "The Look-Out," "Hyacinth," "Ion." Reprinted in *CP* (1983).

NBuU; NBu; CtY (2 copies); PPT; NNC (2 copies); private library (dust jacket).

a.ii First edition, second (corrected) impression, 1925

Title page, collation, contents, text contents, and binding as in **A6a.i**. Paper as in **A6a.i** but measuring 19 × 12.8 cm with bottom edge rough cut; the fourth signature (pp. 39–54) in copies at NBuU and CtY watermarked 'SUEDE | [*D* within a diamond] | FINISH | MADE IN U.S.A.'

Dust jacket of light yellow (C90) laid paper with horizontal chain lines. Front cover, within a green (C132) ornamental rule frame: '[three-line quote from Louis Untermeyer] | [three-line quote from Conrad Aiken] | [rule] | [between two vertical rules] COLLECTED | POEMS OF | *H.D.* | [rule] | [seven-line quote from the *Times Literary Supplement*]'. Spine: 'COLLECTED | POEMS | OF | *H.D.* | 2nd | Edition | [in green: publisher's device] | Boni & Liveright'. Back cover: '*Amy Lowell on* | *H.D.*' above fifteen-line statement, first letter green drop initial. On the front inner flap, in green: '*COLLECTED POEMS OF H.D. $2.50*'. Below this is an advertisement for Robinson Jeffers's *Roan Stallion* and *Tamar* with a woodcut portrait of Jeffers. On the back inner flap is an advertisement for three verse anthologies.

The typographical errors on pp. 191 and 214 have been corrected in this second impression, although that on p. 30 remains.

Published November 1925.

NBuU; CtY; NN.

a.iii First edition, third impression, 1926

Collation, contents, text contents, paper, and binding as in **A6a.i** with altered copyright: 'COPYRIGHT, 1925 BY | HORACE LIVERIGHT, INC. | [short rule] | *All rights reserved* | First printing, April, 1925 | Second printing, November, 1925 | Third printing, November 1926 | PRINTED IN THE UNITED STATES OF AMERICA'.

Private library.

a.iv   First edition, fourth impression, 1929

Collected Poems | *of* | *H.D.* | [deep orange (C51)] [publisher's device] | [black] *New York* | *HORACE LIVERIGHT* | *1929*

Collation, contents, and text contents as in **A6a.i** with altered copyright: 'COPYRIGHT, 1925 BY | HORACE LIVERIGHT, INC. | [short rule] | *All rights reserved* | First printing, April, 1925 | Second printing, November, 1925 | Third printing, November 1926 | Fourth printing, March 1929 | PRINTED IN THE UNITED STATES OF AMERICA'.

Paper and binding as in **A6a.i** with altered spine imprint: 'HORACE | LIVERIGHT'.

Published March 1929.

Private library.

a.v   First edition, fifth impression, 1931

Collected Poems | *of* | *H.D.* | [deep orange (C51)] [publisher's device] | [black] *New York* | *HORACE LIVERIGHT* | *1929*

Collation, contents, and text contents as in **A6a.i** with altered copyright: 'COPYRIGHT, 1925 BY | HORACE LIVERIGHT, INC. | [short rule] | *All rights reserved* | First printing, April, 1925 | Second printing, November, 1925 | Third printing, November 1926 | Fourth printing, March 1929 | Fifth printing, March 1931 | PRINTED IN THE UNITED STATES OF AMERICA'.

Paper and binding as in **A6a.i** except gatherings sewn with white and light yellow thread and altered spine imprint: 'HORACE | LIVERIGHT'.

PU, NNC.

a.vi   First edition, sixth impression, 1940

[within an ornamental rule frame] [rule] | COLLECTED | POEMS OF | [in hollow letters] H.D. | [rule: upper and lower rule connected by vertical rules on either side of the title] | SIXTH PRINTING | [publisher's device] | LIVERIGHT PUBLISHING CORPORATION | NEW YORK

Collation as in **A6a.i** with omission of [π1–2] and addition of [307–308]. Cream laid paper with vertical chain lines, 18.8 × 12.8 cm. Bottom and fore edges rough cut. Endpapers of heavier wove paper, light orange yellow (C70). Covers of dark blue (C183) cloth, 19.4 × 13.9 cm. Front cover gilt-stamped: 'COLLECTED | POEMS OF | H.D.' Gilt-stamped spine title as in **A6a.i-v** with altered publisher's imprint at foot: '[publisher's device] | LIVERIGHT'. Variant binding at CtY of deep red (C16) cloth.

Dust jacket of light blue (C171) laid paper with horizontal chain lines. Front cover in dark blue (C183): within an ornamental rule frame, '[three-line quote by Louis Untermeyer] | [three-line quote by Conrad Aiken] | [rule] | COLLECTED | POEMS OF | *H.D.* | [rule: upper and lower rules connected by short vertical rules on either side of the title] | [seven-line quote from the London *Times Literary Supplement*]'. Spine: 'COLLECTED | POEMS | OF | *H.D.* | SIXTH | EDITION | [publisher's device]'. The back of the dust jacket contains advertisements for ten books. The front inner flap has a twenty-six-line statement on H.D., including a six-line quote from Amy Lowell, under the heading 'COLLECTED POEMS OF | *H.D.*' At top of flap: '306 Pages $2.50'. The back inner flap has an advertisement for 'THE LYRIC PSALTER' edited by Dr. Harry H. Mayer.

P. i: half title, '*Collected Poems* | *H.D.*'; p. ii: blank; pp. iii–viii, 1–306: as in **A6a.i**; pp. 307–308: blank.

In a letter to May Sarton dated 27 September [1940] (in the Berg Collection at the New York Public Library), H.D. wrote: "Boni slipped over a re-print of my 'Poems' without my consent, rather low trick ... considering ... however, if you see it or any possible 'press', realize it was all against my wishes!"

Text contents as in **A6a.i**.

NBuU; CtY; PU; NNC.

A7 *H.D.*

a.i First edition, 1926

[cover title] [a thick decorative border surrounds a box of a thick rule around a thin rule; within a central box created by horizontal rules at top and bottom, two vertical rules further divide the space into three panels; in the center is a decorative compartment] [at the top] H.D. | [within the decorative compartment] [dot] THE [dot] | PAMPHLET POETS | [at foot of central panel] [publisher's device] | [at foot] SIMON & SCHUSTER : *PUBLISHERS* | *NEW YORK* : 37 WEST FIFTY-SEVENTH STREET

[1]^{16}; pp. [1–3] 4–29 [30] 31 [32]. Cream wove paper watermarked 'AMERICAN EGG SHELL', 21.3 × 13.9 cm. A single double-stapled gathering.

P. 1: cover title; p. 2: advertisements for The Pamphlet Poets; at foot: 'COPYRIGHT 1926 BY SIMON AND SCHUSTER INCORPORATED'; p. 3: description of editorial goals; at foot: 'Grateful acknowledgement is hereby | made to H.D. and to the publishers, Boni | and Liveright, for permission to reprint the | poems, copyrighted by them, which are | contained in this pamphlet, and for their | cordial cooperation in the publication of | this entire series. | SIMON AND SCHUSTER'; p. 4: contents; at foot: 'PRINTED IN THE U.S.A.'; pp. 5–6: introduction under the heading 'H.D.'; pp. 7–29: text; p. 30: blank; p. 31: thirty-four-line bibliographical description of H.D.'s work under the heading 'HOW TO KNOW H.D.'; in the bottom left corner: 'MORTIMER-WALLING CO. | PRINTING—NEW YORK'; p. 32: list of the editorial advisory committee for the series.

Published 8 November 1926 at 25 cents.

The contents page lists a poem titled "DREAD" on p. 13 which does not occur there or elsewhere. This is a typographical error for "OREAD," also listed as being on p. 13 and indeed printed there.

Contains "H.D." (by Hughes Mearns), "Pear Tree," "Pursuit," "The Gift," "Oread," "Sheltered Garden," "Loss," "Adonis," "The Pool," "From 'The Tribute,'" "Orchard," "Cuckoo Song," "A Song from 'Hymen,'" "Heat."

NBuU; CtY; PU; PPT; NNC.

a.ii   First edition, second impression (?), 1926

Collation, contents, text contents, and paper as in **A7a** with altered cover title: '[below the title] *Price 25 Cents*'.

Copies of this impression exist at PPT and Pennsylvania State University. Simon and Schuster has no record of having printed the pamphlet.

A8   *Palimpsest*

a.i   First edition (Dijon: Darantière), 1926

Palimpsest: - | παλίμψηστος : a palimpsest, i.e. a | parchment from which one writing has been | erased to make room for another. | [in lower left corner] H.D.

$[\pi]^2$ *^{4} 1–21^8 22^4; pp. [i–xii] [1–3] 4–131 [132–135] 136–244 [245–247] 248–338 [339–344]. Smooth cream wove paper, 18.8 × 13.8 cm. Uncut edges. $[\pi]_{1\text{-}2}$ and 22$_{3\text{-}4}$ form cover leaves and free endpapers. Pale yellow brown (C76) laid paper wrappers with horizontal chain lines, watermarked with a large oval in which the she-wolf suckles Romulus and Remus, beneath: 'ROMA'. Wrapped around π_1 and 22_4 and glued to the spine. Front cover, 19.8 × 14.3 cm, repeats the title page. Spine, tail to head: '[thick-thin rule] Palimpsest: - H.D. [thin-thick rule]'. Back cover has a list of seven Contact Editions titles, a two-line note concerning others forthcoming, and the publisher's imprint.

Pp. i–vi: blank; p. vii: half title, 'Palimpsest'; p. viii: copyright, 'Copyrighted by H.D. 1926 | Published by Contact Editions, | Paris, Ile Saint-Louis, Quai d'Anjou, 29'; p. ix: title page; p. x: blank; p. xi: eleven-line poem in italics 'TO BRYHER'; p. xii: contents; p. 1: section title, 'HIPPARCHIA | '*I cast my lot with cynics, not | with women seated at the distaff.*' | Hipparchia.—Antipater of Sidon.'; p. 2: blank; pp. 3–131: text; p. 132: blank; p. 133: section title, 'MUREX | "*Who fished the murex up?*" '; p. 134: blank; pp. 135–244: text; p. 245: section title, 'SECRET NAME | "*But Isis held her peace; never a | word did she speak, for she knew that Ra | had told her the names that all men | know; his true Name, his Secret Name, | was still hidden in his breast.*" | Hieratic papyrus of the XXth dynasty.'; p. 246: blank; pp. 247–338: text; p. 339: printer's imprint, 'PRINTED | AT DIJON (FRANCE) | BY | MAURICE DARANTIERE | M. CM. XXVI'; pp. 340–344: blank.

CtY copy 2, variant binding: lacks π_2; wrappers trimmed to leaf. Bound in paper over boards, 19.6 × 14.5 cm, with leather shelfback and corners. The decorative paper is mottled light brown (C57) with a pattern of alternating diamonds and flowers, dark gray blue (C187) outside with light yellow brown (C74) centers. Gilt-stamped on spine: '[rule] | [rule] | PALIMP-|SEST | [rule] | [double rule]'. PU copy also with variant binding: lacking π_1 and $22_{3,4}$. Edges trimmed to 18.4 × 13.1 cm, and a binder's leaf added at front and back. Endpapers a heavy wove paper, medium gray (C265). Covers are dark green (C147) cloth. On the spine, gilt-stamped from head to tail: '[triple rule] | PALIMPSEST.—H.D. | [triple rule]'. CtY copy 3 is a unique author's edition with a tipped in leaf, $\pi_2 + 1$, inscribed in ink, 'H.D. | London 1926'. It contains extensive corrections in H.D.'s hand which have been incorporated into **A8b**.

Contains "Hipparchia," "Murex," "Secret Name."

NBuU; CtY (3 copies); PPT; CaOTU.

a.ii   First American edition (Contact Editions French sheets), 1926

Title page and text contents as in **A8a.i**.

$*^4$ $1-21^8$ 22^4; pp. [i–viii] [1–3] 4–131 [132–135] 136–244 [245–247] 248–338 [339–344]. Paper as in **A8a.i** but measuring 19.2 × 13.6 cm; fore and bottom edges rough cut, top edge stained black. Heavy cream wove endpapers. Covers of black decorative paper over boards, 19.3 ×

14.3 cm, deep red (C13) cloth back. Cover pattern of gold hieroglyphs. Spine gilt-stamped: 'PALIMPSEST | BY H.D. | [below] HOUGHTON | MIFFLIN CO.'

Dust jacket of red (C11) wove paper, printed in deep blue (C179). Wavy irregular diagonal lines extend up from left to right. Signed at lower edge 'O. CHAPMAN'. Front cover: '[at top within a thick-rule panel] PALIMPSEST | BY H.D. | [below within a second thick-rule panel] In its snaring of the elusive overtones of | life this first venture into the novelist's | field by one of the most distinguished of | contemporary poets thrusts forward the | established frontiers of prose fiction. | *Edition limited to seven hun-|dred copies for sale in America.*' Spine: 'Palimpsest | By | H.D. | [publisher's device] | Houghton | Mifflin Co.' Back cover has advertisements for twenty-four new fiction titles from Houghton Mifflin. Front inner flap at top, '$3.50'. Below, an advertisement for the new revised edition of Willa Cather's *My Ántonia*. Back inner flap, an advertisement for *The Testament of Dominic Burleigh* by Godfrey Elton.

Pp. i–ii: blank; p. iii: half title, 'Palimpsest'; p. iv: blank; p. v: title page; p. vi: colophon and copyright, 'THIS AMERICAN EDITION CONSISTS | OF SEVEN HUNDRED COPIES | Boston and New York | HOUGHTON MIFFLIN COMPANY | 1926'; p. vii: eleven-line poem in italics titled 'TO BRYHER'; p. viii: contents; from p. 1 as **A8a.i**.

Published 22 October 1926 in an edition of 700 copies at $3.50.

In "A Note on the Text" in the second edition (p. 245), Matthew Bruccoli noted that *Palimpsest* was published in Paris by Contact Editions in 1926. Seven hundred sets of the unbound sheets were sent to Houghton Mifflin in Boston, and these copies have different preliminary matter in the first gathering of four leaves. The first gathering for Houghton Mifflin was supplied with the sheets of the text. All the text sheets—those for Contact and those for Houghton Mifflin—were almost certainly printed at the same time.

CU-Riv; CtY (2 copies); PU; PPT; NN; NNC.

b   Second American edition, 1968

[in hollow letters] H.D. | PALIMPSEST | [device] | SOUTHERN ILLINOIS UNIVERSITY PRESS | CARBONDALE AND EDWARDSVILLE | FEFFER & SIMONS, INC. | LONDON AND AMSTERDAM

$[1–7]^{16} [8]^{12} [9]^{16}$; pp. [i–iv] vii–ix [x–xii] [1–2] 3–238 [239–240] 241–268. Cream wove paper, 20.8 × 12.2 cm. Endpapers of a heavier dark orange yellow (C72) wove paper. Covers, orange yellow (C68) cloth boards, 21.5 × 12 cm. Gilt-stamped on the spine: 'H.D. | [from head to tail] PALIMPSEST | Southern | Illinois | University | Press'.

Dust jacket of heavy yellow (C87) wove stock. At top of front cover are two simulated woodblocks containing the large capital letters *H* and *D* in red brown (C42) on a gray red brown (C46) floral background. Below this: 'PALIMPSEST | [figure of Pallas Athene] | *CROSSCURRENTS / Modern Fiction* / Edited by HARRY T. MOORE'. Spine, from head to tail: '[light red brown (C42)] H.D. | [black] PALIMPSEST | [light red brown] Southern Illinois University Press'. The front inner flap has a thirty-six-line description of the text and the author, together with extracts from two reviews by Babette Deutsch and Mark Van Doren, printed in white.

P. i: 'CROSSCURRENTS / MODERN FICTION'; p. ii: 'CROSS-CURRENTS / MODERN FICTION | HARRY T. MOORE, *Textual Editor* | MATTHEW J. BRUCCOLI, *Textual Editor* | PREFACE BY | HARRY T. MOORE | A NOTE ON THE TEXT BY | MATTHEW J. BRUCCOLI'; p. iii: title page; p. iv: copyright, 'Published by special arrangement with Norman Holmes Pearson | Robert Mcalmon's "Forewarned as regards H D's Prose," pub-|lished by permission of Mrs. Robert L. Wilson | Preface by *Harry T. Moore* and A Note on the Text by *Matthew* | *J. Bruccoli*, COPYRIGHT © 1968 by SOUTHERN ILLINOIS | UNIVERSITY PRESS | All rights reserved | Crosscurrents / Modern Fiction edition, November, 1968 | Library of Congress Catalog Number 68-25566 | Printed in the United States of America | Designed by *Andor Braun*'; p. v: eleven-line poem in italics titled 'To Bryher'; p. vi: blank; pp. vii–ix: preface; p. x: blank; p. 1: 'PALIMPSEST | παλίμψη-στος: | a palimpsest, i.e. a | parchment from which one writing has been | erased to make room for another.'; p. 2: blank; pp. 3–238: text; p. 239: appendix; p. 240: blank; pp. 241–244: 'Forewarned as regards H D's Prose | *By Robert McAlmon*'; pp. 245–268: 'A Note on the Text'.

Published 25 November 1968 in an edition of 4,000 copies at $7.95.

Contains "Preface" (by Harry T. Moore), "Hipparchia," "Murex," "Secret Name," "Forewarned as Regards HD's Prose" (by Robert McAlmon), "A Note on the Text" (by Matthew J. Bruccoli).

NBuU; CU-Riv; PPT; NNC.

A9 *Hippolytus Temporizes*

a   First edition, 1927

[red orange (C34)] HIPPOLYTUS TEMPORIZES | [black] *A Play in Three Acts* | BY | H.D. | [illustration of Hippolytus trampled by horses] | BOSTON AND NEW YORK | HOUGHTON MIFFLIN COMPANY | [in Gothic letter] The Riverside Press Cambridge | 1927

[1–19]⁴; pp. [i–xii] [1] 2–42 [43] 44–95 [96] 97–139 [140]. Cream laid paper with vertical chain lines, 24.3 × 15.8 cm, watermarked 'Hamilton's Victorian'; edges uncut. Endpapers of same laid paper. Covers of red orange (C38) paper over boards, 24.7 × 16.5 cm. Paper decorated with wavy diagonals of alternating grayish red (C20) and flecked metallic gold. Black cloth shelfback. Gilt-stamped at top of spine, from tail to head: HIPPOLYTUS TEMPORIZES *by* H.D.' In a black cardboard box with a paper title label, 8.2 × 2 cm, pasted at top of spine, printed from head to tail: 'HIPPOLYTUS TEMPORIZES | [to the left of above] *by H.D. - Author of Palimpsest'.*

P. i: half title, 'HIPPOLYTUS TEMPORIZES'; p. ii: blank; p. iii: title page; p. iv: copyright page, 'COPYRIGHT, 1927, BY HOUGHTON MIFFLIN COMPANY | ALL RIGHTS RESERVED'; p. v: 'MOST of the lyrics and certain portions of this play and | of an earlier version have appeared in; *The Outlook, The | Chapbook* (London); *Poetry* (Chicago); *This Quarter* | (Paris); and *A Miscellany of American Poetry* (1925).'; p. vi: blank; pp. vii–viii: a forty-one-line poem in italics beginning 'I worship the greatest first—' (beneath at p. viii: 'ISLES OF GREECE | Spring, 1920'); p. ix: 'PEOPLE OF THE PLAY [12 lines]'; p. x: blank; p. xi: 'THE ARGUMENT [18 lines]'; p. xii: blank; p. 1–139: text; p. 140: colophon, 'THIS EDITION CONSISTS OF FIVE HUNDRED AND FIFTY COPIES, | OF WHICH FIVE HUNDRED ARE FOR SALE, PRINTED AT THE | RIVERSIDE PRESS, CAMBRIDGE, MASSACHUSETTS, IN APRIL, | 1927.'

Published 29 April 1927 in an edition of 550 copies; 500 for sale at $5.00.

Contains *Hippolytus Temporizes*. Two songs from act 2 are reprinted as sections 4 and 5 of "Songs from Cyprus" in *Red Roses for Bronze*, 1931.

CtY copy 2 inscribed 'H.D. Aldington | [overstruck] Am Strand | Villa Verena | Kusnacht | bei Zurich | Corrections of Feb. 26—1955'. CtY copies 3 and 4 contain further corrections, and the back flyleaf of copy 5 has a list of 'ERRATA' in H.D.'s hand.

NBuU; NBu; CU-SC; CU-Riv; CtY (six copies); PPT; NNC.

b Second (corrected) edition, 1986

[within a single-rule frame: dark red (C16) *Hippolytus Temporizes* | [black: short swelling rule | HD | [dark red] a play in three acts | [black: rule] | BLACK SWAN BOOKS

[1]^{16} [2–5]^{16}; pp. [i–ii] [1–3] 4–156 [157–160]. Frontis. tipped in after [1]^{16}. White wove paper, 21.4 × 13.8 cm. Light gray (C264) laid paper endpapers with vertical chain lines. Covers purple red (C257) cloth boards, 22.2 × 14.4 cm. Gilt-stamped on front cover: '*Hippolytus Temporizes* [row of Greek frets] | [row of Greek frets]] HD'. Gilt-stamped on spine, from head to tail: 'HD / *Hippolytus Temporizes* [publisher's device]'.

Dust jacket of white stock. At top of front cover is a 3-cm purple red (C259) strip printed in white: 'HD / *Hippolytus Temporizes*'. Below in light gray (C264) is a photograph of Artemis from the Parthenon frieze. Spine, from head to tail: '[purple red] HD [medium gray (C265)] / *Hippolytus Temporizes* [purple red] [publisher's device]'. Medium gray back cover. Between two short, white rules, a ten-line quotation from H.D.'s "Compassionate Friendship" in purple red. At the top of the front inner flap is a 3-cm medium gray strip printed in purple red: '$20.00 | HD / *Hippolytus Temporizes* | a play in three acts'. Beneath, a thirty-five-line statement about the play printed in purple red and continued on the back inner flap for another thirty lines. At the bottom of the back flap: '[purple red] *Cover photograph: Artemis from the | Parthenon frieze* | Published by | BLACK SWAN BOOKS LTD. | P.O. Box 327 | REDDING RIDGE, CT 06876 | [medium gray: to the right] [publisher's device]'.

P. i: blank; p. ii: frontispiece; p. 1: title page; p. 2: copyright page, twenty-two lines; p. 3: contents page; pp. 4–5: 'proem', forty-one-line poem beginning 'I worship the greatest first —'; p. 6: 'People of the Play'; p. 7: 'The Argument,' fifteen lines in italic; p. 8–138: text; pp. 139–151: 'Afterword: *The Flash of Sun on the Snow*'; pp. 152–156: 'Note on the Text'; pp. 157–158: blank; p. 159: advertisement for fifteen Black Swan titles; p. 160: blank. At the heading of each page from p. 4 through p. 156 is a line of Greek frets in line with the page number.

Published January 1986 in an edition of 1,000 at $20.00.

Contains "Proem," "The Argument," *Hippolytus Temporizes*, "Afterword" (by John Walsh), "Note on the Text" (by John Walsh).

Corrections in this edition were based on H.D.'s 1955 corrections to the 1927 edition.

CaOTU; personal copy.

A10 *Hedylus*

a.i First edition (American binding), 1928

HEDYLUS | BY H[dot]D | PRINTED BY | THE SHAKESPEARE HEAD PRESS | STRATFORD-UPON-AVON | FOR BASIL BLACKWELL OXFORD | AND HOUGHTON MIFFLIN COMPANY | BOSTON AND NEW YORK | M CM XXVIII

[a]^4 b-m^8 n^6; pp. [i–viii] [1] 2–23 [24] 25–31 [32] 33–185 [186–188]. Cream wove paper, uncut edges, 19.3 × 12.6 cm, watermarked 'BASIL BLACKWELL OXFORD'. Binding of decorative paper over boards with black cloth back, 19.6 × 13.4 cm. Decorative cover paper in a checked

pattern of alternating black, purple blue (C194), and gilt squares. Gilt-stamped on the spine: 'HEDYLUS | [short rule] BY H.D. | [below] HOUGHTON | MIFFLIN CO.'

Dust jacket of beige-coated white stock. Front cover: upper and lower scalloped borders connected by rays. A woman's figure stands on the lower border. Below the upper border: 'HEDYLUS | by H.D. | author of PALIMPSEST'. Spine: '[thick-thin rule] | HEDYLUS | By H.D. | [thin-thick rule] | [below] [thick-thin rule] | HOUGHTON | MIFFLIN | COMPANY | [thin-thick rule]'. The back cover has advertisements for seven Houghton Mifflin novels under the heading '*Novels of Distinction*'. At top of front inner flap, '$4.50'. Below this is an ad for *The Tale of Genji* by Lady Muraski. Back inner flap has an ad for *Against the Sun* by Godfrey Elton.

Pp. i–ii: blank; p. iii: half title, 'HEDYLUS'; p. iv: blank; p. v: title page; p. vi: limitation, 'SEVEN HUNDRED AND SEVENTY-FIVE | COPIES OF THIS BOOK HAVE BEEN | PRINTED IN GREAT BRITAIN BY THE | SHAKESPEARE HEAD PRESS STRATFORD-|UPON-AVON, OF WHICH SEVEN HUNDRED | AND FIFTY ARE FOR SALE IN GREAT | BRITAIN AND THE UNITED STATES | OF AMERICA'; p. vii: dedication, 'TO KENNETH MACPHERSON | for September 1 1927'; p. viii: 'The wild field-flowers of HEDYLUS and | POSIDIPPUS with SIKELEDES' anemones. | THE GARLAND OF MELEAGER'; p. 1–185: text; pp. 186–188: blank.

Page numbers are printed at the top of the pages except for pages with chapter headings where they are printed in smaller numerals below the text. The exceptions are chapters 3 and 4 (pp. 24 and 32) where page numbers are omitted.

Published 19 October 1928 in an edition of 520 copies at $4.50.

Contains *Hedylus*.

CtY; PU; NN; NNC; NBu.

a.ii   First edition (English binding), 1929

Title page, collation, contents, text contents as in **A10a.i**. Cream wove paper, 18.5 × 12.1 cm, watermarked 'BASIL BLACKWELL OXFORD'. Endpapers of smooth white wove paper. Covers gray orange (C39) paper over boards, 19.2 × 13.3 cm, with black cloth back. Stamped in black at top of front cover is a device, within a single-rule frame, depicting four pillars supporting a lintel over which are four arches. A herm stands between the two central pillars in front of a landscape. Printed on the lintel is 'HEDYLUS'. Gilt-stamped on spine: 'HEDYLUS | [device] | H.D. | [below] BLACKWELL'.

Published 26 January 1929 in an edition of 775 copies at 6s. Of this printing 520 copies were sent to Houghton Mifflin who released them on 19 October 1928.

NBuU; CU-Riv; CtY (3 copies); PPT.

b.i   Second (corrected) American edition, 1980

[within a single-rule frame: in medium brown (C58)] HEDYLUS | [black: short swelling rule] | H.D. | [rule] BLACK SWAN BOOKS

[1–5]¹⁶; pp. [i–ii] [1–6] 7–156 [157–160]. Frontis., inserted after [1]₁, is a photograph of H.D. taken by Man Ray circa 1922. White laid paper with vertical chain lines, 21.5 × 13.7 cm. Endpapers of heavier red (C12) wove paper. Covers of purple (C14) cloth boards, 22.2 × 14.5 cm. Gilt-stamped on front cover: 'HEDYLUS [a Greek fret] | [the same Greek fret] HD'. Gilt-stamped from head to tail on spine, within a single-rule frame: 'HD | [rule] | HEDYLUS | [rule] | [publisher's device]'.

Dust jacket of pink gray (C10) stock. Top front: a black frame containing a single pink gray rule frame, within which is printed in pink gray 'HEDYLUS'. Below: 'HD | [short rule of Greek fret]'. Spine, from head to tail: 'HD | [rule] | HEDYLUS | [rule] | [publisher's device]'. The back has a large mazelike device above a short rule of Greek fret. Front inner flap reads: '$15.00 | HEDYLUS *by H.D.*', followed by a thirty-five-line excerpt from the afterword. The back inner flap has publisher's advertisements.

P. i: blank; p. ii: front.; p. 1: title page; p. 2: copyright page, twelve lines; p. 3: contents; p. 4: dedication, '*To Perdita*'; p. 5: half title, 'HEDYLUS'; p. 6: 'The wild field-flowers of Hedylus and | Posidippus with Sikeledes' anemones. | *The Garland of Meleager*'; pp. 7–141: text; pp. 142–146: 'The Egyptian Cat'; pp. 147–150: 'Afterword'; pp. 151–156: 'Note on the Text'; pp. 157–158: blank; p. 159: publisher's advertisements; p. 160: blank.

Published in November 1980 in an edition of 1,000 copies at $15.00.

The "Note on the Text" states in part: "The present text of *Hedylus* differs primarily in two regards from that published in 1928 by Basil Blackwell in Oxford (and in America by Houghton Mifflin of Boston): this edition adheres to the paragraphing indicated by H.D. in both typescript and galley proofs . . . and encompasses revisions made by H.D. in a notebook kept between January 1951 and May 1953 while she was rereading and rethinking Hedylus."

Contains *Hedylus*, "The Egyptian Cat" (by Perdita Schaffner), "Afterword" (by John Walsh), "Note on the Text" (by John Walsh).

NBuU; NNC; PPT.

b.ii Second (corrected) English edition (photo-offset from **A10b.i**), [1980]

[within a single-rule frame] HEDYLUS | [short swelled rule] | HD | [rule] | CARCANET NEW PRESS LIMITED

[1–10]⁸; pp. [i–ii] [1–6] 7–156 [157–158]. Cream wove paper, 21.4 × 13.5 cm. Endpapers of a heavier medium orange (C53) wove paper. Covers of yellow brown (approximately C74) textured paper over boards. Spine, gilt-stamped from head to tail: 'HD HEDYLUS [publisher's device]'.

Dust jacket of light yellow (C86) with all printing in dark brown (C59). Front cover, equidistant between two parallel rules: 'HD | HEDYLUS | [head of Greek statue]'. Spine, from head to tail: 'HD HEDYLUS [publisher's device]'. Back cover: thirty-two Carcanet titles, advertising, and address. Front inner flap: '[short double rules] | [fifteen-line statement on the book] | [short double rules] | *This is the fifth title by HD to be pub-|lished by Carcanet. Others include:* | TRIBUTE TO FREUD | END TO TORMENT | HERMETIC DEFINITION | TRILOGY | [short double rules] | *Cover design by Sue Richards* | SBN 85635 3582—£4.95'. On the back flap is a twenty-three-line description of *End to Torment*.

P. i: half title; p. ii: frontis., photo of H.D. by Man Ray; p. 1: title page; p. 2: copyright page, seventeen lines; p. 3: contents; p. 4: dedication as in **A10a.ii**; p. 5: half title, 'HEDYLUS'; p. 6: quote from Meleager as in **A10a.ii**; pp. 7–141: text; p. 142–146: 'The Egyptian Cat'; pp. 147–150: 'Afterword'; pp. 151–156: 'Note on the Text'; pp. 157–158: blank.

Published 4 June 1981 at £4.95.

Text contents as in **A10b.i**.

NBuU; CtY; NDP.

A11 *Red Roses for Bronze*

a First edition, 1929

[within a single-rule frame] | [next three lines in decorative letters resembling leaves] RED ROSES | FOR BRONZE | "H.D." | [publisher's device] | NEW YORK: RANDOM HOUSE | 1929

[1]⁴; pp. [1–8]. Cream laid paper with vertical chain lines watermarked 'RH' within a decorative frame, 24.7 × 15.7 cm. Bottom edge uncut. Covers from light yellow brown (C76) stock with vertical chain lines watermarked 'Handcraft', 25.2 × 15.7 cm. Front cover: 'RED ROSES | FOR BRONZE | "H.D." | [short rule] | [drawing of a face and a

rose partially tinted purple pink (C247)] | [short rule] | THE POETRY QUARTOS | Random House, New York, 1929'.

Pp. 1–2: blank; p. 3: title page; p. 4–6: text; at bottom of p. 6, colophon, '[short rule] | THE POETRY QUARTOS | [short rule] | 475 copies for RANDOM HOUSE, printed in Silvermine, Conn'c't, U.S.A. | [device] {P.J.} [device] | Copyright, 1929, by "H.D." '; pp. 7–8: blank.

Published 15 May 1929 in an edition of 475 (515 with overrun) copies at $1.00 for an individual pamphlet, $10.00 for the complete set of twelve.

The *Poetry Quartos* was a set of twelve pamphlets, each containing a new poem by an American poet. According to documents in the Random House Archive at Columbia University, the publication was conceived by Paul Johnston, a fine-press publisher from Connecticut, whose work interested Bennett Cerf at Random House. H.D.'s name was not on any of the original lists discussed by the two men. Ezra Pound's name, however, was, and he submitted H.D.'s poem in his response to Johnston's request; Pound never sent a poem of his own. In October 1928, after months of negotiating with Cerf over who to include in the set, Johnston suggested H.D., even though he thought the poem rather long. Cerf agreed, and a check was sent to H.D. in care of Pound in December.

Johnston ordered the handmade paper from Germany. He originally had requested watermarks with P.J. in one corner and R.H. in the other. The papermaker, however, left out Johnston's initials and put "RH" in both corners. Johnston also had ordered handmade cover stock from a German firm who reneged on their contract at the last minute. Because he could not find an American handmade paper whose color was "lively enough" for him, Johnston ended up using machine-made paper, thus abandoning his original plan for an entirely handmade book.

The Poetry Quartos also included poems by Genevieve Taggard, Robert Frost, Vachel Lindsay, Edwin Arlington Robinson, Louis Untermeyer, Alfred Kreymbourg, Elinor Wylie, Theodore Dreiser, William Rose Benét, Conrad Aiken, and Witter Bynner.

Contains *Red Roses for Bronze*. Reprinted in *Red Roses for Bronze*, 1931, and *CP*(1983).

NBuU; CtY (2 copies); PU; NN; NNC.

A12 *Borderline*

a First edition, 1930

BORDERLINE | In the Cast | PETE (A Negro) . . . . PAUL ROBESON | ADAH (His Wife) . . . . ESLANDA ROBESON |

Astrid . . . . Helga Doorn | Thorne (Helga's husband) . . .
Gavin Arthur | The Cafe Manageress . . . . . . Bryher | The Barmaid . . .
. . . . . . Charlotte Arthur | The Pianist . . . . Robert Herring | The
Old Lady . . . . Blanche Lewin

[A]-B⁸C⁴; pp. [1–4] 5–39 [40]. Photos from the film inserted following pp. 8, 24, 36. Cream wove paper, 18.4 × 13.7. Covers of heavy yellow white stock. Front cover has a collage of faces and scenes from the film. Printed over the collage at the bottom in light orange yellow (C70) outlined in black: 'BORDERLINE'. Below the title at the bottom of the front cover is a .5-cm-wide black strip on which is printed in light gray (C264): 'A POOL FILM WITH PAUL ROBESON'. Cover glued at the spine.

Pp. 1–2: blank; p. 3: title page; p. 4: blank; p. 5–39: text; p. 40: within a single-rule frame, 'Impressed by | THE MERCURY PRESS LTD. | LONDON ILFORD CHELMSFORD | [beneath the above names] Tel.: Central 5316-7 Tel.: Ilford 0051-52 Tel.: Chelmsford 516 | ENGLAND | 1930'.

Contains *Borderline.* Reprinted in **B20** and **C172**.

CtY; PPT.

A13 *Red Roses for Bronze*

a.i First edition, 1931

RED ROSES | FOR | BRONZE | By | H.D. | 1931 | Chatto & Windus | London

[π]⁴ A-I⁸ K²; pp. [i–iv] v [vi] vii–viii 1–147 [148]. Cream wove paper 20.2 × 12.5 cm. Top edge stained dark red (C16); other edges uncut. Endpapers of a heavier smooth wove cream paper. Covers dark red (C16) linen cloth, 20.8 × 13.3 cm. Gilt-stamped on spine: '[ornamental rule] | RED | ROSES | FOR | BRONZE | [asterisk] | H.D. | [ornamental rule] | [below] *CHATTO | AND WINDUS*'.

Dust jacket of cream wove paper printed in red (C11). Front cover, within a floriated rule frame: 'RED ROSES | FOR | BRONZE | [asterisk] | POEMS | BY | H.D. | LONDON | *Chatto & Windus*'. On the spine: '[rule] | RED | ROSES | FOR | BRONZE | [asterisk] | H.D. | [rule]'. The front inner flap has a sixteen-line statement on H.D. in red. At foot: '*6 s. NET*'.

P. i: half title, 'RED ROSES | FOR BRONZE'; p. ii: blank; p. iii: title page; p. iv: 'PRINTED IN GREAT BRITAIN | ALL RIGHTS RESERVED'; p. v: *'NOTE* | I am particularly indebted to POETRY |

QUARTOS, RANDOM HOUSE for courtesy | in allowing me to reprint *Red Roses for* | *Bronze*. [¶] The *Songs for Cyprus* were originally written | for the play *Hippolytus Temporizes*, and | appeared in that volume. | [¶] Other poems, here included, first appeared in | A MISCELLANY OF AMERICAN POETRY, | 1925 and 1926; IMAGIST ANTHOLOGY, | 1930; POETRY, SATURDAY REVIEW OF | LITERATURE, NEW REPUBLIC, ETC. | H.D.'; p. vi: blank; pp. vii–viii: contents; p. 1–148: text. At bottom of p. 148: '[short rule] | Printed in Great Britain by T. and A. CONSTABLE LTD. | at the University Press, Edinburgh'.

Published 22 October 1931 in an edition of 2,000 at a price of 6s. According to Michael Bott, there were actually 2,024 published, including the overplus. Of these, 520 went to Houghton Mifflin for the American edition. Of the remainder, 500 were sold and 1,004 copies in unbound sheets were used as packing in 1936 and 1939.

Contains "Red Roses for Bronze," "In the Rain," "If You Will Let Me Sing," "Choros Translations (from The Bacchae)," "Chance Meeting," "Sea-Choros (from Hecuba)," "Wine Bowl," "Trance," "Myrtle Bough," "Choros Sequence (from Morpheus)," "Halcyon," "Songs from Cyprus," "Let Zeus Record," "White Rose," "Calliope," "All Mountains," "Triplex," "Birds in Snow," "Chance," "When I Am a Cup," "Sigil," "Epitaph," "The Mysteries." Reprinted in *CP* (1983).

CtY (4 copies); CU-Riv; PPT; CaOTU; NN; NNC.

a.ii First American edition (English sheets with reset preliminaries), 1932

RED ROSES | FOR | BRONZE | By | H.D. | [publisher's device, ship in an oval] | BOSTON & NEW YORK | *Houghton Mifflin Company* | 1931

$[\pi]^4$ A-I^8 K^2; [i–iv] v–viii 1–147 [148]. Cream wove paper, 20 × 12.5 cm. Fore and bottom edges rough cut. Top edge stained black. Endpapers of heavier smooth cream wove paper. Covers of a shiny bronze cloth imprinted with a floral pattern, 20.5 × 13 cm. Gray brown (C62) cloth back. Stamped on the spine in pale green (C149): '[rule] | RED | ROSES | FOR | BRONZE | [asterisk] | H.D. | [rule] | [below] HOUGHTON | MIFFLIN CO.' Variant binding at NBu has no floral pattern imprinted on the covers.

Dust jacket of gray brown (C46). Printed in white on the front cover: '[device, vertical line of six alternating arcs] | RED | ROSES | FOR | BRONZE | *Poems by* | H.D. | [repeated device]'. Spine printed in white from head to tail: '*RED ROSES FOR BRONZE Poems by H.D.* | H.M.CO. | [publishers' device]'. On the back cover is a list of six titles published by Houghton Mifflin under the heading 'Poetry'. On the front inner flap in the top right corner: '$3.00'. Beneath: '[short double rule] | RED ROSES

FOR | BRONZE | *Poems by H.D.* | [short rule] | [twenty-eight-line blurb on H.D.'s poetry, including a nineteen-line quote from May Sinclair]'. Back inner flap has an advertisement for *The Serpent in the Cloud* by Theodore Morrison.

Contents as in **A13a.i** with colophon added on p. v: 'The American edition of this book is | limited to five hundred and twenty copies, | of which five hundred are for sale'; and 'NOTE' moved to p. vi.

Published 20 January 1932 in an edition of 520 copies at $3.00.

Text contents as in **A13a.i**.

NBuU; NBu; PPT.

a.iii First American edition, second impression (photo-offset from **A13a.i**), 1970

RED ROSES | FOR | BRONZE | *By* | H.D. | {Hilda Doolittle Aldington} | AMS PRESS | NEW YORK

$[1-5]^{16}$; pp. [i–iv] v [vi] vii–viii 1–147 [148–152]. Cream wove paper, 21.4 × 13.7 cm. Endpapers of a heavier wove paper. Covers medium blue (C182) cloth, 22.2 × 14 cm. Spine gilt-stamped from head to tail: 'RED ROSES FOR BRONZE H.D. [horizontally] AMS'. Variant binding at CtY is gray brown (C61) cloth. Gilt-stamped on spine from head to tail: 'RED ROSES FOR BRONZE [short rule] DOLITTLE [*sic*] "H.D." [short rule] | AMS'. The binding at PU is the same except the printing has been reversed so that it reads from tail to head.

Contents and text contents as in **A13a.i** with altered copyright, p. iv: 'Reprinted from the edition of 1931, London | First AMS EDITION published 1970 | Manufactured in the United States of America | International Standard Book Number: 0-404-02145-X | Library of Congress Catalog Number: 72-119651 | AMS PRESS, INC. | NEW YORK, N.Y. 10003'; pp. 149–152: blank.

CU-Riv; CtY; PU.

A14   *THE USUAL STAR*

a   First edition, 1934

THE USUAL STAR | BY | H.D. | LONDON | 1928 [i.e., Dijon: Darantière, 1934].

$[1-7]^8 [8]^4$; pp. [1–8] 9–89 [90–92] 93–115 [116–120]. Cream wove paper, 18.9 × 13.9 cm. Uncut edges. Covers of a smooth cream wove paper glued at the spine. Front cover: 'THE USUAL STAR | BY | H.D.' Spine, from tail to head: 'THE USUAL STAR'.

Pp. 1–2: blank; p. 3: half title, 'THE USUAL STAR'; p. 4: colophon, *'This edition of one hundred copies | has been privately printed for the author's friends. | No copies are for sale. All rights reserved.'*; p. 5: title page; p. 6: blank; p. 7: section title, 'THE USUAL STAR'; p. 8: blank; pp. 9–89: text; p. 90: blank; p. 91: section title, 'Two Americans | Vaud | 1930.'; p. 92: blank; pp. 93–116: text; p. 117: printer's imprint, 'PRINTED | BY | IMPRIMERIE DARANTIERE | AT DIJON FRANCE | M. CM. XXXIV'; pp. 118–120: blank.

Publication date and place are printed in the printer's imprint on p. 117. The dates and place-names that appear on the title page and section title pages refer to the events in the stories. CtY copy 5 is a unique author's copy which has two extra binder's leaves, one at the front and one at the back. Edges have been trimmed to 17.5 × 12.9 cm. Endpapers of a light yellow brown (C76) wove paper with a pattern of small black triangles. Covers are gray brown (C62) leather, 18.4 × 13.8 cm, indented around the outer edge. Gilt-stamped on the cover: 'THE USUAL STAR'. CtY copy 2 is inscribed: 'H.D. to N.H.P. (corrected copy)'. CtY copy 4 is inscribed: 'New corrections - 1959 - May 9–10'. Corrections are of numerous typographical errors made by Darantière in setting up the book.

Contains "The Usual Star," "Two Americans." "Two Americans" reprinted in *New Directions* 51 (1987): 58–68. See **C174**.

NBuU; CtY (5 copies); PPT; NN.

A15   *KORA AND KA*

a   First edition, 1934

KORA AND KA | BY | H.D. | [at lower right] VAUD | 1930. [i.e., Dijon: Darantière, 1934]

[1–6]⁸ [7]⁴; pp. [1–8] 9–23 [24] 25–40 [41] 42–53 [54–56] 57–70 [71] 72–87 [88] 89–101 [102–104]. Cream wove paper, 18.8 × 13.8 cm; uncut edges. Covers of a heavier smooth cream wove paper, 19.2 × 14 cm, glued at the spine. Cover: 'KORA AND KA | BY | H.D.' Spine from tail to head: 'KORA AND KA'. CtY copy 3 is a unique author's copy with two extra binder's leaves, one at the front and one at the back. Edges have been trimmed to 17.5 × 12.9 cm. Endpapers of light yellow brown (C76) wove paper with pattern of small black triangles. Covers of deep gray brown (C62) leather, 18.8 × 13.8 cm indented around the outer edge. Gilt-stamped on the cover: 'KORA AND KA'.

Pp. 1–2: blank; p. 3: half title, 'KORA AND KA'; p. 4: colophon, '*This edition of one hundred copies | has been privately printed for the author's friends. | No copies are for sale. All rights reserved.*'; p. 5: title page; p. 6: blank; p. 7: section title, 'KORA AND KA'; p. 8: blank; p. 9–54: text; p. 55: section title, 'MIRA-MARE | VAUD | 1930.'; p. 56: blank; pp. 57–102: text; p. 103: printer's imprint, 'PRINTED | BY | IMPRIMERIE DARANTIERE | AT DIJON FRANCE | M. CM. XXXIV'; p. 104: blank.

CtY copy 2 is inscribed: 'H.D. to N.H.P. (Corrected copy)'. CtY copy 5 is inscribed: 'May 5 - 6 - 7 - 1959 more corrections H.D.' Corrections are of numerous typographical errors made by Darantière in setting up the book.

Contains "Kora and Ka," "Mira-Mare."

NBuU; CtY (5 copies); PPT; NN.

b   First American edition, 1978

H[dot]D | [short rule, yellow green (C115)] | KORA & KA | BIOS : BERKELEY

[1–3]^8; pp. [1–6] 7–17 [18–20] 21–32 [33–34] 35–42 [43–48]. Cream wove paper, 18.9 × 8.7 cm, watermarked 'Utopian'. Endpapers of the same wove paper. Covers yellow green (C131) cloth, 19.3 × 9.1 cm. White paper title label, 4.9 × 0.9 cm, pasted on spine, printed from head to tail: '[thick-thin rule] | KORA & KA | [thin-thick rule]'.

Dust jacket of white coated wove paper. Front cover stippled gray black. In the center of the front cover is a photograph of the stem of a plant. Spine, head to tail: 'KORA & KA *by* HD'.

Pp. 1–2: blank; p. 3: title page; p. 4: copyright, 'Copyright 1978 by the Estate of Hilda Doolittle Aldington'; p. 5: section title, 'I | [short rule] | [large dot]'; p. 6: blank; p. 7–17: text; p. 18: blank; p. 19: section title, 'II | [short rule] | [large dot]'; p. 20: blank; pp. 21–32: text; p. 33: section title, 'III | [short rule] | [large dot]'; p. 34: blank; pp. 35–43: text; p. 44: blank; p. 45: colophon, '*Six hundred copies were designed and | printed by Wesley B. Tanner. One hundred | of these have been bound in cloth.*'; pp. 46–48: blank.

Contains *Kora and Ka*.

NBuU; CU-SC; CtY; NNC.

A16   *Nights*

a   First edition, 1935

NIGHTS | BY | JOHN HELFORTH [Dijon: Darantière, 1935]

[1–8]⁸; pp. [1–10] 11–40 [41–44] 45–58 [59] 60–66 [67] 68–73 [74] 75–89 [90] 91–95 [96] 97–99 [100] 101–104 [105] 106–109 [110] 111–115 [116] 117–120 [121] 122–124 [125–128]. Cream wove paper, 19 × 14 cm. Edges uncut. Cover of heavy smooth cream wove paper glued at the spine. Front cover: 'NIGHTS | BY | JOHN HELFORTH'. Spine, from tail to head: 'NIGHTS'.

Pp. 1–2: blank; p. 3: half title, 'NIGHTS'; p. 4: colophon, '*This edition of 100 copies, has been printed | by friends of the author for private circulation. | All rights reserved.*'; p. 5: title page; p. 6: blank; p. 7: contents; p. 8: blank; p. 9: section title, '*PART I* | [short rule] | *PROLOGUE*'; p. 10: blank; pp. 11–41: text; p. 42: blank; p. 43: section title, '*PART II* | [short rule] | *NIGHTS*'; p. 44: blank; pp. 45–125: text; p. 126: blank; p. 127: printer's imprint, 'PRINTED | BY | IMPRIMERIE DARANTIERE | AT DIJON FRANCE | M. CM. XXXV'; p. 128: blank.

The chapter heading on p. 68 is misspelled 'NIHTG III'. On H.D.'s two copies at Yale she has written above the title on the front cover 'Dark Star—'. CtY copy 1 has extensive revisions and comments in H.D.'s hand, correcting typographical errors.

Contains "Prologue," "Nights."

NBuU; CU-SC; CtY (2 copies); NN.

b   First American edition, 1986,

[in hollow caps] NIGHTS | *by* H.D. {John Helforth} | Introduction by PERDITA SCHAFFNER | *A NEW DIRECTIONS BOOK*

[1–8]⁸; pp. [i–viii] ix–xvi [xvii–xviii] [1–2] 3–29 [30–32] 33–106 [107–110]. Cream wove paper, 17.4 × 12.9 cm. Covers of pale orange yellow (approximately C73) heavy wove stock. Front cover: '[medium rule] | [double rule] | [thick rule] | [rule] | NIGHTS | [triple rules] | by | H.D. | {John Helforth} | [thick rule] | [triple rules] | [medium rule] | [rule] | *New Directions*'. Spine, from head to tail: 'H.D. NIGHTS *New Directions*'.

Dust jacket of tan wove stock. The jacket design repeats cover, but the title and the thick rule below the author's name are red (C12). The jacket spine repeats the book spine. On the front inner flap: 'H.D. (John Helforth) | [in red] NIGHTS | Introduction by Perdita Schaffner | [twenty-six-line commentary continued to back flap] | *Jacket design by George Laws* | A NEW DIRECTION BOOK | FPT ISBN 0-8112-0979-2 $19.95'. Back inner flap: '[eight-line quote from Sandra Gilbert] | [eight-line quote from William Pratt] | [list of eight titles by H.D.] | NEW DIRECTIONS | 80 Eighth Avenue, New York 10011'.

P. i: half title, 'NIGHTS'; p. ii: blank; p. iii: list of eight other titles by H.D.; p. iv: blank; p. v: title page; p. vi: copyright, '*Copyright © 1986 by Perdita Schaffner*' | [twenty-one lines]'; p. vii: section title, 'INTRODUCTION'; p. viii: blank; pp. ix–xvi: text; p. xvii: half title, 'NIGHTS'; p. xviii: blank; p. 1: section title, 'Part I: Prologue'; p. 2: blank; pp. 3–29: text; p. 30: blank; p. 31: section title, 'Part II: Nights'; p. 32: blank; pp. 33–106: text; p. 107: blank; p. 108: colophon, '[device] | NIGHTS *has been set in Monotype Goudy Modern* | *and printed letter press, from the type,* | *at A. Colish, Inc. in Mount Vernon, New York.* | *It was designed by Bert Clarke.*'; pp. 109–110: blank.

Published 1 May 1986 in an edition of 2,500 copies at $19.95.

Contains "Introduction," "Part I: Prologue," "Part II: Nights."

NBuU; NNC.

A17 *The Hedgehog*

a.i First edition, 1936

THE HEDGEHOG | BY H.D. | [short swelling rule] | [circular device of a hedgehog against a background of mountains] | [short swelling rule] | THE BRENDIN | PUBLISHING COMPANY | 1936

[A]⁴ B-L⁴; pp. [i–viii] [1] 2–6 [7] 8–10 [11] 12–14 [15] 16–18 [19] 20–21 [22] 23–25 [26] 27–28 [29] 30–32 [33] 34–36 [37] 38–40 [41] 42–45 [46] 47–49 [50] 51–53 [54] 55–57 [58] 59–61 [62] 63–66 [67] 68–69 [70] 71–72 [73] 74–77 [78–80]. Cream wove paper, 21.7 × 17.7 cm, watermarked 'PARCHMENT BASINGWERK'. Endpapers of the same wove paper. Covers of yellow green (C136) paper over boards, 22.2 × 17.9 cm. On the front cover, a box of five rules of increasing thinness within which is printed: 'THE | HEDGEHOG | H.D.' At the top of the spine, from tail to head: 'THE HEDGEHOG'.

Dust jacket of gray green (C120) laid paper with vertical chain lines, watermarked with a crown surmounting 'Abbey Mills | Greenfield'. The design on the jacket cover and spine repeats that of the book.

Pp. i–ii: blank; p. iii: half title, 'THE HEDGEHOG'; p. iv: blank; p. v: title page; p. vi: 'PRINTED IN ENGLAND'; p. vii: contents; p. viii: blank; p. 1–77: text; p. 78: blank; p. 79: colophon, '300 COPIES OF THIS BOOK HAVE | BEEN PRINTED AT THE CURWEN | PRESS, PLAISTOW, LONDON. THE | DRAWINGS ARE BY GEORGE PLANK | *VAUD, 1925* | [large circular device in which the initials *HD* are interwoven with leaves]'; p. 80: blank.

Published in an edition of 300 copies for the friends of H.D.

Contains "1. Alpen-Rose," "2. Vipers," "3. Herisson," "4. Big Little Boots," "5. Echo," "6. Wild Bird," "7. Face to Face," "8. Weltgeist," "9. André," "10. One of Us," "11. Erlking," "12. Gentian-Blue," "13. A Way of Laughing," "14. Doctor Berne Blum," "15. Roselein," "16. In the Mirror," "17. Finding a Book," "18. A Voice," "19. Prayer to the Moon."

NBuU; CtY; PU; PPT.

There is an advertisement for *The Hedgehog* that collates [A]^2; pp. [1–4]. P. 1: cover title (title page as in **A17a.i**); p. 2: publication announcement of *The Hedgehog*; p. 3: specimen page, p. 29 of *The Hedgehog*; p. 4: order form. Paper as in **A17a.i**. CtY (3 copies).

a.ii First American edition (photo-offset from **A17a.i** with altered title page and reset preliminaries), 1988

THE HEDGEHOG | [decorative rule] | [circular device of a hedgehog against a background of mountains] | BY H.D. | INTRODUCTION BY PERDITA SCHAFFNER | WOODCUTS BY GEORGE PLANK | A NEW DIRECTIONS BOOK

[1–6]^8; pp. [i–vii] vii–xii [xiv–xvi] [1] 2–6 [7] 8–10 [11] 12–14 [15] 16–18 [19] 20–21 [22] 23–25 [26] 27–28 [29] 30–32 [33] 34–36 [37] 38–40 [41] 42–45 [46] 47–49 [50] 51–53 [54] 55–57 [58] 59–61 [62] 63–66 [67] 68–69 [70] 71–72 [73] 74–77 [78–80]. Cream wove paper, 21.4 × 18.1 cm. Covers of yellow green (C136) cloth, 22.3 × 19 cm. Stamped on the spine, from head to tail: 'H.D. THE HEDGEHOG [publisher's device] NEW DIRECTIONS'.

Dust jacket of pale yellow (C89) heavy wove paper. Front cover: '[yellow green (C136)] THE HEDGEHOG | [black decorative rule] | [woodcut illustration of hedgehog in a circle within a square rule] | [yellow green (C136)] 'BY | H.D.'. Spine, from head to tail: 'H.D. [yellow green] THE HEDGEHOG [black] [publisher's device] NEW DIRECTIONS'. Back cover: '[initials *H.D.* as on p. 79 in a circle within a square rule] | [yellow green (C136)] NEW DIRECTIONS 80 EIGHTH AVENUE NEW YORK 10011'. Front inner flap: 'FPT ISBN 0-8112-1069-3 >$12.95 | H.D. | [yellow green] THE HEDGEHOG | INTRODUCTION BY | PERDITA SCHAFFNER | WOODCUTS BY *GEORGE PLANK* | [twenty-six-line description of the story continued on back flap] | [publisher's device] | [yellow green] A NEW DIRECTIONS BOOK'. Back inner flap: '[six-line statement by Susan Gubar] | [five-line statement by Alicia Ostriker] | [list of eleven New Directions titles also by H.D.] | *Jacket woodcuts by George Plank;* | *design by Sylvia Frezzolini* | [yellow green] NEW DIRECTIONS | 80 Eighth Avenue, New York 10011'.

P. i: half title, 'THE HEDGEHOG'; p. ii: other books by H.D. [ten titles]; p. iii: title page; p. iv: copyright, 'Copyright © 1988 by Perdita Schaffner | [twenty-nine lines];' p. v: contents page; p. vi: blank; pp. vii–xiii: 'Introduction'; p. xiv: blank; p. xv: half title, 'THE HEDGEHOG'; p. xvi: blank; pp. 1–77: text; p. 78: blank; p. 79: circular device in which the initials *H.D.* are flanked above and beneath by palm leaves; p. 80: blank.

Published 28 September 1988 in an edition of 3,000 at $12.95. Printed at the same time were 3,000 sheets to be held for future paperback edition.

Contains text of *The Hedgehog* as in **A17a.i** and "Introduction" by Perdita Schaffner.

NBuU.

A18 *Euripides'* Ion

a.i First edition, 1937

EURIPIDES | ION | *Translated with notes* | *By* | H.D. | 1937 | CHATTO & WINDUS | LONDON

[A]⁶ B-H⁸ I¹⁰; pp. [i–vi] vii [viii] ix–xi [xii] 1–131 [132]. Cream wove paper, 20.1 × 12.7 cm. Top edge stained red brown (C43); other edges uncut. Endpapers of same wove paper. Covers red orange (C37) cloth, 20.7 × 13.5 cm. Gilt-stamped on the spine: '[broken rule] | [line of six snowflake-like devices] | [broken rule] | *EURIPIDES* | ION | *Translated* | *by* | H.D. | [broken rule] | [line of six snowflake-like devices] | [broken rule] | [below] *CHATTO | AND WINDUS*'. Variant binding at CtY, medium blue (C182) cloth with top edge stained medium blue.

Dust jacket of smooth cream wove paper. Front cover: '[thick, red brown (C43) rule] | *EURIPIDES* | ION | [eight-pointed red brown star outlined in black] | Translated | with commentaries by | H.D. | [thick red brown rule]'. Spine: '*The | ION | of | EURIPIDES | translated | by | H.D. | CHATTO | AND WINDUS*'. Back cover, advertisement for fifteen Chatto & Windus poetry titles. Front inner flap, nineteen-line statement on the translation; at foot: '6s. net'.

P. i: half title, '*ION | of | EURIPIDES*'; p. ii: blank; p. iii: title page; p. iv: publisher's imprint, 'PUBLISHED BY | Chatto & Windus | LONDON | [asterisk] | The Macmillan Company | of Canada, Limited | TORONTO | PRINTED IN GREAT BRITAIN | BY BUTLER AND TANNER LTD., FROME | ALL RIGHTS RESERVED'; p. v: dedication, 'FOR | B. ATHENS 1920 | P. DELPHI 1932'; p. vi: blank; p. vii: [thirteen-line excerpt from Gilbert Murray's *Euripides and His Age*; p. viii: blank;

pp. ix–x: translator's note; p. xi: 'People in the Play'; p. xii: blank; pp. 1–131: text.

In the spring of 1937 1,000 copies were printed at a price of 6s. Of these, 520 were sent to Houghton Mifflin to be bound. Of the remainder, 200 in loose sheets were destroyed by German bombs in October 1940.

CtY copy 2 contains corrections in H.D.'s hand of typographical errors, dated 1954. These corrections are incorporated in **A18b**.

Contains *Euripides* Ion.

NBuU; CtY; CaOTU.

a.ii   First American edition (English sheets), 1937

Title page as in **A18a.i** except for publisher's name: 'Boston & New York | HOUGHTON MIFFLIN COMPANY | 1937'.

Collation and text contents as in **A18a.i**. Paper as in **A18a.i** except top edge black (C267). Endpapers of heavier cream wove paper. Deep red orange (C36) cloth covers, 20.4 × 13.1 cm, with black blue (C188) cloth shelfback. Gilt stamped on spine, from head to tail: 'ION of EURIPIDES *by* H.D.'

Dust jacket of gilt coated stock. Front cover has a black frame, 6.3 × 7.8 cm, printed: '[letters of parallel gold lines] ION | [in gold] OF EURIPIDES by | [letters of parallel gold lines] H.D.' Spine, from head to tail within a black frame, 12.8 × 1.4 cm: 'ION of EURIPIDES *by* H.D.'

Contents as in **A18a.i** with altered publisher's imprint: 'MADE IN GREAT BRITAIN | ALL RIGHTS RESERVED'.

Published 4 May 1937 in an edition of 520 copies at $3.00.

CtY (2 copies).

b   Second (corrected) American edition, 1986

[within a single-rule frame: in deep purple blue (C197) ION | [row of Greek frets] | HD | [in deep purplish blue] a play after Euripides | [rule] | BLACK SWAN BOOKS

[1]^{16} [+ front.] [2]^{16} [3]^{4} [4]^{8} [5–6]^{16}; pp. [i–ii] [1–5] 6–148 [149–152]. Frontis. tipped in before title page. White wove paper, 21.4 × 13.8 cm. Endpapers of light gray (C264) laid paper with vertical chain lines. Covers of dark purple blue (C201) cloth, 22.3 × 14.3 cm. Gilt-stamped on front cover: 'ION [line of Greek frets] | [line of Greek frets] HD'. Gilt-stamped on spine from head to tail: 'HD / ION [publisher's device]'.

Dust jacket of coated white stock. Front cover has a photograph of Tholos at Delphi printed in gray (C265). Printed over the photograph in dark blue (C194): '[to the right] ION | [below and to the left] HD'. Spine, from head to tail: '[dark blue (C194)] HD [gray (C265)] / ION [dark blue (C194)] [publisher's device]'. Back cover is gray (C265). Between two white rules is a twenty-line excerpt from H.D.'s "Notes on Euripides" printed in dark blue. At top of front inner flap is a 3-cm strip of medium gray on which is printed: '[dark blue] $20.00 | HD / ION | a play after Euripides'. Below the gray strip is thirty-seven-line statement printed in dark blue continued on to the back flap for another thirty-six lines. Below the statement on the back inner flap in dark blue: '*Cover photograph: Tholos at Delphi* | Published by | BLACK SWAN BOOKS LTD. | P.O. Box 327 | [to the right of previous two lines: gray] [publisher's device] | REDDING RIDGE, CT 06876'.

P. i: blank; p. ii: frontis., photo of H.D.; p. 1: title page; p. 2: copyright, nineteen lines; p. 3: contents; p. 4: nine-line quote in italics from *Euripides and His Age* by Gilbert Murray; p. 5: half title, 'ION OF EURIPIDES | 1937 | For | B. Athens *1920* | P. Delphi *1932*'; p. 6: 'People of the Play'; p. 7: translator's note; pp. 8–119: text; pp. 120–131: afterword; p. 131: at foot, 'Note on the Text'; pp. 132–133: 'Notes on Euripides'; pp. 134–148: 'The Opening Scenes of ION'; pp. 149–150: blank; p. 151: advertisement for fifteen Black Swan titles; p. 152: blank.

Published July 1986 in an edition of 1,000 at $20.00.

Headings have a line of Greek frets in line with the page numbers. The "Note on the Text" reads: "In 1954 H.D. reread her *Ion* translation, and the present text incorporates the emendations H.D. then made in her copy of the 1937 printing (published by Chatto & Windus), subsequently given to Norman Holmes Pearson and presently in the Collection of American Literature, Beinecke Rare Book and Manuscript Library, Yale University—whose courteous help is thankfully noted."

Contains *Ion*, "Afterword: Dawn Drove the Stars Back" (by John Walsh), "Note on the Text" (by John Walsh), "Notes on Euripides (Excerpts)," "The Opening Scenes of *Ion*."

NBuU; NNC.

A19   *The Walls Do Not Fall*

a.i   First edition, 1944

THE WALLS | DO NOT FALL | by | H.D. | OXFORD UNIVERSITY PRESS | LONDON NEW YORK TORONTO | 1944

[A]⁸B⁸C¹⁰ (C₂ countersigned C*); pp. [i–ii] [1–6] 7–48 [49–50]. Cream laid paper with horizontal chain lines, 20.6 × 12.6 cm, watermarked 'ADELPHI'. [A]₁ and C₁₀ are pastedown endpapers. Covers of heavy light brown (C76) cardboard, 21.2 × 12.9 cm. Front cover: a heavy brown (C55) three-sided rule frame open at the fore edge forming an upright rectangular frame encloses the title flush with the first letters at the left of each line, broken for 7 cm at the four printed title lines: 'H.D. | [within the brown rule] The | WALLS | do not | FALL | [outside the rule at lower left] Oxford | University | Press'. Spine, from tail to head: 'H.D.—THE WALLS DO NOT FALL'. Back cover has a twelve-line blurb on H.D.'s poetry including a six-line excerpt from the poem; first line printed in brown. Below the blurb in brown: '*Price 3s. 6d. net*'.

Pp. i–ii: blank; p. 1: half title, 'THE WALLS | DO NOT FALL'; p. 2: dedication, 'To | BRYHER | *for Karnak 1923* | *from London 1942*'; p. 3: title page; p. 4: copyright, 'OXFORD UNIVERSITY PRESS | AMEN HOUSE, E.C.4 | LONDON EDINBURGH GLASGOW NEW YORK | TORONTO MELBOURNE CAPETOWN BOMBAY | CALCUTTA MADRAS | HUMPHREY MILFORD | PUBLISHER TO THE UNI-VERSITY | PRINTED IN GREAT BRITAIN BY THE BOWERING PRESS, PLYMOUTH'; p. 5: acknowledgments, 'Certain of these poems have | already appeared in *Life and* | *Letters Today*. My thanks are | due to the Editor for per-|mission to include them in this | volume.'; p. 6: blank; pp. 7–48: text; pp. 49–50: blank.

Published 11 May 1944 at 3/6. Mrs. Eve Barrett of Oxford University Press states that the publication records for the three books of the war trilogy were destroyed when the London office of OUP moved to Oxford.

Contains *The Walls Do Not Fall*. Reprinted in *Trilogy*; *CP* (1983).

NBuU; CU-SC; CU-Riv; CtY (4 copies); PU; PPT (2 copies).

a.ii   First American edition (English sheets), 1944

THE WALLS | DO NOT FALL | by | H.D. | OXFORD UNIVERSITY PRESS | LONDON NEW YORK TORONTO | 1944

[A]⁸B-C⁸); pp. [1–6] 7–48. Cream wove paper, 20.1 × 11.1 cm. CtY copy 3 sewn with purple pink (C253) thread. Endpapers of pale orange yellow (C73) wove paper. Covers of deep blue (C179) cloth boards, 20.7 × 11.7 cm. Spine, stamped in silver, from head to tail in hollow letters: 'THE WALLS DO NOT FALL—H. D.'.

Dust jacket of smooth cream wove paper printed in deep blue (C179). Front cover: 'OXFORD UNIVERSITY PRESS | [small six-pointed star] | [ornament] | [title in hollow caps] THE | WALLS | DO | NOT | FALL | *H.D.* | [ornament]'. Spine, from head to tail in hollow caps:

'THE WALLS DO NOT FALL | *by* | H.D. | OXFORD'. Back cover has an advertisement for Oxford University Press. Front inner flap has an eleven-line statement on the poem under the heading 'THE WALLS DO NOT FALL | By H.D.' At bottom: '$2.00'.

P. 1: half title, 'THE WALLS | DO NOT FALL'; p. 2: dedication as in A19a.i; p. 3: title page; p. 4: copyright, 'COPYRIGHT 1944 BY OXFORD UNIVERSITY PRESS, NEW YORK, INC. | PRINTED IN THE UNITED STATES OF AMERICA'; p. 5: acknowledgments; p. 6: blank; pp. 7–48: text.

Published 24 August 1944 at $2.00.

In the U.S. edition the English sheets are sewn differently. The first leaf of [A] in the English edition is a pastedown endpaper, whereas the first leaf of [A] in the U.S. edition has the half title on the recto and the dedication on the verso. Last leaf of [A] is signed B on recto.

Contains *The Walls Do Not Fall.*

NBuU; PU; PPT; CtY; NNC.

A20 *Tribute to the Angels*

a First edition, 1945

TRIBUTE | TO THE ANGELS | by | H.D. | OXFORD UNIVERSITY PRESS | LONDON NEW YORK TORONTO | 1945

[A]-B^{8}C^6; pp. [1–8] 9–42 [43–44]. Cream laid paper with horizontal chain lines, 20.6 × 12.4, watermarked 'ADELPHI'. [A]$_1$ and C$_6$ are pastedown endpapers. Cover of greenish blue (C172) cardboard, 21.2 × 13 cm. Cover: 'H.D. | [title within a single red orange (C38) broken-rule frame] TRIBUTE | to the | ANGELS | Oxford | University Press'. On the spine, from tail to head: 'H.D.—TRIBUTE TO THE ANGELS'. On the back cover is an eleven-line blurb on the poem. The first line is in red orange. Below the blurb in red orange: '*Price 3s. 6d. net*'.

Pp. 1–2: blank; p. 3: half title, 'TRIBUTE TO THE | ANGELS'; p. 4: dedication, 'To | OSBERT SITWELL | . . . *possibly we will reach haven,* | *heaven.*'; p. 5: title page; p. 6: publisher's imprint: 'OXFORD UNIVERSITY PRESS | AMEN HOUSE, E.C.4 | LONDON EDINBURGH GLASGOW NEW YORK | TORONTO MELBOURNE CAPETOWN BOMBAY | CALCUTTA MADRAS | HUMPHREY MILFORD | PUBLISHER TO THE UNIVERSITY | PRINTED IN GREAT BRITAIN BY THE BOWERING PRESS, PLYMOUTH'; p. 7: acknowledgment, 'Certain of these poems have | already appeared in *Life and | Letters Today*. My thanks are | due to the Editor for per-|mission to include them in | this volume.'; p. 8: blank; pp. 9–42: text; pp. 43–44: blank.

Published 11 April 1945 at 3/6. Reprinted in *Trilogy*; *CP* (1983).

CtY copy 4 (inscribed to Norman Holmes Pearson) is a variant copy. Gathering C has an integral extra sheet duplicating pp. 33–34.

Contains *Tribute to the Angels*.

NBuU; CU-Riv; CtY (4 copies); PPT.

b First American edition, 1945

TRIBUTE | TO THE ANGELS | by | H.D. | OXFORD UNIVERSITY PRESS | LONDON NEW YORK

[1–3]⁸; pp. [i–ii] [1–8] 9–42 [43–46]. Cream wove paper, 20.2 × 11.2 cm. Endpapers of smooth cream wove paper. Top edge stained medium blue (C 182). Covers of deep blue (C179) cloth, 20.8 × 11.8 cm. Spine, stamped in silver from head to tail in hollow letters: 'TRIBUTE TO THE ANGELS—H.D.'.

Dust jacket of cream laid paper with vertical chain lines, printed in deep blue; watermark, 'HAMILTON'S VICTORIAN', variously visible. Front cover: 'OXFORD UNIVERSITY PRESS | [ornament] [title in hollow letters] TRIBUTE | TO THE | ANGELS | *by* | *H.D.* | [ornament]'. Spine, from head to tail, in hollow letters: 'TRIBUTE TO THE ANGELS | *by* | *H.D.* | OXFORD'. Back cover has a list of six Oxford University Press titles. Front inner flap, under the heading 'TRIBUTE TO THE ANGELS | by H.D.', has a thirteen-line blurb on the poem. At foot: '2.00'.

Pp. i–ii: blank; p. 1: half title, 'TRIBUTE TO THE | ANGELS'; p. 2: blank; p. 3: title page; p. 4: copyright, 'Copyright 1945 OXFORD UNIVERSITY PRESS | NEW YORK, INC. | FIRST AMERICAN EDITION | LITHO IN THE UNITED STATES OF AMERICA'; p. 5: dedication as in **A20a**; p. 6: blank; p. 7: half title; p. 8: blank; p. 9–42: text; pp. 43–46: blank.

Published 15 November 1945 at $2.00. Allison Crane of Oxford University Press in New York writes: "There is an indication that we printed 750 copies but this is not at all clear and should be given with a query if at all. There is an old mention of this # of copies but it is not clearly marked as the first printing." Reprinted in *Trilogy*; *CP* (1983).

Contains *Tribute to the Angels*.

CtY (2 copies); PPT.

A21 *The Flowering of the Rod*

a   First edition, 1946

THE FLOWERING | OF THE ROD | by | H.D. | GEOFFREY CUMBERLEGE | OXFORD UNIVERSITY PRESS | LONDON NEW YORK TORONTO | 1946

[A]^{8}B-C^{8}D^4; pp. [i–ii] [1–6] 7–50 [51–54]. Cream laid paper with horizontal chain lines, 20.7 × 12.6 cm, watermarked 'ADELPHI'. [A]$_1$ and D$_4$ are pastedown endpapers. Covers of light yellow brown (C76) heavy cardboard, 21.1 × 12.8 cm. Front cover: 'H.D. | The | FLOWERING | of the | ROD | Oxford | University Press'. A three-sided single-rule frame, deep yellow green (C132), partially encloses the title. Spine, from tail to head: 'H.D.—THE FLOWERING OF THE ROD'. Back cover has a nineteen-line blurb on the *Trilogy*, the first line printed in deep yellow green. Below the blurb in deep yellow green: '*Price 3s. 6d. net*'.

Pp. i–2: blank; p. 3: half title, 'THE FLOWERING | OF THE ROD'; p. 4: dedication, 'To | NORMAN HOLMES PEARSON | . . . *pause to give | thanks that we rise again from death and live.*'; p. 5: title page; p. 6: publisher's imprint, 'OXFORD UNIVERSITY PRESS | AMEN HOUSE, E.C.4 | LONDON EDINBURGH GLASGOW | NEW YORK TORONTO MELBOURNE | CAPETOWN BOMBAY | GEOFFREY CUMBERLEGE | PUBLISHER TO THE UNIVERSITY | PRINTED IN GREAT BRITAIN | 8945.6465'; pp. 7–50: text; p. 51: blank; p. 52: printer's imprint, 'PRINTED BY THE BOWERING PRESS, PLYMOUTH'; pp. 53–54: blank.

Published in 1946 at 3/6. It sold for $2.00 in the United States. No separate American edition has been located.

Contains *The Flowering of the Rod*. Reprinted in *Trilogy*; *CP* (1983).

NBuU; CU-Riv; CtY (2 copies); PPT.

A22 *By Avon River*

a   First edition, 1949

BY AVON RIVER | [short rule] | [line of three devices] | [short thick-thin rule] | H.D. | THE MACMILLAN COMPANY | *New York* [raised dot] *1949*

[1]^8 [2–3]^{16} [4]^{12}; pp. [i–iv] [1–4] 5–25 [26–30] 31–98 [99–100]. Cream wove paper, 20.2 × 13.5 cm. Endpapers of a heavier smooth cream paper. Covers of medium blue (C182) grosgrain cloth boards, 20.8 × 13.9 cm.

A blind ornament stamped on front cover. Spine, gilt-stamped from head to tail: 'BY AVON RIVER | [short rule] | BY | H.D. | [from head to tail] MACMILLAN'.

Dust jacket of cream wove paper. Front cover and spine green blue (C173). On an olive (C94) panel with a single white border rule; within a green blue decorated (top and bottom) floral frame: '[white] BY | AVON | RIVER | [rule] | BY H.D. | [rule] | [thick green blue rule]'. Spine: '[within an olive box] [thick green blue rule] | [white: rule] | [from head to tail] BY AVON RIVER | [rule] | BY | H.D. | [rule] | [thick green blue rule] | [below the box: white, from head to tail] MACMILLAN'. Back cover, under the heading (in olive) *'Critical praise for H.D.'* are a seven-line statement by William Rose Benét, a four-line statement by Horace Gregory, and a four-line statement by Marianne Moore, all printed in green blue. The front inner flap has a thirty-line statement in blue gray under the heading 'By Avon River' in olive. At top right edge, from head to tail: '$2.50'. Below: *'Jacket design by Ronald Clyne'*. Back inner flap has a thirty-three-line biographical sketch in green blue under the heading 'H.D.' in olive.

P. i: half title, 'BY AVON RIVER'; p. ii: publisher's imprint; p. iii: title page; p. iv: copyright, 'COPYRIGHT, 1949, BY HILDA ALDINGTON | *All rights reserved*—[five lines in italic] | First Printing | PRINTED IN THE UNITED STATES OF AMERICA'; p. 1: section title, 'GOOD FREND | *Shakespeare Day, 23rd April, 1945* | GOOD FREND FOR IESVS SAKE FORBEARE, | TO DIGG THE DVST ENCLOASED HEARE! | BLESTE BE Y MAN Y SPARES THES STONES, | AND CVRS BE HE Y MOVES MY BONES. | *23rd April, 1564* | *23rd April 1616*'; p. 2: blank; p. 3: dedication, *'For | BRYHER | Shakespeare Day | April 23, 1945 | & | ROBERT HERRING | St. George Day | April 23, 1945'*; p. 4: blank; pp. 5–25: text; p. 26: blank; p. 27: section title, 'THE GUEST | GO, SOUL, THE BODY'S GUEST, | UPON A THANKLESS ARRANT, | FEAR NOT TO TOUCH THE BEST; | THE TRUTH SHALL BE THY WARRANT; | GO, SINCE I NEEDS MUST DIE, | AND GIVE THE WORLD THE LIE!'; p. 28: blank; p. 29: dedication, *'To | BRYHER | from | Seehof | Küsnacht'*; p. 30: eight-line note in italic; pp. 31–96: text; p. 96: text, subscribed, *'September 19 | November 1 | 1946'*; pp. 97–98: birth and death dates of personae; pp. 99–100: blank.

Published 28 June 1949 at $2.50.

Contains "Good Frend" (section title for the following three poems): "The Tempest," "Rosemary," "Claribel's Way to God"; "The Guest."

NBuU; NBu; CU-Riv; CtY (2 copies); PU (2 copies); PPT; CaOTU; NN (2 copies); NNC.

A23 *What Do I Love?*

a   First edition, 1950

[in upper left corner] WHAT | DO | I | LOVE? | [at bottom center] Privately published by | The Brendin Publishing Co., Ltd. | at | 430 Strand, London, W.C.2

[A]¹²; pp. [1–2] 3–24. Cream wove paper, 18.4 × 12.4 cm. Double stapled at the single-gathering centerfold. Cover of pale blue (C185) wove paper. In upper left corner of front cover, printed in dark blue (C197): 'WHAT | DO | I | LOVE?'

P. 1: title page; p. 2: 'PRINTED IN GREAT BRITAIN BY | STEPHEN AUSTIN AND SONS, LTD., HERTFORD'; pp. 3–24: text.

In a letter to Norman Holmes Pearson at the Beinecke Library dated 15 October 1950, H.D. wrote: "But Bryher and Robert [Herring] had a tiny book set up, as for a Xmas card for me to send out, just before L. and L. [*Life and Letters Today*] folded up and they could put things through with the printer. I am posting you a pre-Xmas copy; it is just three poems, I think you have them, a series that I call May 1943, another I call R.A.F., the third and last, Christmas 1944. They hardly fit into any of the Trilogy sequences, but I like them and they do very well in this tiny book that I call "What do I love?" I have left the signature out, as I will sign the copies with Xmas greetings. I have 30 copies here. I think there are 50 altogether." The galleys at CtY have a byline: 'BY | DELIA ALTON', crossed out by H.D. Delia Alton is one of the H.D. personas.

Contains "May 1943," "R.A.F.," "Christmas 1944." Reprinted in *CP* (1983).

CtY.

A24 *Tribute to Freud*

a   First edition, 1956

[within a yellow gray (C93) box] *TRIBUTE TO | FREUD | BY* H.D. | *With unpublished letters | by Freud to the author* | PANTHEON

[1–12]⁸; pp. [i–vi] vii–ix [x] 1–168 [169–171] 172–180 [180–182]. Cream wove paper, 20.1 × 12.4 cm. Top edge stained light gray (C264). Thread differs from copy to copy: white and (a) purple red (C255) or (b) yellow brown (C74) or (c) dark brown (C59). Endpapers of cream wove paper. Covers of medium gray (C265) cloth, 20.8 × 12.9 cm. Stamped on front cover: '[2.8-cm-square red orange (C34) box] | [white] H.D. | [2.8-cm-square red orange box]'. Stamped on spine in red orange: 'H.D. | [white] TRIBUTE | TO | FREUD | [red orange] PANTHEON'.

Dust jacket of orange yellow (C67) stock. Front cover: '[within a red orange box] Tribute to | Freud | by H.D. | with unpublished letters | by Freud to the Author | [below the box] Pantheon'. Spine, from head to tail: 'Tribute to Freud by H.D.' Back cover has an advertisement for *Beethoven and His Nephew* by Richard and Editha Sterba. At top of front inner flap: '$2.50'. Front flap has thirty-one lines of biographical information and a description of the book under the heading: 'H.D. | [in orange red] TRIBUTE TO FREUD'. Back inner flap has a twenty-six-line continuation of this material. At bottom: 'PRINTED IN THE U.S.A.'.

P. i: [in upper right corner] publisher's device; p. ii: blank; p. iii: title page; p. iv: copyright, 'COPYRIGHT 1956 BY PANTHEON BOOKS INC. | 333 SIXTH AVENUE, NEW YORK 14 | LIBRARY OF CONGRESS | CATALOG CARD NUMBER: 56—10963 | MANUFACTURED IN THE UNITED STATES | AMERICAN BOOK—STRATFORD PRESS, INC., NEW YORK'; p. v: dedication, 'To Sigmund Freud | ἀμύμων ἰητηε | "blameless physician" '; p. vi: blank; pp. vii–ix: foreword; p. x: blank; pp. 1–169: text; p. 170: blank; p. 171: section title, 'APPENDIX'; p. 172: note by Norman Holmes Pearson; pp. 173–180: letters by Freud to H.D.; pp. 181–182: blank.

Published 5 September 1956 at $2.50.

Contains "Foreword" (by Merrill Moore), *Tribute to Freud*, "Appendix" (nine letters from Freud to H.D.)

NBuU; CtY; PU; PPT; NNC.

b.i   First English edition, 1971

TRIBUTE | TO | FREUD | by HD | with an introduction | by Peter Jones | [publisher's device] CARCANET PRESS

[A–P]⁴; pp. [i–ii] [1–4] 5–7 [8] 9–117 [118]. White wove paper, 19.6 × 12.5 cm. Endpapers of a lighter white wove paper. Covers of dark blue (C183) cloth. White paper title label, 12.6 × .8 cm, glued to spine, printed from head to tail: '[publisher's device] HD Tribute to Freud'.

Dust jacket of orange yellow (C86) wove paper. On the cover: '[three irregular, wide vertical rules resembling branches; between the second and third rule, from tail to head] HD Tribute to Freud | [between the third rule and the fore edge, from tail to head] with an introduction by Peter Jones'. Spine, [from tail to head]: '[publisher's device] HD Tribute to Freud'. Back cover: '[from tail to head] HD Tribute to Freud | [to the right of the title, two vertical rules similar to those on the front cover] | [to the right of the rules] [publisher's device]'. Front inner flap has a six-line quote from Ernest Jones and a twenty-nine-line description of the book, below which is printed: 'hb £1.50/pb 90p'. Back inner flap has an advertisement for the Carcanet Press.

Pp. i–ii: blank; p. 1: title page; p. 2: copyright, 'Copyright © Norman Holmes Pearson 1971 | © Peter Jones 1971 (Introductory material) | SBN 902145 14 2 | All rights reserved | First published 1956 by Pantheon Books Inc. | First published in this edition 1971 | by Carcanet Press | Pin Farm | South Hinskey, Oxford. | Printed by D. Parchment (OXFORD) Ltd., 60 Hurst Street, Oxford.'; p. 3: contents; p. 4: 'HD (Hilda Doolottle) | 1886–1961 | Sigmund Freud | 1856–1939'; p. 5–7: introduction; p. 8: blank; p. 9: dedication, 'To Sigmund Freud | "blameless physician" '; pp. 10–116: text; p. 117: notes; p. 118: blank.

Contains "Introduction" (by Peter Jones), *Tribute to Freud*, "Notes."

NBuU; CtY.

b.ii   First English edition, paperback, 1971

Title page, collation, contents, and text contents as in **A24b.i**.

White paper, 19.3 × 12.5 cm. Covers of orange (C50) heavy stock, 19.3 × 12.5 cm. Cover design as in **A24b.i** dust jacket. Inside front and back covers have the same design and content as the front and back inner flaps of the dust jacket of **A24b.i**.

NBu.

c.i   Second (revised) American edition, 1974

HD | TRIBUTE TO FREUD | WRITING ON THE WALL [dot] ADVENT | FOREWORD BY | NORMAN HOLMES PEARSON | INTRODUCTION BY | KENNETH FIELDS | [publisher's device] | DAVID R. GODINE | BOSTON

[1–6]^{16} [7]^8 [8]^{16}; pp. [i–vi] vii–xlv [xlvi] [1–2] 3–111 [112–114] 115–187 [188] 189–194. White wove paper, 21.6 × 13.8 cm, watermarked 'WARREN'S OLDSTYLE'. Endpapers of heavy black wove paper. Covers of yellow gray (C93) cloth. Spine stamped from head to tail: 'TRIBUTE TO FREUD H.D. | GODINE'.

Dust jacket of white stock. Front cover and spine are black. Front cover: '[red orange (C36)] TRIBUTE TO | FREUD | [square photograph of a couch on the shore of a mountain lake above which hovers the dreamlike image of a face] | [white] by HD | FOREWORD BY NORMAN HOLMES PEARSON | INTRODUCTION BY KENNETH FIELDS'. Spine, from head to tail: '[red orange] TRIBUTE TO FREUD [white] HD | [black] [publisher's device] | [white] GODINE'. Back cover: '[red orange] [four-line description of the book] | [photograph of Freud in his study] | [five-line statement on the book by Ernest Jones] | [a ten-line excerpt in italic from "Writing on the Wall"]'. At top of front inner flap: 'ISBN 0-87923-074-6 $10.00'. Front and back inner flaps contain a description of the book and biographical information on H.D. under the heading (red orange) 'TRIBUTE TO FREUD | *by H.D.* | *Foreword by Norman Holmes Pearson* | *Introduction by Kenneth Fields*'. At bottom of back inner flap: '*Photograph on jacket front by Mark Silber*'.

P. i: half title, 'TRIBUTE TO FREUD'; p. ii: frontispiece, portrait of H.D. by Islay Lyons; p. iii: title page; p. iv: copyright, 'DAVID R. GODINE, PUBLISHER | 306 DARTMOUTH STREET | BOSTON, MASSACHUSETTS 02116 | COPYRIGHT © BY NORMAN HOLMES PEARSON 1956 | COPYRIGHT © NORMAN HOLMES PEARSON 1974 | © KENNETH FIELDS (INTRODUCTION) 1974 | LCC 73-81064, ISBN 0-87923-074-6'; p. v: contents; p. vi: blank; pp. vii–xvi: foreword; pp. xvii–xlv: introduction; p. xlvi: 'A Note on the Text' (eight lines); p. 1: section title, 'WRITING ON THE WALL | TO SIGMUND FREUD | *blameless physician*'; p. 2: blank; pp. 3–111: text; p. 112: blank; p. 113: section title, 'ADVENT'; p. 114: blank; pp. 115–187: text; p. 188: blank; pp. 189–194: appendix.

Published 15 October 1974 in an edition of approximately 3,000 copies at $15.00.

Contains "Foreword" (by Norman Holmes Pearson), "Introduction" (by Kenneth Fields), "Writing on the Wall," "Advent," "Appendix" (Freud's letters to H.D.).

In an undated letter to Norman Holmes Pearson at the Beinecke, David Godine wrote that the first printing was officially 3,000 but due to a mix-up at the printer he only received 2,650. See also note for **A24c.iii**.

Location: NBuU; NBu.

c.ii   Second (revised) American edition, paperback, 1975

HD | TRIBUTE TO FREUD | WRITING ON THE WALL [dot] ADVENT | FOREWORD BY | NORMAN HOLMES PEARSON | [publisher's device] | McGraw-Hill Book Company | New York · St. Louis · San Francisco · London · Paris · Dusseldorf | Tokyo · Kuala Lumpur · Mexico · Montreal · Panama · Sao Paulo | Sydney · Toronto · Johannesberg · New Delhi · Singapore

Perfect bound in paper wrappers; pp. [i–ii] iii–xii [xiii–xiv] ([1]–194 as in A24c.i). Cream wove paper, 20.1 × 13.3 cm. Paper covers of coated white stock cut flush with text. Front cover illustration of a double window overlooking a beach. At top, the sea is green blue (C168). The sand is gray yellow (C90) speckled with black. A black and white rose is superimposed over the window. In the lower window frame, to the right of the rose stem: 'TRIBUTE | TO FREUD | by HD | Foreword by Norman Holmes Pearson | [to the left of the rose stem] [publisher's device] | McGRAW-HILL | PAPERBACKS | [within a circle] $2.95'. Spine, from head to tail: '[green blue (C168)] [publisher's device] [black] TRIBUTE TO FREUD [green blue] by HD McGRAW-HILL PAPERBACKS [to the left of previous two words] PSYCHOLOGY $2.95'. Back cover: 'TRIBUTE TO FREUD [green blue] PSYCHOLOGY | by HD | [black] [six-line quote from Ernest Jones] | [three paragraph, twenty-three-line description of book] | [to the right of the third paragraph: from tail to head] Cover design by Joan O'Connor | [green blue] [publisher's device] | McGraw-Hill Paperbacks [black] 0-07-027731-1'.

P. i: title page; p. ii: copyright page, thirteen lines; pp. iii–xii: foreword; p. xiii: contents; p. xiv: frontispiece, portrait of H.D. by Islay Lyons; p. 1: section title, 'WRITING ON THE WALL | TO SIGMUND FREUD | *blameless physician*'; p. 2: a note on the text, 'Writing on the Wall to Sigmund Freud, blameless physi-|cian, was written in London in the autumn of 1944, with no | reference to the Vienna notebooks of spring 1933. | [¶] 'Writing on the Wall' appeared in *Life and Letters Today*, Lon-|don, 1945–1946. | H.D.'; pp. 3–111: text; p. 112: blank; p. 113: section title, 'ADVENT'; p. 114: a note on the text, ' "Advent," the continuation of 'Writing on the Wall,' or its | prelude was taken direct from the old notebooks of 1933, | though it was not assembled until December, 1948, Lausanne. | H.D.'; pp. 115–187: text; p. 188: blank; pp. 189–194: appendix.

See note to **A24c.iii**.

Contains "Foreword" (by Norman Holmes Pearson), "Writing on the Wall," "Advent," "Appendix" (Freud's letters to H.D.)

NBuU.

c.iii Second (revised) American edition, second impression (photo-offset from **A24c.ii** with reorganized preliminaries), 1984

HD | TRIBUTE TO FREUD | WRITING ON THE WALL [dot] ADVENT | FOREWORD BY | NORMAN HOLMES PEARSON | A NEW DIRECTIONS BOOK

Perfect bound in paper wrappers; pp. [i–iv] v–xiv ([1]–194 as in **A24c.i**). Cream wove paper, 20 × 12.8 cm. Paper covers of coated white stock cut flush with text. Front cover is a black and white photograph of an elderly Freud. At the bottom: '[white] Tribute to Freud | [black] by H.D.' Black spine printed in white from head to tail: 'Tribute to Freud by H.D. NDP 572'. Back cover, in upper left corner: 'MEMOIR'. Under the heading 'Tribute to Freud | by H.D. | With a foreword by Norman Holmes Pearson' is a twenty-four-line bio-critical description, as well as a four-line quote from Ernest Jones. At the bottom of the back cover: '*Cover photograph by Edmund Engelmen; design by Harold Wortsman* | A NEW DIRECTIONS PAPERBOOK NDP 572 | FPISBN 0-8112-0897-4 >> $6.95'.

P. i: title page; p. ii: copyright, 'Copyright © 1956, 1974 by Norman Holmes Pearson | [twenty-three lines]'; p. iii: contents; p. iv: blank; pp. v–xiv: foreword; p. 1: section title, 'WRITING ON THE WALL | TO SIGMUND FREUD | *blameless physician*'; p. 2: blank; pp. 3–111: text; p. 112: blank; p. 113: section title, 'ADVENT'; p. 114: blank; pp. 115–187: text; p. 188: blank; pp. 189–194: appendix.

Published 31 July 1984 in an edition of 3,000 at $6.95. A second impression of 2,000 copies was printed 19 April 1985 and sold at $7.95.

According to records in the files at New Directions, in 1973 they wanted to be H.D.'s main publisher, but they were thinking of turning mainly to paperbacks and so were interested in someone else doing the cloth bound editions. Norman Holmes Pearson approached David Godine who was interested in acquiring basic rights to the book. At the encouragement of New Directions, however, Pearson awarded the basic rights to New Directions and leased only the cloth rights to Godine. Godine wanted at that time to do a paperback edition, but New Directions held back their permission, thinking to do it themselves. Because of faulty wording in the contract Pearson drew up for Godine, however, both Pearson and Godine were given veto power over awarding paperback rights and Godine promptly exercised this veto in relation to New Directions. In April 1975 Putnam then made an offer of a $1,000 advance for a run of 3,000 books at $1.95, which Godine also turned down, apparently because of New Directions' support for the proposal. Finally Godine agreed to lease the paperback rights to McGraw-Hill for $2,000, which they split with the H.D. Estate. In November 1982 McGraw-Hill let the book go permanently out of print so that the basic rights reverted to Perdita Schaffner, although the clothbound rights remained with Godine.

Text contents as in **A24c.ii**.

NBuU; NBu; CtY.

d Second (revised) English edition (photo-offset from **A24c.iii**), 1985;

Title page as in **A24c.iii** with altered publisher's name: '[in hollow letters] CARCANET'.

Collation and text contents as in **A24c.iii**. White wove paper, 21.5 × 13.4 cm. Paper covers of white stock cut flush with text. Front cover is the same photograph of Freud as front cover of **A24c.iii** enlarged and printed in deep purple (C219). In a ragged white square on the right: '[short deep purple rule] | [in blue green (C164)] H.D. | [short deep purple rule] | [blue green] TRIBUTE TO | FREUD | [short deep purple rule]'. In a ragged white rectangle in the lower right corner, in blue green hollow letters: 'CARCANET'. Deep purple spine printed in white: '[short rule] | H.D. | [short rule] | [from head to tail] TRIBUTE TO FREUD [blue green] CARCANET'. Blue green back cover printed in deep purple; within a circle in the center of the cover is a deep purple photograph of H.D. Below the circle is a nine-line quote from Ernest Jones. At bottom the Carcanet address, below which is: '*Cover design by Stephen Row | Cover photograph by Edmund Engleman | £5.95*'. To the right is the ISBN code in a white square.

Contents as in **A24c.iii** with altered copyright: 'First published in Great Britain in 1970. | Revised edition 1985 by | CARCANET PRESS LTD. | 208–212 Corn Exchange Building, Manchester M43BQ | Copyright © 1956, 1974 by Norman Holmes Pearson | [six lines] | This edition is published by arrangement with New Directions Publishing Co. | agents for the Estate of Hilda Doolittle | The publisher acknowledges financial assistance | from the Arts Council of Great Britain.'

According to information in the files at New Directions, Carcanet was originally going to buy copies of the New Directions reissue, but the plummeting value of the pound made this uneconomical. They consequently photographed the New Directions sheets.

A25 *Selected Poems*

a.i.   First limited edition, 1957

H.D. *SELECTED POEMS* | GROVE PRESS, INC. NEW YORK

$[1-4]^{16}$ (1_2 + 1); pp. [i–ii] [1–6] 7–128. Cream wove paper, 20.2 × 13.5 cm. Endpapers of a heavier cream wove paper. Covers of very light gray (C264) paper with visible dark fibers over boards. Brown (C58) cloth shelfback. In the lower right corner of the front cover is a small circle divided in half, the left half black, the right half purple red (C256). Gilt-stamped at the left edge on the shelf back from tail to head: 'SELECTED POEMS H.D.'. Gilt-stamped on the spine from head to tail: 'SELECTED POEMS H.D. GROVE PRESS"'

P. i: half title, 'H.D. | SELECTED POEMS'; p. ii: dedication, 'To my grandchildren | Valentine, | Nicholas, | and | Elizabeth Bryher'; p. 1: title page; p. 2: copyright, 'Copyright, ©, 1957, by Norman Holmes Pearson | Library of Congress Catalog Card Number: 57-8646 | *H.D. Selected Poems is published in three editions:* | An Evergreen Book (E-71) | A hard bound edition | A specially bound, Limited Edition of 50 numbered copies, | signed by the author | Grove Press, Inc. | by Barney Rosset at Grove Press, Inc. | 795 Broadway New York 3, N.Y. | Typography by Peter Bergman *(The Polyglot Press)* | MANUFACTURED IN THE UNITED STATES OF AMERICA'; p. 3: colophon, '*This is a* | *SPECIALLY BOUND, LIMITED EDITION* | *of* [number supplied in ink] *50 Numbered copies,* | *of which this is copy number* [number supplied in ink] | *H.D.* | *Kusnacht* | *Zurich* | *March 17—1957*; p. 4: blank; pp. 5–6: contents; pp. 7–128: text.

Published 5 September 1957 in an edition of 50 copies.

Contains "The Helmsman," "Adonis," "Sea Heroes," "Never More Will the Wind," "Sea Rose," "Sea Poppies," "Heat," "Orchard," "Acon," "And Pergamos," "Hippolytus Temporizes," "Pear Tree," "Oread," "From Citron Bower," "Pallas," "Along the Yellow Sand," "The Islands," "At Baia," "Fragment 113," "Evadne," "White World," "Love That I Bear," "Lais," "Heliodora," "Helen," "At Ithica [*sic*]," "Lethe," "Where Is the Nightingale," "O Love Cease," "Stars Wheel in Purple," "The Mysteries Remain," "Erige Cor Tuum ad Me in Caelum," "Callypso Speaks," "Bird of the Air," "The Moon in Your Hands," "Fair the Thread," "Georgias Sanctus," "Hymn," "Scribe," "From: The Walls Do Not Fall," "From: Tribute to the Angels," "From: The Flowering of the Rod," "From: Good Frend," "Fire, Flood, and Olive-Tree," "Sigil," "Epitaph."

CtY.

a.ii   First trade edition, 1957

Title page and text contents as in **A25a.i**.

[1–4]¹⁶; pp. [1–6] 7–128. Paper as in **A25a.i**. Gray yellow (C90) cloth, 20.8 × 14.1 cm. Stamped on the cover in dark yellow brown (C78): 'SELECTED POEMS H.D.' Stamped on spine from head to tail in dark yellow brown: 'SELECTED POEMS H.D. GROVE PRESS'.

P. 1: half title as in **A25a.i**; p. 2: dedication as in **A25a.i**; p. 3: title page; p. 4: copyright; pp. 5–6: contents; pp. 7–128: text.

Published 5 September 1957 in an edition of 1,250 copies at $3.00.

NBuU; CtY; PPT; NN; NNC (2 copies).

a.iii   First edition, paperback, 1957

Title page, collation, contents, and text contents as in **A25a.ii**.

Covers of coated white stock cut flush with text, glued at spine. Bottom of front cover and spine covered with discontinuous blocks of red orange

(C34) overlaid with blocks of a netlike pattern of small connected circles. In the upper right corner, at an oblique angle: '[from tail to head] AN EVERGREEN BOOK | $1.45 | [from tail to head] Published by GROVE PRESS'. To the left of above: 'SELECTED POEMS | OF | [in large letters] H.D.' Above and to the left of 'H.D.': *'Felsenthal'*. Spine, from head to tail: 'H.D. SELECTED POEMS OF H.D. E-71 GROVE | PRESS'. Back cover: 'AN EVERGREEN BOOK OF POETRY (E-71)—$1.45 SELECTED POEMS | Of H.D. | [three-paragraph, twenty-one-line description of the poetry] | *Cover design by Francine Felsenthal* | GROVE PRESS, INC., 795 Broadway, New York 3, N.Y.' Inner front and back covers have a list of Evergreen books printed in green (C132).

Published 5 September 1957 in an edition of 2,500 copies at $1.45.

In a letter to Judith Schmidt at Grove Press dated 11 June 1957, Norman Holmes Pearson wrote that he had sent the signatures and loose cover to H.D., and that she was obviously most happy about it: "I am *so* happy with the paperbook," he quoted her. "I rather want to send out just this one. It is so nice to hold and I *love* being an *Evergreen* . . . Please thank Grove again. I could not be happier. Really, I am more elated about my 'Evergreen' than I have ever been about an opus."

NBuU; CtY.

a.iv First English edition (American sheets), 1957

As in **A25a.ii** with white paper label pasted over the publisher's name on the title page, printed: '[publisher's device, a horizontal bow overlaid by three vertical arrows, all within an oval] ANDRE DEUTSCH'. The publisher's name on the spine reads from head to tail in dark yellow brown (C78): 'ANDRE DEUTSCH'.

According to a letter from Judith Schmidt at Grove Press to Norman Holmes Pearson, Grove bound 100 copies for Deutsch with his imprint. He later reordered, taking copies of the Grove Press hardbound edition. He took 25 more copies in September 1958. Sold at 12/6.

NBuU.

a.v First edition, second impression, paperback, 1963

Title page, collation, contents, and text contents as in **A25a.ii**.

Covers of coated white stock cut flush with text. The front cover is filled with a black and white photograph of an elderly H.D. which extends around the spine. In the upper right corner from tail to head: 'EVERGREEN E-71—$1.45 [publisher's device]'. In the lower left corner, in white: 'SELECTED | POEMS OF H.D.' Spine, head to tail: 'SELECTED POEMS OF H.D. [white] [publisher's device] E-71

GROVE PRESS'. Back cover: 'AN EVERGREEN BOOK (E–71)—
$1.45 | Selected Poems of H.D. | [three-paragraph description of the
poetry] | *Photo by B. Obrecht* | GROVE PRESS, INC., 795 Broadway, New
York 3, N.Y.' Inner front and back covers have a list of Evergreen titles.

Grove allowed the book to go out of print in 1962. According to records in
the files at New Directions, in 1963 Norman Holmes Pearson lent Grove
$500.00 to subsidize a reprint of 2,000 copies. Sold for $1.45.

Private library.

a.vi First edition, third impression, paperback

As in **A25a.iii** with altered copyright: below the Library of Congress Catalog number, 'Third printing'. Below the statement of editions: '*Distributed in Canada by McClelland & Stewart Ltd.,* | *25 Hollinger Road, Toronto 16*'.

On the front cover the price reads '$1.95'. On the back cover the price
reads '$1.95', and below it: 'In Canada: 20c additional'. At the bottom of
the back cover: 'GROVE PRESS, INC., 64 University Place, New York 3,
N.Y. | Canadian Distributor: McClelland & Stewart, Ltd., 25 Hollinger
Road, Toronto 16'.

Personal copy.

a.vii First edition, fourth impression, paperback

As in **A25a.iii** with altered copyright: below the Library of Congress number, 'Fourth printing'. There is no information about Canadian publisher or price, either on the copyright page or the back cover.

Sold at $1.95.

Later impressions no longer differentiate the impression number, although
the price rises to $9.95.

Private library.

A26   *Bid Me to Live*

ai. First limited edition, 1960

BID ME | TO LIVE | [short rule] | *(A Madrigal)* | [short rule] | BY H.D. |
[short rule] | GROVE PRESS, INC./NEW YORK

$[1-4]^{16} (1_2 + 1) [5]^{12} [6]^{16}$; pp. [i–ii] [1–6] 7–13 [14] 15–59 [60] 61–73 [74]
75–103 [104] 105–169 [170] 171–184. Cream wove paper, 20.2 × 13.5 cm.
Gatherings sewn with white and light gray (C264) thread. Endpapers of

a heavier cream wove paper. Covers of textured brown pink (C33) paper over boards, 20.8 × 14 cm, with brown (C58) cloth shelfback. Spine gilt-stamped from head to tail: 'BID ME TO LIVE * H.D. | GROVE | PRESS'.

P. i: half title, 'BID ME TO LIVE | *(A Madrigal)*'; p. ii: blank; p. 1: title page; p. 2: copyright, 'Copyright © 1960 by Norman Holmes Pearson | Library of Congress Catalog Card Number: | 60-6345 | First Grove Press Edition 1960 | Distributed in Canada by | McClelland & Stewart Ltd., 25 Hollinger Road | Toronto 16 | Manufactured in the United States of America'; p. 3: colophon, 'This is a specially bound Limited Edition | of 10 numbered copies, *hors commerce*, of | which this is | Copy Number [number supplied in ink] | H.D., | Jan. 25, 1960'; p. 4: blank; p. 5: sixteen-line poem, 'TO ANTHEA', by Robert Herrick; p. 6: blank; pp. 7–13: text; p. 14: blank; pp. 15–59: text; p. 60: blank; pp. 61–73: text; p. 74: blank; pp. 75–103: text; p. 104: blank; pp. 105–169: text; p.: 170: blank; pp. 171–184: text.

Published 27 April 1960 in an edition of 10 copies.

H.D.'s original title for the novel was *Madrigal*, but Barney Rosset informed her through Norman Holmes Pearson that this title was already in use and they would have to find another. She initially agreed to the new title, but after talking with Richard Aldington she wrote to Horace Gregory at Grove on 9 Dec. 1959 pleading to get the original title back: "I want to rush this out in hope of 're-snagging Madrigal as title.' What if there were 50 other 'novels' of the same name? Surely mine takes precedence, written summer 1939 on the eve of War II, bringing War I into focus. The last section or sections, the 'Rico' letter was 'inspired,' I think—& I scrapped the first long ending, to round out the circle or cycle with this 'Rico;' the Ms was left in Suisse, but I retrieved it on my return, I wrote the last 'Rico' sections in Lausanne, winter 1948 or 1949, just ten years after the 1939 beginning with War II between. Well—you see, it does matter to me." Grove's solution was to add "(A Madrigal)" to the title. In a letter to Judith Schmidt at Grove Press dated 15 March [1960], H.D. wrote: "I am so happy to have 'Bid Me to Live'—happier than I have ever been, I think, over any of my books."

Contains *Bid Me to Live*.

CtY.

a.ii   First trade edition, 1960

Title page and text contents as in **A26a.i**.

Collation as in **A26a.i** with deleted colophon page (pp. i–ii). Cream wove paper, 20.2 × 13.3 cm. Endpapers of a heavier cream wove paper. Covers of deep blue (C179) cloth, 20.8 × 13.9 cm. Gilt-stamped on spine from head to tail: 'BID ME TO LIVE [star] H.D. [star] | GROVE | PRESS'.

Dust jacket of coated white stock. Covers and spine covered by a continuous photograph of surf breaking on a beach. Printed in red orange (C35) over the photo on the front cover: 'Bid Me | to Live | A NOVEL BY | H.D.' Spine, from head to tail, in red orange: 'BID ME TO LIVE BY H.D. | GROVE | PRESS'. At upper right of front inner flap: '$3.50'. Below this is a forty-two-line description of the novel and H.D.'s life under the heading 'Bid Me To Live | *A Novel by H.D.*' The description is continued for thirty-five lines on the back inner flap. Below the description on the back inner flap: 'Photo by Lawrence N. Shustak Design by Richard Brodney | GROVE PRESS, INC. | 64 University Place | New York 3, N.Y. | *Distributed in Canada by* | *McClelland & Stewart Ltd.* | *25 Hollinger Road, Toronto 16*'.

P. 1: half title as in **A26a.i**; p. 2: blank; p. 3: title page; p. 4: copyright, 'Copyright © 1960 by Norman Holmes Pearson | Library of Congress Catalog Card Number: | 60-6345 | First Grove Press Edition 1960 | Distributed in Canada by | McClelland & Stewart Ltd., 25 Hollinger Road | Toronto 16 | Manufactured in the United States of America'; pp. 5–184 as in **A26a.i**.

Published 27 April 1960 at $3.50.

CtY (2 copies); PU; PPT; CaOTU; NN (2 copies); NNC.

a.iii   First edition, paperback, 1960

Title page, collation, contents, and text contents as **A26a.ii**.

Cream wove paper, 20.2 × 13.5 cm. Gatherings sewn with white and light gray (C264) thread, glued to paper wrappers. Endpapers of a heavier cream wove paper. Covers of coated white stock cut flush with text. The front cover is taken up with a photograph of the Nelson Monument in Trafalgar Square, over which is printed, in white: '[top right corner] [publisher's device] | $1.95 | [from tail to head] EVERGREEN E-333." Below, in lower right quarter: '[white] Bid me to Live | [yellow green (C135)] a novel by | [yellow(C87)] H.D. | [white] "A rare work of art . . . as timeless | as E.E. Cumming's [*sic*] The Enormous Room." | [yellow] Horace Gregory, *Saturday Review*." White spine printed from head to tail: 'BID ME TO LIVE [yellow] BY [light green blue (C171)] H.D. | [publisher's device] | [black] E-333 [light green blue] GROVE | PRESS.' Back cover: 'AN EVERGREEN BOOK (E-333)—$1.95 | [yellow green (C135)] Bid me to Live | [gray (C264)] a novel by | [yellow green] H.D. | [short, thick, yellow rule] | [black] [fifteen-line description of the novel] | [short, thick, yellow green rule] | [black] [three-line excerpt from a review by Winfield Townley Scott] | [short, thick yellow rule] | [black] [two lines by Norman

Holmes Pearson] | [short, thick yellow green rule] | [black] Cover design by Roy Kuhlman | GROVE PRESS, INC., 64 UNIVERSITY PLACE, NEW YORK 3, N.Y.'

Published 16 April 1960 at $1.95.

NBuU; CtY.

a.iv First edition, second impression (photo-offset from **A26a.ii** with reset title page and new supplementary material), 1983

[blue (C177)] *bid me to live* | [black] H.D. | [blue] *a madrigal* | [black] BLACK SWAN BOOKS

[1–17][16] (1 + front.); pp. [i–ii] [1–6] 7–13 [14] 15–59 [60] 61–73 [74] 75–103 [104] 105–169 [170] 171–211 [212–224]. Cream wove paper, 19 × 13.4 cm. Endpapers of a light gray (C264) laid paper with vertical chain lines. Covers of blue cloth (C177), 19.7 × 13.8 cm. Gilt-stamped on the cover: '*bid me* | *to* | *live* | HD'. Gilt-stamped on spine, head to tail: 'HD *bid me to live* [publisher's device]'. Frontispiece is a photograph of H.D. by Man Ray. Chapters are separated by a drawing of cyclamen by H.D.

Dust jacket of coated cream stock. Front cover is a reproduction of the frontispiece photograph of H.D. by Man Ray. Upper left quarter, in blue (C178): 'Bid Me | to | Live'. Lower right corner, in white: 'HD'. White spine printed from head to tail: 'HD [blue (C178)] *bid me to live* [publisher's device]'. Back cover is blue printed in white. A thirteen-line quote from H.D.'s 'Notes on Recent Writing' is enclosed by two short rules. The top two centimeters of the front inner flap are blue printed in white: '$20.00 | HD *bid me to live*'. Below, continued on back flap, is a three-paragraph summary of the novel. At bottom of the back flap are the publisher's address and logo.

P. i: blank; p. ii: frontispiece; p. 1: title page; p. 2: copyright, 'Copyright © 1960 Norman Holmes Pearson | Copyright © 1983 The Estate of Hilda Doolittle | Copyright © 1983 Perdita Schaffner | Copyright © 1983 Black Swan Books Ltd. | [twelve lines]'; p. 3: contents; p. 4: illustration; p. 5: half title, 'Bid Me to Live | *(A Madrigal)*'; p. 6: sixteen-line poem, 'TO ANTHEA', by Robert Herrick; pp. 7–13: text; p. 14: illustration; pp. 15–59: text; p. 60: illustration; pp. 61–73: text; p. 74: illustration; pp. 75–103: text; p. 104: illustration; pp. 105–169: text; p. 170: illustration; pp. 171–184: text; 185–194: A Profound Animal; 195–204: Afterword; 205–211: Notes on Recent Writing; p. 212: blank; p. 213: list of Black Swan titles; p. 214: printer's imprint, '*Typeset by Type Systems, Inc.* | *Printed by Mercatile Printing Co.* | *Bound by New Hampshire Bindery*'; pp. 215–224: blank.

Published May 1983 in an edition of 1,000 at $20.00.

Contains *Bid Me to Live*," "A Profound Animal" (by Perdita Schaffner), "Afterword" (by John Walsh), "Notes on Recent Writing" (excerpts).

CU-SC; CtY; PU.

a.v First edition, third impression, paperback (photo-offset from **A26a.iv** with reset title page and deleted supplementary material), 1983

H.D. | [ornamental rule] | Bid Me | to Live | *(A Madrigal)* | The Dial Press | New York | [publisher's device]

Perfect bound in paper wrappers; pagination as in **A26a.ii** with addition of four blank leaves, [185–192]. Cream wove paper, 18.9 × 13 cm. Covers of coated white stock cut flush with text. The front cover has a photograph of H.D. within a orange yellow (C72) border. Just within the edge of the photograph is a box of a thin light blue (C180) rule. Superimposed on the photograph in the lower right corner: '[orange yellow shadowed by white] *Bid Me* | *to Live* | [short light blue rule] | [white] *A Novel* | [short light blue rule] | [white] "A rare work of art." | —Horace Gregory'. Orange yellow spine printed head to tail: '[white] *Bid Me to Live* [black] H.D. [publisher's device] The Dial Press'. Black back cover: '[light blue] $7.95 Literature/Fiction | [sixteen-line description of H.D.'s life and the novel] | [white] [three-line quote from [light blue] Winfield Townley Scott] | [white] [two-line quote from [light blue] Norman Holmes Pearson] | [light blue] [photo acknowledgment] | Cover design by Robert Aulicino | The Dial Press | 1 Dag Hammerskjald Plaza | New York, New York 10017 | Printed in U.S.A. 0583 ISBN 0-385-27880-2'.

Contents as in **A26a.ii**, with altered copyright: 'Published by | The Dial Press | 1 Dag Hammerskjold Plaza | New York, New York 10017 | Copyright © 1960 by Norman Holmes | Pearson | [nine lines] | First Dial printing by arrangement with | Black Swan Books Ltd. | [six lines]'; pp. 185–192: blank.

Published 20 May 1983 in an edition of 7,500 copies at $7.95.

Contains *Bid Me to Live*.

Personal copy.

a.vi First English edition (photo-offset from **A26a.iv** with added preliminaries), 1984

[all within a double-rule frame with ornamental corners] Bid Me to Live | H.D. | With a New Introduction by | HELEN McNEIL | and an Afterword by | PERDITA SCHAFFNER | *Virago* | [publisher's device]

Perfect bound in paper wrappers; pp. [i–vi] vii–xix [1–6] 7–13 [14] 15–59 [60] 61–73 [74] 75–103 [104] 105–169 [170] 171–194. Cream wove paper, 19.6 × 12.8 cm. Covers of coated white stock cut flush with text. Top quarter of the cover dark olive green (C126). Printed at the top in yellow green (C117): 'Virago Modern Classics | [white rule] | [white] H.D. | [white rule] | [white] Bid Me to Live'. Bottom three-quarters of front cover has a reproduction of the painting 'Clara' by Dod Proctor. Spine and back cover are all dark olive green. Spine: '[white rule] | [yellow green] [publisher's device] | [white rule] | [white: head to tail] Bid Me to Live 0 86068 429 6'. Back cover: '[yellow green] Virago Modern Classics | [white rule] | [white] H.D. | [white rule] | Bid Me to Live | [twenty-four-line description of the book's contents] | The cover shows | "Clara" by Dod Proctor. | Reproduced by kind permission of | the City Museum and Art Gallery, Stoke-on-Trent. | £3.50 net in UK only Fiction 0 86068 429 6'.

Pp. i–ii: biographical notes under the heading 'H.D. (1886–1961)'; p. iii: title page; p. iv: copyright, 'Published by VIRAGO PRESS Limited 1984 | 41 William IV Street, London WC2N 4DB | First published in U.S.A. by Grove Press Inc., New York, 1960 | First published in Great Britain by Virago Press, 1984 | Virago edition offset from Black Swan Books 1983 edition | Copyright © 1960 Norman Holmes Pearson | Copyright © 1983 The Estate of Hilda Doolittle | Copyright © 1983 Perdita Schaffner | Introduction copyright © Helen McNeil 1984 | *Illustration credit:* by permission of the Collection of American Literature, | Beinecke Rare Book and Manuscript Library, Yale University; and by the | estate of Hilda Doolittle | [seven lines] | Printed and bound in Great Britain by Anchor Brendon Limited | at Tiptree, Essex'; p. v: contents; p. vi: illustration, sketch of cyclamen by H.D.; pp. vii–xix: introduction; pp. 6–184 as in **A26b.i;** pp. 185–194: 'A Profound Animal'.

Published 11 October 1984 in an edition of 6,000 copies at £3.50.

Contains "Introduction" (by Helen McNeil), *Bid Me to Live*, "A Profound Animal" (by Perdita Schaffner).

NBuU; PU.

A27 *Helen in Egypt*

a.i   First edition, 1961

Helen in | Egypt | by | H.D. | Introduction by Horace Gregory | Grove Press, Inc. New York

[1–8]^{16} [9]^{20} [10]^{16}; pp. [i–vi] vii–xi [xii] 1–17 [18] 19–35 [36] 37–65 [66] 67–95 [96] 97–135 [136] 137–151 [152] 153–167 [168] 169–199 [200] 201–215 [216] 217–263 [264] 265–297 [298] 299–315 [316]. Cream wove paper, 20.2 × 13.4 cm. Endpapers of heavier cream wove paper. Top edge stained pale red (C15). Covers of red orange (C38) cloth, 20.7 × 14.2 cm. Gilt-stamped spine: 'H.D. | [rule] | Helen | in | Egypt | [rule] | [below] *Grove Press*'.

Dust jacket of smooth white stock. Bottom two-thirds of front cover and spine red orange (C34). On the front cover this area has a drawing of two Greek figures, presumably Helen and Achilles. Above the colored area: 'Helen in Egypt | by H.D. | INTRODUCTION BY HORACE GREGORY'. At top of spine: 'H.D. | [rule] | Helen | in | Egypt'; below: 'Grove Press'. Top half of back cover has a photograph of an elderly H.D. Below this is a fifteen-line biographical statement. Top right corner of front inner flap: '$5.00'. Under the heading 'HELEN IN EGYPT | By H.D. | *Introduction by Horace Gregory*' is a four-paragraph description of the contents of the poem, completed on the back flap. At bottom of back flap: 'GROVE PRESS, INC. | 64 University Place | New York 3, New York'.

P. i: half title, 'Helen in Egypt'; p. ii: blank; p. iii: title page; p. iv: copyright, 'Copyright © 1961 by Norman Holmes Pearson | *Introduction* copyright © 1961 by Horace Gregory | All Rights Reserved | Library of Congress Catalog Card Number: 61-12764 | First Printing | *Manufactured in the United States of America*'; p. v: contents; p. vi: blank; pp. vii–xi: introduction; p. xii: blank; pp. 1–316: text.

Published 20 October 1961 in an edition of 1,500 at $5.00.

In a letter to Robert Duncan dated 1 July 1961, Marilyn Meeker of Grove Press wrote: "*Esperence* will not be included in the book; some time ago, after much consideration, H.D. decided she did not want it as part of *Helen*. For what reason, I do not know; and Mr. Pearson was unable to persuade her otherwise." Pearson, in a letter to Meeker dated 30 September 1961, quoted Bryher as having written: "Heydt reported Hilda tremendously pleased with Helen and he reads it to her daily." Eric Heydt's cable read: "Hilda happy with Helen for last three days before death."

Contains "Introduction" (by Horace Gregory), "Pallinode, Books 1–7," "Leuke, Books 1–7," "Eidolon, Books 1–6."

Published 1 October 1963 in an edition of 3,500 at $2.45. A total of 5,000 sheets were originally printed in 1961. Of those 1,500 were bound in hard covers. The remaining sheets were stored and eventually bound as paperbacks.

NBuU; CtY; PPT; CaOTU.

a.ii   First edition, paperback, 1963

Title page, collation, paper, contents, text contents as in **A27a.i**.

Gatherings glued into a paper cover. Cover from white coated stock cut flush with text. Front cover as in dust jacket of **A27a.i**, with altered spine, from head to tail: 'HELEN IN EGYPT [red orange (C34)] BY H.D. | [publisher's device] | [black] E-375 | [red orange] GROVE | PRESS'. Back cover: '[at top in red orange] AN EVERGREEN BOOK (E-375)— $2.45 | [black] HELEN IN EGYPT | BY H.D. | [red orange] *Introduction by Horace Gregory*'. Bottom two-thirds of page is red orange and has a brief description of the contents of the poem and quotes from the *Nation, New York Times Book Review, Saturday Review,* and *Library Journal*.

NBuU; CtY; PPT.

a.iii   First edition, second impression (photo-offset from **A27a.i**), 1974

Helen in Egypt | [flowering branch ornament] | by H.D. | *Introduction by Horace Gregory* | A NEW DIRECTIONS BOOK

[1–10]^{16}; pp. [i–iv] vii–xi [xii] 1–304 [305–308]. Cream wove paper, 20 × 13.3 cm. Endpapers of a darker and heavier cream wove paper. Covers of yellow (C83) cloth, 20.8 × 14 cm. Stamped on the spine from head to tail in dark olive brown (C96): 'H.D. Helen in Egypt NEW DIRECTIONS'.

Dust jacket of white coated stock. Front cover: 'Helen in Egypt | by H.D. | [photograph of a wall painting depicting the head of a Greek woman]'. Spine, from head to tail: 'H.D. Helen in Egypt NEW DIRECTIONS'. Back cover has a photo of H.D. in Egypt in 1923. Front inner flap, under the heading 'Helen in Egypt | by H.D.', has an eighteen-line description of the poem's contents. Below: '$9.00 | ISBN 0-8112- 0543-6.' Back inner flap has quotations from the *Nation* (seven lines), the *New York Times Book Review* (four lines), the *Saturday Review* (two lines) and the *Library Journal* (four lines) on *Helen in Egypt*.

P. i: half title, 'Helen in Egypt'; p. ii: two titles also by H.D.; p. iii: title page; p. iv: copyright, 'Copyright © 1969 by Norman Holmes Pearson | Introduction copyright © 1961 by Horace Gregory | [five lines] | Manufactured in the United States of America | First published by Grove Press in 1961 | Published clothbound and as New Directions Paperback 380 in 1974 | Published simultaneously in Canada by McClelland & Stewart, Ltd. | [thirteen lines]'; p. v: contents; p. vi: blank; pp. vii–xi: introduction; p. xii: blank; pp. 1–304: text; pp. 305–308: blank.

Published 27 November 1974 in an edition of 2,000 at $9.00 (raised to $10.50 on 6 April 1984).

Text contents as in **A27a.i**.

CtY (2 copies); CU-Riv; PU.

a.iv   First edition, second impression, paperback, 1974

Title page, collation, contents, text contents, and paper as in **A27a.iii**. Leaves perfect bound in paper wrappers cut flush with text; pp. 305–306, advertisements for New Directions paperbacks; at the tail of spine, 'NDP 380'; back cover, 'POETRY | ISBN: 0-8112-0544-4 | Helen in Egypt | by H.D. [at right, a photograph of H.D.] | [thirteen-line description of the poem's contents] | [five-line quote from the *Nation*] | [three lines of titles by H.D.] | *Cover illustration: wall painting of a woman's head,* | *tomb of Arcus, Tarquinii; design by Gertrude Huston'* | A NEW DIRECTIONS PAPERBOOK NDP 380 $3.25'.

Published 27 November 1974 in an edition of 3,000 at $3.25. On 6 April 1984 there was a second impression of 1,500 at $7.95.

a.v   First English edition (American sheets of **A27a.iii**), 1985

Helen in Egypt | [hieroglyph ornament] | by H.D. | *Introduction by Horace Gregory* | Carcanet

Perfect bound in paper wrappers; pp. [π1–2] [i–vi] vii–xi [xii] 1–304 [305–306]. Cream wove paper, 21.5 × 13.2 cm. Cover of white stock. Front cover and spine are dark orange yellow (C72) marred by yellow brown (C75) discolorations designed to look like cracks and scratches in a wall. Front cover: '[short, yellow brown rule with a hieroglyph in the center] | [white] H.D. | [short yellow brown rule with a hieroglyph in the center] | [white] HELEN | IN | EGYPT | [short yellow brown rule with hieroglyph in center] | [yellow brown hollow letters] CARCANET'. Spine: '[short, yellow brown rule with a hieroglyph in the center] | [white] H.D. | [short yellow brown rule with a hieroglyph in the center] | [white] HELEN | IN | EGYPT | [short yellow brown rule with hieroglyph in center] | [orange yellow (C67)] [owl ornament] | [head to tail in yellow brown] CARCANET'. Back cover is orange yellow and printed in yellow brown: '[photograph of H.D. in Egypt] | [ten-line statement about the poem] | [short rule with hieroglyph in center] | [four-line quote from Gabriel Pearson from the *Times Literary Supplement*] | [short rule with a hieroglyph in the center] | [five-line advertisement for Carcanet Books] | £6.95 *Cover design by Stephen Row* ISBN 0 85635 554 2'.

Pp. π1–2: blank; p. i: half title, 'Helen in Egypt'; p. ii: blank; p. iii: title page; p. iv: copyright, 'Copyright © 1961 by Norman Holmes Pearson | *Introduction* copyright © 1961 by Horace Gregory | All rights reserved | First published by Grove Press (USA) in 1961 | First published in Great Britain in 1985 by | CARCANET PRESS LIMITED | 208–212 Corn Exchange Buildings | Manchester M4 3BQ | [seven lines] | *Printed in England by SRP Ltd., Exeter*'; p. v: contents; p. vi: blank; pp. vii–xi: introduction; p. xii: blank; pp. 1–304: text; pp. 305–306: blank.

Published in 1985 in an edition of 500 copies at £6.95.

According to records in the files at New Directions, Carcanet originally wanted to distribute the New Directions 1984 impression, but since New Directions had just negotiated a new distribution agreement with an English distributor, they couldn't allow Carcanet to act as distributor. They therefore had Carcanet negotiate a regular contract with Laurence Pollinger which included a token advance for 500 copies. In this way, Carcanet was technically publishing the book, not distributing it.

Text contents as in **A27a.i.**

A28 *Hermetic Definition*

a First edition, 1971

[within an ornamental oval frame of roses printed in deep red (C13) and gray green (C122)] Hermetic Definitions | HD | [below] 1971

$[1]^4 [2-5]^8$; pp. [1–72]. White glossy wove paper, 22.6 × 15 cm. Covers of heavy white stock glued at the spine.

Dust jacket of blue gray (C191) textured stock glued at spine. Edges trimmed flush with text. White paper label, 7.4 × .5 cm, glued to the spine, lettered, from head to tail: 'HERMETIC DEFINITIONS [red and gray green rose ornament] HD'.

Pp. 1–2: blank; p. 3: half title, 'HERMETIC DEFINITIONS'; p. 4: blank; p. 5: title page; p. 6: blank; p. 7: section title, 'PART ONE | Red Rose & A Beggar'; p. 8: blank; pp. 9–27: text; p. 28: blank; p. 29: section title, 'PART TWO | Grove of Academe'; p. 30: blank; pp. 31–51: text; p. 52: blank; p. 53: section title, 'PART THREE | Star of Day'; p. 54: blank; pp. 55–64: text; pp. 65–72: blank.

No imprint, colophon, or copyright. This edition was printed from an autograph transcription of the manuscript at the Beinecke Library supplied to Harvey Brown, at that time editor of Frontier Press. The title, "Hermetic Definitions," is printed as it appears on the manuscript, which is an early version of the poem. Inserted in the copy at Yale is a note in the hand of Norman Holmes Pearson: "Illegally published | by Harvey Brown | Frontier Press | West Newbury, Mass. | 1971, in what Brown asserts | was an edition of 1600 copies | 'none for sale'. If so, most | were hidden for later profit. | Note that the title is *Hermetic* | *Definitions* rather than | *Definition* and that the text | differs from New Directions edition. | Text from an earlier version surreptit-|iously obtained by Brown. | 27 March 1973 | Norman Holmes Pearson". According to Harvey Brown and others, he was only one of many who felt extremely frustrated by the fact that much of H.D.'s work was either still in manuscript or out of print at a time when there was a tremendous growth of interest in her work fueled by Robert

Duncan's ongoing publication of *The H.D. Book*. Although this pirated edition does show up in the rare book market selling for $25.00 to $50.00, Harvey Brown continued to distribute the book free to those who asked for it until he died in 1990.

Contains "Red Rose & A Beggar," "Grove of Academe," "Star of Day."

NBuU; CtY.

b.i Second edition, 1972

HERMETIC | DEFINITION | [flowering branch ornament] | *by H.D.* | A NEW DIRECTIONS BOOK

[1–4]^{16}; pp. [i–x] [1–2] 3–55 [56–57] 58–84 [85] 86–117 [118]. Cream wove paper, 19.9 × 13.4 cm. Endpapers of the same wove paper. Covers of gray purple (C245) cloth, 20.7 × 14 cm. Spine gilt-stamped from head to tail: 'HERMETIC DEFINITION H.D. NEW DIRECTIONS'.

Dust jacket of white coated stock. Front cover: reproduction of an Odilon Redon painting in black and white depicting a bouquet of flowers and, to the left, the profile of a woman's head and torso. At top: 'HERMETIC | DEFINITION | by H.D.' Spine, head to tail; 'HERMETIC DEFINITION H.D. NDP343'. Back cover has list of four books of poetry by New Directions. At top of front inner flap: 'HERMETIC | DEFINITION | by H.D. | *Foreword by Norman Holmes Pearson*'. Below and continued on back flap, a four-paragraph description of the contents of the poems, including quotations from H.D. and Robert Duncan. At bottom of front inner flap: '$8.75'. Below the statement on the back inner flap: '*Jacket illustration from a painting by Odilon Redon* | *in the collection of Madame L. Jäggli-Hahnloser;* | *design by Gertrude Huston*'.

P. i: half title, 'HERMETIC DEFINITION'; p. ii: blank; p. iii: title page; p. iv: copyright, 'Copyright © 1958, 1959, 1961, 1969, 1972 by Norman Holmes Pearson | Library of Congress Catalog Card Number: 72-80980 | [five lines] | Parts of some of the poems included in this collection were first published | in *Contemporary Literature, Evergreen Review & The Nation.* | Sections 13 and 14 of "Sagesse" first appeared in *Poetry* as "Regents of | the Night." | First published clothbound and as New Directions Paperbook 343 | in 1972. | Published simultaneously in Canada by McClelland & Stewart, Ltd. | Manufactured in the United States of America | New Directions Books are published for James Laughlin | by New Directions Publishing Corporation, | 333 Sixth Avenue, New York 10014'; pp. v–viii: foreword; p. ix: contents; p. x: blank; p. 1: section title, 'HERMETIC DEFINITION'; p. 2: blank; pp. 3–55: text; p. 56: blank; p. 57: section title, 'SAGESSE | (Summer–Winter 1957)'; pp. 58–84: text; p. 85: section title, 'WINTER LOVE | (Espérence) | (January 3–April 15, 1959)'; pp. 86–117: text; p. 118: blank.

Published 15 November 1972 in an edition of 1,000 at $8.75.

Contains "Foreword" (by Norman Holmes Pearson); "Hermetic Definition" (section title for the following three poems): "Red Rose and a Beggar," "Grove of Academe," "Star of Day"; "Sagesse"; "Winter Love."

NBuU; CU-SC; CtY; PU.

b.ii Second edition, paperback, 1972

Title page, collation, contents, and text contents as in **A28b.i**.

Leaves are 20.1 × 13 cm, perfect bound in paper wrappers; at the bottom of spine, instead of the publisher's name, head to tail: 'NDP 343'; on the back cover, 'POETRY | HERMETIC | DEFINITION | by H.D. | *Foreword by Norman Holmes Pearson* | [sixteen-line description of poem's contents] | [eight-line quote from Robert Duncan] | (*Hermetic Definition is also available in a hardbound edition, $8.75*) | *Cover illustration from painting by Odilon Redon in the | collection of Madame L. Jäggli-Hahnloser; design by Gertrude Huston* | A NEW DIRECTIONS PAPERBACK NDP 343 $3.25'.

Published 15 November 1972 in an edition of 4,000 at $3.25. There was a second impression of 1,000 at $3.95 on 31 March 1980; a third impression of 1,500 at $4.95 on 14 March 1982; and a fourth impression of 1,500 at $6.95 on 23 February 1987.

Personal copy.

b.iii First English edition (photo-offset from **A28b.i**), 1972

HERMETIC | DEFINITION | *by H.D.* | A CARCANET PRESS PUBLICATION

[1–8]⁸; pp. [i–x] [1–2] 3–55 [56–57] 58–84 [85] 86–117 [118]. White laid paper with vertical chain lines, 20.2 × 13.4 cm. Endpapers of a heavier white wove paper. Covers of gray yellow (C90) cloth. Spine gilt-stamped from head to tail: 'HERMETIC DEFINITION / HD [publisher's device]'.

Dust jacket of light blue (C181) stock. Front cover: '[thick white rule] | [black] HD | HERMETIC | DEFINITION | [thin-thick white rule]'. Spine, from head to tail: '[thick white rule] | [black] HERMETIC DEFINITION / HD | [thin-thick white rule] | [publisher's device]'. Back cover: 'Some Carcanet authors and titles'. The front inner flap has the blurb from p. i. At bottom: '£2.20'.

P. i: sixteen-line bio-critical statement under the heading, 'HERMETIC DEFINITION'; p. ii: blank; p. iii: title page; p. iv: copyright, as in **A28b.i** down to 'First published 1972 by Carcanet Press Ltd., Pin Farm, South Hinskey, | Oxford | SBN 856350362—cloth | SBN 856350370—paper | Printed by W & J Mackay Limited, Chatham"; p. v–viii: foreword; pp. ix–x, 1–118 as in **A28b.i**.

Published in an edition of 1,500 copies at £2.20.

Text contents as in **A28b.i**.

CtY.

b.iv   First English edition, paperback, 1972

Title page, collation, contents, and text contents as in **A28b.iii**.

Covers duplicate the dust jacket of **A28b.iii**. Perfect bound in paper wrappers, 20 × 13.5 cm, cut flush with text.

CtY.

A29   *Two Poems*

   a.i   First edition, 1971

2 POEMS BY *H.D.* | with illuminations by WESLEY TANNER | Berkeley—1971—ARIF

[1]¹⁰; pp. [1–20]. Cream wove paper, 23.3 × 15.4 cm. The texts are printed over drawings. Covers of paper over boards with very light gray (C264) cloth shelfback. The cover drawing is of a rural scene with very light greenish blue (C171) sky, pale yellow (C89) clouds, very green yellow (C97) grass, deep purple red (C256) and brilliant yellow (C83) flower and unidentified object in lower right.

Pp. 1–2: blank; p. 3: pointilistic drawing of a rural scene in pale green yellow (C104), light yellow green (C119), deep yellow green (C132), green blue (C169), and light pink (C4) (green hills, pink and yellow mountains beyond, and blue sky); p. 4: blank; p. 5: title page; p. 6: copyright and acknowledgments, 'These poems first appeared in *Life and Letters Today* in | Winter of 1937. Reprinted by permission of Norman | Holmes Pearson, owner of the copyright. Illustrations | copyright 1971 by Wesley Tanner. Printed in U.S.A. | ARIF Press, Box 1069, Berkeley, California 94701.'; pp. 7–15: text; p. 16: colophon, 'Lithographed in December 1970 by Wesley Tanner, | handset and printed in February 1971 by Grabhorn-|Hoyem in an edition of 200 copies in paper wrappers | and 26 copies bound in boards, lettered and signed by | the artist with an additional lithograph on the cover.'; pp. 17–20: blank.

Contains "Star by Day," "Wooden Animal." Reprinted in *CP* (1983).

CtY; PPT.

a.ii   First edition, paperback, 1971

Title page and text contents as in **A29a.i**.

[1]⁸; pp. [1–16]. Paper as in **A29a.i**. Covers of heavy pale yellow green (C104) textured wove paper, 23.7 × 15.9 cm. The drawing on the front cover is the same as that on p. 3 of **A29a.i**. Pp. 1–2: blank; p. 3: title page; p. 4: copyright and acknowledgment as in **A29a.i**; pp. 5–13: text; p. 14: colophon as in **A29a.i**; pp. 15–16 blank.

NBuU; CtY (2 copies); NNC.

A30   *Temple of the Sun*

a   First edition, 1972

TEMPLE OF THE SUN | By | H.D. [gray green (C122)] [publisher's device] | [black] ARIF PRESS | CHRISTMAS | 1972

[1]¹⁴; pp. [1–28]. Wookey Hole mold-made cream laid paper with vertical chain lines, 17.9 × 12 cm. Covers of light gray (C264) wove paper. Front cover: 'TEMPLE | OF THE | SUN | [yellow green (C136)] HD'.

Pp. 1–2: blank; p. 3: half title, 'TEMPLE OF THE SUN'; p. 4: frontispiece, drawing of woman's head and torso in an oval, shaded gray green; p. 5: title page; p. 6: blank; p. 7: section title, 'SATURN'; p. 8: blank; pp. 9–13: text; p. 14: blank; p. 15: section title, 'ZEUS-PROVIDER'; p. 16: blank; pp. 17–22: text; pp. 23–24: blank; p. 25: colophon, 'These fragments from the poem | cycle Temple of the Sun were | written in 1936 and are printed | here with the kind permission of | Norman Holmes Pearson owner | of the copyright. Frontispiece by | Robert Baldock. One hundred & | twenty-five copies have been | printed with Bembo types on | Wookey Hole mould made | paper for the friends of | the Arif Press'; pp. 26–28: blank.

Contains "Saturn," "Zeus-Provider." Reprinted in *CP* (1983).

CtY (2 copies).

A31   *Trilogy*

a.i   First edition, 1973

TRILOGY | *The Walls Do Not Fall* | *Tribute to the Angels* | *The Flowering of the Rod* | [flowering branch ornament] | *by H.D.* | A NEW DIRECTIONS BOOK

[1–6]¹⁶; pp. [i–iv] v–xii [xiii–xiv] [1–2] 3–59 [60–62] 63–110 [111–112] 113–172 [173–178]. Cream wove paper, 20 × 13.1 cm. The gatherings are sewn with white and (at NBuU and NNC) very yellow (C82) or (at CtY) very orange (C48) thread. Endpapers of the same cream wove paper. Covers of red orange (C36) cloth, 20.7 × 13.9 cm. Spine gilt-stamped from head to tail: 'H.D. TRILOGY NEW DIRECTIONS'.

Dust jacket of coated white stock. Front cover: 'TRILOGY | *The Walls Do Not Fall* | *Tribute to the Angels* | *The Flowering of the Rod* | [reproduction of a painting by Odilon Redon of a man reading a book] | by H.D.' Spine: 'H.D. TRILOGY NEW DIRECTIONS'. Back cover has a list of publications by Robert Duncan, Denise Levertov, Ezra Pound, and William Carlos Williams under the heading 'Some Other New Directions Poetry Books'. Front inner flap, under the heading 'TRILOGY | by H.D.', has a twenty-two line description of the contents of the poems, under which is: 'Jacket illustration from a painting by Odilon | Redon, courtesy of the Kunstmuseum, Winterthur, | Switzerland; design by Gertrude Huston | A NEW DIRECTIONS BOOK.' Bottom right corner: '$6.95 | ISBN 0-8112-0490-1'. Back inner flap has a twenty-two-line advertisement for *Hermetic Definitions*.

P. i: half title, 'TRILOGY'; p. ii: 'Also by H.D. | Hermetic Definition'; p. iii: title page; p. iv: copyright and acknowledgment, 'Copyright © 1973 by Norman Holmes Pearson | [twenty-one lines]; pp. v–xii: foreword; p. xiii: contents; p. xiv: blank; p. 1: section title, 'THE WALLS DO NOT FALL | To Bryher | *for Karnak* 1923 | *for London* 1942'; p. 2: blank; pp. 3–59: text; p. 60: blank; p. 61: section title, 'TRIBUTE TO THE ANGELS | To Osbert Sitwell | . . . *possibly we will reach haven,* | *heaven.*'; p. 62: blank; pp. 63–110: text; p. 111: section title, 'THE FLOWERING OF THE ROD | To Norman Holmes Pearson | . . . *pause to give* | *thanks that we rise again from death and live.*'; p. 112: blank; pp. 113–172: text; pp. 173–178: blank.

Published 7 December 1973 in an edition of 1,500 at $6.95.

According to records in the files at New Directions, the book was originally to have appeared in November 1973, but a number of complications delayed it. Grove Press, which was in trouble financially, had decided to keep *Selected Poems* in print, thus complicating the rights question to sections of *Trilogy*. The book was done in conjunction with Carcanet Press in England. It was composed there through Carcanet who sent the negatives to New Directions, splitting the cost. The Birmingham firm doing the setting was shut down by an unannounced strike so that the unfinished work had to be taken to Chatham in September. The galleys were printed in the United States, the page composition was done in England, and the actual printing was done in the United States. Among other complications, Carcanet's compositor neglected to send the dead copy with the page proofs so that there was no way to check the corrections made from the galleys.

Contains "Foreword" (by Norman Holmes Pearson), "The Walls Do Not Fall," "Tribute to the Angels," "The Flowering of the Rod." Reprinted in *CP* (1983).

NBuU; CU-Riv; CtY (2 copies); NNC.

a.ii First edition, paperback, 1973

Title page, collation, contents, and text contents as in **A31a.i**.

Perfect bound in paper wrappers cut flush with text. Pp. 173–174 have advertisements. Paper as in **A31a.i**. Bottom of spine reads, 'NDP 362' instead of the publisher's name. Back cover, in upper left corner: 'POETRY / ISBN: 0-8112-0491-X'. Under the heading 'TRILOGY | by H.D.' is a twenty-line statement comparing *Trilogy* to *The Pisan Cantos* and *The Four Quartets*. Bottom: 'A NEW DIRECTIONS PAPERBOOK NDP 362 $2.95'.

Published 7 December 1973 in an edition of 4,000 (4,063 with overrun) at $2.95. There was a second impression of 1,500 (1,556 with overrun) at $3.95; a third impression of 1,500 (1,537 with overrun) at $5.95 on 25 February 1982; a fourth impression of 1,500 at $5.95 on 31 January 1983; a fifth impression of 1,500 at $7.95 on 20 June 1985; and a sixth impression of 1,500 at $7.95 on 31 January 1987.

NBuU; CU-Riv; CtY (2 copies).

a.iii First English edition (American sheets with canceled title page), 1973

TRILOGY | *The Walls Do Not Fall* | *Tribute to the Angels* | *The Flowering of the Rod* | by H.D. | [publisher's device] | A CARCANET PRESS PUBLICATION

$[A]^8$ ($\pm A_2$) $[B-M]^8$; pp. [i–iii] iv–xii [xiii–xiv] [1–2] 3–172 [173–178]. Cream laid paper, 20.3 × 13.4 cm. Top edge stained yellow green (C130). Endpapers of a heavier light yellow green (C134) laid paper, with horizontal chain lines, watermarked 'Lingua'. Covers of light brown (C57) and black cloth, 20.8 × 13.9 cm. Spine, gilt-stamped from head to tail: 'TRILOGY / H.D.'

Dust jacket of cream wove paper. Front cover, spine, and back cover are yellow green (C99). A single white rule extends around the covers near the top. A white thin-thick rule extends around the covers near the bottom. Front cover: '[below the upper rule] TRILOGY | HD | [just above the lower rule] *The Walls Do Not Fall | Tribute to the Angels | The Flowering of the Rod*'. Spine, from head to tail: '[white rule] | [black] TRILOGY / HD [double white rule] [black] [publisher's device]'. Back cover has a two-column list of Carcanet authors and titles. Front inner flap, under the heading 'TRILOGY | by HD | with a foreword | by Norman Holmes Pearson' has a two-paragraph description of the poem's content. Bottom: '£2.50'. At foot of the back inner flap: 'Mackay, Chatham.'

Contents as in **A31a.i** with the following exceptions: p. ii: 'Also by H.D. | *Hermetic Definition | Tribute to Freud*'; p. iv: copyright, 'Copyright © Norman Holmes Pearson 1973 | [thirteen lines]'. Unnumbered pages in text in **A31a.i** have been numbered.

Text contents as in **A31a.i**.

NBuU; CtY; PPT.

a.iv First English edition, paperback, 1973

Title page, collation, contents, text contents, and paper as in **A31a.iii**. Perfect bound in paper wrappers, 20.3 × 13.4 cm, cut flush with text. Covers duplicate the dust jacket of **A31a.iii**.

A32 *The Poet & The Dancer*

a First edition, 1975

[first two letters dark red (C16)] HD The Poet | & The Dancer | [drawing of a pink rose semienclosed by two gray green (C105) snakes] | FIVE TREES PRESS: SAN FRANCISCO | 1975

[1]⁸ [2]⁶ [3]⁸; pp. [1–44]. Cream wove paper, watermarked 'WARREN'S OLDE STYLE', 20.1 × 13.4 cm. Endpapers of the same cream wove paper with drawings of kelp in yellow green (C102). Covers of light olive gray (C112) cloth, 20.7 × 14 cm. White paper title label, 6.2 × 0.5 cm, pasted to spine, from head to tail: '[first two letters in dark red (C16)] 'HD THE POET & THE DANCER'.

Pp. 1–4: blank; p. 5: title page; p. 6: copyright, 'These poems originally appeared in *Life and Letters Today*, | December, 1935. They are published now with the gener-|ous cooperation of Norman Holmes Pearson and Eileen | & Robert Callahan of the Turtle Island Foundation. | Copyright 1975 / Norman Holmes Pearson | Five Trees Press, 1250 Sandrey Street, San Francisco'; p. 7: section title, 'THE POET'; p. 8: blank; pp. 9–16: text; p. 17: section title, 'THE DANCER'; p. 18: blank; pp. 19–37: text;

p. 38: blank; p. 39: colophon, '*Printed in an edition of* | *600 copies by Kathy Walkup* | *at Five Trees Press, Spring, 1975.* | *One-hundred copies have been* | *hand-bound over boards at the press.* | *Illustrations by Jamie Robles.*'; pp. 40–44: blank.

The first letter of both sections is an enlarged capital printed in dark red.

Contains "The Poet," "The Dancer." Reprinted in *CP* (1983).

NBuU; CtY.

A33   *End to Torment*

a.i   First edition, 1979

end to torment | *A memoir of Ezra Pound by* | [to the right] H.D. | *Edited by Norman Holmes Pearson and Michael King* | *With the poems from "Hilda's Book" by* | EZRA POUND | A NEW DIRECTIONS BOOK

[1–3][16]; pp. [i–vi] vii–xii [1–2] 3–24 [25] 26–65 [66] 67–84. Cream wove paper, 20.1 × 13.5 cm. Endpapers of a heavier cream wove paper. Covers of dark green blue (C174) cloth, 20.8 × 14 cm, with a yellow gray (C93) cloth shelfback. Stamped in silver on the spine from head to tail: 'H.D. end to torment NEW DIRECTIONS'.

Dust jacket of coated white stock. Front cover: '[gray (C265) rule] | end to torment | *A memoir of Ezra Pound by* | [on right, dark gray (C266)] H.D. | [in a gray single-rule frame] [photographs of Ezra Pound on the left and H.D. on the right] | [black] *With the poems from "Hilda's Book" by* | [dark gray] EZRA POUND | [gray rule]'. Spine, from head to tail: '[dark gray] H.D. [black] end to torment NEW DIRECTIONS'. Back cover, under the heading 'Some Comments on H.D. and Her Work', quotes from Denise Levertov, *Contemporary Literature*, the *Nation*, and Robert Duncan. The front and back inner flaps have a two-paragraph bio-critical statement. At bottom of front flap: 'Jacket photograph of H.D. by Man Ray, courtesy of | Perdita Schaffner; photograph of Ezra Pound, cour-|tesy of the Humanities Research Center, University | of Texas; design by Gertrude Huston | A NEW DIRECTIONS BOOK | ISBN: 0-8112-0719-6 $8.50'.

P. i: half title, 'end to torment'; p. ii: photograph of H.D. by Ezra Pound; p. iii: title page; p. iv: copyright, 'Copyright © 1979 by New Directions Publishing Corporation | Copyright © 1979 by The Trustees of the Ezra Pound Literary Property | Trust | Copyright © 1979 by Michael King | [twenty-eight lines]'; p. v: contents; p. vi: blank; pp. vii–xii: foreword; p. 1: section title, 'END TO TORMENT'; p. 2: dedication, 'for Norman'; pp. 3–65: text; p. 66: blank; pp. 67–84: text.

Published 25 June 1979 in an edition of 1,500 at $8.50.

P. 25 has a facsimile of an early Pound poem in manuscript. According to records in the files at New Directions, this book was first discussed in March 1973 and planned for the fall of 1975. Norman Holmes Pearson's death in late 1975 delayed things for some time. Basic rights were left to Bryher by Pearson. Bryher's deteriorating health, however, made it increasingly difficult for her to deal with the practical issues involved. When the manuscript was finally located among Pearson's papers, it was decided to ask Michael King to finish the work, including editing the Pound poems. King's manuscript was ready in April 1977, but legal issues about who controlled rights continued to drag on. Then Donald Gallup sent sections of the galleys to Sheri Martinelli as an act of courtesy, thinking she would be pleased with the manuscript. Instead, she objected vigorously to her inclusion, insisting that her name be replaced with dashes or blank spaces. After being informed that they might be held liable for invasion of privacy, New Directions decided to change her name to a pseudonym throughout the text. They also removed a photograph of the sketch of Pound that Martinelli drew over the poem "Evadne" in H.D.'s copy of *Modern American Poetry*.

Contains "Foreword" (by Michael King), *End to Torment*, "Hilda's Book" (by Ezra Pound).

NBuU; CU-Riv; CtY (2 copies); PPT; CaOTU.

a.ii   First edition, paperback, 1979

Title page, collation, contents, and text contents as in A33a.i.

Perfect bound in paper wrappers, 20.1 × 12.9 cm, cut flush with text. Front cover as front of dust jacket in A33a.i. Back cover: '[gray (C265) rule] | end to torment | *A memoir of Ezra Pound by* | [on right, dark gray (C266)] H.D. | [black] *With the poems from "Hilda's Book" by* | [dark gray] EZRA POUND | *Edited by Norman Holmes Pearson and Michael King*'. Below: [twenty-three lines on book] | [three lines of titles] | [three lines in italics of acknowledgements for cover photo] | A NEW DIRECTIONS PAPERBOOK NDP476 $3.95'.

Published 25 June 1979 in an edition of 4,000 at $3.95. There was a second impression of 1,500 at $4.95 on 3 June 1982.

NBuU; CtY (2 copies).

a.iii   First English edition (photo-offset from A33a.i), 1980

Title page as in A33a.i with altered publisher's imprint: '[publisher's device] | CARCANET NEW PRESS LIMITED'. Collation and contents as in A33a.i with altered copyright: '1980' has been added to each date; at bottom: 'First published in Great Britain in 1980 by | CARCANET NEW PRESS LIMITED | 330 Corn Exchange Buildings | Manchester M4 3BG SBN 85635 318 3 | Printed in Great Britain by Billings, Guilford'.

Cream wove paper, 21.5 × 13.2 cm. Perfect bound in paper wrappers cut flush with text. Deep blue (C194) covers. Front cover: '[white] END TO TORMENT | [on the left, a photograph of Ezra Pound; to the right of the photograph, first line flush with the top] a memoir of | Ezra Pound | by H.D. | [below this, to the right of the Ezra Pound photograph, a photograph of H.D.] | with the poems from "Hilda's Book" | by Ezra Pound'. Spine, from head to tail, in white: 'END TO TORMENT a memoir of Ezra Pound by H.D. [publisher's device]'. Back cover, in white: 'End to Torment: a memoir of Ezra Pound by H.D. | [short rule] | with the poems from "Hilda's Book" by Ezra Pound | EDITED BY NORMAN HOLMES PEARSON AND MICHAEL KING | [twenty-two-line description of text contents] | *Carcanet publish* [sic] *three other titles by H.D.*: | TRIBUTE TO FREUD | TRILOGY | HERMETIC DEFINITION | *Cover photograph of H.D. by Man Ray, courtesy of Perdita Schaffner*; | *photograph of Ezra Pound, courtesy of the Humanities Research Center,* | *University of Texas.* | *Cover design by Sue Richards* | CARCANET PRESS, 330 Corn Exchange, Manchester 4 | £2.95—SBN 85635 318 1'.

Text contents as in **A33a.i**.

At New Directions Publishing.

A34 *Hermione*

a.i First edition, 1981

HER*mione* | [ornament] *by* H.D. [ornament] | A NEW DIRECTIONS BOOK

[1–8]¹⁶; pp. [i–vi] vii–xi [xii] [1–2] 3–139 [140–142] 143–234 [235–236] 237–238 [239–244]. Cream wove paper, 20.2 × 13.2 cm. Endpapers of a slightly heavier cream wove paper. Covers of light blue (C181) cloth, 20.9 × 14 cm. Spine, stamped in silver from head to tail: 'HERmione by H.D. NEW DIRECTIONS'.

Dust jacket of coated white stock. Front cover: a black and white photograph of H.D. over which is printed at the bottom: 'HER*mione* | [ornament] *by* H.D. [ornament]'. Spine: 'HER*mione by* H.D.'. Back cover has an advertisement for *End to Torment*. The front and back inner flaps have a four-paragraph bio-critical statement. At bottom of front inner flap: '$15.00'. At bottom of back inner flap: 'Jacket photograph of Hilda Doolittle | courtesy of Perdita Schaffner; | design by Denise Breslin.'

P. i: half title, 'HER*mione*'; p. ii: 'Also by H.D.' (four titles); p. iii: title page; p. iv: copyright, 'Copyright © 1981 by The Estate of Hilda Doolittle | Copyright © 1981 by Perdita Schaffner | Excerpt from *End to Torment* Copyright © 1979 by New Directions Pub-|lishing Corporation | [twenty lines]'; p. v: dedication, 'To | F . . . . . | for | September 2nd'; p. vi: blank; pp. vii–xi: 'PANDORA'S BOX' (subscribed on p. xi: 'PERDITA SCHAFFNER'); p. xii: blank; p. 1: section title, 'PART ONE'; p. 2: blank; pp. 3–139: text; p. 140: blank; p. 141: section title, 'PART TWO'; p. 142: blank; pp. 143–234: text; p. 235: section title, 'A POSTLUDE'; p. 236: blank; pp. 237–238: text; pp. 239–244: blank.

Published 30 October 1981 in an edition of 2,000 at $15.00.

Contains "Pandora's Box" (by Perdita Schaffner), *Hermione*, "A Postlude" (excerpt from *End to Torment*).

NBuU; CU-SC; CtY (2 copies); PU.

a.ii   First edition paperback, 1981

Title page, collation, contents, text contents, and paper as **A34a.i**.

Pp. 239–40 have advertisements for New Directions books; at the bottom of the spine, 'NDP 526'; on the back cover, 'FICTION | ISBN: 0-8112-0817-6 | HER*mione* | [ornament] *by* H.D. [ornament] | *Introduction by Perdita Schaffner* | [four-paragraph, twenty-four-line description of con-tents] | [two lines: cover photo credit] | [three lines: other titles] | A NEW DIRECTIONS PAPERBOOK NDP 526 $6.95'.

Published 30 October 1981 in an edition of 3,000 copies at $6.95. There was a second impression of 2,000 copies on 31 January 1984.

Personal copy.

a.iii   First English edition (photo-offset from **A34a.i**, with new prelimi-nary material), 1984

[within a double-rule frame with ornamental corners] *HER* | H.D. | With a New Introduction by | HELEN McNEIL | and an Afterword by | PERDITA SCHAFFNER | Virago | [publisher's device]

Perfect bound; pp. [i–iv] v–xi [xii] [1–2] 3–139 [140–142] 143–239 [240–244]. Cream wove paper, 19.6 × 12.8 cm. Perfect bound in paper covers cut flush with text. The top quarter of front cover is dark olive green (C126). At the top, in yellow green (C117): 'Virago Modern Classics | [white rule] | [white] H.D. | [white rule] | Her | [bottom three-quarters of front cover contains the painting *Lady on a Chaise Lounge* by Dod Proctor]. Spine and back cover are dark olive green. Spine: '[white rule] | [yellow green] [publisher's device] | [white rule] | [white; from head to tail] Her

H.D. 0 86068 451 2'. Back cover: [yellow green] 'Virago Modern Classics | [white rule] | [white] H.D. | [white rule] | Her | [twenty-three-line statement on H.D. and the novel] | The cover shows | "A Lady on a Chaise Lounge" by Dod Proctor. | £3.50 net in U.K. only Fiction 0 86068 451 2'.

Pp. i–ii: biographical note under the heading 'H.D. (1886–1961)'; p. iii: title page; p. iv: copyright, 'Published by VIRAGO PRESS Limited 1984 | 41 William IV Street, London WC2N 4DB | First published in U.S.A. by New Directions Books, New York, 1981 | First published in Great Britain by Virago Press, 1984 | Virago edition offset from New Direction Books edition | [nine lines] | Printed in Great Britain by Anchor Brendon Limited | at Tiptree, Essex | To | F . . . | for | September 2nd'; pp. v–xi: introduction; p. xii: blank; p. 1: section title, 'PART ONE'; p. 2: blank; pp. 3–139: text; p. 140: blank; p. 141: section title, 'PART TWO'; p. 142: blank; pp. 143–234: text; pp. 235–239: afterword; pp. 240–242: advertisements; pp. 243–244: blank.

Published 11 October 1984 in an edition of 6,000 copies at £3.95.

Contains "Introduction" (by Helen McNeil), *Her*, "Afterword [Pandora's Box]" (by Perdita Schaffner).

NBuU; PU; CaOTU.

A35   *The Gift*

a.i   First edition, 1982

[within a single-rule frame] The | Gift | [ornament] | H.D. | A NEW DIRECTIONS BOOK

[1–5][16]; pp. [i–viii] ix–xv [xvi–xviii] 1–23 [24] 25–129 [130] 131–142. Cream wove paper, 20.1 × 13.3 cm. Endpapers of a slightly heavier cream wove paper. Covers of red (C12) cloth 21 × 13.9 cm. Spine gilt-stamped from head to tail: 'H.D. The Gift NEW DIRECTIONS'.

Dust jacket of coated white stock. Front cover and spine are black. Front cover has a photograph of the new moon, beneath which in white: 'The | Gift | [ornament] | H.D.' Spine, in white: 'H.D. The Gift NEW DIRECTIONS'. Back cover has advertisements for five titles by H.D. At top of front inner flap: 'ISBN 0-8112-0853-2>$14.95'. Below this and continued on back inner flap is a two-paragraph statement about the book. Below the statement on back inner flap: 'Jacket photograph by Linda Josephson | Scolastic | Kodak Photography Awards 1971; | design by Julie Quan.'

P. i: half title, 'THE GIFT'; p. ii: blank; p. iii: 'ALSO BY H.D.' (5 titles);

p. iv: frontispiece (a photograph of H.D. and her brothers as children); p. v: title page; p. vi: copyright, twenty-six lines; p. vii: photograph of H.D.'s mother, 'To | HELEN | who has | *brought me home* | for Bethlehem Pennsylvania 1741 | from Chelsea London 1941 | *L'amitié passe même le tombeau*'; p. viii: blank; pp. ix–xv: introduction; p. xvi: blank; p. xvii: half title, 'The Gift'; p. xviii: 'The brain comes into play, yes, but it is only | the tool.... The telephone is not the person speaking | over it. The dark room is not the photograph. | *Death and its Mystery*, Camille Flammarion'; pp. 1–23: text; p. 24: blank; pp. 25–129: text; p. 130: blank; 131–142: text.

According to records in the files at New Directions, the New Directions staff first read the manuscript in mid-1980. They felt that for a trade book, the structure was too loose and that the writing did not hang together. Even after Griselda Ohannessian produced an edited version of the text, response was still lukewarm and the manuscript was put away until 1982. When Lawrence Ferlinghetti requested permission to consider the book for publication, Griselda Ohannesian again began to push for its publication by New Directions. At that time John Schaffner read the edited version and was deeply moved by H.D.'s sense of what he called "psychic memory." He then read the original manuscript to make sure that "the important revelation" of the book was "secure and intact." This edited version was then published with the hope that some university press would eventually become interested in the longer, uncut version. For the ensuing controversy, see item **G154**.

Published 17 November 1982 in an edition of 1,500 at $14.95.

Contains "Unless a Bomb Falls . . ." (by Perdita Schaffner) and *The Gift*, which includes the following six sections: "Dark Room," "The Dream," "Because One Is Happy," "The Secret," "What It Was," "Morning Star."

NBuU; CU-SC; CU-Riv; CtY (2 copies); PU.

a.ii   First edition, paperback, 1982

Title page, contents, and text contents as in **A35a.i**.

Perfect bound in paper covers cut flush with text. Front cover duplicates front of dust jacket of **A35a.i**. Spine is white printed in black: 'H.D. The Gift NDP 546'. Back cover: 'H.D. [ornament] | The Gift | *Introduction by Perdita Schaffner* | [statement from dust jacket inner flaps] | A NEW DIRECTIONS PAPERBOOK NDP 546 $5.95'.

Published 17 November 1982 in an edition of 4,000 at $5.95. There was a second impression of 1,500 on 22 July 1984.

Personal copy.

a.iii   First English edition (photo-offset from **A35a.i**), 1984 [within double-rule frame with decorative corners] THE | GIFT | H.D. | Edited by | GRISELDA OHANESSIAN | New introduction to the British edition by | DIANA COLLECOTT | Introduction to the American edition by | PERDITA SCHAFFNER | *Virago* | [publisher's device]

Perfect bound; pp. [i–vi] vii–xix [xx] xxi–xxvii [xxviii] 1–23 [24] 25–129 [130] 131–142 [143–148]. Cream wove paper, 19.6 × 12.7 cm. Paper covers cut flush with text. Front cover is dark olive green (C126). Front cover: '[within white single-rule frame] [white, in upper right corner] [publisher's device] | [in the center is a frame with a thick white border divided into three parts; the upper part of the frame encloses a night sky, medium blue (C182) background dotted with a pale yellow (C89) moon and stars, and the central part of the frame is pale yellow on which is printed in red (C11)] THE GIFT | H.D. | [the lower compartment of the frame contains a reproduction of the painting *Girl Asleep* by Dod Proctor; over the lower left corner of the frame is superimposed a circle surrounded by a white border within which is a photograph of H.D.]'. Spine, from head to tail in white: 'THE GIFT H.D. 0 86068 434 2 | [publisher's device]'. The back cover is dark olive green. In the center, a white single-rule frame surrounds a pale yellow compartment which is enclosed by a white border. Within the compartment is a thirty-two-line statement about the book. Below the compartment: '£3.50 net in U.K. only Autobiography / Literature | 0 86068 434 2'.

Pp. i–ii: biographical note; p. iii: title page; p. iv: copyright, 'Published by VIRAGO PRESS Limited 1984 | 41 William IV Street, London WC2N 4DB | This Virago edition is offset from the New Directions 1982 edition | [eighteen lines]'; p. v: dedication as in A35a.i; p. vi: blank; pp. vii–xix: introduction to the British edition; p. xx: blank; pp. xxi–xxvii: introduction to the American edition; p. xxviii: epigraph from Camille Flammarion as in A35a.i; pp. 1–23: text; p. 24: blank; pp. 25–129: text; p. 130: blank; pp. 131–142: text; pp. 143–146: advertisements; pp. 147–148: blank.

Published 11 October 1984 in an edition of 6,000 at £3.95.

Contains "Introduction to the British Edition" (by Diana Collecott), "Unless a Bomb Falls . . ." (by Perdita Schaffner), and *The Gift*, which includes the following six sections: "Dark Room," "The Dream," "Because One Is Happy," "The Secret," "What It Was," "Morning Star."

CaOTU; NBuU.

A36   *Notes on Thought and Vision*

a.i   First edition, 1982

Notes on Thought and Vision | & | The Wise Sappho | by | H.D. | [publisher's device] | City Lights Books | San Francisco

[1–5]⁸; pp. [i–ii] [1–6] 7–14 [15–16] 17–24 [25] 26–35 [36] 37–53 [54–56] 57–60 [61] 62–69 [70] 71–72 [73–78]. Cream wove paper, 17.7 × 10.6 cm. Endpapers of the same cream wove paper. Covers of dark blue (C183) cloth, 18.4 × 11 cm. Spine gilt-stamped from head to tail: 'H.D. Notes on Thought and Vision City Lights Books'.

Dust jacket of coated cream stock. The front and back covers and spine are dark blue. Front cover: '[white] Notes on | [orange yellow (C66)] THOUGHT & VISION | [white] by | H.D. | [orange yellow and black] [the figure of a Greek woman pulling at her chiton with her left hand and holding a vase in her right hand]'. Spine, in white: 'H.D. Notes on Thought and Vision City Lights Books'. Back cover, in white: 'Thought and Vision | & | The Wise Sappho | *with an introduction by Albert Gelpi* | [two-paragraph, twenty-three-line statement] | City Lights Books'. The inner flaps are white and blank except for the price, $9.95, in the top right corner of the front inner flap.

Pp. i–ii: blank; p. 1: half title, '*Notes on Thought and Vision | & | The Wise Sappho*'; p. 2: blank; p. 3: title page; p. 4: copyright, '[thirteen lines] | First printing: December 1982 | [twelve lines]'; p. 5: contents; p. 6: blank; pp. 7–14: "The Thistle and the Serpent"; p. 15: section title, "Notes on Thought and Vision | *Scilly Islands | July 1919*; p. 16: blank; pp. 17–24: text; p. 25: photograph, 'Charioteer at Delphi'; pp. 26–35: text; p. 36: photograph, 'The Muse Terpsichore'; pp. 37–53: text; p. 54: blank; p. 55: section title, 'The Wise Sappho'; p. 56: blank; pp. 57–69: text; p. 70: blank; pp. 71–72: glossary; pp. 73–76: advertisements; pp. 77–78: blank.

Published in January 1983 in an edition of 300 copies at $9.95.

The last section of "Notes on Thought and Vision" (pp. 52–53) is inadvertently duplicated.

Contains "The Thistle and the Serpent" (by Albert Gelpi), "Notes on Thought and Vision," "The Wise Sappho," "Glossary" (by Anne Janowitz).

NBuU; PU; CU-Riv.

a.ii   First edition, paperback, 1982

Title page, contents, and text contents as in **A36a.i**.

Perfect bound in paper covers cut flush with text. The covers and spine duplicate the dust jacket of **A36a.i** with the exception that bottom of back cover has price, '$4'.

Published in January 1983 in an edition of 3,700 copies at $4.00.

Personal copy.

A37 Priest & A Dead Priestess Speaks

a First edition, 1983

PRIEST | & | A DEAD | PRIESTESS | SPEAKS | [to the right of the previous five lines a light purple (C221) rule extends vertically down the page 20 cm and then horizontally to the left 7.5 cm; to the right of the title and the rule, in orange yellow (C66) hollow letters] H.D. | [above the horizontal rule] Copper Canyon Press: Port Townsend

[1–4]^6; pp. [1–48]. White laid paper with vertical chain lines, 28.5 × 16 cm; fore and bottom edges rough cut. Pp. [1]$_1$ and [4]$_6$ pastedown endpapers. Gatherings sewn with very light purple (C221) thread. Black cloth covers, 29.1 × 16.3 cm. A piece of orange yellow paper has been pasted on the front cover. Silk-screened on it in black are the figures of two men struggling to hold a figure which is a woman from the waist up and a snake from the waist down. Two long black curving lines surround them, and there are irregular black markings at the top and bottom of the paper. To the left of the orange yellow paper is a thin strip of light purple paper. Orange yellow title label pasted to spine, printed, from head to tail: '[ornament] H.D. [ornament] PRIEST & A DEAD PRIEST-ESS SPEAKS'. Bottom of title label dotted with splatter marks of light purple ink.

Line drawings below section titles: on p. 9 a bearded man in an orange yellow cape seated on a stool beneath which is a coiled snake; on p. 29, a woman muffled in a partially orange yellow cloak seated on a stool. The first poem is in fourteen sections, and the second is in seven sections. Each section is numbered with a roman numeral printed in orange yellow.

Pp. 1–4: blank; p. 5: 'H.D.'; p. 6: blank; p. 7: title page; p. 8: blank; p. 9: section title, 'PRIEST'; p. 10: blank; pp. 11–27: text; p. 28: blank; p. 29: section title, 'A DEAD PRIESTESS SPEAKS'; p. 30: blank; pp. 31–40: text; pp. 41–42: blank; p. 43: colophon and copyright, 'This first book issued with the new pressmark, adopted in Copper Canyon's | tenth year, was printed in the summer | by Tree Swenson in an edition of two | hundred and thirty copies with hand-set | twelve point Bembo and twenty-four | point Castellar types on Frankfurt paper. | The book was handbound by Marsha | Hollingsworth who also collaborated | with Tree Swenson on the design of the book. All illustrations are adapted | from Greek vase paintings, the two | on the interior by the printer and the | cover by Phyllis Hopeck, who also | directed the silk-screening of the image | onto Canson paper from the screen | prepared by Drew Elicker. Thanks go | to Centrum, where Copper Canyon | Press is press in residence, and to James | Laughlin who provided the manuscript. | Copyright © 1983 by the Estate of Hilda Doolittle. Published by permission of | New Directions, agents for the Estate. | All rights reserved.'; pp. 44–48: blank.

Published in an edition of 250 copies, December 1983. Prepublication price was $75.00, and thereafter the price was $90.00.

Contains "Priest" and "A Dead Priestess Speaks." Reprinted in *CP* (1983).

NBuU; CU-Riv.

A38 *Collected Poems, 1912–1944*

a.i First edition, 1983

H.D. | [ornament] | Collected | Poems | 1912–1944 | [ornament] | Edited by Louis L. Martz | A New Directions Book

[1–21]¹⁶; pp. [i–viii] ix [x] xi–xxxvi [1–4] 5–42 [43–44] 45–68 [69–70] 71–98 [99–100] 101–143 [144–146] 147–208 [209–210] 211–305 [306–308] 309–365 [366–368] 369–504 [505–508] 509–543 [544–546] 547–574 [575–576] 577–629 [630–636]. Cream wove paper, 22.7 × 15 cm. Endpapers of a heavier cream wove paper. Covers of light gray (C264) cloth. Stamped on spine in blue (C168): '[ornament] | [from head to tail] H.D. Collected Poems [to the left, head to tail] 1912–1944 | NEW DIRECTIONS | [ornament]'.

Dust jacket of coated white stock. Front cover and spine are green blue (C169). Front cover, in white: '[ornament] | H.D. | [ornament] | Collected | Poems | 1912–1944'. Spine, in white: '[ornament] [head to tail] H.D. Collected Poems [to the left] 1912–1944 | NEW DIRECTIONS | [ornament]'. Back cover has a photograph of H.D. printed in blue tones. Below the photo, in blue (C169): 'Photograph of H.D. courtesy of American Literature, the Beinecke Rare Book and Manuscript Library, Yale University'. The front and back inner flaps are printed in blue. Front inner flap: 'FPISBN 0-8112-0876-1 >$35.00 | H.D. | [ornament] | Collected | Poems | 1912–1944 | [ornament] | Edited by Louis L. Martz | [twenty-one-line statement on the book continued to the back inner flap] | A NEW DIRECTIONS BOOK'. Back inner flap: '[twenty-line biographical description of H.D.] | [six titles also by H.D.] | [ornament] | NEW DIRECTIONS | 80 Eighth Avenue, New York, 10011'.

P. i: half title, 'H.D. | [ornament] | Collected | Poems | 1912–1944 | [ornament]'; p. ii: 'Also by H.D.' (six titles); p. iii: title page; p. iv: copyright, thirty lines; p. v: contents; p. vi: blank; p. vii: dedication, 'To the memory of | Norman Holmes Pearson'; p. viii: blank; p. ix: preface; p. x: blank; pp. xi–xxxvi: introduction; p. 1: section title, 'COLLECTED POEMS | 1925'; p. 2: blank; p. 3: section title, 'Sea Garden | 1916'; p. 4: blank; pp. 5–42: text; p. 43: section title, 'The God | 1913–1917'; p. 44: blank; pp. 45–68: text; p. 69: section title, 'Translations | 1915–1920'; p. 70: blank; pp. 71–98: text; p. 99: section title, 'Hymen | 1921'; p. 100: blank; pp. 101–143: text; p. 144: blank; p. 145: section title, 'Heliodora | 1924'; p. 146: blank; pp. 147–208: text; p. 209: section title, 'RED ROSES FOR BRONZE | 1931'; p. 210: blank; pp. 211–305: text; p. 306: blank; p. 307: section title, 'UNCOLLECTED AND | UNPUBLISHED POEMS | 1912–1944'; p. 308: blank; pp. 309–365: text; p. 366: blank; p. 367: section title, 'A Dead Priestess Speaks | Contents | {as prepared by H.D.} | A Dead Priestess Speaks | Electra-Orestes | Calypso | In Our Town | Delphi | Dodona | Sigil | Priest | Master {Magician}'; p. 368: blank; pp. 369–504: text; p. 505: section title, 'TRILOGY'; p. 506: blank; p. 507: section title, 'The Walls Do Not Fall'; p. 508: blank; pp. 509–543: text; p. 544: blank; p. 545: section title, 'Tribute to the Angels'; p. 546: blank; pp. 547–574: text; p. 575: section title, 'The Flowering of the Rod'; p. 576: blank; pp. 577–629: text; p. 630–636: blank.

Published 18 November 1983 in an edition of 2,500 copies at $35.00. There was a second impression in February 1985; 4,000 sheets were printed, of which 750 were bound in boards, while 3,250 were held for the paperback impression.

Contains *Collected Poems* (1925) (section title for the following five collections): *Sea Garden* (1916), "The God, 1913–1917," "Translations, 1915–1920," *Hymen* (1921), *Heliodora* (1924); *Red Roses for Bronze* (1931); "Uncollected and Unpublished Poems, 1912–1944" (section title for the following forty-one poems): "Epigram," "Late Spring," "Amaranth," "Eros," "Envy," "I Said," "Helios and Athene," "Ariadne," "The Shepherd," "At Croton," "Antipater of Sidon," "Gift," "Psyche," "Child Poems," "Projector," "Projector II," "Other Sea-Cities" "A Dead Priestess Speaks" (section title for the following nine poems): "A Dead Priestess Speaks," "Electra-Orestes," "Calypso," "In Our Town," "Delphi," "Dodona," "Sigil," "Priest," "Master {Magician}," "The Dancer," "The Master," "The Poet," "Orestes Theme," "Two Poems for Christmas, 1937," "Fragments from *Temple of the Sun*," "Zeus-Provider," "Archer," "Scribe," "Body and Soul," "Erige Cor Tuum ad Me in Caelum," "Ecce Sponsus," "Ancient Wisdom Speaks," "R.A.F.," "May 1943," "Christmas 1944"; and *Trilogy* (section title for the following three poems): "The Walls Do Not Fall," "Tribute to the Angels," "The Flowering of the Rod."

NBuU; PU; CtY; CU-SC.

a.ii First edition, paperback, 1986

Title page, contents and text contents as in **A38a.i**.

Perfect bound in paper covers cut flush with text. The design of the covers duplicates the dust jacket of **A38a.i**.

Published 12 February 1986 in an edition of 3,250 copies at $15.95. There was a second impression of 2,000 in 1987.

Personal copy.

a.iii   First English edition (photo-offset from **A38a.i**), 1984

H.D. | [ornament] | Collected | Poems | 1912–1944 | [ornament] | Edited by Louis L. Martz | CARCANET PRESS [dot] MANCHESTER

$[1-19]^{16}$ $[20]^{12}$ $[21]^{16}$; pp. [iii–viii] ix [x] xi–xxxvi [1–4] 5–42 [43–44] 45–68 [69–70] 71–98 [99–100] 101–143 [144–146] 147–208 [209–210] 211–305 [306–308] 309–365 [366–368] 369–504 [505–508] 509–543 [544–546] 547–574 [575–576] 577–629 [630]. White wove paper, 21.2 × 13.6 cm. Endpapers of a heavier black (C267) wove paper. Covers of black cloth, 22.1 × 14 cm. Spine gilt-stamped: '*H.D.* | COLLECTED | POEMS | 1912–1944 | [below] CARCANET PRESS'.

Dust jacket of coated white stock. Front and back covers and spine are black. Front cover: '[photograph of H.D. within a triple-rule circle, light blue (C180) within white within light blue] | [light blue] *H.D.* | [white] COLLECTED | POEMS | 1912–1944'. Spine: '[light blue] *H.D.* | [white] COLLECTED | POEMS | 1912–1944 | [light blue] CARCANET PRESS'. Back cover has a six-line quote in light blue from the *New York Times Book Review* and a twelve-line quote in light blue from *The Walls Do Not Fall*. Front inner flap has a thirty-two-line statement in light blue, below which: '[double white rules] | [light blue] Cover design by Sue Richards | ISBN 0 85635 4759 £16.95'. Back inner flap: '[four titles by H.D. in light blue] | [double white rules] | [twenty-eight titles by Carcanet Press in light blue] | [double white rules] | [Carcanet address in white]'.

P. iii: half title, as in **A38a.i**; p. iv: 'Also by H.D.' (six titles); p. v: title page; p. vi: copyright, as in **A38a.i** down to: 'First published in England by Carcanet Press Ltd. in 1984 | [nine lines] | Printed in England by SRP Ltd., Exeter | The Publisher acknowledges the financial assistance of the Arts Council of | Great Britain.'; p. vii: contents; p. viii: dedication, as in **A38a.i**; pp. ix–630: as in **A38a.i**.

Text contents as in **A38a.i**.

CaOTU; PU.

A39 *Selected Poems*

a.i First edition, 1988

HD | SELECTED POEMS | [short rule] | EDITED BY LOUIS MARTZ | A NEW DIRECTIONS BOOK

[1–7]^16; pp. [i–vi] vii–xxvi [1–2] 3–198. Cream wove paper, 20.2 × 13 cm. Endpapers of heavier cream wove paper. Gray red (C19) cloth. Gilt-stamped on spine from head to tail: '*HD SELECTED POEMS* [publisher's device] NEW DIRECTIONS'.

Dust jacket of coated white stock. Front cover: '[photograph of H.D.] [lower right corner: gray red (C18)] *HD* | [light brown (C42)] SELECTED POEMS | EDITED BY LOUIS L. MARTZ'. Spine, head to tail: '[light gray red (C18)] *HD* [light brown] SELECTED POEMS [white] [publisher's device] [light brown] NEW DIRECTIONS'. Back cover is gray red and has a twenty-five-line list of New Directions titles. At top of front inner flap: 'FPT ISBN 0-8112-1065-0 >$18.95'. Below this, under the heading '[gray red] *HD* | [light brown] SELECTED POEMS | [black] EDITED WITH AN INTRODUCTION BY [light brown] LOUIS L. MARTZ', are a three-line quote from the *Boston Herald* and a twenty-eight-line statement continued on the back inner flap, which also has a five-line quote from Alicia Ostriker and a three-line quote from Sandra Gilbert. At the bottom: '*Jacket photograph by Islay Lyons, courtesy of | Perdita Schaffner: design by Sylvia Frezzoni* | [publisher's address].'

P. i: half title, '*HD* | SELECTED POEMS'; p. ii: 'ALSO BY H.D.' (ten titles); p. iii: title page; p. iv: copyright, thirty-five lines; pp. v–vi: contents; pp. vii–xxv: introduction; p. xxvi: acknowledgments (seven lines); p. 1: half title, '*HD* | SELECTED POEMS'; p. 2: blank; pp. 3–198: text.

Contains "Introduction" (by Louis Martz); "From *Sea Garden*" (section title for the following thirteen poems): "Sea Rose," "Sea Lily," "Evening," "Sheltered Garden," "Sea Poppies," "Garden," "Sea Violet," "Orchard," "Sea Gods," "Storm," "Sea Iris," "Hermes of the Ways," "Pear Tree"; "Miscellaneous Poems, 1914–1917" (section title for the following eight poems): "Oread," "The Pool," "Moonrise," "The Tribute (1–6)," "Amaranth," "Eros," "Envy," "Eurydice"; "From *Hymen*" (section title for the following three poems): "Hippolytus Temporizes," "The Islands," "Fragment 113"; "From *Heliodora*, 1924" (section title for the following four poems): "Helen," "Fragment Thirty-Six," "Cassandra," "Toward the Piraeus"; "From *Red Roses for Bronze*, 1931" (section title for the following three poems): "Let Zeus Record," "Epitaph," "The Mysteries"; "Miscellaneous Poems, 1931–1938(?)" (section title for the following seven poems): "Magician," "Sigil (XI, XII, XIV–XIX)," "Calypso," "The Dancer," "The Master," "The Poet," "A Dead Priestess Speaks"; "From *Euripides* Ion" (concluding episode); "From *Trilogy*, 1944–1946" (section title for the following three poems): "The Walls Do Not Fall (1–4, 6–10, 16, 21–23, 39, 40, 43)," "Tribute to the Angels (1–4, 6–8, 16–20, 23–25, 29–32, 35–38, 41, 43)," "The Flowering of the Rod (1–10)," "From *Helen in Egypt*, 1961," (section title for the following poem): "Pallinode (Book One: 1–8; Book Two: 1–4)"; "From *Hermetic Definition*" (section title for the following poem): "Winter Love (2, 5, 6, 16, 19–21, 24, 25, 27, 28)."

Published 30 September 1988 in an edition of 1,500 at $18.95.

NBu.

a.ii First edition, paperback, 1988

Title page, collation, contents, and text contents as in **A39a.i**.

Perfect bound in paper covers cut flush with text. Coated white stock. Covers and spine are black. Front cover: '[photograph of H.D.] [lower right corner: gray (C264)] HD | SELECTED POEMS | EDITED BY LOUIS MARTZ'. Spine, from head to tail: '[gray] SELECTED POEMS [white] [publisher's device] | NEW DIRECTIONS'. Back cover has the material from the inner flaps of **A39a.i** printed in white.

Published 30 September 1988 in an edition of 3,000 at $8.95. A second impression of 2,500 sold at $9.95. Due to problems with the plates of the first impression, the second was entirely reshot from **A39b**.

Personal copy; NBuU.

b First English edition, 1989

[white within a dark gray (C266) box] H.D. | [row of twelve short vertical slashes] | [black] SELECTED | POEMS | *Edited by Louis L. Martz* | [row of twelve short vertical slashes] | CARCANET

$[1–7]^{16}$; pp. [i–vi] vii–xxv [xxvi] [1–2] 3–198. White wove paper, 21.5 × 13.6 cm. Endpapers of heavier white wove paper. Black cloth, 22 × 14 cm. Gilt-stamped spine: '[black in gilt box, 2.4 × 1.4 cm] H.D. | [head to tail] SELECTED POEMS CARCANET'.

Dust jacket of cream laid paper with horizontal chain lines. Covers and spine covered with a woven pattern of alternating lines of orange (C69) and medium gray (C265) strokes. On the front cover in a brown (C75) box: '[white] CARCANET | [orange] SELECTED | [white] H.D. | [orange] POEMS | [white] *Edited by Louis L. Martz*'. Spine: '[white in brown box, 2.4 × 1.4 cm] H.D. | [medium gray, head to tail] SELECTED POEMS CARCANET'. On the back cover in medium gray in white box, ± 6 × 6.5 cm, nine lines from *Hermetic Definition*. On the front inner flap in medium gray: '[thirty-three-line blurb] | ISBN 685635 826 6 £14.95'. On the back inner flap in medium gray beneath a photo of H.D.: 'Carcanet:

The American List | [fifteen names] | Write for a catalog to | CARCANET | 208–212 Corn Exchange | Manchester M4 3BQ | JACKET DESIGN: *Stephen Row*'.

P. i: half title, 'Selected Poems'; p. ii, 'Also by H.D.' (seven titles); p. iii: title page; p. iv: copyright, '[thirty-one lines] | Printed and bound in Great Britain by SRP Ltd., Exeter'; pp. v–vi: contents; pp. vii–xxiv: introduction; p. xxv: acknowledgments; p. xxvi: blank; pp. 1–198 as in **A39a.i**.

Text contents as in **A39a.i**.

An edition of 500 copies printed in 1989 at £14.95, later raised to £16.95.

Personal copy.

B

Contributions to Books and Pamphlets

B1 *Ten Songs for Children Young and Old*

Ed. Walter Rummel. London: Augener, 1914.

Contains "The Mill Fairy," "The Flower Fairy," "The Singer Fairy," "The Cricket," and "The Leaves." Lyrics by H.D., music by Walter Rummel.

Noted but not seen. See **C177**.

B2 *Des Imagistes*

a First edition (book issue), 1914

DES IMAGISTES | AN ANTHOLOGY | [device] | NEW YORK | ALBERT AND CHARLES BONI | 98 FIFTH AVENUE | 1914

$[1-4]^8$; pp. [1-4] 5-54 [55-56] 57-63 [64]. Cream wove paper, 19 × 12.3 cm. Rough-trimmed fore edge; untrimmed bottom edge. Deep blue (±C183) cloth boards, 19.5 × 13.2 cm. On front cover in gilt within a blind-stamped single-rule frame: 'DES IMAGISTES'. Gilt stamped on spine: 'DES | IMAG|ISTES | BONI'.

Published 2 March 1914 at $1.00.

Part of the same impression as the *Glebe* for February 1914 (see **C20**) but with a different binding.

Contains "Sitalkis," "Hermes of the Ways," "Priapus (Keeper of the Orchards)," "Acon," "Hermonax," "Epigram," pp. 20-30.

b English (book) issue, 1914

DES IMAGISTES | AN ANTHOLOGY | [device] | [next four lines hand-stamped in purple] LONDON: THE POETRY BOOKSHOP | 35 DEVONSHIRE STREET | THEOBALDS RD., W.C. | [in some copies] ° | NEW YORK | ALBERT AND CHARLES BONI | 98 FIFTH AVENUE | 1914

Same collation and pagination as **B2a**. Cover of grayish green (±C136) paper over boards, 12.8 × 18.7 cm. Stamped in black on front cover: 'IMAGISTES | THE POETRY BOOKSHOP'. On spine from tail to head: 'IMAGISTES'.

c   Reissue of periodical issue, 1917

[cancellans title page] DES IMAGISTES | AN ANTHOLOGY | NEW YORK | FRANK SHAY, PUBLISHER | 1917

d   Reissue of periodical issue, [circa 1920]

Same title page as the *Glebe* (Feb. 1914). Donald Gallup, in his bibliography of Ezra Pound, lists this as probably having been issued by Frank Shay around 1920 based on physical evidence.

B3 *Some Imagist Poets*

SOME IMAGIST | POETS | AN ANTHOLOGY | [publisher's logo] | BOSTON AND NEW YORK | HOUGHTON MIFFLIN COMPANY | [in Gothic] The Riverside Press Cambridge | 1915

$[1-11]^4$ $[12]^2$ $[13]^4$ $[14]^2$; pp. $[i-ii]^1$ [i-iv] v-vii [viii] ix [x] [1-2] 3-8 [9] 10 [11] 12-13 [14] 15-17 [18-20] 21-30 [31-32] 33-37 [38] 39-48 [49-52] 53 [54] 55-56 [57] 58 [59] 60 [61] 62-63 [64-66] 67 [68] 69-70 [71] 72-73 [74] 75-76 [77] 78 [79-80] 81 [82] 83 [84] 85-91 [92-96]. Cream wove paper, 19.7 × 14.1 cm. Endpapers. Covers of gray green (±C127) wove paper boards, 18 × 14.3 cm. On the cover: 'Some Imagist Poets | An Anthology | THE NEW POETRY SERIES | [publisher's logo] | HOUGHTON MIFFLIN COMPANY | Boston and New York'. [On this copy, the spine is damaged and illegible.] On verso of title page: 'Copyright 1915. Published April 1915'. Also contains poems by Richard Aldington, John Gould Fletcher, F. S. Flint, D. H. Lawrence, and Amy Lowell. Bibliography on p. 93.

Contains the first book appearance of "The Pool," "The Garden," "Sea Lily," "Sea Iris," "Sea Rose," "Oread," "Orion Dead," pp. 21-30.

B4 *The New Poetry*

a First edition, 1917

THE NEW POETRY | AN ANTHOLOGY EDITED BY | HARRIET MONROE | AND | ALICE CORBIN HENDERSON | EDITORS OF "POETRY" | [in Gothic] New York | THE MACMILLAN COMPANY | 1917 | *All rights reserved*

[1–28]⁸; pp. [i–iv] v–xiii [xiv] xv–xxxi [xxxii–xxxiv] 1–383 [384] 385–404 [405–414]. Cream wove paper, 19 × 12.8 cm; rough-trimmed fore edge. Dark green (C137) cloth boards. Gilt-stamped on front cover within a blind-stamped single-rule frame: 'THE NEW POETRY | [three small triangles] | AN ANTHOLOGY'.

First book appearance of "Moonrise." Also includes "Oread," "The Pool," "Hermes of the Ways," "Priapus (Keeper of Orchards)," "The Garden," and "The Shrine," pp. 63–71.

b Second (enlarged) edition, 1923

THE NEW POETRY | AN ANTHOLOGY | OF TWENTIETH-CENTURY VERSE IN | ENGLISH | NEW AND ENLARGED EDITION | EDITED BY | HARRIET MONROE | EDITOR OF *Poetry: A Magazine of Verse* | AND | ALICE CORBIN HENDERSON | [in Gothic] New York | THE MACMILLAN COMPANY | 1923 | *All rights reserved*

[1–44]¹⁶; pp. [i–iv] v–vii [viii] ix–xxxiii [xxxiv] xxxv–xliii [xliv] xlv–lii [liii–liv] [1] 2–611 [612] 613–640 [641–650]. Cream wove paper, 19.8 × 13.4. Heavier wove endpapers. Brown (C47) cloth boards, 21.6 × 14.3 cm; blind-stamped front cover, within a single-rule frame: 'THE NEW POETRY | [three small triangles] | AN ANTHOLOGY'. Gilt-stamped spine: 'THE | NEW | POETRY | MONROE | [three small triangles] | HENDERSON | NEW AND | ENLARGED | EDITION | MACMILLAN'. On verso of title page: 'Set up and electrotyped. Published February, 1917. New and enlarged Edition, April, 1923.'

Contribution as in **B4a** with the addition of "At Baia" and first book appearance of "Hesperides" ("Fragment Thirty-six"), pp. 94–103.

B5 *American Poetry, 1922: A Miscellany*

American Poetry | 1922 | [rule] | A MISCELLANY | Edited By | LOUIS UNTERMEYER

[1–13]⁸ [14]⁴; pp. [i–ii] iii–x [1–2] 3–21 [22–24] 25–38 [39–40] 41–52 [53–54] 55–71 [72–74] 75–76 [77–78] 79–88 [89–90] 91–100 [101–102]

103–123 [124–126] 127–137 [138–140] 141–147 [148–150] 151–167 [168–170] 171–189 [190–192] 193–200 [201–202] 203–205 [206]. Cream wove paper, 18.7 × 12.3 cm; endpapers. Red (C11) paper boards with black cloth shelfback. Front cover stamped in black: 'AMERICAN POETRY | 1922 | [device] | A MISCELLANY'. Spine gilt-stamped: 'American | Poetry | 1922 | [rule] | A | Miscellany'.

Contains the first book appearance of "Holy Satyr," "Lais," "Heliodora," "Toward the Piraeus I–IV," pp. 151–67.

B6 *Miscellany of Poetry, 1920–1922*

A Miscellany of Poetry | 1920–1922 | *Edited by* | *William Keyne Seymour* | *London* | *JOHN G. WILSON* | *350 Oxford Street,* | *W.1*

a² [π]⁴ b–o⁸ p² pp. [i–ii]₁ [i–iv] v–x 1–203 [204–205] 206–210 [211–212]. Cream wove paper, 18.7 × 12.5 cm; endpapers. Blue (C168) paper over boards with yellow (C83) cloth shelfback, 19.1 × 12.9 cm. White paper label printed in black on front cover, within double-rule frame: 'A Miscellany | of Poetry | 1920–1922 | [device] | Edited by | William Keyne Seymor'.

Published December 1922, 1,500 copies.

Contains first book appearance of "We Two," p. 71.

B7 *Contact Collection of Contemporary Writers*

CONTACT COLLECTION OF | CONTEMPORARY WRITERS | [names in column down center of page] Djuna Barnes | Bryher | Mary Butts | Norman Douglas | Havelock Ellis | F.M. Ford | Wallace Gould | Ernest Hemingway | Marsden Hartley | H.D. | John Herrman | James Joyce | Mina Loy | Robert McAlmon | Ezra Pound | Dorothy Richardson | May Sinclair | Edith Sitwell | Gertrude Stein | W.C. Williams

[π]² [1]⁶ 2–21⁸ 22⁴; pp. [i–viii] 1–10 [11] 12–29 [30] 31–40 [41] 42–52 [53] 54–56 [57] 58–74 [75] 76 [77] 78–86 [87] 88–90 [91] 92–113 [114] 115–132 [133] 134–136 [137] 138–140 [141] 142–148 [149] 150 [151] 152–157 [158] 159 [160] 161–162 [163] 164–167 [168] 169–173 [174] 175–177 [178–180] 181–182 [183] 184 [185] 186–189 [190] 191–194 [195] 196–213 [214] 215–216 [217] 218–236 [237] 238–296 [297] 298–302 [303] 304–325 [326] 327–338 [339–344]. Cream wove paper, 19 × 14 cm; rough-trimmed fore and bottom edge; uncut top edge. Light gray (C264) paper cover wrapped over first and last leaf. Printed in black on front and back, tail to head on spine. Glassine outer wrapper.

Published June 1925 at $3.00, ±300 copies. On p. 339: 'Printed at Dijon by Maurice Darrantiére.'

Contains an early version of *Hedylus* (sections XI–XV), pp. [91]–113.

B8 *American Poetry, 1925: A Miscellany*

AMERICAN POETRY | 1925 | [short rule] | A MISCELLANY | [publisher's logo] | NEW YORK | HARCOURT, BRACE AND COMPANY

[1–16]^8 [17]^4; pp. [i–ii] iii–xiv [1–2] 3–26 [27–28] 29–49 [50–52] 53–64 [65–66] 67–69 [70–72] 73–87 [88–90] 91–102 [103–104] 105–119 [120–122] 123–136 [137–138] 139–142 [143–144] 145–164 [165–166] 167–172 [173–174] 175–180 [181–182] 183–187 [188–190] 191–198 [199–200] 201–206 [207–208] 209–222 [223–224] 225–241 [242–244] 245–248 [249–250]. Cream wove paper, 18.8 × 12.5 cm; endpapers. Blue (C182) cloth boards, 19.4 × 12.8 cm, gilt-stamped: 'A MISCELLANY OF | AMERICAN | POETRY | 1925'. Gilt-stamped spine: 'Miscellany | of | American | Poetry | 1925 | [below] HARCOURT | BRACE & CO.'

Dust jacket of mottled pale blue and blue white wove paper with original protective glassine wrapper. On the front within a double-rule thick-thin frame with ornamental corners: '*American Poetry* | *1925* | *A Miscellany* | *72 New Poems by* [two column divided by a vertical rule: on the left] *Conrad Aiken* | *William Rose Benet* | *H.D.* | *T.S. Eliot* | *John Gould Fletcher* | *Alfred Kreymbourg* | *Vachel Lindsay* | *Amy Lowell* | *Edna St. Vincent Millay* | [on the right] *John Crowe Ransom* | *Edwin Arlington* | *Robinson* | *Carl Sandburg* | *Wallace Stevens* | *Sara Teasdale* | *Jean Starr* | *Untermeyer* | *Louis Untermeyer* | *Elinor Wylie*'. On the spine: 'American | Poetry | 1925 | A | Miscellany | Harcourt | Brace & Co.' On the back cover under the heading '*Unusual Collections of Modernist Writing*' are descriptions of twelve titles, below which are the publisher's name and address. The front flap contains a fourteen-line statement on the book under the heading 'AMERICAN POETRY | 1925 | A MISCELLANY'. In the right corner at an angle: '$2.00'. Below the statement: '*Harcourt, Brace and Company* | 383 MADISON AVENUE, NEW YORK'. The back flap contains a fourteen-line advertisement for *The Long Gallery* by Anne Goodwin Winslow.

On the copyright page: 'Copyright, 1925, BY | HARCOURT BRACE AND COMPANY, INC. | First edition, August, 1925 | PRINTED IN THE USA BY | THE QUINN & BODEN COMPANY | RAHWAY, N.J.'

Contains "Songs from Cyprus I–V" and "Let Zeus Record I–VII," pp. 53–64. Reprinted in *Red Roses for Bronze*, 1931, and *CP* (1983).

B9 *The Second American Caravan*

[all within a thin-thick double-rule frame] THE SECOND | AMERI-CAN | CARAVAN | [short rule] | A YEARBOOK | OF AMERICAN | LITERATURE | EDITED BY | ALFRED KREYMBORG | LEWIS MUMFORD | PAUL ROSENFELD | [device] | [short rule] | NEW YORK | THE MACAULAY COMPANY | MCMXXVIII

$[1-27]^{16}$ $[28]^{10}$; pp. [i–vi] vii–ix [x] xi–xii 1–872. Cream wove paper, 23.4 × 15.9 cm; heavier cream wove endpapers. Cream cloth boards stamped in green (C146). Front cover, within a thick-thin double-rule frame: 'THE SECOND | AMERICAN | CARAVAN'. Spine, within a thick-thin double-rule frame: 'THE SECOND | AMERICAN | CARA-VAN | EDITED BY | ALFRED KREYMBORG | LEWIS MUMFORD | PAUL ROSENFELD | [rule] | MACAULAY'.

Published 24 September 1928 at $5.00. Contains the only publication of the story "Narthex," pp. 225–84.

B10 *Imagist Anthology, 1930*

[double title page: on the left, all within a single-rule frame with a star at top and bottom] IMAGIST ANTHOLOGY 1930 | COVICI FRIEDE * NEW YORK | [on the right, all within a single-rule frame with a star at top and bottom] NEW POETRY BY THE IMAGISTS | RICHARD ALDINGTON | JOHN COURNOS * H.D. * JOHN GOULD FLETCHER | F.S. FLINT * FORD MADDOX FORD * JAMES JOYCE | D.H. LAWRENCE * WILLIAM CARLOS WIL-LIAMS | *Forewords by* FORD MADDOX FORD * GLENN HUGHES

$[1-15]^8$; pp. [1–12] 13–21 [22] 23–25 [26–28] 29–43 [44] 45–64 [65–66] 67–81 [82–84] 85–95 [96] 97–105 [106] 107–119 [120–122] 123–127 [128] 129–141 [142] 143–144 [145–146] 147–163 [164–166] 167–169 [170] 171–173 [174–176] 177–179 [180–182] 183–185 [186] 187 [188] 189 [190] 191 [192] 193 [194–196] 197–205 [206] 207–209 [210] 211–221 [222] 223–226 [227–228] 229 [230–240]. Cream wove paper, 20.5 × 13.8 cm; endpapers. Pale blue (C185) cloth boards, 21.1 × 14.4 cm. Light yellow (C86) paper label on spine printed in black: '[star] | [rule] | Imagist | Anthology | 1930 | [rule] | Covici | Friede | [rule] | [star]'.

Published 10 May 1930 at $3.50. Colophon on p. [231]: "The first edition of this work consists of 1000 copies." On verso of title page: "Designed and printed by Paul Johnston at the Fairfield Press." Books by H.D. listed on p. 229: *Collected Poems*, 1925; *Hippolytus Temporizes*, 1927.

Contains "In the Rain," "If You Will Let Me Sing," "Chance Meeting,"

"Choros Translations (From the Bacchae)," pp. 85–119. Reprinted in *Red Roses for Bronze*, 1931, and *CP* (1983).

B11   *The European Caravan*

THE EUROPEAN | CARAVAN | AN ANTHOLOGY OF THE NEW SPIRIT IN | EUROPEAN LITERATURE | Compiled and Edited by | SAMUEL PUTNAM | MAIDA CASTELHUN DARNTON, GEORGE REAVEY | and | J. BRONOWSKI | With Special Introductions by | ANDRÉ BERGE | MASSIMO BONTEMPELLI, JEAN CASSOU | and | E. GIMÉNEZ CABELLERO | PART I | FRANCE, SPAIN, ENGLAND and IRELAND | BREWER, WARREN & PUTNAM | NEW YORK, 1931

$[1-17]^{16}$ $[18]^{10}$ $[19]^{16}$; pp. [1–iv] v–xviii [1–2] 3–41 [42–44] 45–291 [292–294] 295–427 [428–430] 431–577 [578]. Cream laid paper, 20.6 × 13.7 cm, vertical chain lines, watermarked 'C & P'. Heavier cream endpapers. Black cloth boards, 21.5 × 14 cm stamped green (C131) on spine: 'THE | EUROPEAN | CARAVAN | BREWER | WARREN | & PUTNAM'.

Contains the only appearance of "Tatter" and the first book appearance of "Choruses from Morpheus XI–XIII," pp. 481–84. Reprinted *Red Roses for Bronze*, 1931, and *CP* (1983).

B12   *The Cantos of Ezra Pound*

[cover title] THE CANTOS | of | EZRA POUND | *Some Testimonies by* | ERNEST HEMINGWAY | FORD MADDOX FORD | T.S. ELIOT | HUGH WALPOLE | ARCHIBALD MacLEISH | JAMES JOYCE | *and* OTHERS | FARRAR & RHINEHART, Inc. [publisher's logo] PUBLISHERS : NEW YORK

A single gathering stapled twice; pp. [1–2] 3–22 [23–24]. Cream wove paper, 19.5 × 13.2 cm. Unbound.

This pamphlet was published for free distribution in connection with the publication of Ezra Pound's *A Draft of XXX Cantos* by Farrar and Rhinehart in 1933.

Contains the only appearance of an untitled memoir of Pound (section XIII), pp. 17–19.

B13 *Fifty Poets*

[in a semicircle] *FIFTY POETS* | AN | AMERICAN | AUTO-ANTHOL-OGY | [line drawing of two hands holding a bouquet of flowers] | *EDITED BY WILLIAM ROSE BENÉT* | NEW YORK | DODD, MEAD AND COMPANY | PUBLISHERS

[1–10]^8 [11]^4; pp. [i–vi] vii–xii [1–2] 3–149 [150] 151–153 [154–156]. Cream wove paper, 21.5 × 13.8 cm. Endpapers. Green cloth boards, 22.3 × 14.1 cm; single-rule frame blind-stamped on front cover. Spine gilt-stamped: '[triple rules] BENÉT | [triple rules] | [in a black square] *fifty poets* [triple rules] | [flower design] | [triple rules] DODD, MEAD | & COMPANY | [rule]'

Published 19 June 1933 at $2.50.

"The Islands," pp. 76–79. The biographical statement on p. 75 includes excerpts from a previously unpublished letter by H.D. explaining her selection of "The Islands" for the anthology.

B14 *The Oxford Anthology of American Literature*

THE | OXFORD ANTHOLOGY | OF | AMERICAN LITERATURE | CHOSEN AND EDITED BY | WILLIAM ROSE BENÉT | AND | NORMAN HOLMES PEARSON | New York | OXFORD UNIVERSITY PRESS | 1938

[1–54]^{16} [55]^4; pp. [i–iv] vi [vii] viii–x [xi] xii–xvii [xxviii–xxix] xxx [1–2] 3–1575 [1576] 1577–1683 [1684] 1685–1697 [1698] 1699–1705 [1706]. Cream wove paper, 23.3 × 15.6 cm. Deep purple (C256) cloth boards, 23.8 × 16 cm.

Published 27 October 1938 at $4.50. On verso of title page: 'First edition'.

Contains a "A Note on Poetry" by H.D., dated "Dec. 12, 1937, NYC," pp. 1287–88. This note is reprinted in *Agenda* 25.3–4 (1988): 71–74 under the title "Letter to Norman Pearson." See **C176**. Also included are reprintings of "Garden," "Orchard," "Sea Gods," "Oread," "The Pool," "Leda," "The Islands," "Sapphic Fragments Thirty-six and One Hundred Thirteen," "Song," "Lethe," "Lais," "Helen," "*Hippolytus Temporizes* [excerpt]," pp. 1287–94.

B15 *Anthology for the Enjoyment of Poetry*

ANTHOLOGY | *for the* | [next two lines in hollow letters] ENJOYMENT | OF POETRY | [device] | BY MAX EASTMAN | 1 [dot] 9 [dot] 4 [dot]

7 | [short rule] | CHARLES SCRIBNER'S SONS [dot] NEW YORK | CHARLES SCRIBNER'S SONS [dot] LTD [dot] LONDON

Noted but not seen in original binding.

Contains the first book appearance of "Socratic," pp. 3–5.

B16   *The Little Review Anthology*

THE LITTLE REVIEW | ANTHOLOGY | *Edited by* MARGARET ANDERSON | HERMITAGE HOUSE, INC. | New York, 1953

[1–24]^{16}; pp. [1–4] 5–383 [384]. Cream wove paper, 21 × 14 cm; rough-cut fore edge. Heavier cream wove endpapers. Greenish gray (C155) paper over boards with light gray (C264) cloth shelfback. Lower fore edge of front cover stamped in black script: 'MA'. On the spine from head to tail: 'THE LITTLE REVIEW ANTHOLOGY | [in white in a black square] EDITED BY | MARGARET | ANDERSON | [in black below the square] HERMITAGE'.

Contains H.D.'s response to "Confessions-Questionnaire," pp. 364–66. Reprinted from *Little Review* 12 (May 1929). See C103. Also contains "Hermes of the Ways" and "Sitalkis," reprinted in Richard Aldington's "A Young American Poet," pp. 24–28.

B17   *A Return to Pagany*

[double title page: on the left] *A Return to* | [rule] | *The History, Correspondence, and* | *Selections from a Little Magazine* | BEACON PRESS | [on the right] [device, tree within a fence] PAGANY | [rule] | *1929–1932* | *Edited by* STEPHEN HALPERT | *with* RICHARD JOHNS | *Introduction by* KENNETH REXROTH | *Boston*

[1–34]^{16}; pp. [i–xiii] xiv–xvi [xvii] xviii [xix–xx] [1–2] 3–45 [46–47] 48–99 [100–101] 102–122 [123] 124–133 [134–135] 136–165 [166–167] 168–208 [209–210] 211–228 [229] 230–267 [268] 269–279 [280–281] 282–287 [288] 289–306 [307] 308–340 [341] 342–372 [373–374] 375–380 [381] 382–431 [432–433] 435–455 [456–457] 458–483 [484–485] 486–519 [520–524]. Cream wove paper, 25 × 17.5 cm; blue (C194) wove endpapers. Blue paper boards, 26.2 × 18.2 cm, blind-stamped, with red (±C36) cloth shelfback, gilt-stamped from head to tail. Blue, white, and red dust jacket.

Published 27 December 1969 at $12.50. On verso of title page: 'Printed in the United States of America'.

Contains a previously unpublished facsimile TLS from H.D. Aldington to Mr. [Richard] John[s] dated 14 March [1932], p. 444. Also reprints "Electra Orestes; Choros Sequence," pp. 441–43.

B18 *American Film Criticism*

AMERICAN FILM | CRITICISM | From the Beginnings to *Citizen Kane* | Reviews of Significant Films at the Time | They First Appeared | *Edited by* | STANLEY KAUFFMANN | *with* | BRUCE HENSTELL | *Liveright* [publisher's logo] New York

[1–13]^{16} [14]^{12} 15^{16}; pp. [i–iv] v–vii [viii] ix–xxiii [xxiv] [1–2] 3–54 [55–56] 57–208 [209–210] 211–443 [444–448]. Cream wove paper, 22.5 × 15 cm; black endpapers. Reddish orange (C34) cloth boards, 23.3 × 15.5 cm.

Contains H.D.'s review of *The Passion of Joan of Arc*, pp. 216–20.

B19 *Images of H.D.*

Images of H.D. | Eric W. White | [short rule] | *from* The Mystery | H.D. | LONDON / ENITHARMON PRESS / 1976

[1–4]^{8}; pp. [1–14] 15–30 [31–32] 33–58 [59–64]. Pale yellow (C89) laid paper with horizontal chain lines, 24.2 × 15.2 cm; endpapers. Olive (C107) cloth boards. Gilt-stamped spine, from head to tail: 'Images of H.D. / *from* The Mystery'. Three pages of photos sewn in between pp. 24 and 25. Colophon p. [61]: '350 copies of this book have been printed on Glastonbury Book Antique Laid. In addition 50 numbered copies have been printed on Glastonbury Ivory Antique Laid and are signed by Eric White. This is number [number supplied in ink]'.

Contains previously unpublished material from *The Mystery* (chapters 3, 14–19), pp. 33–58.

B20 *The Gender of Modernism*

THE GENDER OF MODERNISM | A CRITICAL ANTHOLOGY | *Edited by Bonnie Kime Scott* | CONTRIBUTING EDITORS | MARY LYNN BROE, MARILYN L. BROWNSTEIN, CAROLYN BURKE, | RONALD BUSH | THADIOUS M. DAVIS | MARI- ANNE DEKOVEN, | SUSAN STANFORD FRIEDMAN, DIANE F. GILLESPIE, NANCY K. | GISH, CLARE HAMSON, SUZETTE HENKE, CORAL ANN JOWELLS, | JANE LILIENFELD, JANE

MARCUS, CELESTE M. SCHENCK, | BONNIE KIME SCOTT, BRENDA R. SILVER, SUSAN M. SQUIER, | AND CHERYL A. WALL | INDIANA UNIVERSITY PRESS BLOOMINGTON AND INDIANAPOLIS

[1–46]¹⁶; pp. [i–vi] vii–xv [xvi–xviii] 1–718. White wove paper, 23.5 × 16.4 cm; medium gray (C265) endpapers. Black cloth boards, 24 × 17 cm. In black within an angled metallic pink (C240) box: 'The GENDER | of MODERNISM'. On the spine: '[in metallic pink] Scott | [from head to tail in black in a metallic pink box] The GENDER | of MODERNISM'.

Contains first book publication of "Responsibilities," "Marianne Moore," and letters to Amy Lowell and Marianne Moore. Also contains "Joan of Arc," "Notes on Thought and Vision," and "Borderline." Introduced by Susan Stanford Friedman. Pp. 85–138.

C

Contributions to Periodicals

C1 "Fate." *Blue and Gray* (literary magazine of the Friend's Central School, Philadelphia) 13.6 (March 1905): 8.
Signed H. This entry is conjectural, based on the research of Emily Wallace. See item **G207**.

C2 "Marion's Two Letters." *Boston Globe* 27 Dec. 1909: 12.
Signed Edith Gray. In a letter to Norman Holmes Pearson at the Beinecke Library dated 20 April 1949, H.D. wrote: "I did some short stories, as (I think) Edith Gray or Grey. I did a few child-story star-articles as Hilda Doolittle for the Sunday Presbyterian paper. I did some column length newspaper stories for the Maclure Syndicate, Mary Marshall got those first published and she and her sister suggested trying Sunday School papers as they paid well. I think I had names given me for those, perhaps I used Edith G. as well." All the pieces published in the *Boston Globe* were syndicated by the Associated Literary Press and sold to subscribing newspapers all over the country. According to Mary Marshall, the *Boston Globe* was a regular subscriber to the syndicate.

C3 "The Purple Plume of Long Ago." *Boston Globe* 8 Feb. 1910: 12.
Signed Edith Gray.

C4 "Prince Frederick's Wooing." *Boston Globe* 24 Feb. 1910: 12.
Signed Edith Gray.

C5 "On Courting Night." *Boston Globe* 31 March 1910: 16.
Signed Edith Gray.

C6 "Shoogy-Shoo." *Boston Globe* 28 April 1910: 11.
Signed Edith Gray.

C7 "His Dreams." *Boston Globe* 13 June 1910: 12
Signed Edith Gray.

C8 "A Reversed Decision." *Forward* 24 Dec. 1910: 427.
Signed Edith Gray.

C9 "Old Tommy." *Comrade* 30 April 1911: 70.
Signed Edith Gray.

C10 "Lady Leicester." *Forward* 21 Oct. 1911: 341.
Signed Edith Gray.

C11 "The Gray Mouse." *Comrade* 10 Feb. 1912: 22.
Signed Edith Gray.

C12 "Winter Woods." *Comrade* 2 March 1912: 34.
Signed Edith Gray.

C13 "Whipporwill." *Comrade* 20 April 1912: 62.
Signed Edith Gray.

C14 "The Griffin of Temple Bar." *Comrade* 27 April 1912: 67.

C15 "Verses, Translations, and Reflections from 'The Anthology.'" *Poetry* 1 (Jan. 1913): 118–22.
Contents: "Hermes of the Ways," "Priapus, Keeper-of-Orchards," "Epigram: After the Greek." "Priapus, Keeper-of-Orchards" also titled "Orchard."

C16 "Sitalkis." *New Freewoman* 1 (Sept. 1913): 114.

C17 "The Forgotten Charge." *Comrade* 27 Sept. 1913: 154.
Signed Edith Gray.

C18 "Two Poems." *Poetry* 3 (Feb. 1914): 164–66.
Contents: "Hermonax," "Acon."

C19 "Four Poems." *Egoist* 1 (2 Feb. 1914): 54–55.
Contents: "Hermes of the Ways," "Incantation (Artemis over the Body of Orion)," "Oread," "Priapus (Keeper-of-the-Orchard)." "Incantation" later retitled "Orion Dead."

C20 "Seven Poems." *Glebe* 1.5 (Feb. 1914): 20–30.
Contents: "Sitalkis," "Hermes of the Ways I and II," "Priapus (Keeper-of-the-Orchards)," "Acon," "Hermonax," "Epigram: After the Greek." Part of the same impression as the anthology *Des Imagistes*. See **B2**.

C21 "Five Poems." *Poetry* 5 (March 1915): 265–68.
Contents: "The Wind Sleepers," "Storm," "The Pool," "The Garden," "Moonrise." "Garden" section 2 often retitled "Heat."

C22 "Mid-Day." *Egoist* 2 (1 May 1915): 74.

Contributions to Periodicals / 97

C23   "Sea Iris." *Little Review* 2 (May 1915): 30.
Included in the article "Some Imagist Poets" by George Lane.

C24   "Huntress." *Greenwich Village* 2.2 (15 July 1915): 57.

C25   "Choruses from Iphigeneia in Aulis." *Egoist* 2 (1 Nov. 1915): 171–72.
Translated by H.D.

C26   "The Cliff Temple." *Egoist* 3 (1 Jan. 1916): 8.

C27   "Two Poems." *Little Review* 2 (Jan.–Feb. 1916): [1–2].
Contents: "Late Spring," "Night."

C28   "The Last Gift." *Egoist* 3 (1 March 1916): 35.
Later retitled "The Gift"; different from "Gift." See **C89**.

C29   "The Helmsman." *Egoist* 3 (1 April 1916): 52.

C30   "Sea Gods." *Egoist* 3 (1 June 1916): 87.

C31   "Cities." *Egoist* 3 (1 July 1916): 102–3.

C32   "Marianne Moore." *Egoist* 3 (Aug. 1916): 118–19.

C33   "The Contest." *Egoist* 3 (Sept. 1916): 132.

C34   Review of *The Farmer's Bride* by Charlotte Mew. *Egoist* 3 (Sept. 1916): 135.

C35   "The Tribute." *Egoist* 3 (Nov. 1916): 165–67.

C36   "Circe." *Egoist* 3 (Dec. 1916): 179.

C37   Review of *Goblins and Pagodas* by John Gould Fletcher. *Egoist* 3 (Dec. 1916): 183–84.

C38   "Two Poems." *Egoist* 4 (Jan. 1917): 88.
Contents: "The God," "Adonis."

C39   "Pygmalion." *Egoist* 4 (Feb. 1917): 21.

C40   "Sea Poppies." *Little Review* 3 (April 1917): 11.

C41   "Eurydice." *Egoist* 4 (May 1917): 54–55.

C42   "The Look-out." *Egoist* 4 (July 1917): 87.

C43   "Cuckoo Song." *Anglo French Review* 1 (June 1919): 416–17.

C44   "Leda." *Chapbook* 1.1 (July 1919): 10–11.

C45 "Hymen." *Poetry* 15 (Dec. 1919): 117–29.
This masque includes lyrics that were later published by themselves under the titles "Never More Will the Wind," "Along the Yellow Sand," "From Citron-Bower," and "Where Love Is King."

C46 "The Islands." *North American Review* 211 (Jan. 1920): [109]–11.

C47 "Sea Heroes." *Coterie* 4 (Easter 1920): 44–46.

C48 "Evadne." *Nation* [London] 27 (10 July 1920): 471.

C49 "Why Have You Sought?" *Nation* [London] 27 (30 July 1920): 558. In *Hymen*.

C50 "Two Poems." *Sphere* 82 (21 Aug. 1920): 160.
Contents: "Lethe," "Thetis."

C51 "Three Poems." *Dial* 69 (Nov. 1920): 507–13.
Contents: "Phaedra Rebukes Hippolyta," "Phaedra Remembers Crete," "Helios." "Pheadra Remembers Crete" later retitled "Phaedra."

C52 "Two Poems." *Contact* o.s. 3 ([Spring 1921]): 8–9.
Contents: "Simaetha," "Prayer."

C53 "Hippolytus Temporizes." *Bookman* 54 (Oct. 1921): 123.

C54 "Hesperides." *Poetry* 19 (Oct. 1921): 26–30.
Contents: "Fragment XXXVI," "Song," "At Baia."

C55 "We Two." *Gargoyle* 3.1 (July 1922): [22].

C56 "Centaur Song." *Gargoyle* 3.2 (August 1922): [10–11].

C57 "The Shrine." *Fortnightly Review* 119 (Jan. 1923): 125–26.

C58 "Two Poems." *Nation and Athenaeum* 27 Jan. 1923: 647.
Contents: "At Ithaca," "Helen."

C59 "At Croton." *Little Review* 9 (Spring 1923): 30–31.

C60 "Cassandra." *Rhythmus* 2.1 (June–July 1923): 48–49.

C61 "Two Poems." *Double Dealer* 5 (Nov. 1923): 207–20.
Contents: "At Eleusis," "Centaur Song." "Centaur Song" appeared previously; see C56.

C62 "Three Poems." *Transatlantic Review* 1 (Feb. 1924): 1–5.
Contents: "Nossis," "Flute Song," "After Troy."

C63 "Leucadian Artemis." *Outlook* [London] 21 June 1924: 427.

C64 "Calliope." *Saturday Review of Literature* 20 Sept. 1924: 125.

C65 "At Athens." *Adelphi* 2 (Dec. 1924): 618.

C66 "People of Sparta." *The Bookman* 60 (Dec. 1924): 417–20.
Translation of Pausanius's *Description of Greece*, book 3.

C67 "North Star." *Outlook* [London] 3 Jan. 1925: 8.
Section 6 from "Let Zeus Record." Also titled "Stars Wheel in Purple."

C68 Review of *The Poems of Sappho* by Edwin Marion Cox. *Saturday Review of Literature* 14 March 1925: 596.

C69 "Hippolytus Temporizes." *This Quarter* 1 (Spring 1925): 97–109.
From "Work in Progress" (act 2, scene 2).

C70 "Antipater of Sidon." *Adelphi* 3 (June 1925): 64.

C71 Review of *The Acropolis of Athens* by M. Schede. *Adelphi* 3 (July 1925): 150.
Unsigned. H.D.'s unsigned reviews in *Adelphi* were identified for Norman Holmes Pearson by H. P. Collins, the editor of the *Adelphi* at the time of their publication, in a letter dated 1 Sept. 1965.

C72 Review of *Greek Social Life* by F. A. Wright. *Adelphi* 3 (July 1925): 151.
Unsigned.

C73 Review of *Lewis and Irene*, trans. Paul Morand. *Adelphi* 3 (July 1925): 152.
Unsigned.

C74 Review of *Little Novels of Sicily* by Giovanni Verga. *Adelphi* 3 (July 1925): 153.
Unsigned.

C75 Review of *The Polyglots* by W. Gerhardi. *Adelphi* 3 (Sept. 1925): 305.
Unsigned.

C76 Review of *The Stages of Greek Religion* by Gilbert Murray. *Adelphi* 3 (Oct. 1925): 378.
Unsigned.

C77 "Hippolytus Temporizes." *The Chapbook* 40 (Oct. 1925): 20–24.
Contents: act 2, scene 1.

C78 "Two Poems." *Poetry* 27 (Nov. 1925): 83–87.
Contents: "All Mountains," "Leucadian Artemis." "Leucadian Artemis" appeared previously; see **C63**.

C79 Review of *Prehellenic Architecture in the Aegean* by E. Bell. *Adelphi* 4 (Aug. 1926): 137.
Unsigned.

C80 Review of *Masterpieces of Greek Drawing and Painting* by Ernst Pfuhl. *Adelphi* 4 (Jan. 1927): 462.
Unsigned.

C81 Review of *The Aryans* by V. Gordon Childe. *Adelphi* 4 (Jan. 1927): 463.
Unsigned.

C82 Review of *The Culture of Ancient Greece and Rome* by F. Poland, E. Reisinger, and R. Wagner. *Adelphi* 4 (Feb. 1927): 523.
Unsigned.

C83 Review of *A Short History of Italian Art* by Adolfo Venturi. *Adelphi* 4 (Feb. 1927): 524.
Unsigned.

C84 Review of *The Formation of the Greek People* by A. Jarde. *Adelphi* 4 (Feb. 1927): 524.
Unsigned.

C85 Review of *Alcamenes and the Establishment of the Classical Type in Greek Art* by Sir Charles Walston [Waldstein]. *Adelphi* 4 (June 1927): 524.
Unsigned.

C86 "Halcyon." *Poetry* 30 (June 1927): 119–26.
Contents: parts 1, 2, 4, 5, 7–10.

C87 "Projector." *Close Up* 1 (July 1927): 46–51.

C88 "The Cinema and the Classics I: Beauty." *Close Up* 1 (July 1927): 22–33.

C89 "Five Poems." *transition* 4 (July 1927): 105–14.
Contents: "Gift," "Psyche," and "Three Child Songs" (section title for the following three poems): "Dream," "No," "Socratic."

C90 "The Cinema and the Classics II: Restraint." *Close Up* 1 (Aug. 1927): 30–39.

C91 "Conrad Veidt: The Student of Prague." *Close Up* 1 (Sept. 1927): 35–44.
Film review of *The Student of Prague*.

C92 "Projector II (Chang)." *Close Up* 1 (Oct. 1927): 35–44.

C93 Film review of *Chang* by Ernest B. Shoedsack and Merian C. Cooper. *Close Up* 1 (Oct. 1927): 82–84.
Unsigned. This item is conjectural, based on the similarity of attention and tone with the poem (see **C92**) inspired by the same film.

C94 Film review of *Out of the Mist*. *Close Up* 1 (Oct 1927): 84–86.
Unsigned. This item is conjectural, based on its similarity to the review of *Chang* which precedes it.

C95 "The Cinema and the Classics III: The Mask and the Movietone." *Close Up* 1 (Nov. 1927): 18–31.
Abridged and reprinted in *intent.* 1.3 (Fall 1989): 1+.

C96 "Boo (*Sirocco* and the Screen)." *Close Up* 2 (Jan. 1928): 38–50.
Film review of *Sirocco* by Noel Coward.

C97 "The King of Kings Again." *Close Up* 2 (Feb. 1928): 21–32.
Film review of *King of Kings* by "Cecil M. de Mille."

C98 Film review of *Expiation* by L. Kuleschow. *Close Up* 2 (May 1928): 38–49.

C99 "Joan of Arc." *Close Up* 3 (July 1928): 15–23.
Film review of *The Passion and Death of a Saint* by Carl Dreyer. Reprinted in *American Film Criticism*, **B18**.

C100 "Russian Films." *Close Up* 3 (Sept. 1928): 18–29.

C101 "Two Poems." *Poetry* 33 (Dec. 1928): 142–43.
Contents: "Birds in Snow," "Triplex."

C102 "An Appreciation." *Close Up* 4 (March 1929): 56–68.
A discussion of the work of G. W. Pabst.

C103 "Confessions-Questionnaire." *Little Review* 12 (May 1929): 38–40.
Part of H.D.'s response to this questionnaire is reprinted in *(HOW)ever* 4 (April 1988): 16. See also **B16**.

C104 "2." *Blues* 1.5 (June 1929): 107–8.
From "Prose Choruses." Reprinted in *Agenda* 25.3-4 (1988) as part of "Four Prose Choruses," pp. 16–23.

C105 "3." *Blues* 1.6 (July 1929): 138–39.
From "Prose Choruses." Reprinted in *Agenda* 25.3-4 (1988) as part of "Four Prose Choruses," pp. 16–23.

C106 Film review of *Turksib*. *Close Up* 5 (Dec. 1929): 488–92.

C107 "Sigil [section 11]." *New Republic* 21 Jan. 1931: 265.
Retitled "The Moon in Your Hands" in *SP* (1957).

C108 "Electra-Orestes—Choros Sequence." *Pagany* 3.2 (Spring 1932): 81–84.

C109 "Pontikonisi (Mouse Island)." *Pagany* 3.3 (July–Sept. 1932): 1–9. Signed Rhoda Peter. In a letter to Richard Johns dated 14 March [1932], H.D. wrote, "I am sending a 1920 Greek sketch to you, under the name, Rhoda Peter. It is rather important to me that the H.D. and the Rhoda Peter are not confused as I find it increasingly difficult to remain MYSELF when writing" (*A Return to Pagany*, ed. Stephen Halpert [Boston: Beacon Press, 1969], 444).

C110 "Magician." *Seed* 1 (Jan. 1933): 2–[6].
Retitled "Master." See A38.

C111 "Apollo at Delphi." *Poetry* 41 (March 1933): 320–25.
Contents: "His Song," "His Presence," "His Ecstasy." Retitled "Delphi." See C159.

C112 "Elegy and Choros." *Poetry* 45 (Dec. 1934): 135–39.
From "Electra-Orestes."

C113 "The Dancer." *Life and Letters Today* 13.1 (Sept. 1935): 84–93.

C114 "The Poet." *Life and Letters Today* 13.2 (Dec. 1935): 80–83.

C115 "Prose Chorus 4." *Caravel* 2.5 (March 1936): [13]–[14].
Contents: "Strophe," "Antistrophe," "Epode." Reprinted in *Agenda* 25.3–4 (1988) as part of "Four Prose Choruses," pp. 16–23.

C116 "Ear-ring." *Life and Letters Today* 14.4 (Summer 1936): 116–28. Signed D. A. Hill. In a letter to Bryher at the Beinecke Library dated 29 May [1936], H.D. wrote: "I find D.A. Hill rather 'thin' but don't care, it's a step out, and the name acts as a focus for a lot of old war-stuff that I will gradually 'eliminate'. Don't TELL about HILL, it better stay like that for the time, if you don't mind." See also Bryher to H.D., 1 June 1936, and H.D. to Bryher 9 June [1936].

C117 "I Sing Democracy." *Life and Letters Today* 17.9 (Autumn 1937): 154–59.
Signed Sylvania Penn. Review of *Whitman* by Edgar Lee Masters. In a letter to Jean Starr Untermeyer dated 29 May [1937] at the Poetry/Rare Book Collection, SUNY Buffalo, H.D. noted: "I wrote a long review of Master's 'Whitman' in L. & L. I don't know whether it appears this, or next issue. Anyhow it says some

of the things I think of America, & though it appears partial to the 'East' it is only in reply to Master's personal flare up *against* the said same! I am not really *parti pris*, but occassionally one can whip oneself up to a little frenzy. I signed the review 'Sylvania Penn', which makes me laugh, too."
Abridged and reprinted as "Autochthon" in *intent.* 1.3 (Fall 1989): 9–10.

C118   "Four Poems." *Life and Letters Today* 17.10 (Winter 1937): 59–65, 70–72.
Contents: "In Our Town," "Orestes Theme," "Star by Day," "Wooden Animal."

C119   "Vincent Van Gogh." *Life and Letters Today* 17.10 (Winter 1937): 138–41.
Signed S. Penn. Review of *Dear Theo: An Autobiography of Vincent Van Gogh, from His Letters*, ed. Irving Stone. Abridged and reprinted as "Come Back" in *intent.* 1.3 (Fall 1989): 8.

C120   "Two Poems." *Poetry* 52 (June 1938): 139–43.
Contents: "Sigil XV," "From Episode I" (section 2 of "Calypso"; reprinted as "Caught" in *Wake* 10 [1951]).

C121   Review of *Two Englishwomen in Rome* by Matilda Lucas. *Life and Letters Today* [Dec. 1938]: 105–6.
Signed Sylvania Penn.

C122   "Fragments from *Temple of the Sun*." *Life and Letters Today* May 1939: 51–56.
Contents: "Saturn" (sections 1 and 2), "Zeus Provider" (sections 1, 2, and 3).

C123   Review of *Venus in Scorpio* by Murray Constantine and Margaret Goldsmith. *Life and Letters Today* June 1940: 330.
Signed S. Penn.

C124   "A Letter from England." *Bryn Mawr Alumnae Bulletin* 21 (July 1941): 22–23.

C125   "Two Poems." *Life and Letters Today* April 1942: [42]–45.
Contents: "Introduction to 'The Coming One'" (section 1 from *The Flowering of the Rod*), "From 'The Coming One' XIX and XX" (sections 21 and 22 from *The Flowering of the Rod*).

C126   "Sea Shell." *Life and Letters Today* Oct. 1942: 17–18.
Section 4 from *The Flowering of the Rod*.

C127   "Worm." *Life and Letters Today* Nov. 1942: 87–88.
Section 6 from *The Flowering of the Rod*.

C128 "Ancient Wisdom Speaks to the Mountain." *Times Literary Supplement* 8 May 1943: 226.
Sections 1–3. Section 2 reprinted as "Picture of a Mountain" in *Wake* 10 (1951).

C129 "Seven New Poems." *Life and Letters Today* July 1944: 47–51.
Contents: *Tribute to the Angels* (sections 1, 4, 5, 15, 19, 20).

C130 "Writing on the Wall (To Sigmund Freud)." *Life and Letters Today* May 1945: 67–98.

C131 "Writing on the Wall (To Sigmund Freud)." *Life and Letters Today* June 1945: 137–54.

C132 "Writing on the Wall (To Sigmund Freud)." *Life and Letters Today* Aug. 1945: 72–89.

C133 "Writing on the Wall (To Sigmund Freud)." *Life and Letters Today* Sept. 1945: 136–51.

C134 "Writing on the Wall (To Sigmund Freud)." *Life and Letters Today* Jan. 1946: 33–45.

C135 "Good Frend, Part I: The Tempest." *Life and Letters Today* April 1947: 34–37.

C136 "Good Frend, Part II: Rosemary." *Life and Letters Today* July 1947: 35–42.

C137 "Hymn (From the Bohemian)." *Life and Letters Today* March 1950: 213.
Retitled "Hymn (for Count Zinzendorf, 1700–1760)" in *SP* (1957).

C138 "To William Morris (1834–1896)." *Life and Letters Today* April 1950: 50.
Retitled "Georgius Sanctus" in *SP* (1957).

C139 "Erige Cor Tuum ad Me in Caelum." *Life and Letters Today* June 1950: 191.
Section 1.

C140 "Last Winter." *Poetry* 77 (Dec. 1950): 125–34.
Originally published as "May 1943" in anonymous chapbook, *What Do I Love*. See **A23**.

C141 "Body and Soul." *Yale Review* 40 (Dec. 1950): 220–22.
Retitled "Fire, Flood, and Olive-Tree" in *SP* (1957).

C142 "Three Poems." *Virginia Quarterly Review* 28 (April 1952): 209–10.
Contents: "Sigil" (section 14), "Scribe," "Archer." "Archer" retitled "Fair the Thread" in *SP* (1957).

C143 "The Revelation." *Nation* 31 Aug. 1957: 94.
Section 2 of "Erige Cor Tuum ad Me in Caelum."

C144 "Three Poems." *Poetry* 91 (Dec. 1957): 149–51.
Contents: "In Time of Gold," "Nails for Petals," "Sometimes and After." Sections 4, 5, and 37 of "Vale Ave."

C145 "Do You Remember?" *Atlantic Monthly* April 1958: 42.
Section 18 of "Vale Ave."

C146 "Sagesse." *Evergreen Review* 2.5 (Summer 1958): 27–36.
Sections 1–10.

C147 "Regents of the Night." *Poetry* 94 (May 1959): 71–73.
Section 13 of "Sagesse."

C148 "Three Recent Poems." *Two Cities* 4 (15 May 1960): 33–34.
Contents: *Helen in Egypt*, Leuke 6:3, Leuke 7:1, Eidolon 4:4.

C149 "The Shell." *Bryn Mawr Alumni Bulletin* 40 (Winter 1960): 31.
"Sagesse," section 18.

C150 "Mary A. Herr, A.B." *Bryn Mawr Alumnae Bulletin* 41 (Spring 1961): 23.

C151 "Acceptance by Miss Doolittle [of Award of Merit for Poetry]." *Proceedings of the American Academy of Arts and Letters and the National Institute of Arts and Letters* no. 11 (1961): 41.
Reprinted in *H.D. Newsletter* 3.1 (1990): [4]–6.

C152 "A Small Grain of Worship." *Nation* 9 Sept. 1961: 143.

C153 "The Death of Martin Presser." *Quarterly Review of Literature* 12 (1965): 241–61.

C154 "Four Poems." *Contemporary Literature* 10 (Autumn 1969): [589]–604.
Contents: "Amaranth," "Eros," "Envy," "Winter Love (Fragments)."

C155 "Selected Letters from H.D. to F. S. Flint: A Commentary on the Imagist Period." Ed. Cyrena Pondrom. *Contemporary Literature* 10 (Autumn 1969): [557]–86.

C156   "The Dream." *Contemporary Literature* 10 (Autumn 1969): [605]–26.
The Gift, chap. 3.

C157   "Helios and Athene." *Iowa Review* 12 (Spring/Summer 1981): 150–54.

C158   "Two Excerpts." *Montemora* 8 (1981): 31–76.
Contents: *The Gift*, chap. 1; *HERmione* (excerpts).

C159   "Delphi." *Poetry* 139 (Jan. 1982): 223–28.
Contents: "His Song," "His Presence," "His Riddle," "His Ecstasy." First appearance of "His Riddle." The other three sections appeared previously; see **C111**.

C160   "Her." *Ms*. Feb. 1982: 66+.
HERmione (excerpts).

C161   "Two Poems." *Southern Review* 18 (April 1982): 338–49.
Contents: "Dodona," "I Said." Sections 4, 5, and 6 of "Dodona" appear in a different form in *Temple of the Sun*.

C162   "Untitled Poem for Silvia Dobson." *Conjunctions* 2 (Spring/Summer 1982): 116.
Reprinted in *Agenda* 25.3-4 (1988): 124.

C163   "A Friendship Traced: H.D. Letters to Silvia Dobson." Ed. Carol Tinker. *Conjunctions* 2 (Spring/Summer 1982): 117–57.

C164   "Sigil VII–XIX." *Antaeus* 44 (Winter 1982): 37–45.

C165   "Other Sea Cities." *Yale Review* 71 (Winter 1982): 165–71.

C166   "Saint Anthony." *Polis* 3 (1982): 5–7.
The text is from an undated typescript in the Beinecke Library. It is apparently a dream transcription from 1940–41.

C167   "Vale Ave." *New Directions in Prose and Poetry* 44. Ed. J. Laughlin et al. New York: New Directions, 1982. Pp. 18–68.

C168   "Fortune Teller." *Iowa Review* 16 (Fall 1986): 18–41.
The previously unpublished second chapter from *The Gift*.

C169   "H.D. by Delia Alton." *Iowa Review* 16 (Fall 1986): 180–221.
Sometimes referred to as "Notes on Recent Writing."

C170   "Art and Ardor in World War I: Selected Letters from H.D. to John Cournos." Ed. Donna Krolik Hollenberg. *Iowa Review* 16 (Fall 1986): 126–55.

C171 "Paint It To-day." *Contemporary Literature* 27 (Winter 1986): [444]–74.
The first four chapters of a previously unpublished novel.

C172 "The *Borderline* Pamphlet." *Sagetrieb* 6 (Fall 1987): [29–49].
Reprint of **A12**.

C173 "To H.C.T.D." *H.D. Newsletter* 1 (Winter 1987): [8].
A previously unpublished poem to Hugh Caswall Tremenheere Dowding written in 1945.

C174 "Two Americans." *New Directions* 51 (1987): 58–68.
Reprinted from **A14**.

C175 "Responsibilities." *Agenda* 25.3-4 (1988): 51–53.
Previously unpublished review of *Responsibilities and Other Poems* by William Butler Yeats probably written about 1916.

C176 "Letter to Norman Holmes Pearson." *Agenda* 25.3-4 (1988): 71–74.
Also titled "A Note on Poetry." First published in *The Oxford Anthology of American Poetry* (1938). See **B14**.

C177 Songs for Children. *H.D. Newsletter* 3.2 (1990): [12–26].
Includes "The Mill Fairy," "The Flower Fairy," "The Singer Fairy," "The Cricket," and "The Leaves." Reprinted from **B1**.

D

Translations

DANISH

Anthology

D1 *Amerikanske stemmer: Etudvalg af amerikansk lyrik fra den forste halvdel af det tyvende århundrede i danks gendigtning ved.* Ed. and trans. Jens Nyholm. Copenhagen: Arne rost-Hansens Forlag, 1968. "Evadne," p. 69.

FRENCH

Books

D2 *Visage de Freud.* Trans. Françoise de Gruson. Paris: Editions Denoël, 1977. 258 pp. Contains the complete text of the 1974 American edition of *Tribute to Freud.* Published as part of the series Freud et son temps.

D3 *HERMIONE.* Trans. Claire Malroux. Paris: Editions des femmes, 1986. 242 pp. Contains the complete text of *HERmione.*

Anthologies

D4 *Anthologie de la nouvelle poésie américaine.* Ed. Eugène Jolas. Paris: Kra, 1928. "Le jardin [Garden]," pp. 59–60.

D5 *Anthologie de la poésie américaine contemporaine.* Ed. Maurice Le Breton. Paris: Editions Denoël, 1948. "Oread," "Garden," "Mid-Day," pp. 209–13. English and French on opposing pages.

D6 *Panorama de la littérature contemporaine aux Etats-Unis.* Introduction, illustrations, documents by John Brown. Paris: Georges Lang, 1954. "Oread," p. 254. Text in English and French.

D7 *Anthologie de la poésie américaine.* Ed. Alain Bousquet. Paris: Librarie Stock, 1956. "At Baia," "Hesperides" (fragment), pp. 154–57.

D8 Bogan, Louise. *Réflections sur la poésie américaine.* Avec une préface de Roger Asselineau. Paris: Vent d'Ouest, 1965. "Verger (Orchard)," p. 125. Translation of *Achievement in American Poetry* (1951).

Periodicals
D9 "Ecrit sur le mur." *Etudes Freudiennes* 3–4 (Sept. 1970): 157–271. Contains the text of "Writing on the Wall."

D10 Two poems. In "H.D. et Freud" by Norman Holland. *Etudes Freudiennes* 3/4 (Sept. 1970): 143–56. Excerpts from *The Walls Do Not Fall* and *Tribute to the Angels*. Trans. Raymond Federman.

GERMAN
Books
D11 *Avon.* Trans. Johannes Urzidil. Berlin and Frankfurt am Main: Suhrkamp Verlages, 1955. 140 pp. Contains complete text of *By Avon River*.

D12 *Trilogie.* Trans. Annemarie and Franz Link. Freiberg i. Br., 1978. 2 vols. Vol. 1: text, pp. 1–146. Vol. 2: commentary, pp. 151–313. Contains complete text of *Trilogy*, as well as commentary.

D13 *Huldigung an Freud: Rückblick aufe. Analyse; mit d. Briefen von Sigmund Freud an H.D.* Trans. Michael Schröter. Frankfurt/M., Berlin: Ulstein Verlag, 1976. 222 pp. Contains complete text of *Tribute to Freud*.

D14 *Das Ende der Qual.* Eine Erinnerung an Ezra Pound. Trans. Andrea Spingler. Zurich: Arche Verlag, 1985. 159 pp. Contains the complete text of *End to Torment* but does not include Pound's "Hilda's Book."

D15 *HERmione.* Trans. Anja Lazarowicz. München: Carl Hauser Verlag, 1987. 285 pp. Contains the complete text of *HERmione*.

Anthologies
D16 *Amerikanische Lyrik,* Vom 17. Jarhundert bis zur Gegenwart. Zweisprachig ausgewählt, herausgegeben und kommentiert von Franz Link. Übersetzungen von Annemarie und Franz Link. Stuttgart: Philip Reclam, 1974. "Oread," "What Song Is Left to Sing," pp. [282–83]. English and German on opposing pages.

D17 *Englisch Horn: Anthologie angelshachsischer Lyrik von den Anfhansen bis zur Gegenwart.* Kohln: Pahidon, 1953. "Leda," p. 222. Trans. Georg von der Voring.

D18 *Von Hopkins bis Dylan Thomas: Englische Gedichte und deutsche Prosaübertragungen.* Herausgegeben und übertragen von Ursula Clemen und Christian Enzensberger. Frankfurt am Main und Hamburg: Fischer Bücherei, 1961. "Oread," "Orchard," "White World," pp. 52–57. English and German on opposite pages.

D19 *Die weiten Horizonte / The Vast Horizons: Amerikanische Lyrik 1638 bis 1980.* Trans. Roswith von Freydorf. Stuttgart: Guido Pressler Verlag, 1985. "Oread," "Adonis," pp. 228–33. English and German on opposite pages.

HUNGARIAN

Anthology

D20 *Észak-Amerikai Költök Antológiája.* Budapest: Kozmosz Könyvek, 1966. "Körtefa [Orchard]," "Höség [Oread]," pp. 117–18. Trans. Hajnal Anna.

ITALIAN

Books

D21 *I segni sul muro.* Trans. Massimo Ferretti. Rome: Casa Editrice Astrolabio, 1973. 140 pp. Contains complete text of "Writing on the Wall."

D22 *H.D.* Trans. Mary de Rachewiltz. Milano: Strenna per gli amici, 1986. 51 pp. "Arise, arise, re-animate" (excerpt from section 13 of "Sagesse"; "Sea Gods"; *Helen in Egypt*, Pallinode book 6; "Winter Love," sections 7 and 8, "I am afraid of loneliness."

Anthologies

D23 Berti, Luigi. *L'imagismo con una piccola antologia.* Cedam: Padova, 1944. "Hermes della strade [Hermes of the Ways]," "Il pero [Pear Tree]," "Il Giardino [The Garden]," pp. [96]–99.

D24 *Poesia americana contemporanea e poesia negra.* Ed. Carlo Izzo. Collectione Fenice. Vol. 12. Bologna: Guanda, 1949. "Pear Tree [Il pero]," "Heat [Afa]," "Helen [Elena]," "Hermes of the Ways [Mercurio della strade]," "In the Rain [Sotto la pioggia]," pp. 256–77. English and Italian on opposite pages. In the second edition [1955], the poems appear on pp. 210–31.

D25 *Poesia americana del '900.* Con testo a fronte introduzioni e note biobibliografiche a cura di Carlo Izzo. Bologna: Guanda, 1963. "Pear Tree [Il pero]," "Heat [Afa]," "Helen [Elena]," *The Walls Do Not Fall*, sections 4,6 [de *Le mura non cadona*], *Tribute to the Angels* 20 [de *Tributo agli angeli*], *The Flowering of the Rod* 10 [de *La fiortura della verga*], "Epitaph [Epitafo]," pp. [178]–99. English and Italian on opposite pages.

D26 *Poesia americana, 1850–1950.* Ed. and trans. Carlo Izzo. 2 vols. Milano: Garzanti, 1971. "Il pero [Pear Tree]," "Afa [Heat]," "Elena [Helen]," "Mercurion delle strade [Hermes of the Ways]," "Sotto la pioggia [In the Rain]," pp. II 42–61.

D27 *Poesia del novecento americano.* Ed. and trans. Tommaso Pisanti. Napoli: Guida, 1978. "Afa [Heat]," "Elena [Helen]," pp. 98–101. English and Italian on opposite pages.

JAPANESE
Book
D28 [*Tribute to Freud*]. Tokyo: Misuzu Shobo, 1983. 243 pp. Contains the complete text of *Tribute to Freud.*

PORTUGESE
Anthology
D29 *Videntes e sonâmbules: Coletanea de poemas norte-americanos.* Ed. Oswaldino Marques. Rio de Janeiro: Ministéio da Educaçao e cultura, 1955. "Lethe," pp. 162–63. Trans. Abgar Renault. English and Portugese on opposite pages.

ROMANIAN
Anthology
D30 *Antologia poezi americane.* Ed. Ion Caraion. Bucuresti: Editura "Univers," 1979. "Livada [Orchard]," "Nimfa [Oread]," "Cor din Morfeu [Choros from Morpheus]," "Caldura [Heat]," pp. 319–[322]. Trans. Ion Caraion.

RUSSIAN
Anthology
D31 [*I Hear America Singing*]. Ed. Iva Aleksandrovich Koskvin. Moscow, 1960. "Garden," "Oead," "Helmsman," "Pear Tree," pp. 138–43.

SPANISH
Anthologies
D32 *Poesia Estado Unidense.* Selección y prólogo de Alfredo Weiss. Buenos Aires: Ediciones Continental, 1944. "Huerto [Heat]," "Leteo [Lethe]," pp. 116–18. Trans. Amparo Rodgriguez Vidal.

D33 *La poesía inglesia: Los contemporáneos.* Seleción, traducción y prólogo de M. Manent. Barcelona: Ediciones Lauro, 1948. "Leteo [Lethe]," "Las estrella giran en la púrpura [Stars Wheel in Purple]," pp. 114–17. English and Spanish on opposite pages.

D34 *Una antología de la lírica nord-americana.* Ed. Agustí Bartra. Mexico, D.F.: Ediciones Lletres, 1951. "El jardin [The Garden]," "Las illes [The Islands]," pp. [163]–68. Trans. Agusti Bartra.

D35 *Antología de la poesía norteamericana contemporánea.* Selección, traduccion y estudio preliminar de Eugenio Florit. Mexico: Gráfica Panamericana, 1955. "Canción [Song]," "El jardin [The Garden]," pp. 43–45. English and Spanish on opposing pages.

D36 *Antología de la poesía norteamericana.* Ed. and trans. Augustí Bartra. Mexico: Libro-Mex Editores, 1957. "Las islas [The Islands]," "La laguna [The Pool]," "Calor [Heat]," "Oréade [Oread]," pp. [200]–205.

D37 *Antología de la poesía norteamericana.* Traducción de Jose Coronel Urtecho y Ernesto Cardenal. Madrid: Aguilar, 1963. "El jardin [The Garden]," "Evadne," "Poema XXIX," pp. 118–27.

D38 *101 poemas: Antología bilingüe de la poesía norteamericana moderna.* Compilador de Salvador Novo. Mexico DF: Editorial Letras, 1965. "Evadne" (trans. Ernesto Cardenal), "Heat" (trans. Juan Ferraté), pp. 296–301. Spanish and English on opposing pages.

D39 *Des imagistes.* Edición de Kevin Power. Madrid: Trieste, 1985. "Sitalkas," "Hermes de los caminos [Hermes of the Ways]," "Príapo [Priapus]," "Acon," "Hermonax," "Epigrama [Epigram]." Trans. John Amador Bedford. This book is a translation of *Des Imagistes* (1914). See B2. English and Spanish on opposing pages.

SWEDISH
Anthology
D40 *Votivtavlor: Tolknihgar.* Trans. Johannes Edfelt. Stockholm: Albert Bonniers Förlag, 1967. "Månuppgång [Moonrise]," "Oreder [Oread]," pp. 70–71.

E

Miscellanea

MUSICAL SETTINGS

E1 De Gravelines, Kyrl. *Oread.* 1917.
Holograph in pencil. 1 Ms. score (1 leaf), 21 × 27 cm. In the collection of the New York Public Library.

E2 Becker, John Joseph. *Two Songs for Voice and Piano.* 1922.
Includes "The Pool" and "Oread." Holograph in ink and pencil. 1 Ms. score (5 pp.). 35 cm. In the collection of the New York Public Library.

E3 Robbins, Reginald C. *Charioteer (Epilogue).* For high voices. Hollywood: Golden West Music Press, 1941.

E4 Robbins, Reginald C. *Lethe.* For high voices. Hollywood: Golden West Music Press, 1941.

E5 Williams, Grace. *The Dancers.* Choral suite for soprano solo, women's choir, string orchestra, and harp or piano. London: Oxford UP Music Dept., 1953.
Includes "Gather for the Festival" from "Songs from Cyprus."

E6 Fetler, Paul. *Oread.* New York: American Music Publishers, 1957.

E7 Nierenberg, Roger. *Fire, Flood, and Olive Tree.* For mixed voices, piano, wood blocks, tom-toms, and bass drum. Delaware Water Gap, Pa.: Shawnee Press, 1957.
1 score (8 pp.) and 1 part, 27 cm.

E8 Rathaus, Karol. *And Pergamos.* New York: Associated Music Publishers, 1962.

E9 Cohen, Edward. *Elegy for Soprano and Six Players.* For soprano, flute, oboe, clarinet, violin, viola, and violoncello. Ship Bottom,

N.J.: Association for the Promotion of New Music, 1977.
Includes "Eurydice" and "Leda." 1 score (49 pp.), 37 cm.

E10 Sampson, David. *The Mysteries Remain.* For B-flat trumpet and organ. Nashville: Brass Press, 1982.
1 score (28 pp.) and 1 part (8 pp.), 28 cm, cover title. Prefatory material includes the poem by H.D.

E11 Kabat, Julie. *Five Poems.* New York: Leonardo Productions, 1984.
Includes "The Moon in Your Hands," "Evadne," "Oread," "Fragment 113," and "The Helmsman." Recorded at St. Michael's Episcopal Church, New York, 15 Dec. 1983. Julie Kabat, voice, glass harmonica, and saw; Ben Hudson, violin. Poem texts printed on record sleeve.

RECORDINGS

E12 H.D. *Helen in Egypt.* Spoken Arts, SA 1042.

E13 H.D. *Helen in Egypt.* Watershed, C-158.
According to a note on the tape, this recording was made in Switzerland between September and November 1955.

E14 MacLeish, Archibald. "Sheltered Garden." *Poet's Gold 3.* RCA, LM 1883.

PROGRAMS, CATALOGS, ETC.

E15 "In Memorium, H.D." 1 leaf, 22 × 17.7 cm. Dated "Zurich, September 27, 1961."
Includes an excerpt from section 13 of "Sagesse," ". . . arise, arise, reanimate." Signed by Perdita and John Schaffner, Bryher, and Norman Holmes Pearson.

E16 *Charles Clinch Bubb and the Clerk's Press.* Catalog for an exhibit at the Ward M. Canaday Center, the University of Toledo Libraries, April–June 1986. [26 pp.], 20.2 × 15 cm.
Includes excerpts from letters from H.D. to Bubb dated 9 Sept. 1916 and [1916 or 1917?] (items 49 and 55).

BROADSIDES AND POSTCARDS

E17 H.D. (Hilda Doolittle) | [red brown (C43)] REVELATION | '*Death, violent and near*' | [twenty-seven-line poem, section 2 of "Erige Cor Tuum ad Me in Caleum"] | [red brown] Dreadnaught Broadside

Pale yellow brown (C76) wove paper, 21.6 × 15.8 cm.
CaOTU.

E18 Recto: text of "Evening" (from *Sea Garden*, 1916). Verso: 'With acknowledgements to Grove Press Inc. | of New York. who kindly gave permission | for this poem to be reprinted.' 'Poemcard 9 Deadalus Press Stoke Ferry Norfolk'.
Light blue (C181) stock, 15.1 × 10 cm.
NBuU.

Part 2

Work on H.D.

F

Reviews of Books by H.D.

Choruses from Iphigeneia in Aulis (1915)

F1 "A Note on the Classical Revival." *Times Literary Supplement* 4 May 1916: 210.

F2 Eliot, T. S. *Poetry* 9 (Nov. 1916): 101–4.

F3 P[ound], E[zra]. "H.D.'s Choruses from Euripides." *Little Review* 5.7 (Nov. 1918): 16–20.

F4 *Nation* 15 Nov. 1919: 246+.

Sea Garden (1916)

F5 *Times Literary Supplement* 5 Oct. 1916: 479.

F6 Fletcher, John Gould. *Egoist* 3 (Dec. 1916): 183–84.

F7 Fletcher, John Gould. "H.D.'s Vision." *Poetry* 9 (Feb. 1917): 266–69.

F8 "The Battle between Rhyme and Imagism." *New York Times Book Review* 4 Feb. 1917: 37.

F9 Lowell, Amy. "Exquisite Cameos and Intaglios." *Poetry Journal* 7 (Aug. 1917): 171–80.

F10 Flint, F. S. "H.D." *Chapbook* 2.9 (March 1920): 22–24.

Choruses, 2d Series (1919)

F11 *Times Literary Supplement* 21 Nov. 1919: 666.

F12 Wescott, Glenway. "Classics in English." *Poetry* 17 (Aug. 1921): 284–88.

Hymen (1921)

F13 *Times Literary Supplement* 27 Oct. 1921: 702.

F14 *Saturday Review* 132 (10 Dec. 1921): 669.

F15 Untermeyer, Louis. "Fire and Ice." *New Republic* 29 (28 Dec. 1921): 134.

F16 "Uniqueness with a Note on Vers Libre." *Times Literary Supplement* 5 Jan. 1922: 8.

F17 Brathwaite, W[illiam] S[tanley]. "A Temperamental Imagist Poet." *Boston Evening Transcript* 14 Jan. 1922, book section: 6.

F18 Lowell, Amy. "The Second Chapter." *New York Evening Post Literary Review* 21 Jan. 1922: 4.

F19 Gawn, Sumett. *Double Dealer* 3.13 (Jan. 1922): 53–54.

F20 Sinclair, May. "The Poems of H.D." *Dial* 72 (Feb. 1922): [203]–7.

F21 Williams-Ellis, A. *Spectator* 25 Feb. 1922: 247.

F22 "Examples of Free Verse at Its Best." *Springfield [Mass.] Sunday Republican* 26 March 1922: 322.

F23 Bryher, Winifred. "Spear-Shaft and Cyclamen-Flower." *Poetry* 19 (March 1922): 333–37.

F24 Anderson, Maxwell. "Temple Music." *Measure* 14 (April 1922): 18.

F25 Barrington, Pauline. *Lyric West* 2.4 (July–Aug. 1922): 33–34.

F26 Van Doren, Mark. "Women as Poets." *Nation* 114 (26 Aug. 1922): 499.

F27 Bryher, Winifred. "Thought and Vision." *Bookman* 56 (Oct. 1922): 225–26.

F28 Moore, Marianne. *Broom* 4.2 (Jan. 1923): 133–35.

Heliodora (1924)

F29 Morgan, Louise. "Flute and Cymbal." *Outlook* [London] 3 May 1924: 306.

F30 Jones, E. B. C. *Nation and Atheneum* 24 May 1924: 250.

F31 "Some Recent Verse." *Saturday Review of Politics, Literature, Science, and Art* 21 June 1924: 640.

F32 Williams-Ellis, A. "We Speak As We Can." *Spectator* 28 June 1924: 1044.

F33 *Times Literary Supplement* 3 July 1924: 416.

F34 Price, Mona. "The Greatest Imagist." *Dublin Magazine* 1 (July 1924): 1055–56.

F35 *New York Evening Post Literary Review* 23 Aug. 1924: 980.

F36 Lucas, F. L. "Turtle and Mock Turtle." *New Statesman* 23 Aug. 1924: 572–73.
Reprinted in *Authors Living and Dead* (New York: Macmillan, 1935), 217–23.

F37 Gorman, Herbert S. "A Poet Who Drinks at the Pierian Spring." *New York Times Book Review* 31 Aug. 1924: 5.

F38 *Dial* 77 (Oct. 1924): 348.

F39 Donelson, J. *Bookman* 60 (Oct. 1924): 226–27.

F40 Untermeyer, Louis. "The Perfect Imagist." *Saturday Review of Literature* 8 Nov. 1924: 260.

F41   Edman, Erwin. *Nation* 12 Nov. 1924: 526.
F42   Guiterman, Arthur. *Outlook* [New York] 31 Dec. 1924: 730.
F43   *Booklist* 21 (Dec. 1924): 101.
F44   Sandoz, Paul. "Staccato." *Voices* 4.2 (Dec. 1924): 56–57.
F45   Seiffert, Marjorie Allen. "Glacial Bloom." *Poetry* 25 (Dec. 1924): 160–64.
F46   Nardi, Marci. *New Republic* 28 Jan. 1925: 266.
F47   MacLeish, Archibald. *Yale Review* 14 (April 1925): 587–92.
F48   McClure, John. *Double Dealer* 7 (April 1925): 152–53.

Collected Poems (1925)

F49   Gorman, Herbert S. *New York Times Book Review* 10 May 1925: 7.
F50   Williams, William Carlos. "H.D.'s Collected Poems Recall Author's Dash into the Raging Deep." *New York Evening Post Literary Review* 5.39 (23 May 1925): 4.
F51   K.S. "H.D. as Leader of Imagists." *Boston Evening Transcript* 29 May 1925, book section: 3.
F52   Auslander, Joseph. "Poets Who Are Poets." *New York World* 21 June 1925: 4.
F53   Hillyer, Robert. *Atlantic Monthly* 136 (July 1925): 10.
F54   Sapir, Edward. "An American Poet." *Nation* 19 Aug. 1925: 211–12.
F55   M[onroe], H[arriet]. *Poetry* 26 (Aug. 1925): 268–75.
F56   Moore, Marianne. "The Bright Immortal Olive." *Dial* 79 (Aug. 1925): 170–73.
F57   [Collins, H. P.] *Adelphi* 3 (Sept. 1925): 305.
F58   Fillmore, Hildegarde. "Poems and Poetical Exercises." *Bookman* 62 (Sept. 1925): 79–81 [80].
F59   Hubbell, Lindley William. "Without Flaw." *Measure* 55 (Sept. 1925): 13–15.
F60   Wilson, James Southall. *Virginia Quarterly Review* 1 (July 1925): 311–20.
F61   Cowley, Malcolm. "Icy Fire." *New York Herald Tribune Weekly Book Review* 11 Oct. 1925: 5.
F62   *Booklist* 22 (Nov. 1925): 63.
F63   Ridge, Lola. "Poems of Pursuit." *Saturday Review of Literature* 26 June 1926: 889.
F64   Moon, Lois Burton. *Lyric West* 5 (July–Aug. 1926): 272.
F65   Sinclair, May. "The Poems of H.D." *Fortnightly Review* 124 (March 1927): 329–45.

Palimpsest (1926, 1968)

F66   Morgan, Louise. *Outlook* [New York] 14 Aug. 1926: 164.
F67   Shanks, E. *Saturday Review* 21 Aug. 1926: 204.

F68   P.J.M. *Manchester Guardian* 3 Sept. 1926: 7.
F69   L.R. *Irish Statesman* 25 Sept. 1926: 69.
F70   [Collins, H. P.] *Adelphi* 4 (Oct. 1926): 268.
F71   "H.D.'s Poetic Experiment in the Art of Fiction." *New York Times Book Review* 21 Nov. 1926: 6.
F72   Storm, Marion. *New York Evening Post Literary World* 27 Nov. 1926: 3.
F73   Deutsch, Babette. "Rapunzel, Rapunzel, Let Down Thy Long Hair." *New York Herald Tribune Weekly Book Review* 28 Nov. 1926: 2.
F74   Van Doren, Mark. *Nation* 22 Dec. 1926: 668.
F75   Fletcher, John Gould. "From 75 B.C. to 1925 A.D." *Saturday Review of Literature* 1 Jan. 1927: 482.
F76   L.B. *Boston Evening Transcript Literary World* 8 Jan. 1927: 3.
F77   *Bookman* 64 (Jan. 1927): 622.
F78   *New Criterion* 5 (Jan. 1927): 160.
F79   Aiken, Conrad. *New Republic* 2 Feb. 1927: 309.
F80   Sage, Robert. "Honey Rather than Wine." *transition* 1 (April 1927): 142–46.
F81   Gregory, Alyse. "A Poet's Novel." *Dial* 82 (May 1927): [417]–19.
F82   G.H.C. "Theorem, Poem, Biography." *larus* 1 (April–May–June 1928): 71–72.
F83   *Contemporary Review* 215 (July 1969): 51.
F84   *Choice* 6 (Feb. 1970): 1752.

Hippolytus Temporizes (1927, 1986)

F85   Troy, William. "White Lightning." *New Republic* 24 Aug. 1927: 24.
F86   Blackmur, R. P. "Ritual." *Hound and Horn* 1 (Sept. 1927): 48–53.
F87   Van Doren, Mark. *Nation* 12 Oct. 1927: 382.
F88   Deutsch, Babette. "Impassable Stairs." *New York Herald Tribune Weekly Book Review* 22 Jan. 1928: 17.
F89   Trueblood, Charles K. "The Poetry of Concentration." *Dial* 84 (Jan. 1928): [63]–65.
F90   Arthur, M. B. *Choice* Sept. 1986: 208.
F91   Muratori, Fred. *Small Press* 4 (Nov./Dec. 1986): 73–74.
F92   Bann, Stephen. "The Mission of Ion." *Agenda* 25.3-4 (1988): 191–96.
      Also reviews *Ion*.

Hedylus (1928, 1980)

F93   "An Imagist Novel." *New York Times Book Review* 18 Nov. 1928: 7.
F94   Frank, Grace. "The Hellas of Dreams." *Saturday Review of Literature* 22 Dec. 1928: 538.

F95 Munson, Gorham B. *Bookman* 68 (Jan. 1929): 575.
F96 Connolly, Cyril. *New Statesman* 23 Feb. 1929: 636.
F97 *Spectator* 142 (9 March 1929): 396–97.
F98 "A Greek Idyll." *Times Literary Supplement* 21 March 1929: 240.
F99 *Dial* 86 (March 1929): 264.
F100 *Nation* 12 June 1929: 722.
F101 *Choice* 18 (April 1981): 1096.
F102 Evans, Stuart. *Times* 28 May 1981: 7.
F103 *Paideuma* 10 (Spring 1981): 190.
F104 Cooke, Judy. "The Voyage In." *New Statesman* 5 June 1981: 23.
F105 Mackinnon, Lachlan. "The I in the Initials." *Times Literary Supplement* 26 June 1981: 719.
F106 Gregory, Horace. *American Book Review* 5.1 (Nov.–Dec. 1982): 20.
F107 Lewis, Peter. "The Artiness of Fiction." *Stand Magazine* 23.1 (1982): 51.
F108 *Review of Contemporary Fiction* Spring 1982: 180–81.
F109 Rasula, Jed. "A Renaissance of Women Writers." *Sulfur* 7 (1983): 160–72 [161–63].
Also reviews *HERmione*, *The Gift*, *Notes on Thought and Vision*, *H.D.: The Life and Work of an American Poet* by Janice Robinson (**H181**), and *Psyche Reborn* by Susan Friedman (**H172**).

Red Roses for Bronze (1929)

F110 Kohn, Walter F. "Con Amore." *New Republic* 2 Jan. 1929: 20.
F111 Hutchison, Percy. *New York Times Book Review* 14 July 1929: 8.

Red Roses for Bronze (1931)

F112 B. "Matt Hilda." *Granta* 28 Nov. 1931: 171.
F113 C.P. "Vertical Verse." *Manchester Guardian* 21 Dec. 1931: 5.
F114 *Times Literary Supplement* 31 Dec. 1931: 1052.
F115 Benét, William Rose. *Saturday Review of Literature* 16 Jan. 1932: 461.
F116 D.V.H. "The Lunatic, the Lover, and the Poet." *Spectator* 6 Feb. 1932: 186.
F117 Deutsch, Babette. "The Glory That Is Greece." *New York Herald Tribune Weekly Book Review* 14 Feb. 1932: 12.
F118 *Pittsburgh Monthly Bulletin* 37 (Feb. 1932): 13.
F119 *Boston Evening Transcript* 5 March 1932, book section: 3.
F120 *Booklist* 28 (March 1932): 301.
F121 *Bookman* 74 (March 1932): iii.
F122 Walton, Eda Lou. "The Poetic Method of H.D." *Nation* 2 March 1932: 264.

F123 "Themes for Bronze." *Contempo* 1 (1 April 1932): 3.
F124 Tod, Margaret. *Voices* 65 (May 1932): 321–22.
F125 Hutchison, Percy. *New York Times Book Review* 31 July 1932: 11.
F126 Flint, F. S. *Criterion* 11 (July 1932): 684–89.
F127 Cunningham, J. V. *Commonweal* 5 Oct. 1932: 541.
F128 Blackmur, R. P. "The Lesser Satisfactions." *Poetry* 41 (Nov. 1932): 94–100.
F129 *Rickword, Edgell. "Three Ages of Poetry." *Sunday Referee* 22 Nov. 1931.
Reprinted in *Essays and Opinions* (Cheshire, Eng.: Carcanet, 1974), 259–61.

The Hedgehog (1936)

F130 Sélincourt, Basil de. "A Little Tale by a Poet." *Manchester Guardian* 5 March 1937: 7.
F131 *Times Literary Supplement* 6 March 1937: 173.
F132 *John O'London's Weekly* 18 June 1937: 467.

Euripides Ion (1937, 1986)

F133 *Spectator* 5 March 1937: 424.
F134 T.B.L.W. *Manchester Guardian* 9 April 1937: 7.
F135 Mithchison, Naomi. "Those Queer Greeks." *Time and Tide* 10 April 1937: 468.
F136 G.B.E. "The Skipper's Guide." *Granta* 21 April 1937: 354–55.
F137 Holmes, John. "Poetry Now." *Boston Evening Transcript Literary World* 22 May 1937: 5.
F138 *London Mercury* 36 (May 1937): 107.
F139 Troy, William. "Roads to Tragedy." *Nation* 12 June 1937: 681–82.
F140 Manton, Guy. *Criterion* 16 (July 1937): 727–30.
F141 Vauxhall, John. *Life and Letters Today* 16.8 (Summer 1937): 166–67.
F142 Earp, F. R. *Classical Review* 51 (Nov. 1937): 171–72.
F143 Lattimore, Richmond. "Euripides as Lyrist." *Poetry* 51 (Dec. 1937): 160–64.
F144 Arthur, M. B. *Choice* Feb. 1987: 136.
F145 Ratner, Rochelle. "Hilda Doolittle (1886–1961)." *Belles Lettres* Nov./Dec. 1987: 3.
Also reviews *Nights*, Guest (**H196**), DuPlessis (**H214**), King (**H216**), and *Women of the Left Bank* by Shari Benstock (**H212**).
F146 Roessel, David. *Classical World* 1987: 230.
F147 Bann, Stephen. "The Mission of Ion." *Agenda* 25.3–4 (1988): 191–96.
Also reviews *Hippolytus Temporizes*.

F148 Guest, Barbara. *Conjunctions* 11 (1988): 280–83. Also reviews *Nights*.

The Walls Do Not Fall (1944)

F149 Sitwell, Osbert. *Observer* 28 May 1944: 3.
F150 *Times Literary Supplement* 3 June 1944: 372.
F151 Mais, S.B.P. *Oxford Mail* 21 June 1944: 2.
F152 Alloway, Lawrence. *Sunday Times* [London] 2 July 1944: 3.
F153 *Scotsman* [Edinburgh] 20 July 1944: 7.
F154 *Glasgow Herald* 24 July 1944.
F155 *H.R. *Birmingham Post* 25 July 1944.
F156 Fausset, H. I'A. *Manchester Guardian* 26 July 1944: 3.
F157 Bottomley, Gordon. *Life and Letters Today* 42 (July 1944): 52–55.
F158 Meres, Francis. *Time and Tide* 19 Aug. 1944: 728.
F159 *News and Book Trade Review* [London] 16 Sept. 1944.
F160 Deutsch, Babette. "The Last of the Imagists." *New York Herald Tribune Weekly Book Review* 1 Oct. 1944: 18.
F161 Bogan, Louise. *New Yorker* 21 Oct. 1944: 89.
F162 Williams, Oscar. "Ladies Day." *New Republic* 23 Oct. 1944: 534.
F163 Gregory, Horace. *Sewanee Review* 52 (Autumn 1944): 585–86.
F164 Atkins, Elizabeth. "A Brilliant New Defense of Poetry." *Poetry* 65 (March 1945): 327–30.
F165 W.P.M. *Dublin Magazine* 20 (Jan.–March 1945): 55–56.
F166 Dupee, F. W. "Imagists and Ex-Imagists." *Nation* 14 April 1945: 421–22.
F167 Blackmur, R. P. *Kenyon Review* 7 (Spring 1945): [339]–40.
F168 Jarrell, Randall. *Partisan Review* 12 (Winter 1945): [120]–26.
F169 Schorer, Mark. *Yale Review* 34 (Winter 1945): 536.
F170 *Virginia Quarterly Review* 31 (Winter 1945): xvi.

Tribute to the Angels (1945)

F171 "From Death to Life." *Times Literary Supplement* 14 April 1945: 176.
F172 *Highland News* [Inverness] 28 April 1945.
F173 *Stonier, G. W. *New Statesman and Nation* 28 April 1945.
F174 *N.C.Y. *Western Morning News* [Plymouth] 7 May 1945.
F175 *Manchester Guardian* 23 May 1945: 3.
F176 *Scotsman* [Edinburgh] 24 May 1945: 7.
F177 *Sunday Times* [London] 27 May 1945: 3.
F178 Gibson, Wilfred. *Manchester Guardian* 29 June 1945: 3.
F179 Sackville-West, Vita. *Observer* 1 July 1945: 3.

F180 Pearson, Norman Holmes. *Life and Letters Today* 46 (July 1945): 58–62.
F181 *Highland News* [Inverness] 4 Aug. 1945.
F182 *Listener* 9 Aug. 1945: 161.
F183 *Whitby Gazette* 25 Aug. 1945.
F184 Jarrell, Randall. *Nation* 29 Dec. 1945: 741.
F185 Kreymborg, Alfred. "A Challenge to Mammon." *Saturday Review of Literature* 29 Dec. 1945: 11.
F186 *New Yorker* 21 (29 Dec. 1945): 68.
F187 Bangay, E. D. *Poetry Review* [London] 36 (Nov.–Dec. 1945): 338–41 [338].
F188 Deutsch, Babette. "Survivors of the Blitz." *New York Herald Tribune Weekly Book Review* 6 Jan. 1946: 16.
F189 *Book Week* 13 Jan. 1946: 8.
F190 Kennedy, Leo. *Chicago Sun Book Week* 13 Jan. 1946: 8.
F191 N[orth], J[essica] N[elson]. "And I John Saw." *Poetry* 67 (March 1946): 341–44.
F192 Davidson, Eugene. *Yale Review* 36 (Autumn 1946): 150.
F193 Fitts, Dudley. *Partisan Review* 13 (Winter 1946): 113–20.
F194 Moss, Howard. *Kenyon Review* 9 (Spring 1947): 295–96. Also reviews *The Flowering of the Rod*.
F195 *Virginia Quarterly Review* 23 (Winter 1947): xviii–xix.

The Flowering of the Rod (1946)

F196 "Love and Resurrection." *Times Literary Supplement* 27 July 1946: 357.
F197 I.H. *Manchester Guardian* 23 Aug. 1946: 3.
F198 Crane, Milton. *New York Times Book Review* 1 Dec. 1946: 46.
F199 *New Yorker* 22 (14 Dec. 1946): 131.
F200 Fitts, Dudley. "Celebration of Man and God." *Saturday Review of Literature* 22 Feb. 1947: 19.
F201 Berryman, John. *Partisan Review* 14 (Jan.–Feb. 1947): [73]–85.
F202 Davidson, Eugene. *Yale Review* 36 (March 1947): 540.
F203 Kunitz, Stanley. "A Tale of a Jar." *Poetry* 70 (April 1947): 36–42.
F204 Flint, F. Cudworth. *Virginia Quarterly Review* 23 (Spring 1947): 287–88.
F205 Moss, Howard. *Kenyon Review* 9 (Spring 1947): 295–96. Also reviews *Tribute to the Angels*.

By Avon River (1949)

F206 *Kirkus Review* 17 (15 March 1949): 173.
F207 A.V.S. "H.D. Pays Tribute to Bard in Poem, Perceptive Essay." *New Haven Register* 3 July 1949: 6.

F208 Wagner, Charles. "Books." *New York Sunday Mirror* 3 July 1949, home ed.: 11.
F209 Scott, W[infield] T[ownley]. *Providence Journal* 3 July 1949: VI–8.
F210 Humphries, Rolfe. *Nation* 9 July 1949: 44.
F211 *Buck, Doris. *Richmond Times-Dispatch* 10 July 1949.
F212 Rogers, W. G. *Cleveland Plain Dealer* 10 July 1949: 17-D.
F213 Sharber, Kate Trimble. *Nashville Banner* 15 July 1949: 22.
F214 Rockwell, Kenneth. "H.D. Sends Her Greetings to a Stratford Address." *Dallas Daily Times Herald* 17 July 1949: 4+.
F215 Rogers, W. G. "Author of the Week." *Sunday Royal Gazette* [Hamilton, Bermuda] 24 July 1949: 5.
F216 Logan, Floyd. *Fort Wayne News-Sentinel* 30 July 1949: 6.
F217 Barrows, Herbert. "The Lyrical World of Shakespeare." *New York Times Book Review* 31 July 1949: 10.
F218 Humphries, Rolfe. *Nation* 9 Aug. 1949: 44.
F219 Bacon, Martha. *Saturday Review of Literature* 20 Aug. 1949: 29.
F220 Freedley, George. *Library Journal* 74 (Aug. 1949): 1099.
F221 Spaeth, J. Duncan. *Philadelphia Inquirer* 10 Sept. 1949.
F222 MacGeorge, Beatrice. *Bryn Mawr Alumnae Bulletin* 30 (April 1950): 10.
F223 Bronner, Milton. "Rosemary for Remembrance from H.D. to Shakespeare." *Louisville Courier-Journal* 11 Sept. 1949, section 3: 14.
F224 Daiches, David. "Shakespeare's World." *New York Herald Tribune Weekly Book Review* 11 Sept. 1949: 3.
F225 Ferril, Thomas Hornsby. *San Francisco Chronicle* 18 Sept. 1949, This World Section: 18.
F226 Nims, John Frederick. "A Strange Little Tribute of Poet to the Bard of Avon." *Tribune Books* [Chicago] 18 Sept. 1949, section 4: 6.
F227 *Freeman, Myra Cohn. *Los Angeles Mirror* 22 Oct. 1949.
F228 H.A.P. *Florida Magazine of Verse* 10.1 (Autumn 1949): 26.
F229 McCauliff, George. *Poetry Chapbook* 8.1 (Fall 1949): [29–30].
F230 Svendsen, Kester. "Hardly Worth the Trouble." *Daily Oklahoman* 13 Nov. 1949, Sunday magazine: 10.
F231 *College English* 11.2 (Nov. 1949): 116.
F232 M.W. *Canadian Forum* 29 (Nov. 1949): 190.
F233 *Times Literary Supplement* 2 Dec. 1949: 798.
F234 *Pittsburgh Press* 1 Jan. 1950, section 2: 34.
F235 Gregory, Horace. "The Moment of Revival." *Poetry* 75 (Jan. 1950): 223–28.
F236 Miller, Margaret Ann. "Flood of Books on Shakespeare Marks

1949 Publisher's Lists." *Arkansas Gazette* [Little Rock] 5 Feb. 1950: 3B.
F237 Tillman, Nathaniel. *Voices* 140 (Winter 1950): 41–42.
F238 **Nassauer Bote* [Limburg] 3 Sept. 1955.
F239 *Günther, Alfred. "Eine Dichter huldigt Shakespeare." *Stuttgarter Zeitung* 22 Oct. 1955.
F240 Haas, Willy. *Sonntagsblatt* 20 Nov. 1955: 13.
F241 *Belzner, Emile. *Rhein-Neckar Zeitung* 3 Dec. 1955.
F242 Gerber, Richard. "Avon." *Neue Zürcher Zeitung* 8 Dec. 1955: 16.
F243 *Die TAT* [Zürich] 17 Dec. 1955: 17.
F244 *Günther, Alfred. *Deutsche Zeitung* 11 Feb. 1956.
F245 Lindeman, Reinhold. "Klang, Kalkül, und Emotion." *Rheinische Post* 18 Feb. 1956: [42].
F246 *Günther, Alfred. "Tausend Exemplare." *Literatur Rundschau* Jahrgang 11, Nummer 12.

Tribute to Freud (1956, 1974, 1984)

F247 *Lee, Charles. *Cleveland Press* 4 Sept. 1956.
F248 Cooley, Franklin A. "A Fine Tribute to Freud." *Richmond Times-Dispatch* 9 Sept. 1956: 12-L.
F249 Dollard, John. "H.D. to Freud with Love." *New York Herald Tribune Weekly Book Review* 9 Sept. 1956: 7.
F250 Davidson, Harry A. "The Poet and the Couch." *New Republic* 10 Sept. 1956: 20.
F251 Barron, Louis. *Library Journal* 81 (15 Sept. 1956): 1996.
F252 *Booklist* 53 (15 Sept. 1956): 37.
F253 *Sharber, Kate Trimble. *Nashville Tennessean* 16 Sept. 1956.
F254 *Publisher's Weekly* 17 Sept. 1956: 1454.
F255 *Cleveland Press* 18 Sept. 1956.
F256 *Jacobson, Josephine. *Baltimore Evening Sun* 6 Oct. 1956.
F257 *Berkeley Gazette* 10 Oct. 1956: 12.
F258 Rogers, Leona. "Freud's Patient Writes Tribute." *Fort Wayne [Ind.] News Sentinel* 13 Oct. 1956: 9.
F259 *M. *Montgomery Advertiser* 17 Oct. 1956.
F260 *Reporter* 18 Oct. 1956: 48.
F261 *Wolfe, Ann F. *Columbus Dispatch* 21 Oct. 1956.
F262 *Springfield [Mass.] Republican* 28 Oct. 1956: 8C.
F263 Boehm, Herbert. *Journal of the Medical Society of New Jersey* Oct. 1956: 528.
F264 Menninger, Karl. *Menninger Library Journal* Oct. 1956: 17.
F265 *Vogue* 1 Nov. 1956: 148.

F266 McLaughlin, Richard. *Springfield [Mass.] Republican* 2 Nov. 1956: 8C.
F267 *Pastoral Psychology* 7 (Nov. 1956): 63.
F268 Fiedler, Leslie. "Memoir and Parable." *Poetry* 89 (Feb. 1957): 326–29.
F269 G[ohdes], C[larence]. *American Literature* 29 (March 1957): 112.
F270 Jones, Ernest. *International Journal of Psychoanalysis* 38 (March–April 1957): 126.
F271 Richardson, Maurice. "Freud and His Doctor." *Observer* 28 Jan. 1973: 34.
F272 *Times Literary Supplement* 23 March 1973: 317.
F273 Jackson, Caroline. *Critical Quarterly* 15.1 (Spring 1973): 95–96.
F274 Beresford, Anne. *Agenda* 11.2/3 (1973): 136–37.
Also reviews *Hermetic Definition*.
F275 Glover, John. "Little Poems." *Stand Magazine* 14.3 (1973): 22–26.
Also reviews *Hermetic Definition*.
F276 *Spectator* 22 June 1974: 771.
F277 [Johnson, Albert H.] *Publisher's Weekly* 2 Sept. 1974: 65.
F278 Mollinger, Robert N. *Library Journal* 99 (1 Dec. 1974): 3133.
F279 Dachslager, E. L. "Writing on the Wall—With Freud." *Houston Post* 29 Dec. 1974, Spotlight: 8.
F280 Litke, James. "The Poet and Dr. Freud." *New Haven Register* 2 Feb. 1975: 4D.
F281 Brin, Ruth F. "H.D.'s Memories of Freud." *Minneapolis Tribune* 9 Feb. 1975: 10D.
F282 Storr, Anthony. "A Relatively Brief Encounter: Consultations with the Master." *Washington Post* 4 March 1975: B5.
F283 Gass, William. "The Anatomy of Mind." *New York Review of Books* 17 April 1975: 3+.
F284 Gass, William. "The Battered Triumphant Sage." *New York Review of Books* 15 May 1975: 9+.
F285 Siggins, Clara M. *Best Sellers* 35 (June 1975): 78.
F286 Peck, John. "Passio Perpeteae H.D." *Parnassus* 3.2 (Spring/Summer 1975): 42–74.
Also reviews *Helen in Egypt*, *Trilogy*, and *Hermetic Definition*.
F287 Harris, Kathryn Gibbs. *Literature and Psychology* 25.2 (1975): 86–88.
F288 *Strausbaugh, John. "Three Misfits." *City Paper* [Baltimore] 31 Aug. 1984.
F289 Becker, Alida. *Philadelphia Inquirer* 23 Sept. 1984: 4-P.
F290 Kiser, Thelma Scott. "New Directions Books Include Play by Tennessee Williams." *Sunday Independent* [Ashland, Ky.] 23 Sept. 1984: 36.

F291 Guest, Barbara. [St. Mark's] *Poetry Project Newsletter* 109 (Nov. 1984): [7]–[8].
F292 Newlove, Donald. "Book Talk." *Gallery Magazine* Feb. 1985: 23.
F293 Gabree, John. "Reading for the Couch." *Newsday* 3 March 1985, Ideas: 16.
F294 Chase, Kathleen. *World Literature Today* Spring 1985: 274.
F295 Freibert, Lucy M. *Arizona Quarterly* Spring 1985: 96.
F296 Hudson, Dora. "Psychic Topography." *Times Literary Supplement* 27 Sept. 1985: 1068.
Also reviews *Helen in Egypt*.
F297 Rettallack, Joan. "H.D., H.D." *Parnassus* 12.2/13.1 (1985): 67–88.
Also reviews *Helen in Egypt, Hermetic Definition, Collected Poems, 1912–1944, End to Torment*, Robinson (**H181**), Guest (**H196**), and Friedman (**H172**).
F298 Elkind, Sue N. "H.D. and Freud." *San Francisco Jung Institute Library Journal* 6.2 (1986): [39]–52.

Selected Poems (1957)

F299 *Publisher's Weekly* 7 Oct. 1957.
F300 Deutsch, Babette. "The Melody Lingers On." *New York Times Book Review* 22 Sept. 1957: 37.
F301 McDonald, Gerald D. *Library Journal* 82 (1 Dec. 1957): 3113.
F302 Brennan, Joseph. *Essence* 16 (Winter 1957): 12.
F303 Duncan, Robert. "In Sight of a Lyre, a Little Spear, a Chair." *Poetry* 91 (Jan. 1958): 256–60.
F304 Eberhart, Richard. "Hölderlin, Leopardi, and H.D." *Poetry* 91 (Jan. 1958): 260–65.
F305 **Publisher's Circular* [London] 28 Feb. 1958.
F306 "Two Poetic Moods." *Times Literary Supplement* 28 March 1958: 172.
F307 Gregory, Horace. *Commonweal* 68 (18 April 1958): 82–83.
F308 *Mercure de France* July 1958: 528.
F309 Skelton, Robin. *National Book League Journal* Nov.–Dec. 1958: 180–81.
F310 Martinelli, Sheri. *Anagogic and Paideumic Review* 6 (1959): [3–12].

Bid Me to Live (1960, 1983)

F311 *Publisher's Weekly* 11 April 1960: 29.
F312 Moore, Harry T. "The Faces Are Familiar." *New York Times Book Review* 1 May 1960: 4.
F313 Hogan, William. *San Francisco Chronicle* 29 April 1960: 29.
F314 Fassett, Catherine Lewis. "Imagist Poet Produces Novel of World War I." *Twin City Sentinel* [Winston-Salem, N.C.] 2 May 1960: 16.

F315 *Newsweek* 2 May 1960: 92.
F316 Gregory, Horace. *Saturday Review of Literature* 28 May 1960: 31–32.
F317 Wermuth, Paul C. *Library Journal* 85 (1 June 1960): 2193.
F318 Scott, Winfield Townley. *New York Herald Tribune Book Review* 12 June 1960: 4.
F319 Kelvin, Norman. "Modern Morals and the Human Heart." *Richmond News Leader* 26 Sept. 1960: 27–28.
F320 *Häusermann, H. W. "Ein Roman über D.H. Lawrence." *Zürich Samstag* 12 Nov. 1960.
F321 Gaffney, Wilbur. "Far Away and Long Ago." *Prairie Schooner* 35 (Summer 1961): 97–98.
F322 Rovit, Earl H. *Books Abroad* 35 (Summer 1961): 289.
F323 *Times Literary Supplement* 29 Sept. 1961: 648.
F324 Tomlinson, Charles. "Two Englands." *Poetry* 99 (Oct. 1961): 54–56.
F325 Bannon, Barbara A. *Publisher's Weekly* 25 March 1983: 50.
F326 Robinson, Janice. "Literary Lovers: Fantasy or Fact?" *San Francisco Chronicle* 7 Aug. 1983, Book Review Section: 1+.
F327 *Choice* (June 1984): 175.
F328 Burgess, Anthony. "Modernist Marriage." *Observer* [London] 21 Oct. 1984: 24.
Also reviews *The Gift* and *HER*.
F329 Barker, Michael. *Books and Bookmen* Nov. 1984: 37.
Also reviews *HERmione*.
F330 Buck, Claire. *Times Literary Supplement* 25 Jan. 1985: 102.
Also reviews *HERmione* and *The Gift*. See also letter by Diana Collecott, *Times Literary Supplement* 15 Feb. 1985, p. 171, responding to review.
F331 Temple, Robert. *Books and Bookmen* Jan. 1985: 35+.
F332 Seed, David. "Discovering Identity." *PN Review* 12.1 (1985): 71–72.
Also reviews *HERmione* and *The Gift*.

Helen in Egypt (1961, 1974, 1985)

F333 *Kirkus Review* 29 (1 Aug. 1961): 706.
F334 Booth, Philip. *Christian Science Monitor* 26 Oct. 1961: 7.
F335 Warner, Rex. *New York Times Book Review* 24 Dec. 1961: 4.
F336 O'Connor, William Van. "The Recent Contours of the Muse." *Saturday Review* 45 (6 Jan. 1962): 68.
F337 Lazenby, Francis D. *Library Journal* 87 (1 Feb. 1962): 563–64.
F338 *Bookmark* 21 (June 1962): 255.

F339 Jacobsen, Josephine. "Helen in Greece and Egypt." *Poetry* 100 (June 1962): 186–89.
F340 Stilwell, Robert. *Books Abroad* 36 (Winter 1962): 82–83.
F341 Swensen, May. *Nation* 23 Feb. 1963: 164.
F342 "Poetic Survivors." *Patriot Ledger* 2 April 1975: 42.
F343 Peck, John. "Passio Perpetuae H.D." *Parnassus* 3.2 (Spring/Summer 1975): 42–74.
Also reviews *Hermetic Definition*, *Trilogy*, and *Tribute to Freud*.
F344 Hudson, Dora. "Psychic Topography." *Times Literary Supplement* 27 Sept. 1985: 1068.
Also reviews *Tribute to Freud*.
F345 Rettallack, Joan. "H.D., H.D.." *Parnassus* 12.2/13.1 (1985): 67–68.
Also reviews *Collected Poems, 1912–1944*, *Hermetic Definition*, *Tribute to Freud*, *End to Torment*, Robinson (**H181**), Guest (**H196**), and Friedman (**H172**).

Hermetic Definition (1971, 1972)

F346 Charles, John W. "Three Late Poems by H.D." *Library Journal* 97 (1 Oct. 1972): 3163.
F347 *Kirkus Review* 40 (15 Oct. 1972): 1227.
F348 *Ancorp News of Books* Nov. 1972: 21.
F349 Kenner, Hugh. *New York Times Book Review* 10 Dec. 1972: 55.
F350 *[Long Beach, Calif.] *Press-Telegram* 13 Dec. 1972.
F351 *[Long Beach, Calif.] *Independent* 14 Dec. 1972.
F352 Moorhead, Andrea. *Osiris* 1 (1972): 26–28.
F353 Norris, Ruth. "Submission to Male Supremacy Sacrifices Poet's Humanity." *Daily World* 6 Feb. 1973: 4.
F354 Sullivan, Shirley. "What Are Poets Saying?" *Journal and Constitution* [Atlanta] 4 Feb. 1973: 6C.
F355 *H.M.M. "Collection Shows Talent of Hilda Doolittle." *Richmond News Leader* 27 Feb. 1973.
F356 *Choice* 9 (Feb. 1973): 1588.
F357 O'Hara, T. *Best Sellers* 1 March 1973: 543.
F358 Dodsworth, Martin. *Manchester Guardian* 15 March 1973: 18.
F359 *American Literature* 45 (March 1973): 147.
F360 *Best Sellers* 32 (1 March 1973): 543.
F361 *Alabama Advertiser-Journal Sunday Magazine* April 1973.
F362 Dillingham, Thomas. *Open Places* Spring/Summer 1973: 56–57.
F363 *Tuatara* 10 (Summer 1973): 82.
F364 Hubbell, Lindley William. "The Last Book of H.D.'s Poetry." *Rising Generation* 1 Aug. 1973: 286–87.

F365 Mayhall, Jane. "Talk Straight as the Greek." *Nation* 8 Oct. 1973: 339–41.

F366 Harris, Kathryn Gibbs. *Literature and Psychology* 23 (2 Nov. 1973): 86–88.

F367 R[egier], W. G. *Prairie Schooner* 47 (Fall 1973): 279.

F368 *Virginia Quarterly Review* 49 (Fall 1973): cxli.

F369 Beresford, Anne. *Agenda* 11.2/3 (1973): 136–37.
Also reviews *Tribute to Freud*.

F370 Glover, John. "Little Poems." *Stand Magazine* 14.3 (1973): 22–26.
Also reviews *Tribute to Freud*.

F371 Smith, Raymond V. *Southern Review* Spring 1975: 475–77.

F372 Reeve, F. D. "H.D. Rediviva." *Poetry* 124 (June 1974): 162–67.
Also reviews *Trilogy*.

F373 Zinnes, Harriet. *M373* Spring–Summer 1974: 122–26 [126].

F374 Peck, John. "Passio Perpetuae H.D.." *Parnassus* 3.2 (Spring/Summer 1975): 42–74.
Also reviews *Trilogy*, *Helen in Egypt*, and *Tribute to Freud*.

F375 Rettallack, Joan. "H.D., H.D.." *Parnassus* 12.2/13.1 (1985): 67–88.
Also reviews *Helen in Egypt*, *Collected Poems, 1912–1944*, *Tribute to Freud*, *End to Torment*, Robinson (**H181**), Guest (**H196**), and Friedman (**H172**).

Trilogy (1973)

F376 "Focus on the Arts." *Bethlehem Globe-Times* 15 Dec. 1973: 7.

F377 *H. *Long Beach [Calif.] Independent Press Telegram* 25 Dec. 1973.

F378 Jennet, M. "H.D.'s Imagist Wisdom." *New Haven Register* 30 Dec. 1973: 4D.

F379 Dodsworth, Martin. "Amazing Gifts and Others." *Guardian* [Manchester] 24 Jan. 1974: 11.

F380 Dodsworth, Martin. "Relief from Coziness." *Guardian* [Manchester] 2 Feb. 1974: 25.

F381 Meacham, Harry. "H.D. Typifies Best Work of Imagists." *Richmond News-Leader* 6 Feb. 1974: 11.

F382 Fuller, John. "Survivals." *New Statesman* 15 Feb. 1974: 230.

F383 Menike, Peter. "Polar Opposites." *New Republic* 16 Feb. 1974: 32.

F384 O'Hara, T. *Best Sellers* 33 (15 Feb. 1974): 499.

F385 Filiatreau, John. "Message of Survival in the Midst of Death." *Louisville Courier Journal and Times* 10 March 1974, section 3: 15.

F386 Porter, Peter. "Across Two Generations." *Observer* 10 March 1974: 33.

F387 "Maximum Dilution." *Times Literary Supplement* 15 March 1974: 267.

F388 *Choice* 11 (April 1974): 257.
F389 McKenzie, James. *Library Journal* 99 (15 June 1974): 1716.
F390 Sandrof, Ivan. *Worcester [Mass.] Evening Gazette* 16 Jan. 1974: 29.
F391 Crozier, Andrew. "Poetry in Series." *Spectator* 22 June 1974: 771.
F392 Asselineau, Roger. *Etudes Anglaises* 27 (April–June 1974): 247.
F393 Reeve, F. D. "H.D. Rediviva." *Poetry* 124 (June 1974): 162–67.
Also reviews *Hermetic Definition.*
F394 Carruth, Hayden. *Hudson Review* 27 (Summer 1974): 308–11.
F395 Schupham, Peter. *Agenda* 12 (Autumn 1974): 40–44.
F396 Graham, Desmond. "New Poetry." *Stand Magazine* 16.2 (1974): 75–78 [75].
F397 Peck, John. "Passio Perpetuae H.D." *Parnassus* 3.2 (Spring/Summer 1975): 42–74.
Also reviews *Hermetic Definition, Helen in Egypt,* and *Tribute to Freud.*

End to Torment (1979, 1980)

F398 *Publisher's Weekly* 22 Jan. 1979: 306.
F399 Lask, Thomas. "Hilda's Book." *New York Times Book Review* 25 Feb. 1979: 47.
F400 *Kirkus Review* 47 (15 March 1979): 361.
F401 Rovit, Earl. *Library Journal* 104 (15 April 1979): 952.
F402 Duke, Maurice. "Ezra Pound Study 'Fond, Intimate.'" *Richmond Times-Dispatch* 10 June 1979: G-5.
F403 [Butscher, Edward]. *Booklist* 75 (June 1979): 1474.
F404 Robb, Christina. "Hilda Doolittle's Ezra Pound Journal." *Boston Globe* 6 July 1979: 31.
F405 Harris, Roger. "Hilda's Lament." *Sunday Star-Ledger* [Newark, N.J.] 8 July 1979, section 4: 27.
F406 *Bronder, Howard. "Woman Poet Writes of Lover, Ezra Pound." *Valley News Dispatch* [Tarentum, Pa.] 12 July 1979.
F407 *Book World* 15 July 1979.
F408 Davenport, Guy. "Poets' Romance." *New York Times Book Review* 15 July 1979: 12+.
F409 *Maxwell, K. N. "H.D.: Pound Wise or Foolish?" *Cleveland Press* 26 July 1979.
F410 Parisi, Joseph. "Loving Memoir of the Brilliant, Bizarre Ezra Pound." *Chicago Sun-Times* 29 July 1979: 13.
F411 *Dudek, Louis. "Land of Mirrors." *Gazette* [Montreal] 11 Aug. 1979.
F412 Wilner, Paul. "Persistence of a Memory." *Newsday* 12 Aug. 1979, Ideas: 22.
F413 *Dudek, Louis. *Toronto Globe and Mail* 18 Aug. 1979.

F414 *Parisi, Joseph. "Young Ezra Pound through H.D.'s Eyes." *Knickerbocker News* [Albany, N.Y.] 25 Aug. 1979.
F415 *M.K. *Cedar Rock* Summer 1979.
F416 *Durance, Mary. "Memoir of Ezra Pound Lacking in Pound." *Citizen* [Ottawa] 15 Sept. 1979.
F417 Ratner, Rochelle. "Ezra Pound & H.D." *Soho Weekly News* 16 Sept. 1979: 58+.
F418 Goskowski, Francis. *Best Sellers* 39 (Oct. 1979): 264.
F419 *Choice* 16 (Oct. 1979): 1016.
F420 *East Bay Review of Books* Fall 1979: 18–19.
F421 *Paideuma* 8.2 (Fall 1979): [363].
F422 Bornstein, George, and Stuart McDougal. *American Literary Scholarship* 1979: [115]–16.
F423 Oderman, Kevin. "The Kind of Remembering That Is Reality." *Denver Quarterly* 14.3 (1979): 117–19.
F424 *Malahat Review* 54 (April 1980): 156.
F425 Heymenn, C. David. "H.D. Hedges, but 'Hilda's Book' Reveals the Fledgling Pound." *Newsart* June 1980: 15+.
F426 Pratt, William. *World Literature Today* 54.4 (Autumn 1980): 635–36.
F427 Weinstein, Norman. "Autobiography." *New Age* 1980: 66+.
F428 *Journal of Modern Literature* 8.3/4 (1980/81): 592.
F429 *Books and Bookmen* 25 (March 1980): 49.
F430 Duffey, Bernard. *American Literature* 53 (May 1981): 324.
F431 Lourdeaux, Stanley. *Contemporary Literature* 22 (Spring 1981): 258–60.
F432 Kerblatt-Blanchenay, Jeanne. *Etudes Anglaises* 34 (July–Sept. 1981): 359–60.
F433 *Key Reporter* [Phi Beta Kappa Society] 47.1 (Autumn 1981): 7.
F434 Buck, Claire. *Agenda* 18.4/19.1 (1981): 186–90.
F435 Beattie, Tori Potts. "Memories of Youth." *Contact II* 5.27 (Fall–Winter 1982/Winter–Spring 1983): 81+.
F436 St. Andrews, B. A. "H.D.: From Scribe's Scribe to People's Poet?" *stone country* 40.3/4 (Spring/Summer 1984): 5–9.
F437 Rettallack, Joan. "H.D., H.D.." *Parnassus* 12.2/13.1 (1985): 67–88.
Also reviews *Helen in Egypt, Hermetic Definition, Collected Poems, 1912–1944, Tribute to Freud*, Robinson (**H181**), Guest (**H196**), and Friedman (**H172**).
F438 *Reinhard, Alice. "Eine Unangepasste." *Tagesauzeigo* 22 July 1987. Also reviews *HERmione*.

Hermione (1981, 1984)

F439   *Publisher's Weekly* 28 Aug. 1981: 321.
F440   *Kirkus Review* 1 Sept. 1981: 1096.
F441   [Bannon, Barbara A.] *Publisher's Weekly* 9 Oct. 1981: 51.
F442   Tartt, Alison. *Library Journal* 15 Oct. 1981: 2048.
F443   Kiser, Thelma Scott. *Ashland [Ky.] Daily Independent* 29 Nov. 1981: 42.
F444   Antertine, Kevin. "H.D.'s Life of Myth and Modernism." *Prodigal Sun* [SUNY Buffalo] 4 Dec. 1981.
F445   See, Carolyn. "H.D.—On Being Geniuses Together." *Los Angeles Times* 7 Dec. 1981: 24.
F446   Driskell, Leon V. *Magill's Literary Annual* 1981: 349–53.
F447   Wagner, Linda W. *Resources for American Literary Study* 11.2 (1981): 340–41.
F448   Gilliland, Gail. "This H.D. Should Just R.I.P." *Philadelphia Inquirer* 2 Jan. 1982: 6-B.
F449   Scharnhorst, Gary. "A Posthumous Novel Better Left Forgotten." *Dallas Morning News* 3 Jan. 1982: 5G.
F450   Dobija, Jane. "Ezra's Girl." *Detroit News* 17 Jan. 1982: 3-G.
F451   "Autobiography with Aliases." *Atlantic Monthly* Jan. 1982: 86.
F452   *Marks, Jim. "Teetering between Friends and Lovers." *Washington Blade* 5 Feb. 1982.
F453   *Kennedy, Joseph Patrick. "The Loves of Her (from the Trunk of Hilda Doolittle)." *Houston Chronicle* 21 Feb. 1982.
F454   Riga, Frank P. *Best Sellers* 41 (Feb. 1982): 408.
F455   Bronder, Howard. "Authors' Lives, Works Provide Book's Impetus." *Valley News Dispatch* [Tarentum, Pa.] 1 May 1982: C1 + [C4].
F456   Freibert, Lucy M. *Arizona Quarterly* 38.1 (Spring 1982): 93–96.
F457   Duval, Joanne. "Poetic Quest for an Enduring Core." *New Directions for Women* May/June 1982: 12.
       Also reviews Robinson (**H181**) and Friedman (**H172**).
F458   Camper, Carol. "The Autobiography of a Future Poet from Pennsylvania." *Contemporary Literature* 23 (Sept. 1982): 377–80.
F459   Cain, Kathleen. "An Imagist Way of Seeing." *Bloomsbury Review* Nov. 1982: 3+.
       Also reviews Robinson (**H181**).
F460   Wagner, Linda. *American Book Review* 5.1 (Nov. 1982): 20–21.
F461   Pratt, William. *World Literature Today* 56 (Fall 1982): 690–91.
F462   King, Michael J. *Paideuma* 11 (Fall 1982): [339]–44.
F463   *Accent* 1982: [item 22].
F464   Allen, Frank. "H.D.'s Poetic Gifts Appear in Memoir, Novel." *Globe-Times* [Bethlehem, Pa.] 13 March 1983: F-2.
       Also reviews *The Gift*.

F465 Rasula, Jed. "A Renaissance of Women Writers." *Sulfur* 7 (1983): 160–72 [161–63].
Also reviews *The Gift*, *Hedylus*, *Notes on Thought and Vision*, Robinson (**H181**), and Friedman (**H172**).

F466 Burgess, Anthony. "Modernist Marriage." *Observer* [London] 21 Oct. 1984: 24.
Also reviews *The Gift* and *Bid Me to Live*.

F467 Barnes, Anne. "Past Impressions That Brighten the Present." *Times* [London] 10 Nov. 1984: 19.

F468 Barker, Michael. *Books and Bookmen* Nov. 1984: 37.
Also reviews *Bid Me to Live*.

F469 Buck, Claire. *Times Literary Supplement* 25 Jan. 1985: 102.
Also reviews *The Gift* and *Bid Me to Live*. See also letter by Diana Collecott, *Times Literary Supplement* 15 Feb. 1985, p. 171, responding to review.

F470 Seed, David. "Discovering Identity." *PN Review* 12.1 (1985): 71–72.
Also reviews *The Gift* and *Bid Me to Live*.

F471 *Reinhard, Alice. "Eine Unangepasste." *Tagesauzeigo* 22 July 1987.
Also reviews *End to Torment*.

F472 Ferchl, Irene. "Schöne Frau Hilda Doolittle's 'Hermione.'" *Stuttgarter Zeitung* 7 Feb. 1987: 46.

F473 *"Kultfigur der Emanzapation." *Mannheimer Moogen* 6 March 1987.

F474 **Basellandschaft Liche Zeitung* 1 April 1987.

F475 Winter, Helmut. "Leuchtende Wörterwelten." *F.A.Z.* 4 April 1987: 26.

F476 Schattenhofer, Monika. "Mücke sticht Marmorstatue." *Frankfurter Literatur-Rundschau* 11 April 1987: 8.

F477 Stromberg, Kyra. "Auf Spurensuche nach dem eigenen Ich." *SZ* [*Süddeutsche Zeitung*] 14 April 1987: 57.

F478 Schmitz, Alexander. "Mal war sie Göttin, mal Kohlenschippe." *Die Welt* 96 (25 April 1987), Geistige: 2.

F479 **Bremer Blatt* April 1987.

F480 *Stromberg, Kyra. "Der Fieberwahn eines Mädchens." *Hannoversche Allgemeine Zeitung* 30 May 1987.

F481 *Schmickl, Gerald. "Ein Mädchen aus der Provinz lernt lieben." *Schöuer Leben/Kurv* 25 June 1987.

F482 *Stromberg, Kyra. "Sie war Ezra Pound's Dryade." *Saarbrücker Zeitung* 4 June 1987.

The Gift (1982, 1984)

F483 *Kirkus Review* 50 (15 Aug. 1982): 947.

F484 Mesic, Penelope. *Booklist* 79 (1 Sept. 1982): 28.

F485 [Bannon, Barbara A.] *Publisher's Weekly* 222 (3 Sept. 1982): 56.
F486 Tartt, Alison. *Library Journal* 107 (Sept. 1982): 1660.
F487 *Dawson, David. *Call-Chronicle* [Allentown, Pa.] 5 Dec. 1982.
F488 *New Yorker* 27 Dec. 1982: 78.
F489 Hunting, Constance. *Sagetrieb* 1 (Winter 1982): 198–99.
F490 *Levinson, Nan. "H.D.'s Gift Is Mystical, Precious." *Washington [D.C.] Times* 25 Jan. 1983.
F491 Allen, Frank. "H.D.'s Poetic Gifts Appear in Memoir, Novel." *Globe-Times* [Bethlehem, Pa.] 13 March 1983: F-2.
Also reviews *End to Torment*.
F492 *Choice* 20 (March 1983): 982.
F493 Dasenbrock, Reed Way. "Pound the Boy and H.D. the Child." *Exquisite Corpse* 1.2 (Feb.–March 1983): 3.
F494 Brownworth, Victoria A. "Childhood Memoir for Adults." *Philadelphia Inquirer* 2 April 1983: 4-D.
F495 Cosgrave, Mary Silva. *Horn Book Magazine* 59 (April 1983): 205.
F496 *Virginia Quarterly Review* 59 (Autumn 1983): 123–24.
F497 Freibert, Lucy M. *Arizona Quarterly* 39 (1983): 89–91.
F498 Lipscomb, Elizabeth Johnston. *Magill's Literary Annual* 1983: 278–82.
F499 Rasula, Jed. "A Renaissance of Women Writers." *Sulfur* 7 (1983): 160–72 [161–63].
Also reviews *Hermione*, *Hedylus*, *Notes on Thought and Vision*, Robinson (**H181**), and Friedman (**H172**).
F500 Rodgers, Martha. *Polis* 4 (1983): 35–36.
F501 Burgess, Anthony. "Modernist Marriage." *Observer* [London] 21 Oct. 1984: 24.
Also reviews *Bid Me to Live* and *HER*.
F502 Buck, Claire. *Times Literary Supplement* 25 Jan. 1985: 102.
Also reviews *HERmione* and *Bid Me to Live*. See also letter by Diana Collecott, *Times Literary Supplement* 15 Feb. 1985, p. 171, responding to review.
F503 Seed, David. "Discovering Identity." *PN Review* 12.1 (1985): 71–72.
Also reviews *HERmione* and *Bid Me to Live*.

Notes on Thought and Vision (1982, 1983)

F504 Allen, Frank. "A Classical Style Was Her Strength." *Philadelphia Inquirer* 11 July 1983: 4-C.
F505 *Choice* 20 (July 1983): 1596.
F506 Rasula, Jed. "A Renaissance of Women Writers." *Sulfur* 7 (1983): 160–72 [161–63].
Also reviews *HERmione*, *Hedylus*, *The Gift*, Robinson (**H181**), and Friedman (**H172**).

Collected Poems, 1912–1944 (1983, 1984, 1986)

F507 Stuttaford, Genevieve. *Publisher's Weekly* 224 (26 Aug. 1983): 379.

F508 Parisi, Joseph. *Booklist* 80 (1 Sept. 1983): 23.

F509 Lipari, Joseph A. *Library Journal* 108 (15 Oct. 1983): 1963.

F510 *Codrescu, Andrei. "Books This Year Have Looked to Past rather than Present for Greatness." *Philadelphia Inquirer* 11 Dec. 1983.

F511 *Allen, Margaret Vanderhaar. "H.D. Writes of Influential Men in Poetry Collection." *Bethlehem Globe-Times* 25 Dec. 1983.

F512 Codrescu, Andrei. "The Bookshelf / Poetry." *Philadelphia Inquirer* 15 Jan. 1984: R-9.

F513 Freibert, Lucy M. *Courier Journal* [Louisville, Ky.] 29 Jan. 1984: D5.

F514 Hamilton, Ian. "At the Right Time, at the Right Place." *Washington Post Book World* 19 Feb. 1984: 3+.

F515 Lucas, John. "Truth, Dare, Slush, or Promise." *New Statesman* 107 (2 March 1984): 23+.

F516 Pollitt, Katha. *New York Times Book Review* 11 March 1984: 7.

F517 Kazin, Alfred. "A Nymph of the New." *New York Review of Books* 29 March 1984: 15–16.

F518 Pearson, Gabriel. "Behind the Mask of the Pythoness." *Times Literary Supplement* 27 April 1984: 447+.
Also reviews Robinson (**H181**) and (**H196**). See also letter from John Lucas, *Times Literary Supplement* 11 May 1984: 523, responding to review.

F519 *Choice* 21 (April 1984): 1134.

F520 Gardner, Frieda. "Humanity Disdained?" *Women's Review of Books* 1.8 (May 1984): 13–14.

F521 *Stanford, Derek. *Books and Bookmen* July 1984.

F522 Chase, Kathleen. *World Literature Today* 58 (Summer 1984): 423.

F523 Ponsot, Marie. *Commonweal* 30 Nov. 1984: 665.

F524 *Virginia Quarterly Review* 60 (Autumn 1984): 136–34.

F525 Eagleton, Terry. *Stand Magazine* 26.1 (Winter 1984/85): 68–72 [69–70].

F526 *English Association* 65 (1984).

F527 Shaw, Marion. "After Imagism." *Poetry Review* [London] 74.1 (1984): 65–67.

F528 Morley, Hilda. *Ironwood* 25 (1985): 159–75.

F529 Morris, Adelaide. *Iowa Review* 15 (1985): 195–203.
Also reviews Guest (**H196**).

F530 Rettallack, Joan. "H.D., H.D." *Parnassus* 12.2/13.1 (1985): 67–88.
Also reviews *Helen in Egypt, Hermetic Definition, Tribute to Freud, End to Torment*, Robinson (**H181**), Guest (**H196**), and Friedman (**H172**).

F531 Guenther, Charles. "A Centennial for H.D.: 50th for New Directions." *St. Louis Post-Dispatch* 9 March 1986: 4B.

F532 *Kiser, Thelma Scott. *Sunday Independent* [Ashland, Ky.] 9 March 1986.

F533 *Stoyva, Johanna. "Unveiling H.D." *Chicago Literary Review* 14 March 1986.

F534 *"Recent Paperbacks." *Boston Globe* 6 April 1986.

F535 *Washington Post Book World* 13 April 1986: 12.

F536 Koestenbaum, Wayne. "Shattering Silences." *New York Native* 5 May 1986: 33+.

F537 Heany, Sean. "Anger, Conversation, and Myth." *Boston Herald* 20 July 1986: 90.

F538 Kolokithas, Dawn. "Spiritual Realism in H.D." *Poetry Flash* 165 (Dec. 1986): 1+.

F539 Unger, Barbara. "The Feminist behind the Modernism." *Contact II* Spring 1988: 70–72.

Nights (First American Edition, 1986)

F540 Hannibal, Mary Ellen. "Long Island Books." *East Hampton [N.Y.] Star* 5 March 1987: II-9.

F541 *Kirkus Reviews* 15 March 1986: 413–14.

F542 Jarolim, Edith. "In Short." *New York Times Book Review* 10 Aug. 1986: 18.

F543 Pekar, Harvey. "Evelyn Scott, H.D., and the Evolution of American Stream of Consciousness Writing." *Austin Chronicle* 15 Aug. 1986: 10.

F544 Thiebaux, Marcelle. "Enigmatic View of Bisexuality." *Newsday* 17 Aug. 1986, Ideas: 22.

F545 Wagner-Martin, Linda. "Another Novel by H.D." *American Poetry Review* March–April 1987: 17.
Also reviews *H.D.: Woman and Poet*, ed. Michael King (**H216**).

F546 Jacobs, Rita D. *World Literature Today* 61 (Spring 1987): [285].

F547 Guest, Barbara. *Conjunctions* 11 (1988): 280–83.
Also reviews *Ion*.

Miscellanea

F548 *Poetry and Drama* 2.6 (June 1914): 179–80.
Reviews *Des Imagistes*.

F549 Lane, George. *Little Review* 2.3 (May 1915): 27–35 [29–31].
Reviews *Some Imagist Poets, 1915*.

F550 *Poetry* 6 (June 1915): 150–53.
Reviews *Some Imagist Poets, 1915*.

F551 Aiken, Conrad. "Imagism or Myopia?" *Poetry Journal* 3.6 (July 1915): 233–41.
Reviews *Some Imagist Poets, 1915*.

F552 Aldis, Mary. *Little Review* 3.4 (June–July 1916): 26–31 [29].
Reviews *Some Imagist Poets, 1916*.

F553 Monroe, Harriet. *Poetry* 8 (Aug. 1916): 255–59.
Reviews *Some Imagist Poets, 1916*.

F554 "Tendencies in American Poetry." *New York Times Book Review* 18 Nov. 1917: 481.
Reviews *Tendencies in Modern American Poetry* by Amy Lowell.

F555 Kreymborg, Alfred. "As Others See Us." *Poetry* 12 (July 1918): 214–24.
Reviews *The New Poetry* by Harriet Monroe.

F556 McClure, John. *Double Dealer* 4 (Nov. 1922): 253–54.
Reviews *American Poetry 1921*.

F557 Nicholl, Louise. "Their Own Editors." *Measure* 21 (Nov. 1922): 15–17 [16].
Reviews *American Poetry 1922*.

F558 Norris, William A. "With a Little Song." *New York Evening Post Literary Review* 30 Dec. 1922: 347–48 [348].
Reviews *Bookman's Anthology of Verse*.

F559 *Dial* 77 (Sept. 1924): 266.
Reviews *Best Poems of 1923*, ed. Thomas Moult.

F560 Hubbell, Lindley William. "The Stretched Meter of an Antique Song." *Voices* 4.1 (Nov. 1924): 25–26.
Reviews *Exile and Other Poems* by Richard Aldington.

F561 Moore, Virginia. "Anthology of American Verse." *New York Evening Post Literary Review* 20 Feb. 1926: 5.
Reviews *American Poetry 1925*.

F562 Eisenberg, Emmanuel. "Escaping into Reality." *Voices* 5.7 (May 1926): 262–65.
Reviews *Modern Poetry* by H. P. Collins.

F563 Beach, Joseph Warren. "Modern British Poetry." *Poetry* 29 (Oct. 1926): 52–56.
Reviews *Modern Poetry* by H. P. Collins.

F564 *Hound and Horn* 1 (Sept. 1927): 66.
Discussion of "Cinema and the Classics" in review of *Close-Up*.

F565 Hitchcock, Henry Russell, Jr. *Hound and Horn* 2 (Sept. 1928): 95–98.
Reviews *Close-Up*.

F566 Howe, Anne. "Blouagh! Or Romping with the Whimsigists." *This Quarter* 2.4 (April/May/June 1930): 725–31 [728].
Reviews *Imagist Anthology 1930*.

F567 M[onroe], H[arriet]. "Imagism Today and Yesterday." *Poetry* 36 (July 1930): 213–18 [217].
Reviews *Imagist Anthology 1930*.

F568 Blakeston, Oswell. *New English Weekly* 19 July 1934: 332–33.
Reviews *Gaunt Island* by Kenneth MacPherson.

F569 Fletcher, John Gould. "Herald of Imagism." *Southern Review* 1 (Winter 1935): 813–27 [820].
Reviews *Amy Lowell: A Chronicle* by S. Foster Damon.

F570 *Times Literary Supplement* 16 July 1954: 455.
On Gilbert Murray with comparison to H.D.

F571 Hardy, John Edward. "The Place of the Imagists." *Poetry* 78 (Aug. 1951): 294–97 [297].
Reviews *Imagism: A Chapter for the History of Modern Poetry* by Stanley Coffman.

F572 Gibbons, Kathryn Gibbs. *Books Abroad* 37 (Spring 1963): 203–4.
Reviews Thomas Burnett Swann's *The Classical World of H.D.* (H78).

F573 Combellack, C. R. B. *Comparative Literature* 15 (Winter 1963): 60–65.
Reviews Swann (H78).

F574 Will, Frederick. *Journal of English and Germanic Philology* 63.1 (Jan. 1964): 179–81.
Reviews Swann (H78).

F575 *Publisher's Weekly* 8 Jan. 1982: 78.
Reviews Robinson (H181).

F576 Donohue, Dennis. "Her Deepest Passion Was D. H. Lawrence." *New York Times Book Review* 14 Feb. 1982: 3+.
Reviews Robinson (H181). See also letter from Rachel DuPlessis, Albert Gelpi, Susan Gubar, and Sandra Gilbert, *New York Times Book Review* 4 April 1982: 37, responding to review.

F577 *Hunter, William B., Jr. "Hilda Doolittle: A Window on the Literary 20's and 30's." *Houston Chronicle* 21 Feb. 1982.
Reviews Robinson (H181).

F578 Milazzo, Lee. "A Talented Poet Unlucky at Love." *Dallas Morning News* 21 Feb. 1982: 5G.
Reviews Robinson (H181).

F579 Kenner, Hugh. "Love among the Modernists." *Washington Post Book World* 7 March 1982: 8+.
Reviews Robinson (H181).

F580 Whitman, Alden. *Philadelphia Inquirer* 7 March 1982: section 12: 7.
Reviews Robinson (H181).

F581 Waterman, Cary. "H.D.: Life of a Poet." *Minneapolis Tribune* 28 March 1982: 14G.
Reviews Robinson (H181).

F582 Allen, Frank. "Misinterpreting H.D.'s Roots." *Bethlehem Globe-Times* 28 May 1982: D1+.
Reviews Robinson (**H181**).

F583 Sharpe, Pat. "From Image to Epic Quest." *In Print* 11.4 (April 1982): 1–2.
Reviews Friedman (**H172**) and Robinson (**H181**).

F584 Duval, Joanne. "Poetic Quest for an Enduring Core." *New Directions for Women* May/June 1982: 12.
Reviews Robinson (**H181**) and Friedman (**H172**). Also reviews *HERmione*.

F585 Crowder, Richard. *American Literature* 54 (Oct. 1982): 457–60.
Reviews Robinson (**H181**).

F586 Gregson, Ian. *Essays in Criticism* 32 (Oct. 1982): 381–84.
Reviews Friedman (**H172**).

F587 Prioleau, Elizabeth. *American Literature* 54 (Oct. 1982): 456–57.
Reviews Friedman (**H172**).

F588 Cain, Kathleen. "An Imagist Way of Seeing." *Bloomsbury Review* Nov. 1982: 3+.
Reviews Robinson (**H181**) and *HERmione*.

F589 Kouidis, Virginia. *Southern Humanities Review* 17 (1982): 378–79.
Reviews Robinson (**H181**).

F590 Pettigeld, Phoebe. "A Helen from Bethlehem." *New Leader* 5 April 1983: 18–19.
Reviews Robinson (**H181**).

F591 MacKnight, Nancy. "H.D.: The Life of an American Poet." *Sagetrieb* 2 (Spring 1983): [143]–45.
Reviews Robinson (**H181**).

F592 *Publisher's Weekly* 18 Nov. 1983: 66.
Reviews Robinson (**H181**).

F593 Gilbert, Sandra. "H.D.? Who Was She?" *Contemporary Literature* 24 (1983): 496–511.
Reviews Robinson (**H181**) and Friedman (**H172**).

F594 Kazin, Alfred. "A Nymph of the New." *New York Review of Books* 29 March 1984: 15.
Reviews Guest (**H196**).

F595 Pearson, Gabriel. "Behind the Mask of the Pythoness." *Times Literary Supplement* 27 April 1984: 447–48.
Reviews *Collected Poems, 1912–1944*, Robinson (**H181**), and Guest (**H196**).

F596 Ratner, Rochelle. "H.D.: Feministe?" *New Women's Times Feminist Review* 29 (Sept./Oct. 1983): 6+.
Reviews Robinson (**H181**) and Friedman (**H172**). Reprinted in *Trying to Understand What It Means to Be a Feminist: Essays on Women Writers* (New York: Contact II Publications, 1984), 5–8.

F597 Hatlen, Burton. Review of *Ideogram: History of a Poetic Method* by Laszlo K. Géfin. *Sagetrieb* 2.2 (Summer–Fall 1983): [137]–45 [138–39].

F598 Gies, Judith. "Hilda Doolittle: Poet in Ceaseless Search of Herself." *Newsday* 29 Jan. 1984: 16+.
Reviews Guest (**H196**).

F599 La Rocque, Paula. "The Legend of H.D." *Dallas Morning News* 8 April 1984: 4G.
Reviews Guest (**H196**).

F600 Toll, Seymour. "Hilda Doolittle: Pagan Mystic of Bethlehem, Pa." *Philadelphia Inquirer* 8 April 1984: R-2.
Reviews Guest (**H196**).

F601 Crawford, Fred. "Approaches to Biography." *Review* 7 (1985): 215–38.
Reviews Robinson (**H181**) and Guest (**H196**).

F602 Butterick, George. *Sulfur* 12 (1985): 144–47.
Reviews Guest (**H196**).

F603 Becker, Alida. "New Paperbacks." *Philadelphia Inquirer* 14 Sept. 1986: 4-S.
Reviews DuPlessis (**H214**).

F604 Overmeyer, J. *Choice* 24 (Dec. 1986): 623.
Reviews DuPlessis (**H214**).

F605 *Small Press Book Review* 2.4 (Jan./Feb. 1987): 8.
Reviews *H.D.: Woman and Poet*, ed. Michael King (**H216**).

F606 Wagner-Martin, Linda. "Another Novel by H.D." *American Poetry Review* March–April 1987: 17.
Also reviews *Nights*.

F607 Dickie, Margaret. *American Literature* 59 (May 1987): 302.
Reviews DuPlessis (**H214**).

F608 Baym, Nina. "Women of the Left Bank." *American Literature* 59 (Oct. 1987): 472–75 [474].
Reviews *Women of the Left Bank* by Shari Benstock (**H212**).

G

Articles about H.D. in Periodicals

G1 [Monroe, Harriet]. "Notes." *Poetry* 1.4 (Jan. 1913): 135.

G2 Aldington, Richard. "Modern Poetry and the Imagists." *Egoist* 1 (1 June 1914): 201–3.

G3 Aldington, Richard. "Free Verse in England." *Egoist* 1 (15 Sept. 1914): 351–52.

G4 Aldington, Richard. "A Young American Poet." *Little Review* 2.1 (March 1915): 22–25.

G5 Flint, F. S. "The Poetry of H.D." *Egoist* 2 (1 May 1915): 72–3.
Reprints "Hermes of the Ways I" and "Pines" (i.e., "Oread").

G6 Monro, Harold. "The Imagists Discussed." *Egoist* 2 (1 May 1915): 77–80 [79].
Reprints "Oread" in full.

G7 Sinclair, May "Two Notes: I. On H.D.; II. On Imagism." *Egoist* 2 (1 June 1915): 88–89.
A reply to Harold Mono's article in *Egoist* 2 (**G6**).

G8 Aldington, Richard. "The Imagists." *Greenwich Village* 2.2 (July 1915): 54–57.
Reprinted in *Bruno Chapbooks* no. 16.

G9 Fletcher, John Gould. "Three Imagist Poets." *Little Review* 3.4 (June–July 1916): 32–41.

G10 M[onroe], H[arriet]. "To the Wilderness." *Poetry* 10 (Aug. 1917): 259–63 [263].

G11 H[enderson], A[lice] C[orbin]. "Imagism: Secular and Esoteric." *Poetry* 11 (March 1918): 339–43 [341–42].

G12 M[onroe], H[arriet]. "Sara Teasdale's Prize." *Poetry* 12 (Aug. 1918): 264–69.
Discusses H.D.'s *Sea Garden*, among other books, as more deserving of prize from Columbia.

G13 Flint, F. S. "Presentation: A Note on the Art of Writing; on the

Artfulness of Some Writers and on the Artlessness of Others." *Chapbook* 2.9 (March 1920): 17–24 [22–24].

G14 Felton, Henry. "On H.D." *Coterie* 4 (Easter 1920): 40–43.

G15 Aldington, Richard. "The Art of Poetry." *Dial* 69 (Aug. 1920): 166–80.

G16 Untermeyer, Louis. "Return of the Vers Libertine." *Nation* 7 June 1922: 696.

G17 Bodenheim, Maxwell. "Concerning 'Free Verse.'" *Nation* 6 Sept. 1922: 233.

G18 Untermeyer, Louis. "The Perfect Imagist." *Saturday Review of Literature* 8 Nov. 1924: 260.

G19 Bregy, Katherine. "American Poetry in Action and Reaction." *Catholic World* 121 (Spring 1925): 764–67.

G20 Monroe, Harriet. "Comment: H.D." *Poetry* 26 (Aug. 1925): 268–75.

G21 Burnshaw, Stanley. "Vers-Libre in Full Bloom: A Note on the Prosody of Andre Spire: II." *Poetry* 32 (Sept. 1928): 334–41 [340–41].

G22 Doggett, Frank. "H.D.: A Study in Sensitivity." *Sewanee Review* 37 (Jan.–March 1929): 1–9.

G23 "Hilda Doolittle." *Wilson Bulletin for Librarians* 5 (Jan. 1931): 356.

G24 Cunningham, J. V. "Envoi." *Hound and Horn* 6 (Oct.–Dec. 1932): [124]–30.
A discussion of the history of *Poetry* (Chicago) with numerous references to H.D.

G25 Emerson, Dorothy. "H.D." *Scholastic* 26 Jan. 1935: 13.
Includes photograph. Reprints in full "Sea Gods" and "Pear Tree."

G26 Tietjens, Eunice. "The Orient's Gift to American Poetry." *Asia* 36 (Nov. 1936): 746–49 [748].
Reprints "The Pool."

G27 Marsh, Edward. "A Number of People III." *Harper's Magazine* (July 1939): [171]+.
Mention of H.D. in a letter from D. H. Lawrence to Marsh dated 29 Jan. 1917.

G28 Aldington, Richard. "Des Imagistes." *Saturday Review of Literature* 16 March 1940: 3–4.
Excerpt from chapters 7 and 9 of *Life for Life's Sake*. Reprinted in *The Saturday Review Gallery*, ed. Jerome Beatty, Jr. (New York: Simon and Schuster, 1959), 269–75.

G29 Aldington, Richard. "Farewell to Europe." *Atlantic* 166 (Oct. 1940): 518–29.
Excerpt from chapters 6–10 of *Life for Life's Sake*.

G30 Sitwell, Edith. "Lecture on Poetry since 1920." *Life and Letters Today* 39 (Nov. 1943): 70–97.
Reprints "Pear Tree" in full.

G31 Jacobs, Willis. "H.D.'s 'Oread.'" *Explicator* 10.7 (May 1945): item 45.
Reprints "Oread" in full.

G32 Thomas, Macklin. "Analysis of the Experience in Lyric Poetry." *College English* 9 (March 1948): 317–21 [320].
Reprints "Oread" in full.

G33 Williams, William Carlos. "Something for a Biography." *General Magazine and Historical Chronicle* 50 (Summer 1948): 211–13.

G34 Watts, Harold H. "H.D. and the Age of Myth." *Sewannee Review* 56 (1948): 287–303.
Reprinted in *Hound and Quarry* (London: Routledge and Kegan Paul, 1953). See H59.

G35 "H.D. at Seventy." *New York Herald Tribune* 28 Aug. 1956: 17.

G36 Lüdeke, Henry. "Hilda Doolittle." *Neue Zeuricher Zeitung* 10 Sept. 1956: 3.

G37 Patmore, Brigit. "Conversations with Lawrence." *London Magazine* 4 (June 1957): 31–45.

G38 Emery, Clark. Notes on *Selected Poems*. *Anagogic and Paideumic Review* 6 (1959): [17].

G39 Major, Clarence. "To Preserve a Living Tradition." *Anagogic and Paideumic Review* 6 (1959): [113–16].

G40 Martinelli, Sheri. Commentary on Clark Emery's notes (G38). *Anagogic and Paideumic Review* 6 (1959): [18–19].

G41 Martinelli, Sheri. Discussion of *Bid Me to Live*. *Anagogic and Paideumic Review* 6 (1959): [20–22].

G42 Jones, A. R. "Notes toward a History of Imagism." *South Atlantic Quarterly* 60 (Summer 1961): 262–85 [268–69].

G43 Gregory, Horace. "Speaking of Books." *New York Times Book Review* 22 Oct. 1961: 2.
Reprints "Orchard," "Helen," "Heat," "Oread," and an excerpt from *Bid Me to Live*, as well as excerpts on H.D. from Richard Aldington's *Life for Life's Sake* and Douglas Bush's *Mythology and the Romantic Tradition in English Poetry*.

G44 Levertov, Denise. "H.D.: An Appreciation." *Poetry* 100.3 (June 1962): 182–86.
Reprinted in *The Poet in the World* (New York: New Directions, 1973), 244–48.

G45 Gibbons, Kathryn Gibbs. "The Art of H.D." *Mississippi Quarterly* 15 (Fall 1962): 152–60.

G46 Reche, Denis. "Pour Ezra Pound." *Tel Quel* 11 (Fall 1962): 17–24.

G47 Duncan, Robert. "From the Day Book." *Origin*, 2d ser. 10 (July 1963): 1–47.
A random sampling of *The H.D. Book*, pt. 2, made by Cid Corman.

G48 Moore, Harry T. "Richard Aldington in His Last Years." *Texas Quarterly* Autumn 1963: 60–74.

G49 Duncan, Robert. "The H.D. Book: Chapter 5." *Aion: A Journal of Tradionary Science* 1 (Dec. 1964): [7–29].
Reprinted in *Stony Brook* 1 (Fall 1968): 4–19.

G50 Bianchi, Ruggero. "Saffo in America: Hilda Doolittle." *Studi Americani* 11 (1965): 197–211.

G51 Edward, Oliver. "Helen in Egypt." *Times* [London] 12 May 1966: 16.

G52 Duncan, Robert. "Beginnings: Chapter 1 of the H.D. Book Part 1." *Coyote's Journal* 5/6 (1966): 8–31.

G53 Fields, Kenneth. "The Poetry of Mina Loy." *Southern Review* 3.3 (July 1967): 597–607.

G54 Duncan, Robert. "Rites of Participation." *Caterpillar* 1 (Oct. 1967): 6–29.
The H.D. Book, pt. 1, chap. 6.

G55 Duncan, Robert. "The H.D. Book, Part 1: Chapter 2." *Coyote's Journal* 8 (1967): 27–35.

G56 Duncan, Robert. "Rites of Participation." *Caterpillar* 2 (Jan. 1968): 125–54.
The H.D. Book, pt. 1, chap. 6 [pt. 2].

G57 Duncan, Robert. "Two Chapters from H.D." *Triquarterly* 12 (Spring 1968): 67–98.
The H.D. Book, pt. 1, chap. 3 and 4.

G58 Duncan, Robert. "The H.D. Book: Part 2, Ch. 1." *Sumac* 1 (Fall 1968): 101–46.

G59 Duncan, Robert. "From the H.D. Book. Part I: Beginnings, Ch. 5: Occult Matters." *Stony Brook* 1/2 (Fall 1968): 4–19.

G60 Duncan, Robert. "The H.D. Book: Part II, Nights and Days, Chapter 2." *Caterpillar* 6 (Jan. 1969): 16–38.

G61 Hoyem, Andrew. "I Like to (B)eat People Up." *Poetry* 113 (March 1969): 426–28 [426].

G62 Duncan, Robert. "The H.D. Book: Part II, Nights and Days, Chapter 4." *Caterpillar* 7 (April 1969): 27–60.

G63 Duncan, Robert. "The H.D. Book: Part 2, Ch. 3." *IO* 6 (Summer 1969): 117–40.

G64 Dembo, L. S. "Norman Holmes Pearson on H.D.: An Interview." *Contemporary Literature* 10 (Autumn 1969): 435–46.

G65 Duncan, Robert. "From the H.D. Book, Part II, Chapter 5 [section 1]." *Stony Brook* 3/4 (Fall 1969): 336–47.

Reprinted with **G80** in *Sagetrieb* 4.2/3 (Fall/Winter 1985): [39]–85. See **G165**.

G66 Engel, Bernard F. "H.D.: Poems That Matter and Dilutations." *Contemporary Literature* 10 (Autumn 1969): 507–22.

G67 Holland, Norman. "H.D. and the 'Blameless Physician.'" *Contemporary Literature* 10 (Autumn 1969): 474–506.

G68 Pondrom, Cyrena N. "Selected Letters from H.D. to F. S. Flint: A Commentary on the Imagist Period." *Contemporary Literature* 10 (Autumn 1969): 557–86.

Pondrom contributed both a general introduction to the letters and introductory notes for almost every individual letter.

G69 Riddel, Joseph N. "H.D. and the Poetics of 'Spiritual Realism.'" *Contemporary Literature* 10 (Autumn 1969): 447–73.

G70 Wagner, Linda Welshimer. "*Helen in Egypt*: A Culmination." *Contemporary Literature* 10 (Autumn 1969): 523–36.

G71 Weatherhead, A. Kingsley. "Style in H.D.'s Novels." *Contemporary Literature* 10 (Autumn 1969): 537–56.

G72 Boughn, Michael. "Unity in H.D.'s *War Trilogy*." *Iron* 5 (1969): 6–30.

G73 Holland, Norman. "Freud and H.D." *International Journal of Psychoanalysis* 50 (1969): 309–15.

Translated and reprinted as "H.D. et Freud." *Etude Freudienne* 3/4 (Sept. 1970): 143–56.

G74 Greenwood, E. B. "H.D. and the Problem of Escapism." *Essays in Criticism* 21 (Oct. 1971): 365–76.

G75 Duncan, Robert. "Glimpses of the Last Day (From Chapter 11 of *The H.D. Book*)." *Io* 10 (1971): 212–15.

G76 Schulman, Grace. "Women the Inventors." *Nation* 11 (Dec. 1972): 594–96.

G77 Hubell, Lindley W. "The Last Book of H.D.'s Poetry." *Eigo Seinen* 119 (Aug. 1973): 286–87.

G78 Scoggan, John. "Charles Olson's Imago Mundi, H.D.'s Flowering of the Rod: A Study of the Soul in a Recent Poetics." *Archai* 3/4 (1974): 1–94.

G79 Friedman, Susan Stanford. "Who Buried H.D.? A Poet, Her Critics, and Her Place in 'The Literary Tradition.'" *College English* 36 (March 1975): 801–14.

Reprinted in *Feminist Criticism: Essays on Theory, Poetry, and Prose* (Metuchen, N.J.: Scarecrow Press, 1978), 92–110.

G80 Duncan, Robert. "The H.D. Book." *Credences* 1.2 (July 1975): 50–94.

Includes pt. 2, chap. 5 (section 2), 7, and 8. Chapter 5 reprinted with item **G65** in *Sagetrieb* 4.2/3 (Fall/Winter 1985): [39]–85. See **G165**.

G81 Schaffner, Perdita. "Merano, 1962." *Paideuma* 4 (Fall/Winter 1975): 513–18.

G82 Eder, Doris. "Freud and H.D." *Book Forum: An International Transdisciplinary Quarterly* 1 (1975): 365–69.

G83 Sisson, C. H. "H.D." *Poetry Nation* 4 (1975): 85–91.
Reprinted in *The Avoidance of Literature: Collected Essays* (Manchester: Carcanet, 1978), [481]–87.

G84 Satherwaite, Alfred. "John Cournos and 'H.D.'" *Twentieth Century Literature* 22 (Dec. 1976): 394–410.

G85 Wallace, Emily. "Afterword: The House of the Father's Science and the Mother's Art." *William Carlos Williams Newsletter* 2.2 (1976): 4–5.

G86 Gates, Norman T. "Richard Aldington and Marianne Moore." *Marianne Moore Newsletter* 1.1 (Spring 1977): 16–18.

G87 Newlin, Margaret. "'Unhelpful Hymen': Marianne Moore and Hilda Doolittle." *Essays in Criticism* 27 (July 1977): 216–30.

G88 Gage, John T. "Images and Critical Method." *Style* 11 (Fall 1977): 355–74 [360–61].

G89 Quinn, Vincent. "H.D.'s 'Hermetic Definition': The Poet as Archtypal Mother." *Contemporary Literature* 18 (Winter 1977): 51–61.

G90 Friedman, Susan Stanford. "Creating a Woman's Mythology: H.D.'s *Helen in Egypt*." *Women's Studies* 5 (1977): 163–97.

G91 Link, Franz H. "Bild und Mythos in der Dichtung Hilda Doolittle." *Literaturweissenschaftliches Jahrbuch*, Neue Folge/Achtzennter Band (1977): 271–303.
Reprinted in *Zwei amerikanische Dichterinnen: Emily Dickinson und Hilda Doolittle*, Schriften zur Literaturwissenschaft 2 (Berlin: Duncker und Humbolt, 1979).

G92 "H.D." *Poetry Society of America Bulletin* Feb. 1978: 11–12.
Synopsis of the H.D. symposium held Jan. 1978 and broadcast on WBAI-FM (N.Y.) on 8 March 1978.

G93 Kerblat-Houghton, Jeanne. "*Helen in Egypt*: Variations sur un thème sonore." *G.R.E.S.* 2 (April 1978).

G94 Gubar, Susan. "The Echoing Spell of H.D.'s *Trilogy*." *Contemporary Literature* 19 (Spring 1978): 196–218.
Revised and reprinted in *Shakespeare's Sisters: Feminist Essays on Women Poets*, ed. Sandra M. Gilbert and Susan Gubar (Bloomington: Indiana UP, 1979), 153–64.

G95 Clare, John. "Form in Vers-libre." *English* 27 (Summer/Autumn 1978): 150–70 [153].

G96 Romig, Evelyn M. "An Achievement of H.D. and Theodore Roethke: Psychoanalysis and the Poetics of Teaching." *Literature and Psychology* 28 (1978): 105–11.

G97 Sievert, Heather Rosario. "H.D.: A Symbolist Perspective." *Comparative Literature Studies* 16 (March 1979): 48–57.

G98 Riddel, Joseph. "H.D.'s Scene of Writing—Poetry as (and) Analysis." *Studies in the Literary Imagination* 12 (Spring 1979): 41–59.
Reprinted in *American Critics at Work: Examinations of Contemporary Literary Theory*, ed. Victor A. Kramer (Troy, N.Y.: Whitston, 1984), 143–75.

G99 DuPlessis, Rachel Blau. "Romantic Thralldom in H.D." *Contemporary Literature* 20 (Summer 1979): 178–203.

G100 Friebert, Lucy. "Conflict and Creativity in the World of H.D." *Journal of Women's Studies* 1 (Summer 1979): 258–71.

G101 Duncan, Robert. "The H.D. Book, Part II: Nights and Days, Chap. 9." *Chicago Review* 30.3 (Winter 1979): 37–88.

G102 DuPlessis, Rachel Blau. "Family, Sexes, Psyche: An Essay on H.D. and the Muse of the Woman Writer." *Montemora* 6 (1979): 137–56.

G103 Friedman, Susan Stanford. "Psyche Reborn: Tradition, Re-Vision, and the Goddess as Mother-Symbol in H.D.'s Epic Poetry." *Women's Studies* 6 (1979): 147–60.

G104 Gubar, Susan. "Mother, Maiden, and the Marriage of Death: Woman Writers and an Ancient Myth." *Women's Studies* 6 (1979): 301–15 [306–7].

G105 Rovit, Earl. "Our Lady-Poets of the Twenties." *Southern Review* 16.1 (Jan. 1980): 65–85.

G106 Friebert, L. M. "From Semblance to Selfhood: The Evolution of Woman in H.D.'s Neo-Epic *Helen in Egypt*." *Arizona Quarterly* 36 (Summer 1980): 165–75.

G107 Faas, Eckbert. "An Interview with Robert Duncan." *Boundary 2* 8.2 (Winter 1980): 1–19 [14–17].

G108 Gilbert, Sandra M. "Costumes of the Mind: Transvestism as Metaphor in Modern Literature." *Critical Inquiry* 7 (Winter 1980): 391–417 [414].

G109 Firchow, Peter E. "Rico and Julia: The Hilda Doolittle–D. H. Lawrence Affair Reconsidered." *Journal of Modern Literature* 8 (1980): 51–76.

G110 Mandel, Charlotte. "Garbo/Helen: The Self-Projection of Beauty by H.D." *Women's Studies* 7 (1980): 127–35.

G111 Morris, Adelaide. "Reading H.D.'s 'Helios and Athene.'" *Iowa Review* 12 (Spring/Summer 1981): 155–63.

G112 Gehman, Geoff. "The Resurrection of Hilda Doolittle." *Globe-Times* [Bethlehem, Pa.] 18 Sept. 1981: D-1+.

G113 DuPlessis, Rachel Blau, and Susan Stanford Friedman. "'Woman Is Perfect': H.D.'s Debate with Freud." *Feminist Studies* 7 (Fall 1981): 417–30.

G114 Gubar, Susan. "Blessings in Disguise—Cross-Dressing as Re-Dressing for Female Modernists." *Massachusetts Review* 22 (Autumn 1981): [477]–[508] [501–2].

G115 King, Michael. "Go Little Book: Ezra Pound, Hilda Doolittle, and 'Hilda's Book.'" *Paideuma* 10.2 (Fall 1981): [347]–60.

G116 Friedberg, Anne. "Approaching *Borderline*." *Millenium Film Journal* 7–9 (Fall/Winter 1980–81): 130–39.

G117 Auerbach, Nina. "'Magi and Maidens'—The Romance of the Victorian Freud." *Critical Inquiry* 8 (Winter 1981): 281–300 [298–300].

G118 Gubar, Susan. "The Blank Page and the Issue of Female Creativity." *Critical Inquiry* 8 (Winter 1981): 243–63 [254–55].

G119 Duncan, Robert. "From the H.D. Book, Part Two: Nights and Days, Ch. 11." *Montemora* 8 (1981): 79–113.

G120 Friedman, Susan, and Rachel Blau DuPlessis. "'I Had Two Loves Separate': The Sexualities of H.D.'s *Her*." *Montemora* 8 (1981): 7–30.

G121 Rodgers, Martha. "H.D.—A Tribute." *Polis* 2 (1981): 31–33.

G122 Friedman, Susan Stanford, and Rachel Blau Duplessis. "This Fascinating Genius Called H.D." *Ms.* 10 (Feb. 1982): 65–66.

G123 Beck, Joyce Lorraine. "Dea Awakening: A Reading of H.D.'s *Trilogy*." *San Jose Studies* 8 (Spring 1982): 59–70.

G124 French, William. "'Saint Hilda,' Mr. Pound, and Rilke's Parisian Panther at Pisa." *Paideuma* 11.1 (Spring 1982): [79]–87.

G125 Gelpi, Albert. "Hilda in Egypt." *Southern Review* 18 (Spring 1982): 233–50.
Revised and reprinted in *Coming to Light: American Women Poets in the Twentieth Century*, ed. Diane Wood Middlebrook and Marilyn Yalom (Ann Arbor: U of Michigan P, 1985), 74–91.

G126 Kerblat-Blanchney, Jeanne. "'Ce que recèlent les mots' dans *The Walls Do Not Fall*." *Revue Français d'Etudes Américaines* 7 (Nov. 1982): 373–81.

G127 Bernstein, Michael Andre. "Bring It All Back Home: Derivations and Quotations in Robert Duncan and the Poundian Tradition." *Sagetrieb* 1.2 (Fall 1982): 176–89.

G128 Ostriker, Alicia. "The Thieves of Language: Women Poets and Revisionist Mythmaking." *Signs: Journal of Women in Culture and Society* 8 (Autumn 1982): 68–90.

G129 Rasula, Jed. "The Compost Library." *Sagetrieb* 1.2 (Fall 1982): 190–219 [213].

G130 Kumin, Maxine. "'Stamping a Tiny Foot against God': Some American Women Poets between the Two Wars." *Quarterly Journal of the Library of Congress* 39 (Winter 1982): 48–61 [52–55].

G131 Schultz, Robert. "A Detailed Chronology of Ezra Pound's London Years, 1908–1920, Part 1: 1908–1914." *Paideuma* 11.3 (Winter 1982): [456]–72.

G132 Friedberg, Anne. " 'And I Myself Have Learned to Use the Small Projector': On H.D., Woman, History, Recognition." *Wide Angle* 5.2 (1982): 26–31.
Condensed and reprinted in *Telescope* 3.3 (Fall 1984): 171–77.

G133 "Bryher." *Gay News [Literary Supplement]* no. 260 (3–16 March 1983).

G134 Allen, Frank. "Coining New Words: H.D.'s Trilogy of Artistic Growth." *Pennsylvania English* 9.2 (Spring 1983): 19–32.
Includes photographs of Charles Doolittle and Sayre Observatory. Reprinted as "Open Book" in *Seeds of Recognition* by Frank Allen and Margaret Vanderhaar Allen (Bethlehem, Pa.: Friends of H.D., 1984), 9–26.

G135 Gilbert, Susan. "The Rediscovery of H.D." *New York Times Book Review* 7 Aug. 1983: 12+.

G136 Friedman, Susan Stanford. " 'Remembering Shakespeare Always, but Remembering Him Differently': H.D.'s *By Avon River*." *Sagetrieb* 2.2 (Summer–Fall 1983): [45]–70.

G137 Knapp, Peggy A. "Women's Freud(e): H.D.'s *Tribute to Freud* & Gladys Schmitt's *Sonnets for an Analyst*." *Massachusetts Review* 24 (Summer 1983): 338–52.

G138 Materer, Timothy. "H.D., Serenitas, and Canto CXIII." *Paideuma* 12.2–3 (Fall–Winter 1983): [275]–80.

G139 Friedman, Susan Stanford. " 'I go where I love': An Intertextual Study of H.D. and Adrienne Rich." *Signs: Journal of Women in Culture and Society* 9 (Winter 1983): 228–45.
Reprinted in *Coming to Light: American Women Poets in the Twentieth Century*, ed. Diane Wood Middlebrook and Marylin Yalom (Ann Arbor: U of Michigan P, 1985), 233–53.

G140 Arthur, Marilyn. "Psychomythology: The Case of H.D." *Bucknell Review* 28 (1983): 65–79.

G141 Buck, Claire. "H.D. and Freud: Bisexuality and Feminine Discourse." *m/f* 8 (1983): 52–65.

G142 Duncan, Robert. "The H.D. Book: Part 2, Ch. 10." *Ironwood* 22 (1983): 48–64.

G143 Mandel, Charlotte. "The Redirected Image: Cinematic Dynamics in the Style of H.D. (Hilda Doolittle)." *Literature/Film Quarterly* 11 (1983): 36–45.

G144 Ostriker, Alicia. "The Poet as Heroine: Learning to Read H.D." *American Poetry Review* 12.2 (1983): 29–38.
Reprinted in *Writing like a Woman* (Ann Arbor: U of Michigan P, 1983), 7–41.

G145 Howdle, Andrew. "Feminine Hermeticism in H.D.'s *Trilogy*." *Studies in Mystical Literature* 4 (Jan. 1984): 26–44.

G146 Scobey, Katherine. "The Making of a Poet." *New Journal* 16.4 (Feb. 1984): 27–34.

G147 Scalapino, Leslie. "Re-living." *Poetics Journal* 4 (May 1984): 53–55.

G148 Kloepfer, Deborah Kelly. "Flesh Made Word: Maternal Inscription in H.D." *Sagetrieb* 3.1 (Spring 1984): [27]–48.

G149 Wilhelm, James J. "On the Trail of the 'One' Crawfordsville Incident or, the Poet in Hoosierland." *Paideuma* 13 (Spring 1984): [11]–47 [12–14].

G150 Gubar, Susan. "Sapphistries." *Signs: Journal of Women in Culture and Society* 10 (Autumn 1984): 43–62.

G151 Diepeveen, Leonard. "H.D. and the Film Arts." *Journal of Aesthetic Education* 18 (Winter 1984): 57–65.

G152 Jackson, Brendan. "'The Fulsomeness of Her Prolixity': Reflections on 'H.D., "Imagiste."'" *South Atlantic Quarterly* 83 (Winter 1984): 91–102.

G153 Morris, Adelaide. "The Concept of Projection: H.D.'s Visionary Powers." *Contemporary Literature* 25 (Winter 1984): 411–36.

G154 DuPlessis, Rachel Blau. "A Note on the State of H.D.'s *The Gift*." *Sulfur* 9 (1984): 178–82.

G155 Gilbert, Sandra, and Susan Gubar. "Ceremonies of the Alphabet: Female Gramatologies and the Female Authorgraph." *New York Literary Forum* 12 (1984): 23–52 [30–33, 36].

G156 King, Michael. "Williams, Pound, H.D.: A Modern Triangle." *Library Chronicle of the University of Texas at Austin* 29 (1984): 11–33.
Reprinted in *WCW and Others*, ed. Dave Oliphant and Thomas Zigal (Austin, Tex.: Harry Ransom Humanities Research Center, 1985), 86–111.

G157 Smith, Paul. "H.D.'s Identity." *Women's Studies* 10 (1984): 321–37.

G158 Guest, Barbara. "A Poet 'In Exile.'" *Pittsburgh Post-Gazette* 5 March 1985: W–11.

G159 Bawer, Bruce. "H.D. Mother of Us All?" *New Criterion* 2 (March 1984): 63–70.

G160 Camboni, Marina. "H.D.'s *Trilogy*, or the Secret Language of Change." *Litterature d'America: Rivista Trimestrale* 6.27 (Spring 1985): 87–106.

G161 Collecott, Diana. "Remembering Oneself: The Reputation and Later Poetry of H.D." *Critical Quarterly* 27.1 (Spring 1985): 7–22.

G162 Gilbert, Sandra M. "Sexual Linguistics." *New Literary History* 16 (Spring 1985): 515–43 [530].

G163 Pondrom, Cyrena. "H.D. and the Origins of Imagism." *Sagetrieb* 4 (Spring 1985): [73]–97.

G164 Doyle, Charles. "Palimpsests of the Word: The Poetry of H.D." *Queen's Quarterly* 92 (Summer 1985): 310–21.

G165 Duncan, Robert. "From the H.D. Book, Part II, Chapter 5." *Sagetrieb* 4.2/3 (Fall/Winter 1985): [39]–85.
Reprint of items **G65** and **G80**.

G166 Duncan, Robert. "H.D. Book: Book II, Chapter 6" *Southern Review* 21 (Winter 1985): 26–48.

G167 Crawford, Fred D. "Approaches to Biography: Two Studies of H.D." *Review* 7 (1985): 215–38.

G168 Duncan, Robert. "H.D.'s Challenge." *poesis: A Journal of Criticism* 6.3/4 (1985): [19]–34.

G169 Friedman, Susan Stanford. "Palimpsest of Origins in H.D.'s Career." *poesis: A Journal of Criticism* 6.3/4 (1985): [56]–73.

G170 Gelpi, Albert. "Remembering the Mother: A Reading of H.D.'s *Trilogy*." *poesis: A Journal of Criticism* 6.3/4 (1985): [40]–54.

G171 Guest, Barbara. "The Intimacy of Biography." *poesis: A Journal of Criticism* 6.3/4 (1985): [74]–83.

G172 Ostricker, Alicia. "What Do Women (Poets) Want?: Marianne Moore and H.D. as Poetic Ancestresses." *poesis: A Journal of Criticism* 6.3/4 (1985): [1]–9.
Revised and reprinted in *Contemporary Literature* 27.4 (Winter 1986): [475]–92.

G173 Wallace, Emily Mitchell. "Athene's Owl." *poesis: A Journal of Criticism* 6.3/4 (1985): [98]–123.

G174 Dunn, Margaret M. "H.D.'s *Trilogy*: A Portrait of the Artist in Full Bloom." *CEA Critic* 48.3 (Spring 1986): 29–37.

G175 Zajdel, Melody M. "'I See Her Differently': H.D.'s *Trilogy* as Feminist Response to Masculine Modernism." *Sagetrieb* 5.1 (Spring 1986): 7–16.

G176 Collecott, Diana. "H.D." *Women's Review* 11 (Sept. 1986): 46–47.

G177 Smyers, Virginia. "H.D.'s 'New Beginning.'" *HOW(ever)* 3.3 (Oct. 1986): 14.

G178 Collecott, Diana. "Mirror-Images: Images of Mirrors in Poems by Sylvia Plath, Adrienne Rich, Denise Levertov, and H.D." *Revue Français d'Etudes Américaines* 11 (Nov. 1986): 449–60.

G179 Collecott, Diana. "A Double Matrix: Re-reading H.D." *Iowa Review* 16 (Fall 1986): 93–124.

G180 Davis, Dale. "The Matter of Myrrhine for Louis." *Iowa Review* 16 (Fall 1986): 165–73.

G181 Dobson, Silvia. "'Shock Knit within Terror': Living through World War II." *Iowa Review* 16 (Fall 1986): 232–45.

G182 DuPlessis, Rachel Blau. "Language Acquisition." *Iowa Review* 16 (Fall 1986): 252–83.

G183 Friedman, Susan Stanford. "Gender and Genre Anxiety: Elizabeth Barret Browning and H.D. as Epic Poets." *Tulsa Studies in Women's Literature* 5 (Fall 1986): 203–28.

G184 Guest, Barbara. "The Intimacy of Biography." *Iowa Review* 16 (Fall 1986): 58–71.

G185 Morris, Adelaide. "H.D.'s 'H.D. by Delia Alton.'" *Iowa Review* 16 (Fall 1986): 174–78.

G186 Morris, Adelaide. "H.D.'s 'Fortune Teller.'" *Iowa Review* 16 (Fall 1986): 14–17.

G187 Morris, Adelaide. "Introduction [to the H.D. Centennial issue of the *Iowa Review*]." *Iowa Review* 16 (Fall 1986): 1–6.

G188 Schaffner, Perdita. "Running." *Iowa Review* 16 (Fall 1986): 7–13.

G189 Silverstein, Louis. "Reveries of a Cataloguer." *Iowa Review* 16 (Fall 1986): 156–64.

G190 Smith, Paul. "H.D.'s Flaws." *Iowa Review* 16 (Fall 1986): 77–86.

G191 Zajdel, Melody. "Portrait of an Artist as a Woman: H.D.'s Raymonde Ransome." *Women's Studies* 13 (Fall 1986): 127–34.

G192 Baccolini, Raffaella. "Pound's Tribute to H.D., 1961." *Contemporary Literature* 27 (Winter 1986): [435]–39.

G193 Friedman, Susan Stanford, and Rachel Blau DuPlesis. "Foreword [to *Paint It Today*]." *Contemporary Literature* 27 (Winter 1986): [440]–43.

G194 Friedman, Susan Stanford, and Rachel Blau DuPlessis. "H.D.: Centennial Issue." *Contemporary Literature* 27 (Winter 1986): [433]–34.

G195 Gregory, Eileen. "Rose Cut in Rock: Sappho and H.D.'s *Sea Garden*." *Contemporary Literature* 27 (Winter 1986): [525]–52.

G196 Kloepfer, Deborah Kelly. "Fishing the Murex Up: Sense and Resonance in H.D.'s *Palimpsest*." *Contemporary Literature* 27 (Winter 1986): [553]–73.

G197 Milicia, Joseph. "H.D.'s 'Athenians': Son and Mother in *Hedylus*." *Contemporary Literature* 27 (Winter 1986): [574]–94.

G198 Morris, Adelaide. "A Relay of Power and of Peace: H.D. and the Spirit of *The Gift*." *Contemporary Literature* 27 (Winter 1986): [493]–524.

G199 Rasula, Jed. "Rails Gone for Guns." *Zonë* 1 (Winter 1986): 107–20.

G200 Augustine, Jane. "Logos and Etymologies in H.D.'s 'Trilogy.'" *ninth decade* 7 (1986): 38–45.

G201 Hirsh, Elizabeth A. "New Eyes: H.D., Modernism, and the Psychology of Seeing." *Literature and Psychology* 32 (1986): 1–10.

G202 Spicher, Julia. "Wind in the Garden—A Reading of H.D.'s *Sea Garden*." *Mandorla, the Minetta Review* 1986: 88–98.

G203 Burnett, Gary. "H.D. and Lawrence: Two Allusions." *H.D. Newsletter* 1 (Spring 1987): [32]–35.

G204 Friedman, Susan Stanford. "H.D. Chronology: Composition and Publication of Volumes." *H.D. Newsletter* 1 (Spring 1987): [12]–15.

G205 Gregory, Eileen. "Ovid and H.D.'s 'Thetis' (*Hymen* Version)." *H.D. Newsletter* 1 (Spring 1987): [29]–31.

G206 Silverstein, Louis. "The H.D. Papers at Yale University." *H.D. Newletter* 1 (Spring 1987): [7]–9.

G207 Wallace, Emily Mitchell. "Hilda Doolittle at Friends' Central School in 1905." *H.D. Newsletter* 1 (Spring 1987): [17]–28.

G208 Sutton, Walter. "*Trilogy* and *The Pisan Cantos*: The Shock of War." *Sagetrieb* 6 (Spring 1987): 41–52.

G209 Boone, Bruce. "H.D.'s Writing: Herself a Ghost." *Sagetrieb* 6 (Fall 1987): [17]–19.

G210 Boughn, Michael. "Elements of the Sounding: H.D. and the Origins of Modernist Prosodies." *Sagetrieb* 6 (Fall 1987): [101]–22.

G211 Boughn, Michael. "The Bibliographic Record of H.D.'s Contributions to Periodicals." *Sagetrieb* 6 (Fall 1987): [171]–94.

G212 Creeley, Robert. "H.D." *Sagetrieb* 6 (Fall 1987): [15]–16.

G213 Dahlen, Beverly. "Homonymous: A Meditation on H.D.'s *Trilogy*." *Sagetrieb* 6 (Fall 1987): [9]–13.

G214 Dawson, F[ielding]. "On H.D." *Sagetrieb* 6 (Fall 1987): [21]–25.

G215 Faery, Rebecca Blevins. "Love Is Writing': Eros in H.D.'s *Hermione*." *San Jose Studies* 13 (Fall 1987): 56–65.

G216 Finch, Annie R. C. "H.D., 'Imagiste?'" *Cumberland Poetry Review* 7 (Fall 1987): 36–45.

G217 Friedman, Susan Stanford. "H.D. Chronology: Composition and Publication of Volumes." *Sagetrieb* 6 (Fall 1987): 51–55.

G218 Goheen, Cynthia J. "By Impression Re-Called." *San Jose Studies* 13 (Fall 1987): 47–55.

G219 Gregory, Eileen. "Scarlet Experience: H.D.'s *Hymen*." *Sagetrieb* 6 (Fall 1987): [77]–100.

G220 Hansen, Jorgen Christian. "H.D. *Palimpsest*: En introduktion." *Publication on English Themes* 5 (1987): 52–56.

G221 Hatlen, Burton. "Recovering the Human Equation: H.D.'s 'Hermetic Definition.'" *Sagetrieb* 6 (Fall 1987): [141]–69.

G222 King-Smyth, Rosie. "The Spell of the Luxor Bee." *San Jose Studies* 13 (Fall 1987): 77–87.

G223 Kolokithas, Dawn. "The Pursuit of Spirituality in the Poetry of H.D." *San Jose Studies* 13 (Fall 1987): 66–76.

G224 Laity, Cassandra. "H.D.'s Romantic Landscapes: The Sexual Politics of the Garden." *Sagetrieb* 6 (Fall 1987): 57–75.

G225 Larsen, Jeanne. "Myth and Glyph in *Helen in Egypt*." *San Jose Studies* 13 (Fall 1987): 88–101.

G226 Travis, S. "A Crack in the Ice: Subjectivity and the Mirror in H.D.'s *Her*." *Sagetrieb* 6 (Fall 1987): [123]–40.

G227 Schmidt, G. "Doolittle's *The Walls Do Not Fall.*" *Explicator* 46 (Fall 1987): 46.

G228 Dobson, Silvia. "Clouds of Memories: Books H.D. Shared with Me, 1934–1960." *H.D. Newsletter* 1 (Winter 1987): [26]–41.

G229 Mandel, Charlotte. "H.D.'s 'Projector II' and *Chang, a Film of the Jungle.*" *H.D. Newsletter* 1 (Winter 1987): [42]–45.

G230 Olgivie, D. Bruce. "H.D. and Hugh Dowding." *H.D. Newsletter* 1 (Winter 1987): [9]–17.

G231 Roessel, David. "H.D. and Lawrence: Two More Allusions." *H.D. Newsletter* 1 (Winter 1987): [46]–50.

G232 Smyers, Virginia. "H.D.'s Books in the Bryher Library." *H.D. Newsletter* 1 (Winter 1987): [18]–25.

G233 Silverstein, Louis. "Nicknames and Acronyms Used by H.D. and Her Circle." *H.D. Newsletter* 1 (Winter 1987): [4]–5.

G234 Crawford, Fred D. "Misleading Accounts of Aldington and H.D." *English Literature in Transition (1880–1920)* 30 (1987): 49–67.

G235 Dunn, Margaret M. "Altered Patterns and New Endings: Reflections of Change in Stein's *Three Lives* and H.D.'s *Palimpsest.*" *Frontiers: A Journal of Women Studies* 9 (1987): 54–59.

G236 Friedman, Susan Stanford. "Against Discipleship: Collaboration and Intimacy in the Relationship of H.D. and Freud." *Literature and Psychology* 33.3–4 (1987): 89–108.

G237 Lucas, Rose. "Re(reading)-Writing the Palimpsest of Myth." *Southern Review: Literary and Interdisciplinary Essays* 21 (March 1988): 43–57.

G238 Duncan, Robert. "A Note on *The H.D. Book.*" *H.D. Newsletter* 2 (Spring 1988): [6]–7.

G239 Bergman, David. "The Economics of Influence: Gift Giving in H.D. and Robert Duncan." *H.D. Newsletter* 2 (Spring 1988): [11]–16.

G240 Brown, Chris. "A Filmography for H.D." *H.D. Newsletter* 2 (Spring 1988): [19]–24.

G241 Boughn, Michael. "The Bibliographic Record of Reviews of H.D.'s Work." *H.D. Newsletter* 2 (Spring 1988): [27]–47.

G242 Smith, Martha Nell. "Not Each in Isolation." *H.D. Newsletter* 2 (Spring 1988): [48]–51.

G243 Copeland, Donna. "Doolittle's 'Helen.'" *Explicator* 46 (Summer 1988): 33–35.

G244 Ahearn, Barry. "Williams and H.D., or Sour Grapes." *Twentieth Century Literature* 35 (Fall 1988): 299–309.

G245 Roche, Judith. "Myrrh: A Study of Persona in H.D.'s *Trilogy.*" *line* 12 (Fall 1988): 63–110.

G246 Fromm, Gloria G. "The Forging of H.D." *Poetry* 153 (Dec. 1988): 160–72.

G247 Friedman, Susan Stanford. "The Writing Cure: Transference and Resistance in a Dialogic Analysis." *H.D. Newsletter* 2 (Winter 1988): 25–35.

G248 Schoeck, R. J. "Listening to Stones: Reflections on H.D.'s *The Walls Do Not Fall*." *H.D. Newsletter* 2 (Winter 1988): 15–24.

G249 Silverstein, Louis H. "Planting the Seeds: Selections from the H.D. Chronology." *H.D. Newsletter* 2 (Winter 1988): 4–14.

G250 Vanacker, Sabine. "Stein, Richardson, and H.D." *Bête Noir* 6 (Winter 1988): 111–23.

G251 Burnett, Gary. "A Poetics out of War: H.D.'s Responses to the First World War." *Agenda* 25.3–4 (1988): 54–63.

G252 Bruzzi, Zara. "'The Fiery Moment': H.D. and the Eleusinian Landscape of English Modernism." *Agenda* 25.3–4 (1988): 97–112.

G253 Collecott, Diana. "Editorial." *Agenda* 25.3–4 (1988): 3–7.

G254 Collecott, Diana. "Memory and Desire: H.D.'s 'A Note on Poetry.'" *Agenda* 25.3–4 (1988): 64–70.

G255 Dobson, Sylvia. "Remembering H.D." *Agenda* 25.3–4 (1988): 126–44.

G256 Friedman, Susan Stanford. "Exile in the American Grain: H.D.'s Diaspora." *Agenda* 25.3–4 (1988): 27–50.
Reprinted in *Alien and Critical: Women Writers in Exile*, ed. Mary Lynn Broe and Angela Ingram (Durham, N.C.: U of North Carolina P, 1988).

G257 Gregory, Eileen. "Falling from the White Rock: A Myth of Margins in H.D." *Agenda* 25.3–4 (1988): 113–23.

G258 Montefiore, Jan. "'What Words Say': Three Women Poets Reading H.D." *Agenda* 25.3–4 (1988): 172–90.

G259 Moody, A. D. "H.D., 'Imagiste': An Elemental Mind." *Agenda* 25.3–4 (1988): 77–96.

G260 Ostriker, Alicia. "No Rule of Procedure: The Open Poetics of H.D." *Agenda* 25.3–4 (1988): 145–54.

G261 Pondrom, Cyrena N. "*Trilogy* and the *Four Quartets*: Contrapuntal Visions of Spiritual Quest." *Agenda* 25.3–4 (1988): 155–65.

G262 Renaux, Sigrid. "H.D.'s 'Oread': A Linguistic Approach." *Revista Letras* 37 (1988): 81–98.

G263 Smith, Penny. "Hilda Doolittle and Frances Gregg." *Powys Review* 6.2 (1988): 46–51.

G264 Walsh, John. "Introduction: 'Water Flows Uphill.'" *Agenda* 25.3–4 (1988): 10–13.
Introduction to H.D.'s "Prose Corybantic" and "Four Prose Choruses."

G265 Renaux, Sigrid. "H.D.'s 'Lethe': A Linguistic Approach." *Estudos Anglo-Americanos* 12–13 (1988–89): 30–41.

G266 Campbell, Bruce. "H.D.'s 'Hermetic Definition' and the Order of Writing." *American Poetry* 6.3 (Spring 1989): 15–21.

G267 Gardiner, Jeffrey. "Dionysian Presences." *American Poetry* 6.3 (Spring 1989): 2–14.

G268 Zilboorg, Caroline. "A New Chapter in the Lives of H.D. and Richard Aldington: Their Relationship with Clement Shorter." *Philological Quarterly* 68 (Spring 1989): 241–62.

G269 Zilboorg, Caroline. "Two Poems for H.D." *Journal of Modern Literature* 16.1 (Summer 1989): 174–77.

G270 Jarnot, Lisa. "H.D. and the Poetics of Revelation." *intent.* 1.3 (Fall 1989): 2–4.

G271 Schaum, Melita. "Lyric Resistance: Views of the Political in the Poetics of Wallace Stevens and H.D." *Wallace Stevens Journal: A Publication of the Wallace Stevens Society* 13 (Fall 1989): 191–205.

G272 Laity, Cassandra. "H.D. and A. C. Swinburne: Decadence and Modernist Women's Writing." *Feminist Studies* 15 (Fall 1989): 461–84.
Reprinted as "H.D. and A. C. Swinburne: Decadence and Sapphic Modernism" in *Lesbian Texts and Contexts: Radical Revisions*, ed. Karla Jay, Joanne Glasgow, and Catharine R. Stimpson (New York: New York UP, 1990).

G273 Witte, Sarah E. "H.D.'s Recension of the Egyptian Book of the Dead in *Palimpsest*." *Sagetrieb* 8.1–2 (Spring–Fall 1989): 121–47.

G274 Burnett, Gary. "The Identity of 'H': Imagism and H.D.'s *Sea Garden*." *Sagetrieb* 8.3 (Winter 1989): 55–75.

G275 Sword, Helen. "Orpheus and Eurydice in the Twentieth Century: Lawrence, H.D., and the Poetics of the Turn." *Twentieth Century Literature* 35.4 (Winter 1989): 407–28.

G276 Zilboorg, Caroline. "Letters across the Abyss: The H.D.–Adrienne Monnier Correspondence." *Sagetrieb* 8.3 (Winter 1989): 115–34.

G277 Collecott, Diana. "H.D. and Mass Observation." *line* 13 (1989): 153–61.

G278 Chisholm, Dianne. "H.D.'s Autoheterography." *Tulsa Studies in Women's Literature* 9.1 (Spring 1990): 79–106.

G279 Collecott, Diana. "What Is Not Said: A Study in Textual Inversion." *Textual Practice* 4.2 (June 1990): 236–58.

G280 Fuchs, Miriam. "H.D.'s Self-Inscription: Between Time and 'Out of Time' in *The Gift*." *Southern Review* 26.3 (July 1990): 542–54.

G281 Gregory, Eileen. "Virginity and Erotic Liminality: H.D.'s *Hippolytus Temporizes*." *Contemporary Literature* 32.2 (Summer 1990): 133–60.

G282   Hughes, Gertrude Reif. "Making It Really New: Hilda Doolittle, Gwendolyn Brooks, and the Feminist Potential of Modern Poetry." *American Quarterly* 42 (September 1990): 375–402.

G283   Augustine, Jane. "Modernist Moravianism: H.D.'s Unpublished Novel *The Mystery*." *Sagetrieb* 9.1–2 (Spring/Fall 1990): 65–78.

G284   Shugar, Dana. "Faustine Re-Membered: H.D.'s Use of Swinburne's Poetry in *Hermione*." *Sagetrieb* 9.1–2 (Spring–Fall 1990): 79–94.

G285   Camboni, Marina. "Time in a Room: H.D.'s *Bid Me to Live*." *RSA, Journal of American Studies* 1 (1990).

G286   Collecott, Diana. "H.D.'s 'Gift of Greek,' Bryher's 'Eros of the Sea.'" *H.D. Newsletter* 3.1 (1990): [11]–14.

G287   Smyers, Virginia. "'Classical' Books in the Bryher Library." *H.D. Newsletter* 3.1 (1990): [15]–25.

G288   Zilboorg, Caroline. "H.D. and R.A.: Early Love and the Exclusion of Ezra Pound." *H.D. Newsletter* 3.1 (1990): [26]–34.

G289   Spoo, Robert. "'Authentic Sisters': H.D. and Margaret Cravens." *H.D. Newsletter* 3.1 (1990): [35]–43.

G290   Gregory, Eileen. "H.D.'s Volumes of Dickinson's Poems; and, A Note on Candor and Iniquity." *H.D. Newsletter* 3.1 (1990): [44]–46.

G291   Babcock, Robert. "H.D.'s 'Pursuit' and Sappho." *H.D. Newsletter* 3.2 (1990): [43]–47.

G292   Brown, Chris. "H.D. and Rummel's *Songs for Children*: A Lyrical Collaboration." *H.D. Newsletter* 3.2 (1990): 4–11.
       See also C177.

G293   Roessel, David. "H.D.'s Troy: Some Bearings." *H.D. Newsletter* 3.2 (1990): [38]–42.

G294   Augustine, Jane. "*The Mystery* Unveiled: The Significance of H.D.'s 'Moravian' Novel." *H.D. Newsletter* 4.1 (Spring 1991): [9]–17.

G295   Clack, Jerry. "Helen in Vienna." *H.D. Newsletter* 4.1 (Spring 1991): [27]–31.

G296   Hengen, Shannon. "H.D.'s *Prosodie à clef*: St. John Perse and *Hermetic Definition*." *H.D. Newsletter* 4.1 (Spring 1991): [32]–36.

G297   Hollenberg, Donna Krolik, and Louis H. Silverstein. "The Challenge of Editing the H.D.-Pearson Correspondence." *H.D. Newsletter* 4.1 (Spring 1991): [18]–26.

G298   Williams, Henry L. "H.D.'s Moravian Heritage." *H.D. Newsletter* 4.1 (Spring 1991): [4]–8.

Miscellanea

G299   *New Canterbury Literary Society Newsletter* 9 (Winter 1981–82): 1. Note on publication of *HERmione*.

G300 *New Canterbury Literary Society Newsletter* 10 (Summer 1982): 1.
Discusses Frank Allen's review of Robinson. See **F582**

G301 *New Canterbury Literary Society Newsletter* 10 (Autumn 1982): 1.
Discusses review of *Collected Poems, 1912–1944* in *American Book Review*.

G302 *New Canterbury Literary Society Newsletter* 12.1 (Spring 1984): 1.
Discusses Robinson (**H181**), Friedman (**H172**), and *Collected Poems, 1912–1944*.

G303 *New Canterbury Literary Society Newsletter* 12.3 (Autumn 1984): 3–4.
Discusses Robinson and Martz's criticism of H.D. in the introduction to *Collected Poems, 1912–1944*.

G304 [Wilkerson, David J.] *New Canterbury Literary Society Newsletter* 14 (Summer 1986): 4.
Discusses Fred J. Crawford's presentation on "Richard Aldington and H.D."

G305 Freidberg, Anne. "The Pool Films." *H.D. Newsletter* 1 (Spring 1987): [10]–11.

Addenda

G306 Gelpi, Albert. "Two Ways of Spelling It Out: An Archetypal-Feminist Reading of H.D.'s *Trilogy* and Adrienne Rich's *Sources*." *Southern Review* 26.2 (Spring 1990): 266–84.

G307 Hogue, Cynthia. "(Re)Placing Woman: The Politics and Poetics of Gender in H.D.'s *Helen in Egypt*." *American Poetry* 8 (Fall 1990): 87–99.

H

Books and Parts of Books about H.D.

H1 Lowell, Amy. *Tendencies in Modern American Poetry.* New York: Macmillan, 1917. Pp. 235–43.

H2 Aiken, Conrad. *Skepticisms.* New York: Alfred Knopf, 1919. Pp. 92–93.

H3 Untermeyer, Louis. "H.D. and the Imagists." *The New Era in American Poetry.* New York: Henry Holt, 1919. Pp. 291–308.

H4 Waugh, Arthur. *Tradition and Change: Studies in Contemporary Literature.* London: Chapman and Hall, 1919. P. 126.

H5 Wilkinson, Marguerite. *New Voices: An Introduction to Contemporary Poetry.* New York: Macmillan, 1919. Pp. 88–90, 102–4.
Revised 1936 edition contains further discussion of H.D. on pp. 410, 417.

H6 Eliot, T. S. "Euripides and Professor Murray." *The Sacred Wood.* London: Methuen, 1920. Pp. 64–70 [69–70].

H7 Monro, Harold. *Some Contemporary Poets (1920).* London: Leonard Parsons, 1920. Pp. 101–4.

H8 Heuffer, Ford Maddox. *Thus to Revisit: Some Reminiscences.* New York: E. P. Dutton, 1921. Pp. 9, 64, 104, 136, 157, 162, 163, 166, 171, 197.

H9 [Lowell, Amy]. *A Critical Fable.* Boston: Houghton Mifflin, 1922. Pp. 52–54.

H10 Cook, Howard Willard. *Our Poets of Today.* New York: Moffat, Yard, 1923. Pp. 255–58.

H11 Haney, John Louis. *The Story of Our Literature.* New York: Charles Scribner's Sons, 1923. Pp. 231–32.

H12 Untermeyer, Louis. "H.D." *American Poetry since 1900.* New York: Henry Holt, 1923. Pp. 309–16.

H13 Weirick, Bruce. *From Whitman to Sandburg in American Poetry: A Critical Survey.* New York: Macmillan, 1924. Pp. 155–56.
H.D. is mistakenly referred to as "Helena Doolittle."

H14 Collins, H. P. "H.D.'s Method" and "The Position of H.D." *Modern Poetry*. New York: Houghton Mifflin, 1925. Pp. 154–86, 187–202.

H15 Monroe, Harriet. "H.D." *Poets and Their Art*. New York: Macmillan, 1926. Pp. 92–99.

H16 Moore, Marianne "'NEW' Poetry since 1912." *Anthology of Magazine Verse for 1926*. Ed. William Stanley Braithwaite. Boston: B. J. Brimmer Co., 1926. Pp. 172–79.

H17 Richards, I. A. *Principles of Literary Criticism*. London: Routledge and Kegan Paul, 1926. Pp. 199–200.
Reprinted in Norman C. Stagberg and Wallace L. Anderson, *Poetry as Experience* (New York: American Book Co., 1952), 28–29.

H18 Untermeyer, Louis. *Collected Parodies*. New York: Harcourt Brace, 1926. Pp. 47, 313.

H19 Fairclough, Henry Rushton. *The Classics and Our Twentieth Century Poets*. Stanford, Calif.: Stanford UP, 1927. Pp. 31–37.
Reprinted New York: AMS Press, 1967.

H20 Vines, Sherard. *Movements in Modern English Poetry and Prose*. Oxford: Oxford UP, 1927. Pp. 64, 69, 70, 226.
Reprinted Folcroft Library Editions, 1970.

H21 Kreymborg, Alfred. *Our Singing Strength*. New York: Coward-McCann, 1929. Pp. 347–53 and passim.

H22 Taupin, René. *L'influence du symbolisme français sur la poésie américaine (de 1910 à 1920)*. Paris: Librarie Ancienne Honoré Champion, 1929. Pp. 100–105, 158–65.
Translated by William Pratt and Anne Rich Pratt as *The Influence of French Symbolism in Modern American Poetry* (New York: AMS Press, 1985).

H23 Lowell, Amy. *Poetry and Poets—Essays*. Boston: Houghton Mifflin, 1930. P. 117 and passim.

H24 Hughes, Glenn. "H.D.: The Perfect Imagist." *Imagism and the Imagists: A Study in Modern Poetry*. Stanford, Calif.: Stanford UP, 1931. Pp. 109–24.
Reprints a letter from H.D. to Glenn Hughes, pp. 110–11.

H25 Lewisohn, Ludwig. *The Story of American Literature*. New York: Modern Library, 1932. Pp. 375, 377, 386.

H26 Bullough, Geoffrey. *The Trend of Modern Poetry*. London: Oliver and Boyd, 1934. Pp. 76–77.

H27 Vocadlo, Otakar. *Soucasna literatura spojenych statu—odzvoleni presidenta Wilsona po velkou hospodarskou krisi*. Praze: Vydal Jan Laichter, 1934. Pp. 69–72 and passim.

H28 Cournos, John. *Autobiography*. New York: G. P. Putnam, 1935. Pp. 268–69, 273, and passim.

H29 Damon, S. Foster. *Amy Lowell*. Boston: Houghton Mifflin, 1935. Passim.

H30 Deutsch, Babette. *This Modern Poetry*. New York: W. W. Norton, 1935. Pp. 64–69.

H31 Whitall, James. *English Years*. New York: Harcourt, 1935. Pp. 54–58, 177–79, and passim.

H32 Bush, Douglas. *Mythology and the Romantic Tradition in English Poetry*. Cambridge: Harvard UP, 1937. Pp. 497–506.

H33 Fletcher, John Gould. *Life Is My Song*. New York: Farrar & Rinehart, 1937. Pp. 77–81, 146–50, and passim.

H34 Gilkes, Martin. *A Key to Modern English Poetry*. London: Blackie & Son, 1937. Pp. 48–49.

H35 Brooks, Cleanth, and Robert Penn Warren. *Understanding Poetry*. New York: Holt, Rinehart and Winston, 1938. Pp. 86–88.

H36 McAlmon, Robert. *Being Geniuses Together*. London: Secker and Warburg, 1938. Passim.
Revised and reprinted with extra material by Kay Boyle (New York: Doubleday, 1968; San Francisco: North Point Press, 1984).

H37 Monroe, Harriet. *A Poet's Life—Seventy Years in a Changing World*. New York: Macmillan, 1938. Passim.

H38 Palmer, Herbert. *Post-Victorian Poetry*. London: J. M. Dent & Sons, 1938. Pp. 325–29.

H39 Fairchild, Hoxie Neale. *Religious Trends in English Poetry*. 7 vols. 1939; reprinted New York and London: Columbia UP, 1962. 5:461–66. See also 7:283–86.

H40 Untermeyer, Louis. *From Another World: The Autobiography of Louis Untermeyer*. New York: Harcourt, Brace, 1939. Pp. 107–8, 113, 319.
Quotes letter from H.D. regarding Amy Lowell, p. 113.

H41 Berti, Luigi. "H.D." *Boccaporto*. 2 vols. Firenze: Parenti, 1940. 1:185–91.

H42 Fletcher, John Gould. "Hilda Doolittle." *We Moderns*. Gotham Book Mart Catalogue No. 42. New York: Gotham Book Mart, 1940. P. 22.

H43 Millet, Fred. *Contemporary American Authors*. New York: Harcourt, Brace, 1940. Pp. 72, 143, 328–29.
Reprinted by AMS Press, 1970.

H44 Aldington, Richard. *Life for Life's Sake*. New York: Viking, 1941. Pp. 111–12, 134–39, and passim.

H45 Cargill, Oscar. *Intellectual America—Ideas on the March*. New York: Macmillan, 1941. Pp. 245–47.

H46 Daniels, Earl. *The Art of Reading Poetry*. New York: Farrar and Rinehart, 1941. Pp. 195–99.
Reprinted in Norman C. Stagberg and Wallace L. Anderson, *Poetry as Experience* (New York: American Book Co., 1952), 28–29.

H47 Kunitz, Stanley. *Twentieth Century Authors.* New York: H. W. Wilson Company, 1942. P. 391.
Also appears in the first supplement, p. 283.

H48 Berti, Luigi. *L'imagismo, con una piccola antologia.* Padona: Cedam, 1944. Pp. 57–61 and passim.

H49 Tate, Allen. *Sixty American Poets, 1896–1944.* Washington, D.C.: Library of Congress, 1945. Pp. 5–7.

H50 Gregory, Horace, and Marya Zaturenska. *A History of American Poetry, 1900–1940.* New York: Harcourt, Brace & Co., 1946. Pp. 192–200.

H51 Winters, Ivor. *In Defense of Reason.* Denver: Alan Swallows, 1947. Pp. 51, 118–19, and passim.

H52 Le Breton, Maurice, ed. *Anthologie de la poésie américaine contemporaine.* Paris: Les Editions Denöel, 1948. Pp. 28–29, 50–51. See also **D5**.

H53 Paige, D. D. *The Letters of Ezra Pound, 1907–1941.* New York: Harcourt, Brace, 1950. Passim.

H54 Rajan, B. "Imagism: A Reconsideration." *Modern American Poetry.* Ed. B. Rajan. London: Dennis Dobson, 1950. Pp. 81–94.

H55 Coffman, Stanley. *Imagism: A Chapter for the History of Modern Poetry.* Norman: U of Oklahoma P, 1951. Pp. 145–48 and passim.

H56 Sergeant, Howard. *Tradition in the Making of Modern Poetry.* London: Britannicus Liber Ltd., 1951. 100–109.

H57 Williams, William Carlos. *The Autobiography of William Carlos Williams.* New York: Random House, 1951. Pp. 67–70 and passim.

H58 Deutsch, Babette. *Poetry in Our Time.* New York: Henry Holt & Co., 1952. Pp. 96–99.

H59 Watts, Harold H. "H.D. and the Age of Myth." *Hound and Quarry.* London: Routledge and Kegan Paul, 1953. Pp. 209–22. Reprinted from *Sewanee Review.* See **G34**.

H60 Brown, John, ed. *Panorama de la littérature contemporaine aux Etats-Unis.* Paris: Georges Lang, 1954. Pp. 253–54. Reprints "Oread" in French and English.

H61 Moore, Harry T. *The Intelligent Heart—The Story of D. H. Lawrence.* New York: Farrar, Straus and Young, 1954. Pp. 230, 236, 237, 240, 248, 414–15.
Revised and reprinted as *The Priest of Love.* New York: Farrar, Straus and Giroux, 1974.

H62 Moore, Merrill. Foreword. *Tribute to Freud.* By H.D. New York: Pantheon Books, 1956. Pp. vii–ix.

H63 DeFord, Sara. *Lectures on Modern Poetry.* Tokyo: Hokuseido Press, 1957. Pp. 95–101.

H64 Nehls, Edward. *D. H. Lawrence: A Composite Biography.* Vol. 1. Madison: U of Wisconsin P, 1957. Passim.

H65 Aiken, Conrad. *A Reviewer's ABC.* New York: Meridian Books, 1958. Pp. 154–55.

H66 Gregory, Horace. *Amy Lowell—Portrait of the Poet in Her Time.* New York: Thomas Nelson, 1958. Pp. 80–87, 110–15, and passim.

H67 Butler, E[liza] M[arian]. *Paper Boats.* London: Collins, 1959. Pp. 183–84.

H68 Ciardi, John. *How Does a Poem Mean.* Boston: Houghton Mifflin, 1959. P. 975.

H69 Nehls, Edward. *D. H. Lawrence: A Composite Biography.* Vol. 3. Madison: U of Wisconsin P, 1959. Passim.

H70 Pearson, Norman Holmes. "H.D." *Phoenix Profiles.* Bryn Mawr, Pa.: Bryn Mawr College, 1959. Pp. [8]–[9].
Pamphlet printed on the occasion of the fiftieth reunion of the class of 1909. Pearson's article reprinted in the *Encyclopedia Americana.*

H71 Selver, Paul. *Orage and the New Age Circle: Reminiscences and Reflections.* London: George Allen & Unwin, 1959. P. 35.

H72 Norman, Charles. *Ezra Pound.* New York: Macmillan, 1960. Pp. 4–6, 88–91, and passim.

H73 Carne-Ross, D. S. "Translation and Transposition." *The Craft and Context of Translation.* Ed. William Arrowsmith and Roger Shattuck. Austin: U of Texas P, 1961. Pp. 3–21.
Reprinted Garden City, N.Y.: Anchor Books, 1964.

H74 Gregory, Horace. Introduction. *Helen in Egypt.* By H.D. New York: Grove Press, 1961. Pp. vii–xi.

H75 Rexroth, Kenneth. "The Poet as Translator." *The Craft and Context of Translation.* Ed. William Arrowsmith and Roger Shattuck. Austin: U of Texas P, 1961. Pp. 22–37.
Reprinted Garden City, N.Y.: Anchor Books, 1964.

H76 Bryher, [Winifred]. *The Heart to Artemis—A Writer's Memoirs.* New York: Harcourt, Brace & World, 1962. Pp. 182–83, 196–98, 189–92, 196–202, 241–42, 261–62, 270–71, and passim.

H77 Knoll, Robert E., ed. *Robert McAlmon and the Lost Generation: A Self Portrait.* Lincoln: U of Nebraska P, 1962. Passim.

H78 Swann, Thomas Burnett. *The Classical World of H.D.* Lincoln: U of Nebraska P, 1962.
Reviewed by Frederic Will, *JEGP* 63.1 (Jan. 1964): 179–81. See also **F573–74**.

H79 Coffman, Stanley. "Imagism." *The Concise Encyclopedia of English and American Poetry.* Ed. Stephen Spender and Donald Hall. London: Hutchison, 1963.

H80 Pratt, William. Introduction. *The Imagist Poem.* New York: Dutton, 1963. Pp. 11–39.

H81 Spiller, Robert E., et al., eds. *The Literary History of the United States.* 3d ed. New York: Macmillan, 1963. Pp. 1187, 1188–89.

H82 Gross, Harvey. *Sound and Form in Modern Poetry: A Study of Prosody from Thomas Hardy to Robert Lowell.* Ann Arbor: U of Michigan P, 1964. Pp. 105–12.

H83 Stead, C. K. *The New Poets.* London: Hutchinson UP, 1964. Pp. 101–14.

H84 Ward, A. C. *Twentieth-Century English Literature, 1901–1960.* 1928, 1940. New York: Barnes and Noble, 1964. Pp. 188–89.

H85 Hutchins, Patricia. *Ezra Pound's Kensington.* London: Faber and Faber, 1965. Pp. 35–36, 69, 130, 134–35, 156.

H86 Moore, Harry T. *Richard Aldington: An Intimate Portrait.* Ed. Alister Kershaw and Frédéric-Jacques Temple. Carbondale: Southern Illinois UP, 1965. Pp. 80–105.

H87 Randall, Sir Alec. *Richard Aldington: An Intimate Portrait.* Ed. Alister Kershaw and Frederic-Jacques Temple. Carbondale: Southern Illinois UP, 1965. Pp. 110–21.

H88 Untermeyer, Jean Starr. *Private Collection.* New York: Alfred A. Knopf, 1965. Pp. 84–86.

H89 Dembo, L. S. "Imagism and Aesthetic Mysticism." *Conceptions of Reality in Modern American Poetry.* Berkeley and Los Angeles: U of California P, 1966. Pp. 10–41 and passim.

H90 Fletcher, Ian. "Some Anticipations of Imagism." *A Catalogue of the Imagist Poets.* New York: J. Howard Woolmer, 1966. Pp. 39–53.

H91 Goodwin, K. L. *The Influence of Ezra Pound.* London: Oxford UP, 1966. Pp. 9–13, 15–16, 189–95, and passim.
Reprints excerpts from a letter from H.D. to Glen Hughes, originally printed in *Imagism and the Imagists: A Study in Modern Poetry* (Stanford, Calif.: Stanford UP, 1931), 110–11.

H92 Moore, Harry T., and Warren Roberts. *D. H. Lawrence and His World.* New York: Viking, 1966. P. 60.

H93 Kaufman, J. Lee. *Encyclopedia of World Literature in the Twentieth Century.* Ed. Wolfgang Bernard Fleischman. 4 vols. New York: Fredrick Ungar, 1967. 1:293.

H94 Reck, Michael. *Ezra Pound—A Close-Up.* New York: McGraw-Hill, 1967. Pp. 8–10, 19–20.

H95 Quinn, Vincent. *Hilda Doolittle.* New York: Twayne, 1967.

H96 Weatherhead, A. Kingsley. *The Edge of the Image: Marianne Moore, William Carlos Williams, and Some Other Poets.* Seattle: U of Washington P, 1967. Pp. 16–17, 144. Includes "Oread."

H97 Bruccoli, Matthew. "A Note on the Text." *Palimpsest.* By H.D. Carbondale: Southern Illinois UP, 1968. Pp. 245–68.

H98 Lucas, Frank L. "Turtle and Mock-Turtle." *Authors Dead & Living.* New York: Macmillan, 1926. Pp. 217–23.
Review of *Heliodora* reprinted from the *New Statesman.* See **F36**. Reprinted Freeport, N.Y.: Books for Libraries Press, 1968.

H99 McAlmon, Robert. "Forewarned as Regards H.D.'s Prose." *Palimpsest.* By H.D. Carbondale: Southern Illinois UP, 1968. Pp. 241–44.

H100 Moore, Harry T. Preface. *Palimpsest.* By H.D. Carbondale: Southern Illinois UP, 1968. Pp. vii–ix.

H101 Patmore, Brigit. *My Friends When Young.* London: Heinemann, 1968. Passim.

H102 Waggoner, Hyatt H. *American Poets from the Puritans to the Present.* Boston: Houghton Mifflin, 1968. Pp. 358–64, 683–84.

H103 Delavenay, Emile. *D. H. Lawrence: L'homme et la genèse de son oeuvre: Les années de formation, 1885–1919.* 2 vols. Paris: Librarie Klincksieck, 1969. Passim.
Translated by Katharine Delavenay as *D. H. Lawrence: The Man and His Work: The Formative Years, 1885–1919.* London: Heinemann, 1972.

H104 Hamburger, Michael. *The Truth of Poetry: Tensions in Modern Poetry from Baudelaire to the 1960s.* London: Weidenfeld and Nicholson, 1969. Pp. 300–301.

H105 Press, John. *A Map of Modern English Verse.* Oxford: Oxford UP, 1969. Pp. 49–51.

H106 Richardson, Kenneth, ed. *Twentieth Century Writing: A Reader's Guide to Contemporary Literature.* London and New York: Newnes Books, 1969. P. 273.

H107 Untermeyer, Louis. *The Pursuit of Poetry.* New York: Simon and Schuster, 1969. Pp. 60–61.

H108 Brown, Harry Matthew, and John Milstead. *What the Poem Means: Summaries of 1,000 Poems.* New York: Scott, Foresman, 1970. Pp. 65–66.

H109 Furbank, P. N. *Reflections on the Word "Image."* London: Secker and Warburg, 1970. Pp. 42–46.

H110 Myers, Robin. *A Dictionary of Literature in the English Language from Chaucer to 1940.* 2 vols. Oxford: Pergamon Press, 1970. 1:260.

H111 Stock, Noel. *The Life of Ezra Pound.* New York: Pantheon, 1970. Pp. 23, 104, 107, 115–16, 121, 129–30, and passim.

H112 Vines, Sherard. *Movements in Modern English Poetry and Prose.* 1927. New York: Folcroft Library Editions, 1970. Pp. 64, 69, 70.

H113 Ward, A. C. *Longman Companion to Twentieth Century Literature.* London: Longman, 1970. P. 241.

H114 Jones, Peter. Introduction. *Tribute to Freud.* By H.D. Oxford: Carcanet Press, 1971. Pp. 5–7.

H115 Feder, Lillian. *Ancient Myth in Modern Poetry.* Princeton: Princeton UP, 1971. Pp. 17–18.

H116   Kenner, Hugh. *The Pound Era.* Berkeley and Los Angeles: U of California P, 1971. Pp. 53, 174–78, and passim.

H117   Kronenberger, Louis, ed. *Brief Lives: A Biographical Guide to the Arts.* New York: Little, Brown & Co., 1971. P. 234.

H118   McCormick, John. *American Literature, 1919–1932: A Comparative History.* London: Routledge & Kegan Paul, 1971. Pp. 118, 160.

H119   Mottram, Eric, and Malcolm Bradbury, eds. *The Penguin Companion to American Literature.* Vol. 3 of *The Penguin Companion to Literature.* Baltimore: Penguin Books, 1971. P. 77.

H120   Rexroth, Kenneth. *American Poetry in the Twentieth Century.* New York: Herder and Herder, 1971. Pp. 36–38.

H121   Jones, Peter. Introduction. *Imagist Poetry.* London: Penguin, 1972. Pp. 13–42.

H122   Pearson, Norman Holmes. Foreword. *Hermetic Definition.* By H.D. New York: New Directions, 1972. Pp. [v–viii].

H123   Wolle, Francis. *A Moravian Heritage.* Boulder, Colo.: Empire Reproduction and Printing, 1972. Pp. 55–60.

H124   Brooks, Cleanth, R. W. B. Lewis, and Robert Penn Warren, eds. *American Literature: The Makers and the Making.* 2 vols. New York: St. Martin's, 1973. Pp. 2047–55.

H125   Holland, Norman. "Freud and H.D." *Freud As We Knew Him.* Ed. Hendrick Ruitenbeek. Detroit: Wayne State UP, 1973. Pp. 449–62.
Reprinted from the *International Journal of Psycho-analysis.* See **G73**.

H126   Holland, Norman. "H.D. and the 'Blameless Physician.'" *Freud As We Knew Him.* Ed. Hendrick Ruitebbeek. Detroit: Wayne State UP, 1973. Pp. 463–94.
Reprinted from *Contemporary Literature.* See **G67**.

H127   Holland, Norman N. *Poems in Persons: An Introduction to the Psychoanalysis of Literature.* New York: W. W. Norton & Co., 1973.

H128   Pearson, Norman Holmes. Foreword. *Trilogy.* By H.D. New York: New Directions, 1973. Pp. v–xii.

H129   Fields, Kenneth. Introduction. *Tribute to Freud.* By H.D. Boston: David R. Godine, 1974. Pp. xvii–xlv.

H130   Gates, Norman T. *The Poetry of Richard Aldington: A Critical Evaluation and Anthology of Uncollected Poems.* University Park: Pennsylvania State UP. Passim.

H131   Juhasz, Susan. *Metaphor and the Poetry of Williams, Pound, and Stevens.* Lewisburg, Pa.: Bucknell UP, 1974. Pp. 21–26.

H132   Klaich, Dolores. *Woman + Woman: Attitudes toward Lesbianism.* New York: Simon & Schuster, 1974. Pp. 75–85.

Translated into French by Martine Laroche as *Femme à femme* (Paris: Éditons des Femmes, 1976).

H133 Pearson, Norman Holmes. Introduction. *Tribute to Freud.* By H.D. New York: New Directions, 1974. Pp. v–xiv.

H134 Stauffer, Donald Barlow. *A Short History of American Poetry.* New York: E. P. Dutton, 1974. Pp. 275–78.

H135 Day, Martin S. *A Handbook of American Literature.* Queensland: U of Queensland P, 1975. P. 350.

H136 Ford, Hugh. *Published in Paris: American and British Writers, Painters, and Publishers in Paris, 1920–1939.* New York: Macmillan, 1975. Pp. 43–73.

H137 Gould, Jean. *Amy: The World of Amy Lowell and the Imagist Movement.* New York: Dodd, Mead & Co., 1975. Passim.

H138 Harmer, J. B. *Victory in Limbo: Imagism, 1908–1817.* London: Secker and Warburg, 1975. Pp. 15, 35–36, 38–43, 61–66, 90, 105, 111–12, 140–43, 152–53, 156–57.

H139 Kaplan, Cora. *Salt and Bitter and Good.* New York: Paddington Press, 1975. Pp. 223–26.

H140 Kenner, Hugh. *A Homemade World: The American Modernist Writers.* New York: Alfred A. Knopf, 1975. Pp. 7–8.

H141 Ruihley, Glenn Richard. *The Thorns of a Rose: Amy Lowell Reconsidered.* Hamden, Conn.: Archon, 1975. Pp. 80–85.

H142 Smoller, Sanford J. *Adrift among Geniuses: Robert McAlmon, Writer and Publisher of the Twenties.* University Park, Pa., and London: Pennsylvania State UP, 1975. Pp. 35–36, 38–39, 45–46, 180–81, 302–3, 307–10, and passim.

H143 Ward, A. C. *American Literature, 1880–1930.* New York: Cooper Square, 1975. Pp. 180–82.

H144 Bradbury, Malcolm, and James McFarlane. *Modernism, 1890–1930.* New York: Penguin, 1976. Pp. 228–29, 232–33.

H145 Heymann, C. David. *Ezra Pound: The Last Rower.* New York: Viking, 1976. Pp. 21–22.

H146 Lynch, Beverly. "Love, Beyond Men and Women: H.D." *Lesbian Lives: Biographies of Women from "The Ladder."* Ed. Barbara Grier and Coletta Reid. Oakland, Calif.: Diana Press, 1976. Pp. 259–72.

H147 Mills, Gordon. *Hamlet's Castle: The Study of Literature as a Social Experience.* Austin: U. of Texas P., 1976. Pp. 117–21.

H148 Perkins, David. *A History of Modern Poetry from the 1890's to the High Modernist Mode.* Cambridge: Harvard UP, 1976. Pp. 339–400.

H149 White, Eric Walter. *Images of H.D.* London: Enitharmon Press, 1976.
Also includes "The Mystery" by H.D. See **B 19**.

H150   Thurley, Geoffrey. "Phenomenalist Idioms: Doolittle, Moore, Levertov." *The American Moment: American Poetry in the Mid-Century.* London: Edward Arnold, 1977. Pp. 109–25.

H151   Watts, Emily Stipes. *The Poetry of American Women from 1632 to 1945.* Austin: U of Texas P, 1977. Pp. 152–58 and passim.

H152   Williams, Ellen. *Harriet Monroe and the Poetry Renaissance: The First Ten Years of Poetry, 1912–1922.* Chicago: U of Illinois P, 1977. Passim.

H153   Duffey, Bernard. *Poetry in America—Expression and Its Values in the Times of Bryant, Whitman, and Pound.* Durham: Duke UP, 1978. Pp. 196–211.

H154   Nagy, N. Cristoph de. "Lebensgang und Lebensende der amerikanischen Poetin H.D." In *Über den Tod von Albert Steffen, Béla Bartok, H.D.* Bern: Francke, 1978. Pp. 44–57.

H155   Ronald, Ann. "The Female Faust." *Feminist Criticism: Essays on Theory, Poetry, and Prose.* Metuchen, N.J.: Scarecrow Press, 1978. Pp. [211]–21 [212, 219].

H156   Sisson, C. H. "H.D." *The Avoidance of Literature: Collected Essays.* Manchester: Carcanet, 1978. Pp. [481]–87.
Reprinted from *Poetry Nation* 4 (1975): 85–91.

H157   Boulton, James T., and Andrew Robertson. *The Letters of D. H. Lawrence.* 3 vols. Cambridge: Cambridge UP, 1979-. Vol. 1, passim; vol. 2, passim.

H158   Firchow, Peter. "Hilda Doolittle, 1886–1961." *American Writers: A Collection of Literary Biographies.* Supplement 1, part 1. Ed. Leonard Unger. New York: Charles Scribner's Sons, 1979. Pp. 253–75.

H159   Healey, Claire. "Hilda Doolittle." *American Women Writers: A Critical Reference Guide from Colonial Times to the Present.* 4 vols. Ed. Lina Mainero. New York: Frederick Ungar, 1979. 1:523–26.

H160   Jones, Peter. *An Introduction to Fifty American Poets.* London and Sydney: Pan Books, 1979. Pp. 143–51.

H161   Kammer, Jeanne. "The Art of Silence and the Forms of Women's Poetry." *Shakespeare's Sisters: Feminist Essays on Women Poets.* Ed. Sandra M. Gilbert and Susan Gubar. Bloomington and London: Indiana UP, 1979. Pp. 153–64.

H162   King, Michael. Foreword. *End to Torment.* By H.D. Ed. Michael King and Norman Holmes Pearson. New York: New Directions, 1979. Pp. vii–xii.

H163   Link, Franz. Commentary on *Trilogie.* Trans. Annamarie and Franz Link. 2 vols. Freiburg i. Br., 1978. 2:151–313.

H164   Mason, Mary Grimley, and Carol Hurd, eds. *Journeys: Autobiographical Writing by Women.* Boston: G.K. Hall, 1979. Pp. 165–67.

H165 Ackroyd, Peter. *Ezra Pound and His World.* New York: Charles Scribner's Sons, 1980. Pp. 12–14, 27–28.

H166 Bernikow, Louise. "Lovers: Paris in the Twenties." *Among Women.* New York: Harper & Row, 1980. Pp. 155–92.

H167 Gould, Jean. *American Women Poets: Pioneers of Modern Poetry.* New York: Dodd, Mead, 1980. Pp. 151–76.

H168 Rosenmeier, Rosamond. "Doolittle, Hilda (H.D.)." *Notable American Women: The Modern Period.* Ed. Barbara Sicherman et al. Cambridge: Harvard UP, 1980. Pp. 198–201.

H169 Schaffner, Perdita. "The Egyptian Cat." *Hedylus.* By H.D. Redding Ridge, Conn.: Black Swan Books, 1980. Pp. 142–46.

H170 Zajdel, Melody M. "Hilda Doolittle (H.D.)." *American Writers in Paris, 1920–1939.* Vol. 4 of *Dictionary of Literary Biography.* Ed. Karen Lane Rood. Detroit: Gale, 1980. Pp. 112–20.

H171 Freeman, Lucy, and Herbert S. Strean. "The Poet Patient." *Freud and Women.* New York: Frederick Ungar, 1981. Pp. 117–22.

H172 Friedman, Susan Stanford. *Psyche Reborn: The Emergence of H.D.* Bloomington: Indiana UP, 1981.

H173 Gage, John. *In the Arresting Eye: The Rhetoric of Imagism.* Baton Rouge: Louisiana State UP, 1981. Passim.

H174 Marianai, Paul. *William Carlos Williams: A New World Naked.* New York: McGraw-Hill, 1981. Pp. 44–52, 93–97, 235–39, and passim.

H175 Paul, Sherman. *The Lost America of Love: Rereading Robert Creeley, Edward Dorn, and Robert Duncan.* Baton Rouge: Louisiana State UP, 1981.
Excerpts from and discussion of Robert Duncan's *H.D. Book.*

H176 Revell, Peter. "'The Meaning That Words Hide': H.D.'s *Trilogy.*" *Quest in Modern American Poetry.* New York: Vision and Barnes and Noble, 1981. Pp. 171–98.

H177 Schaffner, Perdita. "Pandora's Box." *HERmione.* By H.D. New York: New Directions, 1981. Pp. vii–xi.

H178 Gelpi, Albert. "The Thistle and the Serpent." *Notes on Thought and Vision.* By H.D. San Francisco: City Lights Books, 1982. Pp. 7–14.

H179 Kerblat-Blanchenay, Jeanne. "The Rose Loved of Lover or the Heroines in the Poems of the 20's by H.D." *The Twenties: Actes du GRENA.* Aix en Provence: Université de Provence, 1982. Pp. 45–64.

H180 Kerblatt-Houghton, Jeanne. "Après la guerre de Troie: *Helen in Egypt* de H.D." In *Le mythe du héros.* C[entre] A[xois] [de] R[echerches] A[nglais] 3. Aix-en-Provence: Pubs. U. de Provence, 1982. Pp. 201–13.

H181 Robinson, Janice. *H.D.: The Life and Work of an American Poet.* Boston: Houghton Mifflin, 1982.

H182 Schaffner, Perdita. "Unless a Bomb Falls . . . ." *The Gift.* By H.D. New York: New Directions, 1982. Pp. ix–xv.

H183 Breslin, James. *From Modern to Contemporary: American Poetry, 1945–65.* Chicago: U of Chicago P, 1983.
Discussion of Denise Levertov's debt to H.D., pp. 157–59.

H184 Friedman, Susan Stanford. "Hilda Doolittle (H.D.)." *Modern American Poets.* Vol. 45, 2 ser., *Dictionary of Literary Biography.* Ed. Peter Quartermain. Detroit: Gale Research Company, 1983.

H185 Kerblatt-Blanchenay, Jeanne. "*End to Torment*: Etudes d'interrogation dans la mémoire de H.D." In *All Men Are Created Equal: Idéologies, rêves, et réalités.* Ed. Jean-Pierre Martin. Aix-en-Provence: Pubs. U. de Provence, 1983. Pp. 147–67.

H186 Lorenz, Clarissa M. *Lorelei Two: My Life with Conrad Aiken.* Athens: U of Georgia P, 1983.

H187 Martz, Louis. Introduction. *H.D.: Collected Poems, 1912–1944.* Ed. Louis Martz. New York: New Directions, 1983. Pp. xi–xxxvi.

H188 Nyran, Dorothy, ed. *Modern American Literature.* Vol. 4 of *A Library of Literary Criticism.* New York: Frederick Ungar, 1983. Pp. 132–34.

H189 Ostricker, Alicia. *Writing like a Woman.* Ann Arbor: U of Michigan P, 1983. Pp. 7–41.

H190 Rosenthal, M. L., and Sally M. Gall. *The Modern Poetic Sequence: The Genius of Modern Poetry.* Oxford: Oxford UP, 1983. Pp. 477–78.

H191 Schaffner, Perdita. "A Profound Animal." *Bid Me to Live (A Madrigal).* By H.D. 1960. Redding Ridge, Conn.: Black Swan Books, 1983. Pp. 185–94.

H192 Smith, Paul. "Wounded Woman: H.D.'s Post-Imagist Writing." *Pound Revised.* London: Croom Helm, 1983. Pp. 110–32.

H193 Wallace, Emily Mitchell. "Youthful Days and Costly Hours." *Ezra Pound and William Carlos Williams—The University of Pennsylvania Conference Papers.* Philadelphia: U of Pennsylvania P, 1983. Pp. [14]–58 [39–40, 46–48].

H194 Watts, Harold H. "H.D." *20th-Century Poetry.* Vol. 9 of *Great Writers Student Library.* London: Macmillan, 1983. Pp. 152–54.
Includes bibliography.

H195 Collecott, Diana. Introduction. *The Gift.* By H.D. London: Virago Press, 1984.

H196 Guest, Barbara. *Herself Defined: The Poet H.D. and Her World.* New York: Doubleday, 1984.

H197 Hughes, Gertrude. "Arms and the Woman: H.D.'s Revisionary Epic." *Genius and Gender: Revisionary Visions of Emily Dickin-*

son, H.D., Elizabeth Bishop, Gwendolyn Brooks, and Adrienne Rich. Middletown, Conn.: Wesleyan UP, 1984. Pp. 135–57.

H198 McNeil, Helen. Introduction. *Her.* By H.D. London: Virago Press, 1984. Pp. v–xi.

H199 McNeil, Helen. Introduction. *Bid Me to Live.* By H.D. London: Virago Press, 1984. Pp. vii–xix.

H200 Pound, Omar, and A. Walton Litz, eds. *Ezra Pound and Dorothy Shakespear: Their Letters, 1909–1914.* New York: New Directions, 1984. Passim.
Biographical note, pp. 342–43.

H201 Ridgeway, Christopher. Introduction. *Death of a Hero.* By Richard Aldington. 1929. London: Hogarth Press, 1984. Pp. [v]–[vi].

H202 Ahrends, Günther. "Wandlungers in der Naturkonzeption in der amerikanischen Lyrik des 20. Jahrhunderts." *Englische und amerikanische Naturdichtung im 20. Jahrhundert.* Ed. Günther Ahrends and Hans Ulrich. Tübingen: Gunter Narr, 1985. Pp. 370–95.

H203 Schuhmann, Kuno. "Kontaktaufnahmen: Imagistische Dichtun und Natur." *Englische und amerikanische Naturdichtung im 20. Jahrhundert.* Ed. Günther Ahrends and Hans Ulrich. Tübingen: Gunter Narr, 1985. Pp. 278–93.

H204 DuPlessis, Rachel Blau. *Writing beyond the Ending.* Bloomington: Indiana UP, 1985. Pp. 66–83 and passim.

H205 Grahn, Judy. *The Highest Apple.* San Francisco: Spinsters Ink, 1985.

H206 Jaffe, Nora Crow. "'She Herself Is the Writing': Language and Sexual Identity in H.D." *Literature and Medicine.* Vol. 4 of *Psychiatry and Literature.* Ed. Peter W. Graham. Baltimore and London: Johns Hopkins UP, 1985. Pp. 86–111.

H207 King, Michael. "Williams, Pound, H.D.: A Modern Triangle." *WCW & Others.* Ed. Dave Oliphant and Thomas Zigal. Austin, Tex.: Harry Ransom Humanities Research Center, 1985. Pp. 11–33.
Includes photographs. Reprinted from *Library Chronicle of the University of Texas at Austin* 29 (1984): 11–33.

H208 McDougal, Stuart Y. "Dreaming a Renaissance." In *Ezra Pound among the Poets.* Ed. George Bornstein. Chicago: U. of Chicago P., 1985. Pp. 63–80.

H209 Robinson, Alan. *Poetry, Painting, and Ideas, 1885–1914.* London: Macmillan, 1985. Passim.

H210 Schumann, Kuno. "Kontaktaufrahmen: Imagistische Dichtung und Natur." *Englische und amerikanische Naturdichtung im 20. Jahrhundert.* Ed. Günther Ahrends and Hans Ulrich. Tübingen: Gunter Narr, 1985. Pp. 278–93.

H211 Waggoner, Hyatt. "Hilda Doolittle." *Encyclopedia Americana.* 30 vols. Danbury, Conn.: Grolier, 1985. 9:292.

H212 Benstock, Shari. *Women of the Left Bank: Paris, 1900–1940.* Austin: U of Texas P, 1986. Pp. 311–56 and passim.

H213 DeShazer, Mary K. "Write, Write, or Die: The Goddess Muse of H.D." *Inspiring Women: Reimagining the Muse.* New York: Pergamon Press, 1986. Pp. 67–110.

H214 DuPlessis, Rachel Blau. *H.D.: The Career of That Struggle.* Bloomington and Indianapolis: Indiana UP, 1986.

H215 Gilbert, Susan M., and Susan Gubar. "Tradition and the Female Talent." *The Poetics of Gender.* Ed. Nancy K. Miller. New York: Columbia UP, 1986. 200–22.

Reprinted from *Literary History: Theory and Practice*, Proceedings of the Northeastern University Center for Literary Studies (Boston: 1984), vol. 2.

H216 King, Michael, ed. *H.D.: Woman and Poet.* Orono, Maine: National Poetry Foundation, 1986.

Contains (*a*) "Introduction," by Michael King, pp. [15]–24; (*b*) "Keeper of the Flame," by Perdita Schaffner, pp. [27]–33; (*c*) "For H.D.," by Mary de Rachewiltz, pp. [35]–36; (*d*) "Woof and Heave and Surge and Wave and Flow," by Silvia Dobson, pp. [37]–48; (*e*) "Letters from H.D.," by May Sarton, pp. [49]–57; (*f*) "H.D., C. G. Jung, & Küsnacht: Fantasia on a Theme," by John Walsh, pp. [59]–64; (*g*) "Family, Sexes, Psyche: An Essay on H.D. and the Muse of the Woman Writer," by Rachel Blau DuPlessis, pp. [69]–90; (*h*) "Modernism and the 'Scattered Remnant': Race and Politics in the Development of H.D.'s Modernist Vision," by Susan Stanford Friedman, pp. [91]–116; (*i*) "Staring at the Pacific and Swimming in It," poem by Alicia Ostriker, pp. [119]–20; (*j*) "A Weaving at the Zollbrücke in Zürich," poem by John Peck, pp. [121]–24; (*k*) "Praxilla's Silliness," poem by Rachel Blau DuPlessis, pp. [125]–29; (*l*) "Lesbos," poem by Sandra M. Gilbert, pp. [131]–33; (*m*) "Biography," poem by Barbara Guest, pp. [135]–40; (*n*) "Heliodora's Greece," by Dale Davis, pp. [143]–56; (*o*) "'A Primary Intensity between Women': H.D. and the Female Muse," by Mary K. DeShazer, pp. [157]–71; (*p*) "Remembering the Mother: A Reading of H.D.'s *Trilogy*," by Albert Gelpi, pp. [173]–90; (*q*) "Mother as Muse and Desire: The Sexual Politics of H.D.'s *Trilogy*," by Deborah Kelly Kloepfer, pp. [191]–206; (*r*) "H.D. Imagiste and Her Octopus Intelligence," by L. S. Dembo, pp. [209]–25; (*s*) "Autobiography and Prophecy: H.D.'s *The Gift*," by Adelaide Morris, pp. [227]–36; (*t*) "What's in a Box?: Psychoanalytic Concept and Literary Technique in H.D.," by Janice S. Robinson, pp. [237]–57; (*u*) "'But Am I Wrong?': A Study of Interrogation in *End to Torment*," by Jeanne Kerblatt-Houghton, pp. [259]–77; (*v*) "*Bid Me to Live*: Within the Storm," by Joseph Milicia, pp. [279]–98; (*w*) "Magical Lenses: Poet's Vision beyond the Naked Eye," by Charlotte Mandel, pp. [301]–17; (*x*) "Images at the Crossroads: The 'H.D. Scrapbook'," by Diana Collecott, pp. [319]–67; (*y*) "Approaching *Borderline*," by Anne Friedberg, pp. [369]–90; (*z*) "An Annotated Bibliography of Works about H.D.: 1969–1985" by Mary S. Mathis and Michael King, pp. [393]–511.

H217 Lazarowicz, Anja. "Schreiben heilt die Seele über Hilda Doolittle—H.D." *Bogen 19* [Der Bogen erscheint mindestans dreimal jährlich]. München: Carl Hanser Verlag, 1986.

H218 Ostricker, Alicia. *Stealing the Language: The Emergence of Women's Poetry in America.* Boston: Beacon Press, 1986. Passim.

H219 Drake, William. *The First Wave: Women Poets in America, 1915–1945.* New York: Collier/Macmillan, 1987. Pp. 142–43.

H220 Gelpi, Albert. *A Coherent Splendor: The American Renaissance, 1910–1950.* Cambridge: Cambridge UP, 1987. Pp. 253–320.

H221 Hanscombe, Gillian, and Virginia L. Smyers. *Writing for Their Lives: The Modernist Women, 1910–1940.* London: Women's Press, 1987. Pp. 14–46 and passim.

H222 Winks, Robin W. *Cloak and Gown: Scholars in the Secret War, 1939–1961.* New York: William Morrow, 1987. Pp. 310–13.

H223 Di Prima, Diane. *The Mysteries of Vision: Some Notes on H.D.* Santa Barbara, Calif.: am here books, 1988.

H224 Fritz, Angela DiPlace. *Thought and Vision: A Critical Reading of H.D.'s Poetry.* Washington, D.C.: Catholic U of America P, 1988.

H225 Gilbert, Sandra M., and Susan Gubar. *No Mans Land: The Place of the Woman Writer in the Twentieth Century.* Vol. 1. *The War of the Words.* New Haven and London: Yale UP, 1988. Passim.

H226 Smith, Paul. "An End to Torment: H.D.'s Metonymic Course." *Faith of a (Woman) Writer.* Ed. Alice Kessler-Harris and William McBrien. Westport, Conn.: Greenwood, 1988. Pp. 273–78.

H227 Theweleit, Klaus. *Orpheus (und) Eurydike.* Vol. 1. of *Buch der Könige.* Basel, Frankfurt a. M.: Stroemfeld/Roter Stern, 1988.

H228 Bloom, Harold, ed. *H.D.* Modern Critical Views. New York and Philadelphia: Chelsea House Publishers, 1989.
Contains (*a*) "Introduction," by Harold Bloom; (*b*) "H.D.: An Appreciation" (**G44**), by Denise Levertov; (*c*) "*Tribute to Freud* and the H.D. Myth," by Norman Holland; (*d*) "Style in H.D.'s Novels" (**G71**), by A. Kingsley Weatherhead; (*e*) "Who Buried H.D.? A Poet, Her Critics, and Her Place in the 'Literary Tradition'" (**G79**), by Susan Stanford Friedman; (*f*) "The Echoing Spell of H.D.'s *Trilogy*" (**G94**), by Susan Gubar; (*g*) "Introduction to *The Collected Poems*" (**H187**), by Louis Martz; (*h*) "The Concept of Projection: H.D.'s Visionary Powers" (**G153**), by Adelaide Morris; (*i*) "H.D.: Hilda in Egypt" (**G125**), by Albert Gelpi; (*j*) "The H.D. Book: Part 2, Chapter 6" (**H166**), by Robert Duncan.

H229 Burnett, Gary. *H.D. between Image and Epic: The Mysteries of Her Poetics.* Modern Literature Series 111. Ann Arbor: UMI Research Press, 1989.

H230 Doyle, Charles. *Richard Aldington: A Biography.* Carbondale: Southern Illinois UP, 1989. Passim.

H231 Gilbert, Sandra M., and Susan Gubar. *No Mans Land: The Place of the Woman Writer in the Twentieth Century.* Vol. 2. *Sexchanges.* New Haven and London: Yale UP, 1989. Pp. 231–38 and passim.

H232 Hirsh, Elizabeth A. "Imaginary Images: 'H.D.,' Modernism, and the Psychoanalysis of Seeing." In *Discontented Discourses: Feminism/Textual Intervention/Psychoanalysis.* Ed. Marleen S. Barr and Richard Feldstein. Urbana: U of Illinois P, 1989. Pp. 141–59.

H233 Kloepfer, Deborah Kelly. *The Unspeakable Mother: Forbidden Discourse in Jean Rhys and H.D.* Ithaca, N.Y.: Cornell UP, 1989.

H234 Nelson, Cary. *Repression and Recovery: Modern American Poetry and the Politics of Cultural Memory, 1910–1945.* Madison: U of Wisconsin P, 1989. Pp. 82 and passim.

H235 Segal, Charles. *Orpheus: The Myth of the Poet.* Baltimore: Johns Hopkins UP, 1989.

H236 Shucard, Alan, Fred Moramarco, and William Sullivan. *Modern American Poetry, 1865–1950.* Boston: Twayne, 1989. Pp. 77–83 and passim.

H237 Warner-Martin, Linda. "H.D.'s Fiction: Convolutions to Clarity." In *Breaking the Sequence: Women's Experimental Fiction.* Ed. Ellen G. Friedman and Miriam Fuchs. Princeton: Princeton UP, 1989. Pp. 148–60.

H238 Ecker, Gisela. "'Die Gluckselige Einheitlichkeit des Weibes' und 'Woman Is Perfect'—Lou Andreas-Salome und H.D. in der Schule bei Freud." In *Femmes Frauen Women.* Ed. Françoise Rossum-Guyon. Amsterdam: Rodopi, 1990.

H239 Friedman, Susan Stanford. *Penelope's Web: Gender, Modernity, H.D.'s Fiction.* Cambridge: Cambridge UP, 1990.

H240 Friedman, Susan Stanford. "Introduction." In *The Gender of Modernism: A Critical Anthology.* Ed. Bonnie Kime Scott. Bloomington and Indianapolis: Indiana UP, 1990.
Introduces a selection of texts by H.D. See **B20**.

H241 Friedman, Susan Stanford, and Rachel Blau DuPlessis, eds. *Signets: Reading H.D.* Madison: U of Wisconsin P, 1990.
Contains (*a*) "A Sketch of H.D.: The Egyptian Cat," by Perdita Schaffner; (*b*) "A Photobiography of H.D.," by Susan Stanford Friedman, Rachel Blau DuPlessis, and Louis H. Silverstein; (*c*) "Selections from the Poem *Biography*," by Barbara Guest (**H216**); (*d*) "Herself Delineated: Chronological Highlights of H.D.," by Louis H. Silverstein; (*e*) "Dating H.D.'s Writing," by Susan Stanford Friedman; (*f*) "A Relay of Power and of Peace: H.D. and the

Spirit of *The Gift*," by Adelaide Morris (**G198**); (*g*) "H.D. and the Origins of Imagism," by Cyrena N. Pondrom (**G163**); (*h*) "H.D.'s Romantic Landscapes: The Sexual Politics of the Garden," by Cassandra Laity (**G224**); (*i*) "Rose Cut in Rock: Sappho and H.D.'s *Sea Garden*," by Eileen Gregory (**G195**); (*j*) "Images at the Crossroads: H.D.'s 'Scrapbook,'" by Diana Collecott (**H216**); (*k*) "Fishing the Murex Up: Sense and Resonance in H.D.'s *Palimpsest*," by Deborah Kelly Kloepher (**G196**); (*l*) "'I had two loves separate': The Sexualities of H.D.'s *HER*," by Susan Stanford Friedman and Rachel Blau DuPlessis (**G120**); (*m*) "Return of the Repressed in H.D.'s Madrigal Cycle," by Susan Stanford Friedman; (*n*) "Excerpts from 'Language Acquisition,'" by Rachel Blau Duplessis; (*o*) "The Concept of Projection: H.D.'s Visionary Powers," by Adelaide Morris (**G153, H228**); (*p*) "The Echoing Spell of H.D.'s *Trilogy*," by Susan Gubar (**G94, H228**); (*q*) "Remembering the Mother: A Reading of H.D.'s *Trilogy*," by Albert Gelpi (**G170, H216**); (*r*) "No Rule of Procedure: The Open Poetics of H.D.," by Alicia Ostriker (**G260**); (*s*) "*The H.D. Book*: Part II, Chapter 10," by Robert Duncan (**G142**); (*t*) "Creating a Women's Mythology: H.D.'s *Helen in Egypt*," Susan Stanford Friedman (**G90**); (*u*) "Romantic Thralldom in H.D.," by Rachel Blau DuPlessis (**G99**); (*v*) "Imaginary Images: 'H.D.,' Modernism, and the Psychoanalysis of Seeing," by Elizabeth A. Hirsh (**H232**).

H242 Gray, Richard. *American Poetry of the Twentieth Century*. New York, London: Longman, 1990. Pp. 39, 52–53, 57–60, and passim.

H243 Gregory, Eileen. "Angels and Apocalypse: H.D.'s *Tribute to the Angels*." In *A Gathering of Angels: A Publication of Papers Presented at the Conference A Gathering of Angels, February 24–26, 1989.* Ed. Robert Sardello. Dallas: Dallas Institute of Humanities and Culture, 1990. Pp. 87–97.

H244 Kries-Schinck, Annette. *We Are Voyagers, Discoverers: H.D.'s Trilogy and Modern Religious Poetry*. Heidelberg: C. Winter, 1990.

H245 Zillborg, Caroline. "H.D.'s Influence on Richard Aldington." *Richard Aldington: Reappraisals*. Ed. Charles Doyle. English Literary Studies Monograph Series no. 49. Victoria, B.C.: U of Victoria P, 1990. Pp. 26–44.

H246 Hollenberg, Donna Krolik. *H.D.: The Poetics of Childbirth and Creativity*. Boston: Northeastern UP, 1991.

I

Dissertations and Theses about H.D.

I1 Salmon, J. C. "Hilda Doolittle." M.A. thesis. Boston U, 1938.

I2 Frank, Kathryn G. "The Art of Hilda Doolittle." M.A. thesis. University of Pittsburgh, 1957.

I3 Fulsom, Ralph Edward. "An Investigation of the Structural Aspects of Free Verse As They Affect the Oral Reader." *DA* 17 (1957): 3120–21. Northwestern U.

I4 Kaufman, J. Lee. "Theme and Meaning in the Poetry of H.D." *DA* 20 (1959): 1790.

I5 Galloway, Ruth D. "Theme and Imagery in the Poetry of Hilda Doolittle." M.A. thesis. West Texas State University, 1965.

I6 Geisheker, Mary Rose. "Des Imagistes: Toward a Poetic Revolution." *DAI* 33 (1973): 3644A–45A. U of Wisconsin.

I7 Milicia, Joseph. "A Study of Palimpsest: A Novel of H.D." M.A. thesis. Columbia U, 1964.

I8 Harrington, Elaine. Thesis. Montclair State College (N.J.), 1970.

I9 Milicia, Joseph, Jr. "The Fiction of H.D. (Hilda Doolittle)." *DAI* 33 (1972): 320A. Columbia U.

I10 Friedman, Susan Stanford. "Mythology, Psychoanalysis, and the Occult in the Late Poetry of H.D." *DAI* 34 (1973): 6638A. U of Wisconsin, Madison.

I11 Robinson, Janice Stevenson. "H.D.'s 'Helen in Egypt': A Recollection." *DAI* 35 (1973): 1121. U of California, Santa Cruz.

I12 Holland, Joyce. "H.D.: The Shape of a Career." *DAI* 35 (1975): 7906A.

I13 Nadeau, Richard M. "The Flower Magicians Bartered For." Thesis. Bard College, 1975. Senior project submitted to the Division of Languages and Literature.

I14 Desy, Peter Michael. "H.D. and the Search for the Absolute." *DAI* 39 (1978): 5501. Kent State U.

I15 Steele, Joy Cogdell. "Time and American Autobiography: Four Twentieth Century Writers." *DAI* 39 (1978): 3559A. U of Iowa.

I16 Wright, Patrick Stephen. "Scientific Lyricism: A Study of H.D.'s Modernist Writing." M.A. thesis. Simon Fraser U, 1979.

I17 Zajdel, Melody McCollum. "The Development of a Poetic Vision: H.D.'s Growth from Imagist to Mythologist." *DAI* 40 (1979): 5445A. Michigan State U.

I18 Bock, Layeh Aronson. "The Birth of Modernism: Des Imagistes and the Psychology of William James." *DAI* 41 (1980): 666A. Stanford U.

I19 Crowell, Joan Therese. "A Study of H.D.: Her Life and Work." Ph.D. diss. Dalhousie University, 1980.

I20 Levine-Keating, Helene. "Myth and Archtype from a Female Perspective: An Exploration of Twentieth Century North and South American Women Poets." *DAI* 41 (1980): 664A. New York U.

I21 DeShazer, Mary Kirk. "The Woman Poet and Her Muse: Sources and Images of Female Creativity in the Poetry of H.D., Louise Bogan, May Sarton, and Adrienne Rich." *DAI* 43 (1982): 1967A. U of Oregon.

I22 Fritz, Angela DiPlace. "The Thematic Development in the Poetry of H.D." *DAI* 43 (1982): 2991A–92A. Washington State U.

I23 Scoggan, John William. "De(con)structive Poetics: Readings of Hilda Doolittle's *The War Trilogy*." *DAI* 44 (1982): 167A. U of British Columbia.

I24 Seidman, Barbara Ann. "The Filmgoing Imagination: Filmmaking and Filmgoing as the Subjects of Modern American Literature." *DAI* 42 (1982): 4827A. U of Illinois, Urbana-Champaign.

I25 Boles, Joseph David. "Clio in Crisis: The Historiographic Impulse in the Writings of H.D." *DAI* 43 (1983): 3592A. Rutgers U.

I26 Funt, Karen Lorraine Bryce. "Reading, Psychoanalysis, Dialectics." *DA* 44 (1983): 3071A. State U of New York, Buffalo.

I27 Gardner, Frieda. "H.D.'s Palimpsests." *DAI* 44 (1983): 492A. U of Minnesota.

I28 King, Rosalie Anne. "Bee, Angels, Myrrh: Studies in H.D.'s 'Trilogy.'" *DAI* (1983): 1787A. U of California, Santa Cruz.

I29 Kloepfer, Deborah Kelly. "'Companions of the Flame': The Relationship between the Mother and Language in Jean Rhys and H.D." *DA* 44 (1983): 2473A. State U of New York, Buffalo.

I30 Schultz, Stephen Paul. "The Imagination of H.D.: Hilda Doolittle and 'Hermetic Definition.'" *DA* 44 (1983): 2145A. State U of New York, Buffalo.

I31 Combellick, Katherine Ann. "Feminine Forms of Closure: Gilman, Deming, and H.D." *DA* 45 (1984): 182A. State U of New York, Binghamton.

I32 Funt, Karen Lorraine Bryce. "Reading, Psychoanalysis, Dialectics." *DAI* 44 (10) (1984): 3071A.

I33 Shapiro, Daniel. "The Shape of Poetry, 1910–1920: Convention, Reform, and Revolution." *DAI* 45 (9A) (1984): 2871. U of Toronto (Canada).

I34 Van Gerven, Claudia. "'But to an Outcast and a Vagabond': Authority and Rhetoric in the Poetry of H.D." *DAI* 45 (1984): 2106A. U of Colorado, Boulder.

I35 Sievert, Heather Rosario. "H.D.: A Symbolist Perspective." *DAI* 46 (1985): 2288A. New York U.

I36 Hollenberg, Donna Krolik. "Nursing the Muse: The Childbirth Metaphor in H.D.'s Poetry." *DAI* 47 (1986): 537A. Tufts U.

I37 Shikina, Seiji. "The Adaptation of Haiku Form to the Poetry of the Imagists." *DAI* 47 (6) (1986): 2162A. U of Southwestern Louisiana.

I38 Wasserman, Rosanne. "Helen of Troy: Her Myth in Modern Poetry." *DAI* 47 (1986): 1340A. City U of New York.

I39 Meggison, Lauren Louise. "Keepers of the Flame: Hermeticism in Yeats, H.D., and Borges." *DAI* 48 (2) (1987): 386A. U of California, Irvine.

I40 Dunn, Margaret M. "'The Inevitable Triad': Self and Other in the Fiction and Poetry of H.D." *DAI* 48 (5) (1987): 1202A–3A. Indiana U.

I41 Phelan, Margaret M. "H.D. and Marianne Moore: Correspondences and Contradictions." *DAI* 49 (1) (1987): 92A. Rutgers The State U of New Jersey–New Brunswick.

I42 Siegel, Carol Roberta. "D. H. Lawrence and Traditions in Women's Literature." *DAI* 48 (9) (1987): 2336A. U of California, Berkeley.

I43 Burnett, Gary Dean. "The Mysteries between Image and Epic: H.D.'s Poetry and Poetics in Transition." *DAI* 49 (5) (1988): 1140A.

I44 Altman, Meryl Beth. "Interlocutions: Men, Women, and Modernisms in American Poetry." *DAI* 50 (1) (1989): 137A.

I45 Augustine, Jane. "The Mystery: H.D.'s Unpublished Moravian Novel Edited and Annotated: Towards a Study in the Sources of a Poet's Religious Thinking." *DAI* 49 (8) (1989): 2216A.

I46 Freeman, Clara Jean. "Magdalene Before and After: H.D.'s Poetic Sequences." *DAI* 49 (9) (1989): 2652A.

I47 Case, Laurie. "H.D. and Her Poetry: An Adult Developmental Approach to the Question of Women's Creative Productivity." *DAI* 51 (5) (1990): 2603B.

I48 Cramer, Patricia. "Matriarchal Myth-Making for a Post-Patriarchal Age: The Anti-War Writing of Virginia Woolf and Hilda Doolittle." *DAI* 50 (7) (1990): 2060A–61A.

I49 Baccolini, Raffaella. "Tradition, Identity, Desire: H.D.'s Revisionist Strategies in *By Avon River, Winter Love*, and *Hermetic Definition*." *DAI* 50 (11) (1990): 3582A.

I50 Hirsh, Elizabeth Anne. "Modernism Revised: Formalism and the Feminine: Irrigaray, H.D., Barnes." *DAI* 50 (12) (1990): 3961A.

I51 Buck, Claire. "Reading the Feminine Self: H.D./Freud/Psychoanalysis." *DAI* 50 (12) (1990): 3959A–60A.

I52 Dodd, Elizabeth Caroline. "Reticence and the Lyric: The Development of a Personal Classicism among Four Women Poets of the Twentieth Century." *DAI* 50 (12) (1990): 3945A–46A.

I53 Hogue, Cynthia Anne. "Figuring Woman (Out): Feminine Subjectivity in the Poetry of Emily Dickinson, Marriane Moore, and H.D." *DAI* 51 (4) (1990): 1228A–29A.

I54 Cleary, Rosemary Joan. "Haunting Households, Heidegger, and Holy Ghosts: A Psychology of the Family within the Economy of Culture." *DAI* 51 (6) (1990): 3112B.

J

Miscellanea

Articles and Published Letters

J1 *Poetry* 7.2 (Nov. 1915): 103–5.
Announcement of the award of $50.00 to H.D. for the Helen Haire Levinson guarantor's prize.

J2 "Hilda Doolittle Exhibit on at Yale." *New York Herald Tribune* 16 Sept. 1956: 58.

J3 *"Poet Hilda Doolittle, on Yale Visits, Assails Imagist Label Used to Describe Her Work." *New Haven Register* 16 Sept. 1956.
Includes photograph of H.D., Norman Holmes Pearson, and Bryher (identified as "Mrs. Bryher, a distant relative of H.D.")

J4 *Bulletin of the Poetry Society of America* Oct. 1960: 15.
Announcement of H.D.'s induction as member. Includes photo on p. 21 with the caption, "H.D. in Kusnacht."

J5 Collins, H. P. *Times* [London] 17 Oct. 1961: 15.
A letter on the occasion of H.D.'s death.

J6 "Friends of H.D. Will Promote Bethlehem Poet." *Globe-Times* [Bethlehem, Pa.] 23 June 1979: 11.

J7 Ratner, Amy. "A World-Famous Poet Remembered at Home." *Express* [New York] 3 Sept. 1982: D-10.

J8 Darragh, Tim. "Doolittle Gets Praise and a State Marker." *Morning Call* 11 Sept. 1982: 90.

J9 Salisbury, Stephan. "Bethlehem Pays Proud Tribute to a Great Native Poet—H.D." *Philadelphia Inquirer* 11 Sept. 1982: 1D+.

J10 Stumpf, Ron. "H.D. Honored: State Marks Birthplace of Late Bethlehem Poet." *Globe-Times* [Bethlehem, Pa.] 9 Nov. 1982: 12.

Catalogues and Programs

J11 *Les années vingt: Les écrivans américains à Paris et leurs amis, 1920–1930.* Paris: Centre Culturel Américain, 1959.
This is the catalog of the Paris USIA Exposition in 1959. It includes

a photo of H.D. (no. 22) and a list of items relating to her in the exposition (pp. 97–98).

J12 Program of the Brandeis University Creative Arts Awards. Annual Presentation Ceremony, New York, 7 April 1959: [7].
On the occasion of H.D.'s receipt of the Brandeis University Medal for Poetry.

J13 Poetry Society of London. *A Programme of Tribute to H.D.* 20 Nov. 1964.

J14 Program for the Manhattan Theater Club, Writers in Performance: *Tribute to H.D.*, 16 May 1978. Readings by Marylin Hacker, Avaci Petrides, Charlotte Mandel, and Adrienne Rich.
The program includes a brief quote by H.D. on Kenneth MacPherson.

J15 Program for the Dedication of the Official State Marker for Hilda Doolittle (H.D.). Cosponsored by The Friends of H.D., Pennsylvania Historical and Museum Commission, and Moravian College Library, Sept. 10, 1982 at 3:30 P.M., 10 E. Church Street, Bethlehem, Pa.

J16 Allen, Frank. "H.D.: Bethlehem Poet, Greek Flower." *Musikfest '85: Souvenir Program Book, August 17–25, Bethlehem, Pa.* Bethlehem: Bethlehem Musikfest Association, 1985. Pp. 46–47.

J17 Program for *Euripides* Ion, translation and commentary by H.D. Produced for the H.D. Centennial Conference, University of Maine at Orono, June 5–7, 1986. Directed by C. F. Terrell. Original music by Don Stratton.
P. [4] contains a statement by C. F. Terrell titled, "H.D.'s Version of Euripides' *Ion*."

Photographs and Postcards

J18 *Close-Up* July 1927: 17.
Photograph of H.D. from Kenneth MacPherson's film *Wingbeat*.

J19 Virago Collectors Cards no. 16.
Includes a photograph of H.D. along with a brief biographical statement.

J20 *Pennsylvania English* 9.1 (Fall 1982).
Includes a photograph of H.D. on the cover and a brief note inside the cover.

J21 *San Francisco Review of Books* 9.2 (Nov.–Dec. 1982): 1.
Includes a photograph of H.D. on the cover.

J22 "Long Live Poetry." City Lights [Bookstore] 1985 Literary Calendar. Ed. Nancy J. Peters. San Francisco: City Lights Books. P. 18.
Photo of H.D. in Egypt, 1923.

J23 "The Women Writers: 1986 Calendar." Ed. Elaine Goldman Gill and Mary Gilliland. Trumansburg, N.Y.: Crossing Press, 1986.

Includes a photograph of H.D. on p. 41, a brief discussion of her on p. [111], and excerpts from *Trilogy* on pp. [42–43].

J24   Postcard. Crossing Cards, Trumansburg N.Y.
Photograph of H.D. by Man Ray.

J25   Postcard. Crossing Cards, Trumansburg N.Y.
Photograph of H.D.

Obituaries

J26   "Hilda Doolittle, Poet, Dead at 75." *New York Times* 29 Sept. 1961: 35.

J27   *New York Herald Tribune* 29 Sept. 1961: 14.

J28   *Times* [London] 29 Sept. 1961: 15.
Includes a tribute to H.D. by Herbert Read.

J29   *New Haven Journal-Courier* 30 Sept. 1961: 4.

J30   *Washington Post* 2 Oct. 1961: A6.

J31   *Time* 6 Oct. 1961: 86.

J32   *Publisher's Weekly* 180 (23 Oct. 1961): 34.

J33   "Hilda Doolittle Returns Home." *Globe-Times* [Bethlehem, Pa.] 31 Oct. 1961: 6.

J34   Moore, Marianne. "H.D." *Bryn Mawr Alumnae Bulletin* 42 (Fall 1961): 20.

J35   Günther, Alfred. "In memoriam H.D." *Neue Zürcher Zeitung* 1 Dec. 1961, blatt 7: 1.

Index of Titles by H.D.

Acceptance of Award of Merit for Poetry, C151
Acon, A2, 6, 25, 38; B2; C18, 20; D39
Adonis, A6, 7, 25, 38; C38; D19
Advent, A24b
After Troy, A5, 6, 38; C62
All Mountains, A13, 38; C78
Along the Yellow Sand, A25; C45
Amaranth, A38, 39; C154
Ancient Wisdom Speaks, A38; C128
And Pergamos, A25; E8
Antipater of Sidon, A38; C70
Antistrophe, C115
Apollo at Delphi, C111
An Appreciation, C102
Archer, A38; C142
Ariadne, A38
Art and Ardor in World War I: Selected Letters from H.D. to John Cournos, C170
At Athens, C65
At Baia, A4, 6, 25, 38; B4b; C54; D7
At Croton, A38; C59
At Eleusis, A5, 6, 38; C61
At Ithaca, A5, 6, 25, 38; C58
Autochthon, C117
Avon, D11

Beauty, C88
Because One Is Happy, A35
Bid Me to Live, A26; F311–32; G285; H191, 199, 216
Bird of the Air, A25
Birds in Snow, A13, 38; C101
Body and Soul, A38; C141
Boo (*Sirocco* and the Screen), C96
Borderline, A12; B20; C172; G116; H216
By Avon River, A22; D11; F206–46; G136; I49

Calliope, A13, 38; C64
Callypso Speaks, A25
Calypso, A38, 39; C120, 188
The Cantos of Ezra Pound, B12
Cassandra, A5, 6, 38, 39; C60
Caught, C120
Centaur Song, A5, 6, 38; C56, 61
Chance, A13, 38
Chance Meeting, A13, 38; B10
Charioteer, A5, 6, 38; E3
Child Poems, A38
Choros Sequence (from Morpheus), A13, 38; B11; D30
Choros Translations (from the Bacchae), A13, 38; B10
Choruses from Iphigeneia in Aulis, A1, 6, 38; C25; F1–4, 11–12
Choruses from Odyssey, A6, 38
Choruses from the Hippolytus of Euripides, A1, 6, 38
Christmas 1944, A23, 38
The Cinema and the Classics, C88, 90, 95
Circe, A3, 4, 6, 38; C36
Cities, A2, 6, 38; C31
Citron Bower, A25; C45
The City Is Peopled, A2, 6, 38
Claribel's Way to God, A22
The Cliff Temple, A2, 6, 38; C26
Collected Poems, A6; F49–65
Collected Poems, 1912–1944, A38; F507–39; G301–3; H187, 228
Come Back, C119
The Coming One, C125
Confessions-Questionnaire, B16; C103
Conrad Veidt: The Student of Prague, C91
The Contest, A2, 6, 38; C33
The Cricket, B1; C177

Cuckoo Song, A4, 6, 7, 38; C43

The Dancer, A32, 38, 39; C113
Dark Room, A38
A Dead Priestess Speaks, A37, 38, 39
The Death of Martin Presser, C153
Delphi, A38; C111, 159
Demeter, A4, 6, 38
Do You Remember? C145
Dodona, A38; C161
Dream, A38; C89
The Dream, A35; C156

Ear-ring, C116
Ecce Sponsus, A38
Egypt, A4, 6, 38
Electra-Orestes, A38; B17; C108, 112
Elegy and Choros, C112
End to Torment, A33; D14; F398–438; H162
Das Ende der Qual, D14
Envy, A38, 39; C154
Epigram, A38; B2
Epigram: After the Greek, C15, 20; D39
Epigrams, A5, 6, 38
Episode I (excerpt), C120
Epitaph, A13, 25, 38; D25
Epode, C115
Erige Cor Tuum ad Me in Caelum, A25, 38; C139, 143; E17
Eros, A38, 39; C154
Euripides Ion, A18, 39; F133–48; J17
Eurydice, A6, 38, 39; C41; E9
Evadne, A4, 6, 25, 38; C48; D1, 37, 38; E11
Evening, A2, 6, 38, 39; E18

Fair the Thread, A25; C142
Fate, C1
Fire, Flood, and Olive-Tree, A25; C141; E7
The Flower Fairy, B1; C177
The Flowering of the Rod, A21, 25, 31, 38, 39; C125, 126, 127; D25; F196–206; G79
Flute Song, A5, 6, 38; C62
The Forgotten Charge, C17
Fortune Teller, C168; G186
Four Prose Choruses, C104, 105, 115; G264
Fragment Forty, A5, 6, 38

Fragment Forty-one, A5, 6, 38
Fragment 113, A4, 6, 25, 38–39; B13; E11; *see also* Not Honey
Fragment Sixty-eight, A5, 6, 38
Fragment Thirty-six, A5, 6, 38; B4b, 13; C54
Fragments from *Temple of the Sun*, A38; C122
A Friendship Traced, C163

Garden, A2, 6, 38, 39; B3–4, 13; C21; D4, 5, 31, 34, 35, 37
Georgias Sanctus, A25; C138
Gift, A38; C28, 89
The Gift, A35; C156, 158, 168; F483–503; G154, 198, 280; H182, 195, 216
The Gift, A2, 6, 7, 38; C28
The God, A6, 38
The God, A6, 38; C38
Good Frend, A22, 25; C135–36
The Gray Mouse, C11
The Griffin of Temple Bar, C14
Grove of Academe, A28
Grown Up, A38
The Guest, A22

Halcyon, A13, 38; C86
H.D., A7
H.D. by Delia Alton, C169; G185
Heat, A7, 25; C21; D24, 25, 26, 27, 30, 32, 36, 38; G43
The Hedgehog, A17; F130–32
Hedylus, A10; B7; F93–109; G197; H169
Helen, A5, 6, 25, 38; B14; C58; D24, 25, 26, 27; G43, 243
Helen in Egypt, A27, 39; C148; D22; E12–13; F333–45; G93, 225; H180, 241; I11
Heliodora, A5, 6, 38; F29–48
Heliodora, A5, 6, 25, 38; B5
Helios, A4, 6, 38; C51
Helios and Athene, A38; C157; G111
The Helmsman, A2, 6, 25, 38; C29; D31; E11
Her, C160
Hermes of the Ways, A2, 6, 38, 39; B2, 4, 16; C15, 19, 20; D23, 24, 26, 39; G5
Hermetic Definition, A28, 39; F346–76; G266, 296; H122; I30, 49

Hermione, A34; C158, 160; D2, 15; F439–82, 584, 588; G120, 215, 226, 284, 299; H177, 198, 241
Hermonax, A5, 6, 38; B2; C18, 20; D39
Hesperides, B4b; C54; D7
Hipparchia, A8
Hippolytus Temporizes, A9; B14; C69, 77; F85–92; G281
Hippolytus Temporizes, A4, 6, 25, 38, 39
His Dreams, C7
His Ecstasy, A38; C111, 159
His Presence, A38; C111, 159
His Riddle, A38; C159
His Song, A38; C111, 159
Holy Satyr, A5, 6, 38; B5
Huldigung an Freud, D13
Huntress, A2, 6, 38; C24
Hyacinth, A5, 6, 38
Hymen, A4, 6, 38; F13–28; G205, 219
Hymen, A4, 6, 7, 38; C45
Hymn (for Count Zinzendorf, 1700–1760), A25; C137
Hymn (From the Bohemian), C137

I Said, A38; C161
I Segni sul muro, D21
I Sing Democracy, C117
If You Will Let Me Sing, A13, 38; B10
If Your Eyes Had Been Blue, A38
Des Imagistes, B2; C20; D39
In Our Town, A38; C118
In the Rain, A13, 38; B10; D24, 26
In Time of Gold, C144
Incantation (Artemis over the Body of Orion), C19
Ion, A5, 6, 38; F92
The Islands, A4, 6, 25, 38, 39; B13–14; C46; D34, 36

Joan of Arc, B18, 20; C99

The King of Kings Again, C97
Kora and Ka, A15

Lady Leicester, C10
Lais, A5, 6, 25, 38; B5, 14
The Last Gift, C28
Last Winter, C140
Late Spring, A38; C27
The Leaves, B1; C177

Leda, A4, 6, 38; B14; C44; D17; E9
Let Zeus Record, A13, 38, 39; B8
Lethe, A5, 6, 25, 38; B14; C50; D29, 32, 33; E4; G265
A Letter from England, C124
Letter to Norman Holmes Pearson, B14; C176
Letters to F. S. Flint, C155
Letters to John Cournos, C170
Letters to Silvia Dobson, C163
Leucadian Artemis, C63
The Look-out, A5, 6, 38; C42
Loss, A2, 6, 7, 38
Love That I Bear, A25

Magician, A38; C110
Marianne Moore, B20; C32
Marion's Two Letters, C2
Mary A. Herr, A.B., C150
The Mask and the Movietone, C95
Master, A38; C110
The Master, A38, 39
May 1943, A23, 38; C140
Mid-Day, A2, 6, 38; C22; D5
The Mill Fairy, B1; C177
Mira-Mare, A15
The Moon in Your Hands, A25; C107; E11
Moonrise, A5, 6, 38, 39; B4; C21; D40
Morning Star, A35
Murex, A8
Myrtle Bough, A1, 38
The Mysteries, A13, 38
The Mysteries Remain, A25; E10
The Mystery, B19; G283, 294; H149; I45

Nails for Petals, C144
Narthex, B9
Never More Will the Wind, A25; C45
Night, A2, 6, 38; C27
Nights, A16; F540–47
No, A38; C89
North Star, C67
Nossis, A5, 6, 38; C62
Not Honey, A4; *see also* Fragment 113
Note on Poetry, B14; C176; G253
Notes on Recent Writing, A26; C169
Notes on Thought and Vision, A36; B20; F504–7; H178

O Love Cease, A25
Odyssey, A5, 6
Old Tommy, C9
On Courting Night, C5
Orchard, A2, 6, 7, 25, 38, 39; B14; C15; D8, 18
Oread, A5, 6, 7, 25, 38, 39; B3–4, 14; C19; D5, 6, 16, 18, 19, 30, 36, 40; E1, 2, 6, 11; G5–6, 43, 262; H96
Orestes Theme, A38; B3; C118
Orion Dead, A5, 6, 38; C19
Other Sea Cities, A38; C165

Paint It Today, C171; G193
Palimpsest, A8; F66–84; G196, 235, 273; H99–100, 241; I8
Pallas, A25
The Passion of Joan of Arc, B18, 20; C99
Pear Tree, A2, 6, 7, 25, 38, 39; D23, 24, 25, 26, 31; G25
People of Sparta, C66
Phaedra, A4, 6, 38; C51
Phaedra Rebukes Hippolyta, C51
Phaedra Remembers Crete, C51
Picture of a Mountain, C128
Pines, G5; *see also* Oread
The Poet, A32, 38, 39; C114
The Poetry Quartos, A11
Pontikonisi (Mouse Island), C109
The Pool, A5, 6, 7, 38, 39; B3–4, 14; C21; D36; E2; G26, 30–32, 43
Prayer, A4, 6, 38; C52
Priapus, Keeper-of-Orchards, B2–4; C15, 19, 20; D39
Priest, A37, 38
Prince Frederick's Wooing, C4
Prisoners, A2, 6, 38
Projector, A38; C87
Projector II (Chang), A38; C92; G229
Prose Choruses, C104, 105, 119; G264
Psyche, A38; C89
The Purple Plume of Long Ago, C3
Pursuit, A2, 6, 7, 38; G291
Pygmalion, A6, 38; C39

R.A.F., A23, 38
Red Rose and a Beggar, A28
Red Roses for Bronze, A11, 13, 38; F110–29
Regents of the Night, C147
Responsibilities, B20; C175

Restraint, C90
The Revelation, C143; E17
A Reversed Decision, C8
Review of:
  The Acropolis of Athens by M. Schede, C71
  Alcamenes and the Establishment of the Classical Type in Greece by Charles Walston (Waldstein), C85
  The Aryans by V. Gordon Childe, C81
  Chang by Ernest B. Shoedsack and Merian C. Cooper, C92
  The Culture of Ancient Greece and Rome, C82
  Dear Theo, ed. Irving Stone, C119
  Expiation by L. Kuleschow, C98
  The Farmer's Bride by Charlotte Mew, C34
  The Formation of the Greek Poeple by A. Jarde, C84
  Goblins and Pagodas by John Gould Fletcher, C37
  Greek Social Life by F. A. Wright, C72
  Lewis and Irene by Paul Morand, C73
  Little Novels of Sicily by Giovanni Vergal, C74
  King of Kings by Cecil B. de Mille, C97
  Masterpieces of Greek Drawing and Painting by Ernst Pfuhl, C80
  Out of the Mist, C94
  Panhellenic Architecture in the Aegean by E. Bell, C79
  The Passion and Death of a Saint by Carl Dreyer, B18, 20; C99
  The Poems of Sappho, trans. Edwin Marion Cox, C68
  The Polyglots by W. Gerhardi, C75
  Responsibilities and Other Poems by W. B. Yeats, B20; C175
  Sirocco by Noel Coward, C96
  A Short History of Italian Art by Adolfo Venturi, C83
  The Stages of Greek Religion by Gilbert Murray, C76
  The Student of Prague by Conrad Veidt, C91
  Turksib, C106
  Two Englishwomen in Rome, C121

Venus in Scorpio by Murray Constantine and Margaret Goldsmith, C123
Whitman by Edgar Lee Masters, C117
Rosemary, A22; C136
Russian Films, C100

Sagesse, A28; C146, 147, 149; D22
Saint Anthony, C166
Saturn, A30; C122
Scribe, A25, 38; C142
Sea Garden, A2, 6, 38; F5–10; G12, 195, 202, 275; H241
Sea Gods, A2, 6, 38, 39; B14; C30; G26
Sea Heroes, A4, 6, 25, 38; C47
Sea Iris, A2, 6, 38, 39; B3; C23
Sea Lily, A3, 6, 38, 39; B3
Sea Poppies, A2, 6, 25, 38, 39; C40
Sea Rose, A2, 6, 25, 38, 39; B3
Sea Shell, C126
Sea Violet, A2, 6, 38, 39
Sea-Choros (from Hecuba), A13, 38
The Secret, A35
Secret Name, A8
Selected Letters from H.D. to F. S. Flint, C155; G68
Selected Poems, A25, 39; F299–310
Seven New Poems, C129
She Contrasts Herself with Hippolyta, A4, 6, 38
She Rebukes Hippolyta, A4, 6, 38
The Shell, C149
Sheltered Garden, A2, 6, 7, 38, 39; E14
The Shepherd, A38
Shoogy-Shoo, C6
The Shrine, A2, 6, 38; B4; C57
Sigil, A13, 25, 38, 39; C107, 120, 142, 164
Simaetha, A4, 6, 38; C52
The Singer Fairy, B1; C177
Sitalkis, A5, 6, 38; B2, 16; C16, 20; D39
A Small Grain of Worship, C152
Socratic, A38; B14; C89
Sometimes and After, C144
Song, A4, 6, 38; B14; C54; D35
Songs for Children, C177
Songs from Cyprus, A13, 38; B8; E5
Star by Day, A29; C118

Star of Day, A28
Stars Wheel in Purple, A25; C67; D33
Storm, A2, 6, 38, 39; C21
Strophe, C115

Tatter, B11
Telesila, A5, 6, 38
The Tempest, A22; C135
Temple of the Sun, A30; C122, 161
Ten Songs for Children Young and Old, B1; C177
Thetis, A4, 5, 6, 38; C50; G205

3, C109

Three Child Songs, C89
To H.C.T.D., C173
To William Morris, C138
Toward the Piraeus, A5, 6, 38, 39; B5
Trance, A13, 38
The Tribute, A3, 6, 7, 38, 39; C35
Tribute to Freud, A24; D2, 13, 21, 28; F247–98; H114, 129, 228
Tribute to the Angels, A20, 25, 31, 38, 39; C129; D25; F171–95; H243
Trilogie, D12; H163
Trilogy, A31, 38; F376–97; G72, 94, 123, 145, 170, 174–75, 200, 208, 213, 245, 261; H128, 216, 228, 244; I23, 28; J23
Triplex, A13, 38; C101

2, C108

Two Americans, A14; C174
Two Poems, A29
Two Poems for Christmas, 1937, A38

Untitled Poem for Sylvia Dobson, C162
The Usual Star, A14

Vale Ave, C144–45, 167
Verses, Translations, and Reflections from "The Anthology," C15
Vincent Van Gogh, C119
Visage de Freud, D2

The Walls Do Not Fall, A19, 25, 31, 38, 39; D10, 25; F149–70; G126, 227, 248
Wash of Cold River, A5, 6, 38

We Two, A5, 6, 38; B6; C55
What Do I Love? A23; C140
What It Was, A35
When I Am a Cup, A13, 38
Where Is the Nightingale, A25
Where Love Is King, C45
Whipporwill, C13
White Rose, A13, 38
White World, A6, 25, 38; D18
The Whole White World, A4
Why Have You Sought, A4, 6, 38; C49

The Wind Sleepers, A2, 6, 38; C21
Wine Bowl, A13, 38
Winter Love, A28, 39; C154; D22; I49
Winter Woods, C12
The Wise Sappho, A36
Wooden Animal, A29; C118
Worm, C127
Writing on the Wall, A24b; C130, 131, 132, 133, 134; D9, 21

Zeus-Provider, A30, 38; C122

General Index to Names and Titles

Accent, F463
Achievement in American Poetry, D8
"An Achievement of H.D. and Theodore Roethke: Psychoanalysis and the Poetics of Teaching," G96
Ackroyd, Peter, H165
Acropolis of Athens, C71
"Across Two Generations," F386
"The Adaptation of Haiku Form to the Poetry of the Imagists," I37
Adelphi, C65, 70–76, 79–85; F57, 70
Adrift among Geniuses: Robert McAlmon, Writer and Publisher of the Twenties, H142
"After Imagism," F527
"Afterword: The House of the Father's Science and the Mother's Art," G85
"Against Discipleship: Collaboration and Intimacy in the Relationship of H.D. and Freud," G236
Agenda, C104–5, 115, 162, 175; F92, 147, 274, 369, 395, 434; G251–61, 264
Ahearn, Barry, G244
Ahrend, Günther, H202–3, 210
Aiken, Conrad, A2a.iii, 6a.i, iv, 11, F79, 551; H2, 65
Aion: A Journal of Tradionary Science, G49
Alabama Advertiser-Journal Sunday Magazine, F361
Albert and Charles Boni, B2
Alcamenes and the Establishment of the Classical Type in Greek Art, C85
Aldington, Richard, A1b, 3, 26a; B10; F560; G2–4, 8, 15, 28–29; H44, 201
Aldis, Mary, F552
Alien and Critical: Women Writers in Exile, G256

All Men Are Created Equal: Idéologies, rêves et réalités, H185
Allen, Frank, F464, 491, 504, 582; G134, 300; J16
Allen, Margaret Vanderhaar, F511; G134
Alloway, Lawrence, F152
"Altered Patterns and New Endings: Reflections of Change in Stein's *Three Lives* and H.D.'s *Palimpsest*," G235
Altman, Meryl Beth, I44
Alton, Delia (H.D.), A23; C169
"Amazing Gifts and Others," F379–80
American Academy of Arts and Letters, C151
American Book Review, F106, 460; G301
American Critics at Work: Examinations of Contemporary Literary Theory, G98
American Film Criticism, B18
American Literary Scholarship, F422
American Literature, F269, 359, 430, 585, 587, 607
American Literature, 1880–1930, H143
American Literature, 1919–1932: A Comparative History, H118
American Literature: The Makers and the Making, H124
American Moment: American Poetry in the Mid-Century, H150
"An American Poet," F54
American Poetry, G266–67, 307
"American Poetry in Action and Reaction," G19
American Poetry in the Twentieth Century, H120
American Poetry, 1921, F556
American Poetry, 1922, F557

American Poetry, 1922: A Miscellany, B5
American Poetry, 1925, F561
American Poetry, 1925: A Miscellany, B7
American Poetry of the Twentieth Century, H242
American Poetry Review, F545, 606; G144
American Poetry since 1900, H12
American Poets from the Puritans to the Present, H102
American Quarterly, G282
American Women Poets: Pioneers of Modern Poetry, H167
American Women Writers: A Critical Reference Guide from Colonial Times to the Present, H159
American Writers: A Collection of Literary Biographies, H158
American Writers in Paris, 1920–1939, H170
Amerikanische Lyrik, D16
Amerikanske stemmer: Etudvalg af amerikansk lyrik fra den forste halvdel af det tyvende århundrede i danks gendigtning ved, D1
Among Women, H166
AMS Press, A13a.iii
Amy Lowell, H29
Amy Lowell: A Chronicle, F569
Amy Lowell—Portrait of the Poet in Her Time, H66
Amy: The World of Amy Lowell and the Imagist Movement, H137
Anagogic and Paideumic Review, F310; G38–41
"Analysis of the Experience in Lyric Poetry," G32
"The Anatomy of Mind," F283
Anchor Brendon, A26a.vi, 34
Ancient Myth in Modern Poetry, H115
Ancorp News of Books, F348
"And I John Saw," F191
"'And I Myself Have Learned to Use the Small Projector': On H.D., Woman, History, Recognition," G132
Anderson, Margaret, B16
Anderson, Maxwell, F24
Anderson, Wallace L., H17, 46
Andre Deutsch, A25a.iii
"Angels and Apocalypse: H.D.'s *Tribute to the Angels*," H243

"Anger, Conversation, and Myth," F537
Anglo-French Review, A4a; C43
Anna, Hajnal, D20
Les années vingt: Les écrivans américains à Paris et leurs amis, J11
"An Annotated Bibliography of Works about H.D.: 1969–1985," H216
"Another Novel by H.D.," F545, 606
Antaeus, C164
Antertine, Kevin, F444
Anthologie de la nouvelle poésie américaine, D4
Anthologie de la poésie américaine, D7
Anthologie de la poésie américaine contemporaine, D5
Anthologie de la poésie américaine contemporaine, H52
Anthology for the Enjoyment of Poetry, B15
"Anthology of American Verse," F561
Una antología de la lirica nord-americana, D34
Antología de la poesía norteamericana, D36
Antología de la poesía norteamericana, D37
Antología de la poesía norteamericana Contemporánea, D35
Antologia poezi americane, D30
"Approaches to Biography," F601
"Approaches to Biography: Two Studies of H.D.," G167
"Approaching *Borderline*," G116; H216
"Après la guerre de Troie: *Helen in Egypt* de H.D.," H180
Archai, G78
ARIF Press, A29, 30
Arizona Quarterly, F295, 456, 497; G106
Arkansas Gazette, F236
"Arms and the Woman: H.D.'s Revisionary Epic," H197
Arrowsmith, William, H73, 75
"The Art of H.D.," G45
"The Art of Hilda Doolittle," I2
"The Art of Poetry," G15
The Art of Reading Poetry, H46
"The Art of Silence and the Forms of Women's Poetry," H161
Arthur, Charlotte, A12
Arthur, Gavin, A12

Arthur, M. B., F90, 144
Arthur, Marilyn, G140
"The Artiness of Fiction," F107
The Aryans, C81
"As Others See Us," F555
Ashland [Ky.] Daily Independent, F443
Asia, G26
Asselineau, Roger, D8; F392
"At the Right Time, at the Right Place," F514
"Athene's Owl," G173
Atkins, Elizabeth, F164
Atlantic, G29
Atlantic Monthly, A145; F53, 451
Auerbach, Nina, G117
"Auf Spurensuche nach dem eigenen Ich," F477
Augustine, Jane, G200, 283, 294; I45
Aulicino, Robert, A26a.v
Auslander, Joseph, F52
Austin Chronicle, F543
"'Authentic Sisters': H.D. and Margaret Cravens," G289
"Author of the Week," F215
"Authors' Lives, Works Provide Book's Impetus," F455
Authors Living and Dead, F36; H98
Autobiography, H28
"Autobiography," F427
"Autobiography and Prophecy: H.D.'s The Gift," H216
"The Autobiography of a Future Poet from Pennsylvania," F458
The Autobiography of William Carlos Williams, H57
"Autobiography with Aliases," F451
The Avoidance of Literature: Collected Essays, G83; H156
"Avon," F242
A.V.S., F207

B., F112
Babcock, Robert, G291
Baccolini, Rafaella, G192; I49
Bacon, Martha, F219
Baldock, Robert, A30
Ballantyne Press, A1a
Baltimore Evening Sun, F256
Bangay, E. D., F187
Bann, Stephen, F92, 147
Bannon, Barbara A., F325, 441, 485

Barker, Michael, F329, 468
Barnes, Anne, F467
Barnes, Djuna, B7
Barr, Marleen S., H232
Barrington, Pauline, F25
Barron, Louis, F251
Barrows, Herbert, F217
Bartra, Agustí, D34, 36
Basellandschaft Liche Zeitung, F474
Basil Blackwell, A10a
"The Battered Triumphant Sage," F284
"The Battle between Rhyme and Imagism," F8
Bawer, Bruce, G159
Baym, Nina, F608
Beach, Joseph Warren, F563
Beacon Press, B17; C109
Beattie, Tori Potts, F435
Beck, Joyce Lorraine, G123
Becker, Alida, F289, 603
Becker, John Joseph, E2
Bedford, John Amador, D39
"Bee, Angels, Myrrh: Studies in H.D.'s 'Trilogy,'" I28
"Behind the Mask of the Pythoness," F518, 595
Being Geniuses Together, H36
Bell, E., C79
Belles Lettres, F145
Belzner, Emile, F241
Benét, William Rose, A11, 22; B13–14; F115
Benstock, Shari, F145, 608; H212
Beresford, Anne, F274, 369
Berg, André B11
Bergman, David, G239
Bergman, Peter, A25a
Berkeley Gazette, F257
Bernikow, Louise, H166
Bernstein, Michael André, G127
Berryman, John, F201
Berti, Luigi, D23; H41, 48
Best Poems of 1923, F559
Best Sellers, F285, 357, 360, 384, 418, 454
Bête Noir, G250
Bethlehem Globe-Times, F376, 464, 491, 511, 585; G112; J6, 10, 33
"Bethlehem Pays Proud Tribute to a Great Native Poet—H.D.," J9
Betjeman, John, A2a.iii

Bianchi, Ruggero, G50
"The Bibliographic Record of H.D.'s Contributions to Periodicals," G211
"The Bibliographic Record of Reviews of H.D's Work," G241
"*Bid Me to Live*: Within the Storm," H216
"Bild und Mythos in der Dichtung Hilda Doolittle," G91
"Biography," H216, 241
Bios, A15b
Birmingham Post, F155
"The Birth of Modernism: Des Imagistes and the Psychology of William James," I18
Black Swan Books, A9b, 10b, 18b, 26a.iv, v, vi
Blackmur, R. P., F86, 128 167
Blakeston, Oswell, F568
"Blank Page and the Issue of Female Creativity," G118
"Blessings in Disguise—Cross-Dressing as Re-Dressing for Female Modernists," G114
Bloom, Harold, H228
Bloomsbury Review, F459, 588
"Blouagh! Or Romping with the Whimsigists," F566
The Blue and Gray, C1
Blues, C104–5
Boccaporto, H41
Bock, Layeh Aronson, I18
Bodenheim, Maxwell, G17
Boehm, Herbert, F263
Bogan, Louise, D8, F161
Bogen 19, H217
Boles, Joseph David, I25
Boni and Liveright, A6
Bontempelli, Massimo, B11
Book Forum: An International Transdisciplinary Quarterly, G82
Book Week, F189
Book World, F407
Booklist, F43, 62, 120, 252, 403, 484, 508
The Bookman (New York), A4a, 5; C53, 66; F27, 39, 58, 77, 95, 121
The Bookman's Anthology of Verse, F558
Bookmark, F338
Books Abroad, F322, 340, 572
Books and Bookmen, F329, 331, 429, 468, 521

"Books This Year Have Looked to Past rather than Present for Greatness," F510
Boone, Bruce, G209
Booth, Philip, F334
Bornstein, George, F422; H208
Boston Evening Transcript, F17, 51, 76, 119, 137
Boston Globe, C2, 3, 4, 5, 6, 7; F404, 534
Boston Herald, F537
Bottomley, Gordon, F157
Boughn, Michael, G72, 210–11, 241
Boulton, James T., H157
Boundary 2, G107
Bousquet, Alain, D7
Bowering Press, A19, 20, 21
Boyle, Kay, H36
Bradbury, Malcolm, H119, 144
Brathwaite, W[illiam] S[tanley], F17
Breaking the Sequence: Women's Experimental Fiction, H237
Bregy, Katherine, G19
Bremer Blatt, F479
Brendin Publishing Company, A17a.i, 23
Brennan, Joseph, F302
Breslin, Denise, 34a.i–ii
Breslin, James, H183
Brewer, Warren & Putnam, B11
Brief Lives: A Biographical Guide to the Arts, H117
"The Bright Immortal Olive," F56
"A Brilliant New Defense of Poetry," F164
Brin, Ruth F., F281
"Bring It All Back Home: Derivations and Quotations in Robert Duncan and the Poundian Tradition," G127
Broe, Mary Lynn, G256
Bronder, Howard, F406, 455
Bronner, Milton, F223
Bronowski, J., B11
Brooks, Cleanth, H35, 124
Broom, F28
Brown, Chris, G240, 292
Brown, Harry Matthew, H108
Brown, Harvey, A28a
Brown, John, D6; H60
Brownworth, Victoria A., F494
Bruccoli, Matthew, A8a.ii; H97
Bruno Chapbooks, G8

Bruzzi, Zara, G252
Bryher, A4, 8, 12, 19, 22, 23, 31, 33; B7; C116; F23, 27; H76
"Bryher," G133
Bryn Mawr Alumnae Bulletin, C124, 149–50; F222; J34
Bubb, Charles Clinch, A1b, 3; E16
Buch der Könige, H227
Buck, Doris, F211
Buck, Claire, F330, 434, 469, 502; G141; I51
Bucknell Review, G140
Bulletin of the Poetry Society of America, J4
Bullough, Geoffrey, H26
Burgess, Anthony, F328, 466, 501
Burnett, Gary, G203, 251, 274; H229; I43
Burnshaw, Stanley, G21
Bush, Douglas, G43; H32
"'But Am I Wrong?': A Study of Interrogation in *End to Torment*," H216
"'But to an Outcast and a Vagabond': Authority and Rhetoric in the Poetry of H.D.," I34
Butler, E[liza] M[arian], H67
Butscher, Edward, F403
Butterick, George, F602
Butts, Mary, B7
"By Impression Re-Called," G218
Bynner, Witter, A11

Cabellero, E. Gimenez, B11
Cain, Kathleen, F459, 588
Callahan, Eileen, A32
Callahan, Robert, A32
Call-Chronicle [Allentown, Pa.], F487
Camboni, Marina, G160, 285
Campbell, Bruce, G266
Camper, Carol, F458
Canadian Forum, F232
The Cantos of Ezra Pound, Some Testimonies, B12
Caraion, Ion, D30
Caravel, C115
Carcanet Press, A10b.ii, 24b.i, ii, d, 27a.v, 28b.iii, 31a.iii, 33a.iii, 38a.iii, A39b; F129
Cardenal, Ernesto, D37–38
Cargill, Oscar, H45
Carne-Ross, D. S., H73

Carruth, Hayden, F394
Case, Laurie, I47
Cassou, Jean, B11
A Catalogue of the Imagist Poets, H90
Caterpillar, G54, 56, 60, 62
Cather, Willa, A8a.ii
Catholic World, G19
"'Ce que recèlent les mots' dans *The Walls Do Not Fall*," G126
CEA Critic, G174
Cedar Rock, F415
"Celebration of Man and God," F200
"A Centennial for H.D.: 50th for New Directions," F531
"Ceremonies of the Alphabet: Female Gramatologies and the Female Authorgraph," G155
Cerf, Bennett, A11
"A Challenge to Mammon," F185
"The Challenges of Editing the H.D.-Pearson Correspondence," G297
Chang, C93–94
Chapbook (London), A9; C44, 77; F10; G13
Charles, John W., F346
Charles Clinch Bubb and the Clerk's Press, E16
"Charles Olson's Imago Mundi, H.D.'s Flowering of the Rod: A Study of the Soul in a Recent Poetics," G78
Charles Scribner's Sons, B15
Chase, Kathleen, F294, 522
Chatto & Windus, A13a, 18a
Chicago Literary Review, F533
Chicago Sun Book Week, F190
Chicago Sun-Times, F410
Chicago Tribune Books, F226
Childe, Gordon, C81
"Childhood Memoir for Adults," F494
Chisholm, Dianne, G278
Chiswick Press, A2
Choice, F84, 90, 101, 144, 327, 356, 388, 419, 492, 505, 518, 604
Christian Science Monitor, F334
Ciardi, John, H68
Citizen [Ottawa], F416
City Lights Books, A36; J21–22
City Paper, F288
Clack, Jerry, G295
Clare, John, G95

Clarke, Bert, A16b
"'Classical' Books in the Bryher Library," G287
Classical Review, F142
"A Classical Style Was Her Strength," F504
Classical World, F146
The Classical World of H.D., F572; H78
The Classics and Our Twentieth Century Poets, H19
"Classics in English," F12
Cleary, Rosemary Joan, I54
Clemen, Ursula, D18
Clerk's Press, A1b, 3
Cleveland Plain Dealer, F212
Cleveland Press, F247, 255, 409
"Clio in Crisis: The Historiographic Impulse in the Writings of H.D.," I25
Cloak and Gown: Scholars in the Secret War, 1939–1961, H222
Close-Up, C87–88, 90–100, 102, 106; F564–65; J18
"Clouds of Memories: Books H.D. Shared with Me, 1934–1960," G228
Clyne, Ronald, A22
Codrescu, Andrei, F510, 512
Coffman, Stanley, F571; H55, 79
Cohen, Edward, E9
A Coherent Splendor: The American Renaissance, 1910–1950, H220
"Coining New Words: H.D.'s Trilogy of Artistic Growth," G134
Colish, A., A16b
Collecott, Diana, A35a.iii; F330, 469, 502; G161, 175, 178–79, 253–54, 277, 279, 286; H195, 216, 241
Collected Parodies, H18
"Collection Shows Talent of Hilda Doolittle," F355
College English, F231; G32, 79
Collins, H. P., C71; F57, 70, 562, 563; H14; J5
Columbus Dispatch, F261
Combellack, C. R. B., F573
Combellick, Katherine Ann, I31
Coming to Light: American Women Poets in the Twentieth Century, G125, 139
"Comment—H.D.," G20
Commonweal, F127, 307, 523
"'Companions of the Flame': The Relationship between the Mother and Language in Jean Rhys and H.D.," I29
Comparative Literature, F573
Comparative Literature Studies, G97
"The Compost Library," G129
The Comrade, C9, 11–14, 17
"Con Amore," F110
"The Concept of Projection: H.D.'s Visionary Powers," G153; H228, 241
Conceptions of Reality Modern American Poetry, H89
"Concerning 'Free Verse,'" G17
The Concise Encyclopedia of English and American Poetry, H79
"Conflict and Creativity in the World of H.D.," G100
Conjunctions, C162–63; F148, 547
Connolly, Cyril, F96
Constable and Company, A2
Constantine, Murray, C123
Contact, A4a, C52
Contact II, F435, 539
Contact Collection of Contemporary Writers, B7
Contact Editions, A8a.i
Contempo, F123
Contemporary American Authors, H43
Contemporary Literature, A28b, 33; C154–56; C171; F431, 458, 593; G64, 66–71, 89, 94, 99, 153, 172, 192–98, 281; H126
Contemporary Review, F83
"Conversations with Lawrence," G37
Cook, Howard Willard, H10
Cooke, Judy, F104
Cooley, Franklin A., F248
Cooper, Merian C., C93
Copeland, Donna, G243
Copper Canyon Press, A37
Corman, Cid, G47
Cosgrave, Mary Silva, F494
"Costumes of the Mind: Transvestism as Metaphor in Modern Literature," G108
Coterie, C47; G14
Cournos, John, B9; C170; H28
Coward, Noel, C96
Cowley, Malcolm, F61
Cox, Edwin Marion, C68
Coyote's Journal, G52, 55
C.P., F113

"A Crack in the Ice: Subjectivity and the Mirror in H.D.'s *Her*," G226
The Craft and Context of Translation, H73, 75
Cramer, Patricia, I48
Crane, Milton, F198
Crawford, Fred, F601; G167, 234, 304
"Creating a Woman's Mythology: H.D.'s *Helen in Egypt*," G90; H241
Credences, G80
Creeley, Robert, G212
Criterion, F126, 140
A Critical Fable, H9
Critical Inquiry, G108, 117–18
Critical Quarterly, F273; G161
Crossing Press, J23
Crowder, Richard, F585
Crowell, Joan Therese, I19
Crozier, Andrew, F391
Culture of Ancient Greece and Rome, C82
Cumberland Poetry Review, G216
Cunningham, J. V., F127; G24
Curwen Press, A17a.i

D. H. Lawrence: A Composite Biography, H64, 69
"D. H. Lawrence and Traditions in Women's Literature," I42
D. H. Lawrence: L'homme et la genèse de son oeuvre: Les années de formation, 1885–1919, H103
D. H. Lawrence: The Man and His Work: The Formative Years, 1885–1919, H103
Dachslager, E. L., F279
Dahlen, Beverly, G213
Daiches, David, F224
Daily Oklahoman, F230
Daily World, F353
Dallas Daily Times Herald, F214
Dallas Morning News, F449, 578, 599
Damon, S. Foster, F569; H29
The Dancers, E5
Daniels, Earl, H46
Darnton, Maida Castelhun, B11
Darragh, Tim, J8
Darrantière, Maurice, A8a.i, 14, 15a, 16; B6
Dasenbrock, Reed Way, F493
"Dating H.D.'s Writing," H241
Davenport, Guy, F408

Davidson, Eugene, F192, 202
Davidson, Harry A., F250
Davis, Dale, G180; H216
Dawson, David, F487
Dawson, Fielding, G214
Day, Martin S., H135
De Gravelines, Kyrl, E1
"Dea Awakening: A Reading of H.D.'s *Trilogy*," G123
Deadalus Press, E18
Dear Theo: An Autobiography of Vincent Van Gogh, from His Letters, C119
Death of a Hero, H201
"De(con)structive Poetics: Readings of Hilda Doolittle's *The War Trilogy*," I23
DeFord, Sara, H63
Delavenay, Emile, H103
Delavenay, Katharine, H103
Dembo, L. S., G64; H89, 216
Denver Quarterly, F423
Description of Greece, C66
DeShazer, Mary K., H213, 216; I21
Desy, Peter Michael, I14
"A Detailed Chronology of Ezra Pound's London Years, 1908–1920, Part 1: 1908–1914," G131
Detroit News, F450
Deutsch, Babette, A8a.ii; F73, 88, 117, 160, 188, 300; H30, 58
Deutsche Zeitung, F244
"The Development of a Poetic Vision: H.D.'s Growth from Imagist to Mythologist," I17
Di Prima, Diane, H223
Dial, A4a; C51; F20, 38, 56, 81, 89, 99; F559; G15
Dial Press, A26a.v
"Eine Dichter huldigt Shakespeare," F239
Dickie, Margaret, F607
Dictionary of Literary Biography, H170, 184
A Dictionary of Literature in the English Language from Chaucer to 1940, H110
Diepeveen, Leonard, G151
Dillingham, Thomas, F362
"Dionysian Presences," G267
Discontented Discourses: Feminism / Textual Intervention / Psychoanalysis, H232
"Discovering Identity," F332, 470, 503

Dobija, Jane, F450
Dobson, Silvia, C162–63; G181, 228, 255; H216
Dodd, Elizabeth Caroline, I52
Dodd, Mead and Company, B12
Dodsworth, Martin, F358, 379
Doggett, Frank, G22
Dollard, John, F249
Donelson, J., F39
Donohue, Dennis, F576
"Doolittle Gets Praise, and a State Marker," J8
"Doolittle's 'Helen'," G243
"Doolittle's *The Walls Do Not Fall*," G227
Doorn, Helga (H.D.), A12
Double Dealer, A5; C61; F19, 48, 556
"A Double Matrix: Re-reading H.D.," G179
Douglas, Norman, B7
Dowding, Hugh C. T., C173
Doyle, Charles, G164; H230
A Draft of XXX Cantos, B12
Drake, William, H219
Dreadnaught, E17
"Dreaming a Renaissance," H208
Dreiser, Theodore, A11
Driskell, Leon V., F446
Dublin Magazine, F34, 165
Dudek, Louis, F411, 413
Duffey, Bernard, F430; H153
Duke, Maurice, F402
Duncan, Robert, A27a.i, 28b, 33; F303; G47, 49, 52, 54–60, 63, 65, 75, 80, 101, 119, 142, 165–66, 168, 238; H228, 241
Dunn, Margaret M., G174, 235; I40
Dupee, F. W., F166
DuPlessis, Rachel Blau, F145, 576, 603, 604, 607; G99, 101, 113, 120, 122, 154, 182, 193–94; H204, 214, 216, 241
Durance, Mary, F416
Duval, Joanne, F457, 584
D.V.H., F116

Eagleton, Terry, F525
Earp, F. R., F142
East Bay Review of Books, F420
East Hampton [N.Y.] Star, F540
Eberhart, Richard, F304

"The Echoing Spell of H.D.'s *Trilogy*," G94; H228, 241
Ecker, Gisela, H238
"The Economics of Influence: Gift Giving in H.D. and Robert Duncan," G239
Eder, Doris, G82
Edfelt, Johannes, D40
The Edge of the Image: Marianne Moore, William Carlos Williams, and Some Other Poets, H96
Edman, Erwin, F41
Edward, Oliver, G51
Egoist, A1b, c, 2, 4a, 5; C19, 22, 25, 26, 28, 29, 30, 31, 32, 33, 34, 35, 36, 37, 38, 39, 41, 42; F6; G2–3, 5–7
"The Egyptian Cat," A10b.i–ii; H169, 241
Eigo Seinen, G77
Eisenberg, Emmanuel, F562
Elegy for Soprano and Six Players, E10
"Elements of the Sounding: H.D. and the Origins of Modernist Prosodies," G210
Elicker, Drew, A37
Eliot, T. S., B11; F2; H6
Elkind, Sue N., F298
Ellis, Havelock, B7
Elton, Godfrey, A8a.ii
Emerson, Dorothy, G25
Emery, Clark, G38, 40
Encyclopedia Americana, H70, 211
Encyclopedia of World Literature in the Twentieth Century, H93
"*End to Torment*: Etudes d'interrogation dans la mémoire de H.D.," H185
"An End to Torment: H. D.'s Metonymic Course," H226
Engel, Bernard F., G66
Engelmen, Edmund, A24b.i, c.iii, d
*Englisch Horn: Anthologie angelshachsischer Lyrik von den Anfhansen bis zur Gegenwart*m, D16
Englische und amerikanische Naturdichtung im 20. Jahrhundert, H202, 203, 210
English, G95
English Association, F526
English Literary Studies Monograph Series no. 49, H245

English Literature in Transition (1880–1920), G234
English Years, H31
"Enigmatic View of Bisexuality," F544
Enitharmon Press, B19
"Envoi," G24
Enzensberger, Christian, D18
"Escaping into Reality," F562
Essays and Opinions, F129
Essays in Criticism, F586; G74, 87
Essence, F302
Estudos Anglo-Americanos, G265
Észak-Amerikai Költök Antológiája, D20
Etude Freudienne, G73
Etudes Anglaises, F392, 432
Etudes Freudiennes, D9–10
"Euripides and Professor Murray," H6
"Euripides as Lyrist," F143
The European Caravan, B11
Evans, Stuart, F102
"Evelyn Scott, H.D., and the Evolution of American Stream of Consciousness Writing," F543
Evergreen Review, A28b, C146
"Examples of Free Verse at Its Best," F22
"Excerpts from 'Language Aquisition,'" H241
Exile and Other Poems, F560
"Exile in the American Grain: H.D.'s Diaspora," G256
Expiation, C98
Explicator, G31, 227, 243
Express, J7
"Exquisite Cameos and Intaglios," F9
Exquisite Corpse, F493
Ezra Pound, H72
Ezra Pound—A Close-Up, H94
Ezra Pound among the Poets, H208
"Ezra Pound & H.D.," F417
Ezra Pound and Dorothy Shakespear: Their Letters, 1909–1914, H200
Ezra Pound and His World, H165
Ezra Pound and William Carlos Williams—The University of Pennsylvania Conference Papers, H193
"Ezra Pound Study 'Fond, Intimate,'" F402
Ezra Pound: The Last Rower, H145
Ezra Pound's Kensington, H85
"Ezra's Girl," F450

Faas, Eckbert, G107
"The Faces Are Familiar," F312
Faery, Rebecca Blevins, G215
Fairchild, Hoxie Neale, H39
Fairclough, Henry Rushton, H19
Fairfield Press, B10
The Faith of a (Woman) Writer, H226
"Falling from the White Rock: A Myth of Margins in H.D.," G257
"Family, Sexes, Psyche: An Essay on H.D. and the Muse of the Woman Writer," G102; H216
"Far Away and Long Ago," F321
Fassett, Catherine Lewis, F314
Fausset, H. I'A., F156
"Faustine Re-Membered: H.D.'s Use of Swinburne's Poetry in *Hermoine*," G284
F.A.Z., F475
Feder, Lillian, H115
Federman, Raymond, D10
Feldstein, Richard, H232
Felsenthal, Francine, A25a.iv
Felton, Henry, G14
"The Female Faust," H155
"Feminine Forms of Closure: Gilman, Deming and H.D.," I32
"Feminine Hermeticism in H.D.'s *Trilogy*," G145
"The Feminist behind the Modernism," F539
Feminist Criticism: Essays on Theory, Poetry, and Prose, G79; H155
Feminist Studies, G113, 272
Femme á femme, H132
Femmes Frauen Women, H238
Ferchl, Irene, F472
Ferlinghetti, Lawrence, A35
Ferraté, Juan, D38
Ferretti, Massimo, D21
Ferrill, Thomas Hornsby, F225
Fetler, Paul, E6
"The Fiction of H.D. (Hilda Doolittle)," I7
"Der Fieberwahn eines Mädchens," F480
Fiedler, Leslie, F268
Fields, Kenneth, A24c.i; G53; H129
"'The Fiery Moment': H.D. and the Eleusinian Landscape of English Modernism," G252

Fifty Poets, B13
"Figuring Woman (Out): Feminine Subjectivity in the Poetry of Emily Dickinson, Marriane Moore, and H.D.," I53
Filiatreau, John, F385
Fillmore, Hildegarde, F58
"The Filmgoing Imagination: Filmmaking and Filmgoing as the Subjects of Modern American Literature," I24
"A Filmography for H.D.," G240
Finch, Annie R. C., G216
"A Fine Tribute to Freud," F248
Firchow, Peter E., G109; H158
"Fire and Ice," F15
The First Wave: Women Poets in America. 1915–1945, H219
"Fishing the Murex Up: Sense and Resonance in H.D.'s *Palimpsest*," G196; H241
Fitts, Dudley, F193, 200
Five Trees Press, A32
Flammarion, Camille, A35
Fleischman, Wolfgang Bernard, H93
"Flesh Made Word: Maternal Inscription in H.D.," G148
Fletcher, Ian, H90
Fletcher, John Gould, B10; F6, 7, 75, 569; G9; H33, 42
Flint, F. Cudworth, F204
Flint, F. S., B9; C155; F10, 126; G5, 13
"Flood of Books on Shakespeare Marks 1949 Publisher's Lists," F236
Florida Magazine of Verse, F228
Florit, Eugenio, D35
"The Flower Magicians Bartered For," I13
"Flute and Cymbal," F29
"For H.D.," H216
Ford, Ford Maddox, B7, 10, 12; *see also* Heuffer, Ford Maddox
Ford, Hugh, H136
"Forewarned as Regards H.D.'s Prose," H99
"Foreword [to *Paint It Today*]," G193
"The Forging of H.D.," G246
"Form in Vers-libre," G95
Formation of the Greek People, C84
Fort Wayne [Ind.] News Sentinel, F216, 258

Fortnightly Review, C57; F65
Forward, C8, 10
Frank, Grace, F94
Frank, Kathryn G., I2
Frank Shay, B2c
Frankfurter Literatur-Rundschau, F476
"Free Verse in England," G3
Freedley, George, F220
Freeman, Clara Jean, I46
Freeman, Lucy, H171
Freeman, Myra Cohn, F227
Freibert, Lucy M., F295, 456, 497, 513; G100, 106
French, William, G124
Freud, Sigmund, A24
"Freud and H.D.," G73, 82; H125
"Freud and His Doctor," F271
Freud and Women, H171
Freud As We Knew Him, H125–26
Freud et son temps, D2
"Freud's Patient Writes Tribute," F258
Freydorf, Roswith von, D19
Frezzolini, Sylvia, A17a.ii, A39
Friedberg, Anne, G116, 132, 305; H216
Friedman, Ellen G., H237
Friedman, Susan Stanford, F109, 297, 345, 375, 437, 457, 465, 499, 506, 530, 583–84, 587–88, 593, 596; G79, 90, 103, 113, 120, 122, 136, 139, 169, 183, 193–94, 204, 217, 236, 247, 256, 302; H172, 184, 216, 228, 239–41; I10
"Friends of H.D. Will Promote Bethlehem Poet," J6
Fritz, Angela DiPlace, H224; I22
From Another World: The Autobiography of Louis Untermeyer, H40
"From Death to Life," F171
"From Image to Epic Quest," F583
From Modern to Contemporary: American Poetry, 1945–65, H183
"From Semblance to Selfhood: The Evolution of Woman in H.D.'s Neo-Epic *Helen in Egypt*," G106
"From 75 B.C. to 1925 A.D.," F75
"From the Day Book," G47
From Whitman to Sandburg in American Poetry: A Critical Survey, H13
Fromm, Gloria G., G246
Frontier Press, A28a

Frontiers: A Journal of Women Studies, G235
Frost, Robert, A11
Fuchs, Miriam, G280; H237
Fuller, John, F382
Fulsom, Ralph Edward, I3
"'The Fulsomeness of Her Prolixity': Reflections on 'H.D., "Imagiste,"'" G152
Funt, Karen Lorraine Bryce, I26
Furbank, P. N., H109

Gabree, John, F293
Gaffney, Wilbur, F321
Gage, John T., G88; H173
Gall, Sally M., H190
Gallery Magazine, F292
Galloway, Ruth D., I5
Gallup, Donald, A33
"Garbo/Helen: The Self-Projection of Beauty by H.D.," G110
Gardiner, Jeffrey, G267
Gardner, Frieda, F520; I27
Gargoyle (Paris), A5; C55, 56
Gass, William, F283–84
Gates, Norman T., G86; H130
A Gathering of Angels: A Publication of Papers Presented at the Conference A Gathering of Angels, February 24–26, 1989, H243
Gaunt Island, F568
Gawn, Sumett, F19
Gay News [Literary Supplement], G133
Gazette [Montreal], F411
G.B.E., F136
Gehman, Geoff, G112
Geisheker, Mary Rose, I6
Gelpi, Albert, A36; F576; G125, I70, 306; H178, 216, 220, 228, 241
"Gender and Genre Anxiety: Elizabeth Barret Browning and H.D. as Epic Poets," G183
The Gender of Modernism, B20; H240
General Magazine and Historical Chronicle, G33
Genius and Gender: Revisionary Visions of Emily Dickinson, H.D., Elizabeth Bishop, Gwendolyn Brooks, and Adrienne Rich, H197
Geoffrey Cumberlege, A21
Gerber, Richard, F242

Gerhardi, W., C75
G.H.C., F82
Gibbons, Kathryn Gibbs, F572; G45
Gibson, Wilfred, F178
Gies, Judith, F598
Gilbert, Sandra, A16b, 39; F576, 593; G94, 108, 135, 155, 162; H161, 215–16, 225, 231
Gilkes, Martin, H34
Gill, Elaine Goldman, J23
Gilliland, Gail, F448
Gilliland, Mary, J23
"Glacial Bloom," F45
Glasgow, Joanne, G272
Glasgow Herald, F154
Glebe, B2; C20
"Glimpses of the Last Day," G75
"The Glory That Is Greece," F117
Glover, John, F275, 370
"'Die Glückselige Einheitlichkeit des Weibes' und 'Woman Is Perfect'— Lou Andreas-Salome und H.D. in der Schule bei Freud," H238
"Go Little Book: Ezra Pound, Hilda Doolittle, and 'Hilda's Book,'" G115
Godine, David R., A24c.i, iii
Gohdes, Clarence, F269
Goheen, Cynthia J., G218
Goldsmith, Margaret, C123
Goodwin, K. L., H91
Gorman, Herbert S., F37, 49
Goskowski, Francis, F418
Gould, Jean, H137, 167
Gould, Wallace, B7
Grabhorn-Hoyem, A29
Graham, Desmond, F396
Grahn, Judy, H205
Granta, F112, 136
Graves, Robert A2a.iii
Gray, Edith (H.D.), C2, 3, 4, 5, 6, 7, 8, 9, 10, 11, 12, 13
Gray, Richard, H242
Great Writers Student Library, H194
"The Greatest Imagist," F34
"A Greek Idyll," F98
Greek Social Life, C72
Greenwich Village, A2; C24; G8
Greenwood, E. B., G74
Gregory, Alyse, F81
Gregory, Eileen, G195, 205, 219, 257, 281, 290; H241, 243

Gregory, Horace, A22, 26a, 27; F106, 163, 235, 307, 316; G43; H50, 66, 74
Gregson, Ian, F586
G.R.E.S., G93, 96
Grier, Barbara, H146
Gross, Harvey, H82
Grove Press, A25a, 26a, 27; E18
Gruson, Françoise de, D2
Gubar, Susan, A17a.ii; F576; G94, 104, 114, 118, 150, 155; H161, 215, 225, 228, 231, 241
Guenther, Charles, F531
Guest, Barbara, F145, 148, 291, 297, 345, 375, 437, 518, 529, 530, 547, 594–95, 598–602; G158, 171, 184; H196, 216, 241
Guiterman, Arthur, F42
Günther, Alfred, F239, 244, 246; J35

H., F377
Haas, Willy, F240
Hacker, Marylin, J14
Halpert, Stephen, B17; C109
Hamburger, Michael, H104
Hamilton, Ian, F514
Hamlet's Castle: The Study of Literature as a Social Experience, H147
A Handbook of American Literature, H135
Haney, John Louis, H11
Hannibal, Mary Ellen, F540
Hannoversche Allgemeine Zeitung, F80
Hanscombe, Gillian, H221
Hansen, Jorgen Christian, G220
H.A.P., F228
Harcourt, Brace and Company, B8
"Hardly Worth the Trouble," F230
Hardy, John Edward, F571
Harmer, J. B., H138
Harper's Magazine, G27
Harriet Monroe and the Poetry Renaissance: The First Ten Years of Poetry, 1912–1922, H152
Harrington, Elaine, I8
Harris, Kathryn Gibbs, F287, 366
Harris, Roger, F405
Hartley, Marsden, B7
Hatlen, Burton, F597; G221
"Haunting Households, Heidegger, and Holy Ghosts: A Psychology of the Family within the Economy of Culture," I54
Häusermann, H. W., F320
H.D., D22
"H.D.," F10
"H.D.: A Study in Sensitivity," G22
"H.D.: A Symbolist Perspective," G97; I35
"H.D.—A Tribute," G121
"H.D.: An Appreciation," G44; H228
"H.D. and A. C. Swinburne: Decadence and Modernist Women's Writing," G272
"H.D. and A. C. Swinburne: Decadence and Sapphic Modernism," G272
"H.D. and Freud," F298
"H.D. and Freud: Bisexuality and Feminine Discourse," G141
"H.D. and Her Poetry: An Adult Developmental Approach to the Question of Women's Creative Productivity," I47
"H.D. and Hugh Dowding," G230
"H.D. and Lawrence: Two Allusions," G203
"H.D. and Lawrence: Two More Allusions," G231
"H.D. and Marianne Moore: Correspondences and Contradictions," I41
"H.D. and Mass Observation," G277
"H.D. and R.A.: Early Love and the Exclusion of Ezra Pound," G288
"H.D. and Rummel's *Songs for Children*: A Lyrical Collaboration," G292
"H.D. and the Age of Myth," G34; H59
"H.D. and the 'Blameless Physician,'" G67; H126
"H.D. and the Film Arts," G151
"H.D. and the Imagists," H3
"H.D. and the Origins of Imagism," G163; H241
"H.D. and the Poetics of 'Spiritual Realism,'" G69
"H.D. and the Poetics of Revelation," G270
"H.D. and the Problem of Escapism," G74

"H.D. and the Search for the Absolute," I14
"H.D. as Leader of Imagists," F51
"H.D. at Seventy," G35
"H.D.: Bethlehem Poet, Greek Flower," J16
H.D. between Image and Epic: The Mysteries of Her Poetics, H229
H.D. Book, A28a; G47, 49, 52, 54–60, 62–63, 65, 75, 80, 101, 119, 142, 165–66; H175, 228, 241
"H.D., C. G. Jung, & Küsnacht: Fantasia on a Theme," H216
"H.D.: Centennial Issue," G194
"H.D. Chronology: Composition and Publication of Volumes," G204, 217
H.D. et Freud, D10
"H.D. et Freud," G73
"H.D.: Feministe?" F596
"H.D.: From Scribe's Scribe to People's Poet?" F436
"H.D., H.D.," F297, 345, 375, 437, 530
"H.D. Hedges, but 'Hilda's Book' Reveals the Fledgling Pound," F425
"H.D. Honored: State Marks Birthplace of Late Bethlehem Poet," J10
"H.D., 'Imagiste?'" G216
"H.D., 'Imagiste': An Elemental Mind," G259
"H.D. Imagiste and Her Octopus Intelligence," H216
"H.D.: Life of a Poet," F581
"H.D. Mother of Us All?" G159
H.D. Newsletter, C151, 173; G203–7, 228–33, 238–42, 247–49, 286–98, 305
"H.D.—On Being Geniuses Together," F445
"H.D. *Palimpsest*: En introduktion," G220
"The H.D. Papers at Yale University," G206
"H.D. Pays Tribute to Bard in Poem, Perceptive Essay," F207
"H.D.: Poems That Matter and Dilutations," G66
"H.D.: Pound Wise or Foolish?" F409
"H.D. Rediviva," F372, 393
"H.D. Sends Her Greetings to a Stratford Address," F214

"H.D., Serenitas, and Canto CXIII," G138
H.D.: The Life and Work of an American Poet, F109, 297, 326, 345, 375, 437, 457, 459, 465, 499, 506, 518, 530, 585, 588–93, 595, 596, 601; G300, 302–3
"H.D.: The Perfect Imagist," H24
H.D.: The Poetics of Childbirth and Creativity, H246
"H.D.: The Shape of a Career," I12
"H.D. to Freud with Love," F249
"H.D. Typifies Best Work of Imagists," F381
"H.D.? Who Was She?" F593
H.D.: Woman and Poet, F545, 605; H216
"H.D. Writes of Influential Men in Poetry Collection," F511
"H.D.'s 'Athenians': Son and Mother in *Hedylus*," G197
"H.D.'s Autoheterography," G278
"H.D.'s Books in the Bryher Library," G232
"H.D.'s Challenge," G168
"H.D.'s Choruses from Euripides," F3
"H.D.'s Collected Poems Recall Author's Dash into the Raging Deep," F50
"H.D.'s Fiction: Convolutions to Clarity," H237
"H.D.'s Flaws," G190
"H.D.'s 'Fortune Teller,'" G186
"H.D.'s Gift Is Mystical, Precious," F490
"H.D.'s 'Gift of Greek,' Bryher's 'Eros of the Sea,'" G286
"H.D.'s 'H.D. by Delia Alton,'" G185
"H.D.'s 'Helen in Egypt': A Recollection," I11
"H.D.'s 'Hermetic Definition' and the Order of Writing," G266
"H.D.'s 'Hermetic Definition': The Poet as Archtypal Mother," G89
"H.D.'s Identity," G157
"H.D.'s Imagist Wisdom," F378
"H.D.'s Influence on Richard Aldington," H245
"H.D.'s 'Lethe': A Linguistic Approach," G265
"H.D.'s Life of Myth and Modernism," F444

"H.D.'s Memories of Freud," F281
"H.D.'s Method," H14
"H.D.'s Moravian Heritage," G298
"H.D.'s 'New Beginning,'" G177
"H.D.'s 'Oread'," G31
"H.D.'s 'Oread': A Linguistic Approach," G262
"H.D.'s Palimpsests," I27
"H.D.'s Poetic Experiment in the Art of Fiction," F71
"H.D.'s Poetic Gifts Appear in Memoir, Novel," F464, 491
"H.D.'s 'Projector II' and *Chang, a Film of the Jungle*," G229
"H.D.'s *Prosodie à clef*: St. John Perse and *Hermetic Definition*," G296
"H.D.'s 'Pursuit' and Sappho," G291
"H.D.'s Rescension of the Egyptian Book of the Dead in *Palimpsest*," G272
"H.D.'s Romantic Landscapes: The Sexual Politics of the Garden," G224, 240
"H.D.'s Scene of Writing—Poetry as (and) Analysis," G98
"H.D.'s Self-Inscription: Between Time and 'Out of Time' in *The Gift*," G280
"H.D.'s *Trilogy*, or the Secret Language of Change," G160
"H.D.'s *Trilogy*: A Portrait of the Artist in Full Bloom," G174
"H.D.'s Troy: Some Bearings," G293
"H.D.'s Version of Euripides' *Ion*," J17
"H.D.'s Volumes of Dickinson's Poems; and, A Note on Candor and Iniquity," G290
"H.D.'s Writing: Herself a Ghost," G209
Healey, Claire, H159
Heany, Sean, F537
The Heart to Artemis—A Writer's Memoirs, H76
"A Helen from Bethlehem," F590
"Helen in Egypt," G51
"*Helen in Egypt*: A Culmination," G70
"*Helen in Egypt*: Variations sur un thème sonore," G93
"Helen in Greece and Egypt," F339
"Helen in Vienna," G295
"Helen of Troy: Her Myth in Modern Poetry," I38

Helforth, John (H.D.), A16
"Heliodora's Greece," H216
"The Hellas of Dreams," F94
Hemingway, Ernest, B7, 12
Henderson, Alice Corbin, B4; G11
Hengen, Shannon, G296
Henry Holt and Company, A4a.ii
Henstell, Bruce, B18
"Her Deepest Passion Was D. H. Lawrence," F576
"Herald of Imagism," F569
Hermitage House, Inc., B16
Herr, Mary A., C150
Herrick, Robert, A26
Herring, Robert, A12, 23
Herrman, John, B7
Herself Defined: The Poet H.D. and Her World, H196
"Herself Delineated: Chronological Highlights of H.D.," H241
Heuffer, Ford Maddox, H8; *see also* Ford, Ford Maddox
Heydt, Eric, A27a
Heymenn, C. David, F425; H145
Highest Apple, H205
Highland News [Inverness], F172, 181
Hilda Doolittle, H95
"Hilda Doolittle," G23
"Hilda Doolittle," H211
"Hilda Doolittle," I1
"Hilda Doolittle: A Window on the Literary 20's and 30's," F577
"Hilda Doolittle and Frances Gregg," G262
"Hilda Doolittle (1886–1961)," F145
"Hilda Doolittle, 1886–1961," H158
"Hilda Doolittle Exhibit on at Yale," J2
"Hilda Doolittle: Pagan Mystic of Bethlehem PA," F600
"Hilda Doolittle, Poet, Dead at 75," J26
"Hilda Doolittle: Poet in Ceaseless Search of Herself," F598
"Hilda Doolittle Returns Home," J33
"Hilda Doolittle's Ezra Pound Journal," F404
"Hilda in Egypt," G125; H228
"Hilda's Book," A33; F399
"Hilda's Lament," F405
Hill, D. A. (H.D.), C116
Hillyer, Robert, F53

Hirsh, Elizabeth A., G201; H232, 241; I50
A History of American Poetry, 1900–1940, H50
A History of Modern Poetry from the 1890's to the High Modernist Mode, H148
Hitchcock, Henry Russell, Jr., F565
H.M.M., F355
Hogan, William, F313
Hogue, Cynthia Anne, G307; I53
"Hölderlin, Leopardi, and H.D.," F304
Holland, Joyce, I12
Holland, Norman, D10; G67, 73; H125–27, 228
Hollenberg, Donna Krolik, C170; G297; H246; I36
Hollingsworth, Marsha, A37
Holmes, John, F137
A Homemade World: The American Modernist Writers, H140
"Homonymous: A Meditation on H.D.'s *Trilogy*," G213
"Honey Rather than Wine," F80
Hopeck, Phyllis, A37
Horace Liveright, Inc., A6a.iii
Horn Book Magazine, F495
Houghton Mifflin Company, A2a.ii, 5a.ii, 8a.ii, 9a, 10a, 13a.ii, 18a.ii; B3
Hound and Horn, F86, 564, 565; G24, 34
Hound and Quarry, H59
Houston Chronicle, F543, 577
Houston Post, F279
How Does a Poem Mean, H68
Howdle, Andrew, G145
Howe, Anne, F566
HOW(ever), C103; G177
Hoyem, Andrew, G61
H.R., F155
Hubbell, Lindley William, F59, 364, 560; G77
Hudson, Ben, E11
Hudson, Dora, F296, 344
Hudson Review, F394
Hughes, Gertrude Reif, G282; H197
Hughes, Glenn, B9; H24, 91
"Humanity Disdained?" F520
Humphries, Rolfe, F210, 218
Hunter, William B., Jr., F577
Hunting, Constance, F489

Hurd, Carol, H164
Huston, Gertrude, 27a.iii, 28b, 31, 33
Hutchins, Patricia, H85
Hutchison, Percy, F111, 125

"'I go where I love': An Intertextual Study of H.D. and Adrienne Rich," G139
"'I Had Two Loves Separate': The Sexualities of H.D.'s *Her*," G120; H241
"The I in the Initials," F105
"I Like to (B)eat People Up," G61
"'I See Her Differently': H.D.'s *Trilogy* as Feminist Response to Masculine Modernism," G175
"Icy Fire," F61
"The Identity of 'H': Imagism and H.D.'s *Sea Garden*," G274
I.H., F197
"Images and Critical Method," G88
"Images at the Crossroads: The 'H.D. Scrapbook,'" H216, 241
Images of H.D., B18; H149
"Imaginary Images: 'H.D.,' Modernism, and the Psychoanalysis of Seeing," H232, 241
"The Imagination of H.D.: Hilda Doolittle and 'Hermetic Definition,'" I30
"Imagism," H79
Imagism: A Chapter for the History of Modern Poetry, F571, H55
"Imagism: A Reconsideration," H54
"Imagism and Aesthetic Mysticism," H89
Imagism and the Imagists: A Study in Modern Poetry, H24, 91
"Imagism or Myopia?" F551
"Imagism: Secular and Esoteric," G11
"Imagism Today and Yesterday," F567
L'imagismo, con una piccola antologia, D23, H48
Imagist Anthologies, A5
Imagist Anthology, 1930, A13; B9; F566, 567
"An Imagist Novel," F93
The Imagist Poem, H79
"Imagist Poet Produces Novel of World War I," F314
Imagist Poetry, H121

"An Imagist Way of Seeing," F459, 588
Des Imagistes, B2; C20; D39; F548
"Des Imagistes," G28
"Des Imagistes: Toward a Poetic Revolution," I6
"The Imagists," G8
"Imagists and Ex-Imagists," F166
"The Imagists Discussed," G6
"Impassable Stairs," F88
In Defense of Reason, H51
"In memoriam H.D.," J35
In Print, F583
"In Sight of a Lyre, a Little Spear, a Chair," F303
In the Arresting Eye: The Rhetoric of Imagism, H173
Independent [Long Beach, Calif.], F351
" 'The Inevitable Triad': Self and Other in the Fiction and Poetry of H.D.," I40
L'influence du symbolisme français sur la poésie américaine (de 1910 à 1920), H22
The Influence of Ezra Pound, H91
The Influence of French Symbolism in Modern American Poetry, H22
Ingram, Angela, G256
Inspiring Women: Reimagining the Muse, H213
Intellectual America—Ideas on the March, H45
The Intelligent Heart—The Story of D. H. Lawrence, H61
intent., C95, 117; G270
"Interlocutions: Men, Women, and Modernisms in American Poetry," I44
International Journal of Psychoanalysis, F270; G73; H125
"An Interview with Robert Duncan," G107
"The Intimacy of Biography," G171, I84
"Introduction [to the H.D. Centennial issue of the *Iowa Review*]," G187
An Introduction to Fifty American Poets, H160
"Introduction: 'Water Flows Uphill,' " G264
"An Investigation of the Structural Aspects of Free Verse As They Affect the Oral Reader," I3
IO, G63, 75
Iowa Review, C157, 168–70, 529; G111, 179–82, 184–90
Irish Statesman, F69
Iron, G72
Ironwood, F528; G142
Izzo, Carlo, D23, 26

Jackson, Brendan, G152
Jackson, Caroline, F273
Jacobs, Rita D., F546
Jacobs, Willis, G31
Jacobson, Josephine, F256, 339
Jaffe, Nora Crow, H206
Janowitz, Anne, A36
Jarde, A., C84
Jarnot, Lisa, G270
Jarolim, Edith, F542
Jarrell, Randall, F168, 184
Jay, Karla, G272
Jeffers, Robinson, A6a.ii
Jennet, M., F378
"John Cournos and 'H.D.,' " G84
John G. Wilson, B6
John O'London's Weekly, F132
Johns, Richard, B17; C109
Johnson, Albert H., F277
Johnston, Paul, A11; B10
Jolas, Eugène, D4
Jonathan Cape, A5a.i
Jones, A. R., G42
Jones, E. B. C., F30
Jones, Ernest, A24; F270
Jones, Peter, A24b.i; H114, 121, 160
Josephson, Linda, A35
Journal and Constitution [Atlanta], F354
Journal of Aesthetic Education, G151
Journal of English and Germanic Philology, F574
Journal of Modern Literature, F428; G109, 269
Journal of the Medical Society of New Jersey, F263
Journal of Women's Studies, G100
Journeys: Autobiographical Writing by Women, H164
Joyce, James, B7, 10, 12
Juhasz, Susan, H131

Kabat, Julie, E11
Kammer, Jeanne, H161

Kaplan, Cora, H139
Kauffmann, Stanley, B18
Kaufman, J. Lee, H93; I4
Kazin, Alfred, F517, 594
"Keeper of the Flame," H216
"Keepers of the Flame: Hermeticism in Yeats, H.D., and Borges," I39
Kelvin, Norman, F319
Kennedy, Joseph Patrick, F453
Kennedy, Leo, F190
Kenner, Hugh, F349, 579; H116, 140
Kenyon Review, F167, 194, 205
Kerblatt-Blanchenay, Jeanne, F432; H179, 185
Kerblatt-Houghton, Jeanne, G93, 126; H180, 216
Kershaw, Alister, H86–87
Kessler-Harris, Alice, H226
Key Reporter [Phi Beta Kappa Society], F433
A Key to Modern English Poetry, H34
"The Kind of Remembering That Is Reality," F423
King, Michael, A33; F145, 462, 545, 604, 605; G115, 156; H162, 207, 216
King, Rosalie Anne, I28
King of Kings, C97
King-Smyth, Rosie, G222
Kirkus Review, F206, 333, 347, 400, 440, 483, 541
Kiser, Thelma Scott, F290, 443, 532
Klaich, Dolores, H132
"Klang, Kalkül, und Emotion," F245
Kloepfer, Deborah Kelly, G148, 196; H216, 233, 241; I29
Knapp, Peggy A., G137
Knickerbocker News [Albany], F414
Knoll, Robert E., H77
Koestenbaum, Wayne, F536
Kohn, Walter F., F110
Kolokithas, Dawn, F538; G223
"Kontaktaufnahmen: Imagistische Dichtung und Natur," H203, 210
Koskvin, Iva Aleksandrovich, D31
Kouidis, Virginia, F589
Kreymborg, Alfred, A11; B8; F185, 555; H21
Kries-Schinck, Annette, H244
Kronenberger, Louis, H117
K.S., F51
Kuhlman, Roy, A26a.iii

Kuleschow, L., C98
"Kultfigur der Emanzapation," F473
Kumin, Maxine, G130
Kunitz, Stanley, F203, 47

La Rocque, Paula, F599
"Ladies Day," F162
Laity, Cassandra, G224, 272; H241
"Land of Mirrors," F411
Lane, George, C23; F549
"Language Acquisition," G182
Laroche, Martine, H132
Larsen, Jeanne, G225
larus, F82
Lask, Thomas, F399
"The Last Book of H.D.'s Poetry," F364; G77
"The Last of the Imagists," F160
Lattimore, Richmond, F143
Laughlin, James, A2a.iii; C167
Lawrence, D. H., B9; G27, 275; H61
Laws, George, A16b
Lazarowicz, Anja, D15; H217
Lazenby, Francis D., F337
L.B., F76
Le Breton, Maurice, D5; H52
"Lebensgang und Lebensende der amerikanischen Poetin H.D.," H154
"Lecture on Poetry since 1920," G30
Lectures on Modern Poetry, H63
Lee, Charles, F247
"The Legend of H.D.," F599
Lesbian Lives: Biographies of Women from "The Ladder," H146
Lesbian Texts and Contexts: Radical Revisions, G272
"Lesbos," H216
"The Lesser Satisfactions," F128
"Letters across the Abyss: The H.D.–Adrienne Monnier Correspondence," G276
"Letters from H.D.," H216
Letters of D. H. Lawrence, H157
The Letters of Ezra Pound, 1907–1941, H53
Leuchtende Wörterwelten, F475
Levertov, Denise, A33; G44; H183, 228
Levine-Keating, Helene, I20
Levinson, Nan, F490
Lewin, Blanche, A12
Lewis, Peter, F107

Lewis, R. W. B., H124
Lewis and Irene, C73
Lewisohn, Ludwig, H25
Library Chronicle of the University of Texas at Austin, G156; H207
Library Journal, F220, 251, 278, 301, 337, 346, 389, 401, 442, 486, 509
A Library of Literary Criticism, H188
Life and Letters Today, A19, 20, 21, 23, 29, 32; C113–14, 116–19, 121–23, 125–27, 129–39; F141, 157, 180; G30
Life for Life's Sake, G28–29, 43; H44
Life Is My Song, H33
The Life of Ezra Pound, H111
Lindeman, Reinhold, F245
Lindsay, Vachel, A11
line, G245, 277
Link, Annemarie, D12, 16; H163
Link, Franz, D12, 16; G91; H163
Lipari, Joseph A., F509
Lipscomb, Elizabeth Johnston, F498
Listener, F182
"Listening to Stones: Reflections on H. D.'s *The Walls Do Not Fall*," G248
The Literary History of the United States, H81
Literary History: Theory and Practice, H215
"Literary Lovers: Fantasy or Fact?" F326
Literatur Rundschau, F246
Literature and Medicine, H206
Literature and Psychology, F287, 366; G96, 201, 236
Literature/Film Quarterly, G143
Literaturweissenschaftliches Jahrbuch, G91
Litke, James, F280
Litterature d'America: Rivista Trimestrale, G160
Little Novels of Sicily, C74
"Little Poems," F275, 370
Little Review, A2; C23, 27, 40, 59, 103; F3, 549, 552; G4, 9
Little Review Anthology, B16
"A Little Tale by a Poet," F130
Litz, A. Walton, H200
Logan, Floyd, F216
"Logos and Etymologies in H.D.'s 'Trilogy,'" G200
London Magazine, G37

London Mercury, F138
Long Beach [Calif.] Independent Press Telegram, F377
"Long Live Poetry," J22
Longman Companion to Twentieth Century Literature, H113
Lorelei Two: My Life with Conrad Aiken, H186
Lorenz, Clarissa M., H186
Los Angeles Mirror, F227
Los Angeles Times, F445
Lost America of Love: Rereading Robert Creeley, Edward Dorn, and Robert Duncan, H175
Louisville Courier-Journal, F223, 385, 513
Lourdeaux, Stanley, F431
"Love among the Modernists," F579
"Love and Resurrection," F196
"Love, Beyond Men and Women: H.D.," H146
"'Love Is Writing': Eros in H.D.'s *Hermione*," G215
"Lovers: Paris in the Twenties," H166
"The Loves of Her (from the Trunk of Hilda Doolittle)," F453
"Loving Memoir of the Brilliant, Bizarre Ezra Pound," F410
Lowell, Amy, A5a.ii, 6; F9, 18, 554; H1, 9, 23
Loy, Mina, B7
L.R., F69
Lucas, F. L., F36
Lucas, Frank L., H98
Lucas, John, F515, 518
Lucas, Matilda, C121
Lucas, Rose, G237
Lüdeke, Henry, G36
"The Lunatic, the Lover, and the Poet," F116
Lynch, Beverly, H146
Lyons, Islay, A24c.i, 39
"Lyric Resistance: Views of the Political in the Poetics of Wallace Stevens and H. D.," G271
Lyric West, F25, 64
"The Lyrical World of Shakespeare," F217

M., F259
McAlmon, Robert, A8a.ii; B7; H36, 99

Macaulay Company, B9
McBrien, William, H226
McCauliff, George, F229
McClelland & Stewart Ltd., A25a.vi, A26a, 27a.iii, 28b
McClure, John, F48, 556
McCormick, John, H118
McDonald, Gerald D., F301
McDougal, Stuart, F422; H208
McFarlane, James, H144
MacGeorge, Beatrice, F222
McGraw-Hill Book Company, A24c.ii, iii
Mackail, J. W., A1b
McKenzie, James, F389
Mackinnon, Lachlan, F105
MacKnight, Nancy, F591
McLaughlin, Richard, F266
MacLeish, Archibald, B11; E14; F47
Maclure Syndicate, C2
Macmillan Company, A22; B4
McNeil, Helen, A26a.vi, 34a.iii; H198-99
Macpherson, Kenneth, A10a; F568; J14, 18
"Ein Mädchen aus der Provinz lernt lieben," F481
"Magdalene Before and After: H.D.'s Poetic Sequences," I46
"Magi and Maidens'—The Romance of the Victorian Freud," G117
"Magical Lenses: Poet's Vision beyond the Naked Eye," H216
Magill's Literary Annual, F446, 498
Mais, S. B. P., F151
Major, Clarence, G39
"Making It Really New: Hilda Doolittle, Gwendolyn Brooks, and the Feminist Potential of Modern Poetry," G282
"The Making of a Poet," G146
"Mal war sie Göttin, mal Kohlenschippe," F478
Malahat Review, F424
Malroux, Claire, D3
Manchester Guardian, F68, 113, 130, 134, 156, 175, 178, 197, 358, 379-80
Mandel, Charlotte, G110, 143, 229; H216; J14
Mandorla, the Minetta Review, G202
Manent, M., D33
Mannheimer Moogen, F473

Manton, Guy, F140
A Map of Modern English Verse, H105
Mariani, Paul, H174
Marianne Moore Newsletter, G86
Marks, Jim, F452
Marques, Oswaldino, D29
Marsh, Edward, G27
Marshall, Mary, C2
Martin, Richard, A2a.iii
Martinelli, Sheri, A33; F310; G40-41
Martz, Louis L., A38, 39; G303; H187, 228
Mason, Mary Grimle, H164
Massachusetts Review, G114, 137
Masterpieces of Greek Drawing and Painting, C80
Masters, Edgar Lee, C117
Materer, Timothy, G138
Mathis, Mary S., H216
"Matriarchal Myth-Making for a Post-Patriarchal Age: The Anti-War Writing of Virginia Woolf and Hilda Doolittle," I48
"Matt Hilda," F112
"The Matter of Myrrhine for Louis," G180
"Maximum Dilution," F387
Maxwell, K. N., F409
Mayer, Harry H., A6a.iv
Mayhall, Jane, F365
Meacham, Harry, F381
"The Meaning That Words Hide: H.D.'s *Trilogy*," H176
Mearns, Hughes, A7
Measure, F24, 59, 557
Meeker, Marilyn, A27a.i
Meggison, Lauren Louise, I39
"The Melody Lingers On," F300
"Memoir and Parable," F268
"Memoir of Ezra Pound Lacking in Pound," F416
"Memories of Youth," F435
"Memory and Desire: H.D.'s 'A Note on Poetry,'" G254
Menike, Peter, F383
Menninger, Karl, F264
Menninger Library Journal, F264
"Merano, 1962," G81
Mercatile Printing Co., A26a.iv
Mercure de France, F308
Mercury Press, A12
Meres, Francis, F158

Mesic, Penelope, F484
"Message of Survival in the Midst of Death," F385
Metaphor and the Poetry of Williams, Pound, and Stevens, H131
m/f, G141
Middlebrook, Diane Wood, G125, 139
Milazzo, Lee, F578
Milicia, Joseph, G197; H216; I7, 9
Mille, Cecil B. de, C97
Millenium Film Journal, G116
Miller, Margaret Ann, F236
Miller, Nancy K., H215
Millet, Fred, H43
Mills, Gordon, H147
Milstead, John, H108
Minneapolis Tribune, F281, 581
"Mirror-Images: Images of Mirrors in Poems by Sylvia Plath, Adrienne Rich, Denise Levertov, and H.D.," G178
A Miscellany of American Poetry, A5, 9, 13
Miscellany of Poetry, 1920–1922, B6
"Misleading Accounts of Aldington and H.D.," G234
"The Mission of Ion," F92, 147
Mississippi Quarterly, G45
Mithchison, Naomi, F135
M.K., F415
Modern American Literature, H188
Modern American Poetry, A33; H54
Modern American Poetry, 1865–1950, H236
Modern American Poets, H184
"Modern British Poetry," F563
Modern Critical Views, H228
"Modern Morals and the Human Heart," F319
Modern Poetic Sequence: The Genius of Modern Poetry, H190
Modern Poetry, F562, 563; H14
"Modern Poetry and the Imagists," G2
"Modernism and the 'Scattered Remnant': Race and Politics in the Development of H.D.'s Modernist Vision," H216
Modernism, 1890–1930, H144
"Modernism Revised: Formalism and the Feminine: Irrigaray, H.D., Barnes," I50

"Modernist Marriage," F328, 466, 501
"Modernist Moravianism: H.D.'s Unpublished Novel *The Mystery*," G283
Mollinger, Robert N., F278
"The Moment of Revival," F235
Monro, Harold, G6; H7
Monroe, Harriet, B4; F55, 553, 555, 567; G1, 10, 12, 20; H15, 37
Montefiore, Jan, G258
Montemora, C158; G102, 119–20
Montgomery Advertiser, F259
Moody, A. D., G259
Moon, Lois Burton, F64
Moore, Harry T., A8a.ii, 312; G48; H61, 86, 92, 100
Moore, Marianne, A22; F28, 56; G21; J34
Moore, Merrill, A24; H62
Moore, Virginia, F561
Moorhead, Andrea, F352
Moramarco, Fred, H236
Morand, Paul, C73
A Moravian Heritage, H123
Morgan, Louise, F29, 66
Morley, Hilda, F528
Morning Call, J8
Morris, Adelaide, F529; G111, 185–87, 198; H216, 228, 241
Moss, Howard, F194, 205
"Mother as Muse and Desire: The Sexual Politics of H.D.'s *Trilogy*," H216
"Mother, Maiden, and the Marriage of Death: Woman Writers and an Ancient Myth," G104
Mottram, Eric, H119
Moult, Thomas, F559
Movements in Modern English Poetry and Prose, H20, 112
Ms., C160; G122
"Mücke sticht Marmorstatue," F476
Mumford, Lewis, B9
Munson, Gorham B., F95
Muratori, Fred, F91
Murray, Gilbert, A18; C76; F571
Musikfest '85, J16
M.W., F232
My Friends When Young, H101
Myers, Robin, H110
"Myrrh: A Study of Persona in H.D.'s *Trilogy*," G245

"The Mysteries between Image and Epic: H.D.'s Poetry and Poetics in Transition," I43
The Mysteries of Vision: Some Notes on H.D., H223
"The Mystery: H.D.'s Unpublished Moravian Novel Edited and Annotated: Towards a Study in the Sources of a Poet's Religious Thinking," I45
"*The Mystery* Unveiled: The Significance of H.D.'s 'Moravian' Novel," G294
"Myth and Archtype from a Female Perspective: An Exploration of Twentieth Century North and South American Women Poets," I20
"Myth and Glyph in *Helen in Egypt*," G225
Le mythe du héros, H180
Mythology and the Romantic Tradition in English Poetry, G43; H32
"Mythology, Psychoanalysis, and the Occult in the Late Poetry of H.D.," I10

Nadeau, Richard M., I13
Nagy, N. Cristoph de, H154
Nardi, Marcia, F46
Nashville Banner, F213
Nashville Tennessean, F253
Nassauer Bote, F238
Nation [New York], A4a, 5, 28b, 33; C143, 152; F4, 26, 41, 54, 74, 87, 100, 122, 139, 166, 184, 210, 218, 341, 365; G16-17, 76
Nation [London], C48, 49
Nation and Athenaeum, C58; F30
National Book League Journal, F309
National Institute of Arts and Letters, C151
N.C.Y., F174
Nehls, Edward, H64, 69
Nelson, Cary, H234
Neue Zürcher Zeitung, F236, 242; J35
New Age, F427
New Canterbury Literary Society Newsletter, G299-304
"New Chapter in the Lives of H.D. and Richard Aldington: Their Relationship with Clement A. Shorter," G268

New Criterion, F78; G159
New Directions, A14, 17a.ii, 24c.iii, 27a.iii, 28b, 31, 33, 34, 35, 38, 39; C167
"New Directions Books Include Play by Tennessee Williams," F290
New Directions for Women, F457, F584
New Directions in Prose and Poetry, C167, 174
New English Weekly, F568
The New Era in American Poetry, H3
"New Eyes: H.D., Modernism, and the Psychology of Seeing," G201
New Freewoman, C15
New Hampshire Bindery, A26a.iv
New Haven Journal Courier, J29
New Haven Register, F207, 280, 378; J3
New Journal, G146
New Leader, F590
New Literary History, G162
The New Poetry, B4; F555
"New Poetry," F396
New Poetry Series, A2a.ii
"'NEW' Poetry since 1912," H16
The New Poets, H83
New Republic, A13; C107; F15, 46, 79, 85, 110, 162, 250, 383
New Statesman, F36, 96, 104, 382, 515; H98
New Statesman and Nation, F173
New Voices: An Introduction to Contemporary Poetry, H5
New Women's Times Feminist Review, F596
New York Evening Post Literary Review, F18, 35, 50, 72, 558, 561
New York Herald Tribune, G35; J2, 27
New York Herald Tribune Weekly Book Review, F61, 73, 88, 117, 160, 188, 224, 249, 318
New York Literary Forum, G155
New York Native, F536
New York Review of Books, F283-84, 517, 594
New York Sunday Mirror, F208
New York Times, J26
New York Times Book Review, F8, 37, 49, 71, 93, 111, 125, 198, 217, 300, 312, 335, 349, 399, 408, 516, 542, 554, 576; G43, 135
New York World, F52
New Yorker, F161, 186, 199, 488

Newlin, Margaret, G87
Newlove, Donald, F292
News and Book Trade Review, F159
Newsart, F425
Newsday, F293, 412, 544, 598
Newsweek, F315
Nicholl, Louise, F557
"Nicknames and Acronyms Used by H.D. and Her Circle," G233
Nierenberg, Roger, E7
"Nights and Days," G60, 62, 101, 119
Nims, John Frederick, F226
ninth decade, G200
No Mans Land: The Place of the Woman Writer in the Twentieth Century, H225, 231
"No Rule of Procedure: The Open Poetics of H.D.," G260; H241
Norman, Charles, H72
"Norman Holmes Pearson on H.D.: An Interview," G64
Norris, Ruth, F353
Norris, William A., F558
North, Jessica Nelson, F191
North American Review, C46
"Not Each in Isolation," G242
Notable American Women: The Modern Period, H168
"A Note on the Classical Revival," F1
"A Note on *The H.D. Book*," G238
"A Note on the State of H.D.'s *The Gift*," G154
"Notes toward a History of Imagism," G42
Novo, Salvador, D38
"A Number of People III," G27
"Nursing the Muse: The Childbirth Metaphor in H.D.'s Poetry," I36
Nyholm, Jens, D1
"A Nymph of the New," F517, 594
Nyran, Dorothy, H188

Obrecht, B., A25a.v
Observer, F149, 179, 271, 328, 386, 466, 501
"Occult Matters," G59
O'Connor, William Van, F336
Oderman, Kevin, F423
Ohannessian, Griselda, A35
O'Hara, T., F357; 384
Olgivie, D. Bruce, G230
Oliphant, Dave, G156; H207

"On H.D.," G14, 214
"On the Trail of the 'One' Crawfordsville Incident or, the Poet in Hoosierland," G149
101 poemas: Antologiá bilingüe de la poesía norteamericana moderna, D38
Open Places, F362
Orage and the New Age Circle: Reminiscences and Reflections, H71
"The Orient's Gift to American Poetry," G26
Origin, G47
"Orpheus and Eurydice in the Twentieth Century: Lawrence, H.D., and the Poetics of the Turn," G275
Orpheus: The Myth of the Poet, H235
Orpheus (und) Eurydike, H227
Osiris, F352
Ostriker, Alicia, A17a.ii, 39; G128, 144, 172, 260; H189, 216, 218, 241
"Our Lady-Poets of the Twenties," G105
Our Poets of Today, H10
Our Singing Strength, H21
Out of the Mist, C94
Outlook [London], A9, 66; C63, 67, F29
Outlook [New York], F42
Overmeyer, J., F604
"Ovid and H.D.'s 'Thetis' (*Hymen* Version)," G205
Oxford Anthology of American Literature, B14
Oxford Anthology of American Poetry, C176
Oxford Mail, F151
Oxford University Press, A19, 20, 21; B14

Pabst, G. W., C102
Pagany, C108–9
Paideuma, F103, 421, 462; G81, 115, 124, 131, 138, 149
Paige, D. D., H53
"Palimpsest of Origins in H.D.'s Career," G169
"Palimpsests of the Word: The Poetry of H.D.," G164
Palmer, Herbert, H38
Pamphlet Poets, A7
"Pandora's Box," H177
Panorama de la littérature contemporaine

aux Etats-Unis, D6; H60
Pantheon, A24
Paper Boats, H67
Parisi, Joseph, F410, 414, 508
Parnassus, F286, 297, 343, 345, 374, 375, 397, 437, 530
Partisan Review, F168, 193, 201
"Passio Perpeteae H.D.," F286, 343, 374, 397
Passion and Death of a Saint, C99
"Past Impressions That Brighten the Present," F467
Pastoral Psychology, F267
Patmore, Brigit, G37; H101
Patriot Ledger, F342
Paul, Sherman, H175
Pausanius, C66
Pearson, Gabriel, A27a.vi; F518, 595
Pearson, Norman Holmes, A18b, 21, 23, 24, 25a.iii, iv, v, 26a, 27a.i, 28a, b, 29, 30, 31, 32, 33, 38; B14; C2, 71, 176; E15; F180; H70, 122, 127, 133, 162
Peck, John, F286, 343, 374, 397; H216
Pekar, Harvey, F543
Pelican Press, A1c, 4a.ii
Penelope's Web: Gender, Modernity, H.D.'s Fiction, H239
Penguin Companion to American Literature, H119
Penn, Sylvania (H.D.), C117, 119, 121, 123
Pennsylvania English, G134; J20
"The Perfect Imagist," F40; G18
Perkins, David, H148
"Persistence of a Memory," F412
Peter, Rhoda (H.D.), C109
Peters, Nancy J., J22
Petrides, Avaci, J14
Pettigeld, Phoebe, F590
Pfuhl, Ernst, C80
Phelan, Margaret M., I41
"Phenomenalist Idioms: Doolittle, Moore, Levertov.," H150
Philadelphia Inquirer, F221, 289, 448, 494, 504, 510, 512, 580, 600, 603; J9
Philological Quarterly, G268
Phoenix Profiles, H70
"A Photobiography of H.D.," H241
Pisanti, Tommaso, D27
Pittsburgh Monthly Bulletin, F118
Pittsburgh Post-Gazette, G158

Pittsburgh Press, F234
P.J.M., F68
"The Place of the Imagists," F571
Plank, George, A17
"Planting the Seeds: Selections from the H.D. Chronology," G249
PN Review, F332, 470, 503
"Poems and Poetical Exercises," F58
Poems in Persons: An Introduction to the Psychoanalysis of Literature, H127
"The Poems of H.D.," F20
"Poems of H.D.," F65
"Poems of Pursuit," F63
Poems of Sappho, C68
Poesia americana, 1850–1950, D25
Poesia americana contemporanea e poesia negra, D23
Poesia americana del '900, D25
Poesia del novecento americano, D27
Poesia Estado Unidense, D32
La poesía inglesia: Los contemporáneos, D33
poesis: A Journal of Criticism, G168–73
"The Poet and Dr. Freud," F280
"The Poet and the Couch," F250
"The Poet as Heroine: Learning to Read H.D.," G144
"The Poet as Translator," H75
"Poet Hilda Doolittle, on Yale Visit, Assails Imagist Label Used to Describe Her Work," J3
The Poet in the World, G44
"The Poet Patient," H171
"A Poet Who Drinks at the Pierian Spring," F37
"The Poetic Method of H.D.," F122
"Poetic Quest for an Enduring Core," F457, 584
"Poetic Survivors," F342
Poetics Journal, G147
The Poetics of Gender, H215
"A Poetics out of War: H.D.'s Responses to the First World War," G251
Poetry [Chicago], A2, 4a, 5, 9, 13, 28b; C15, 18, 21, 45, 54, 78, 86, 101, 111–12, 120, 140, 144, 147, 159; F1, 7, 12, 23, 45, 55, 128, 143, 164, 191, 203, 235, 268, 303, 304, 324, 339, 372, 393, 550, 553, 555, 563, 567, 571; G1, 10–12, 20–21, 24, 61, 246; J1

Poetry and Drama, F548
Poetry and Poets—Essays, H23
Poetry as Experience, H17, 46
Poetry Bookshop, A2; B2b
Poetry Chapbook, F229
Poetry Flash, F538
Poetry in America—Expression and Its Values in the Times of Bryant, Whitman, and Pound, H153
Poetry in Our Time, H58
"Poetry in Series," F391
Poetry Journal, F9, 551
Poetry Nation, G83; H156
"Poetry Now," F137
Poetry of American Women from 1632 to 1945, H151
"The Poetry of Concentration," F89
"The Poetry of H.D.," G5
"The Poetry of Mina Loy," G53
Poetry of Richard Aldington: A Critical Evaluation and Anthology of Uncollected Poems, H130
Poetry, Painting, and Ideas, 1885–1914, H209
Poetry Project Newsletter, F291
Poetry Quartos, A11
Poetry Review [London], F187, 527
Poetry Society of America Bulletin, G92
Poetry Society of London, J13
Poets and Their Art, H15
Poet's Gold, E14
A Poet's Life—Seventy Years in Changing World, H37
"A Poet's Novel," F81
"Poets' Romance," F408
Poet's Translation Series, A1a
"Poets Who Are Poets," F52
Poland, F., C82
"Polar Opposites," F383
Polis, C166, 500; G121
Pollitt, Katha, F516
Polyglot Press, A25a
Polyglots, C75
Pondrom, Cyrena, C155; G68, 163, 261; H241
Ponsot, Marie, F523
"The Pool Films," G305
Porter, Peter, F386
"Portrait of an Artist as a Woman: H.D.'s Raymonde Ransome," G191
"The Position of H.D.," H14

"A Posthumous Novel Better Left Forgotten," F449
Post-Victorian Poetry, H38
Pound, Ezra, A11, 33; B6; F3
Pound, Omar, H200
Pound, Ezra, H116
Pound Revised, H192
"Pound's Tribute to H.D., 1961," G192
"Pound the Boy and H.D. the Child," F493
"Pour Ezra Pound," G46
Powys Review, G263
Prairie Schooner, F321, 367
Pratt, Anne Rich, H22
Pratt, William, A16.b, 461; F426; H22, 79
"Praxilla's Silliness," H216
Prehellenic Architecture in the Aegean, C79
"Presentation: A Note on the Art of Writing; on the Artfulness of Some Writers; and on the Artlessness of Others," G13
Press, John, H105
Press-Telegram [Long Beach, Calif.], F350
Price, Mona, F34
The Priest of Love, H61
"A Primary Intensity between Women': H.D. and the Female Muse," H216
Principles of Literary Criticism, H17
Prioleau, Elizabeth, F587
Private Collection, H88
Proctor, Dod, A26a.vi, 34a.iii
Prodigal Sun, F444
"A Profound Animal," A26a.iv, vi; H191
Program for Euripides' *Ion*, J17
Program for the Dedication of the Official State Marker for Hilda Doolittle, J15
Program for the Manhattan Theater Club, Writers in Performance, J14
Program of the Brandeis University Creative Arts Awards, J12
"A Programme of Tribute to H.D.," J13
Providence Journal, F209
Psyche Reborn, F109, 297, 345, 375,

437, 457, 465, 499, 506, 530, 583–84, 587–88, 593, 596; H172
"Psyche Reborn: Tradition, Re-Vision, and the Goddess as Mother-Symbol in H.D.'s Epic Poetry," G103
Psychiatry and Literature, H206
"Psychic Topography," F296, 344
"Psychomythology: The Case of H.D.," G140
Publication on English Themes, G220
Published in Paris: American and British Writers, Painters, and Publishers in Paris, 1920–1939, H136
Publisher's Circular, F305
Publisher's Weekly, F254, 277, 299, 311, 325, 398, 439, 441, 485, 507, 575, 592; J32
The Pursuit of Poetry, H107
"The Pursuit of Spirituality in the Poetry of H.D.," G223
Putnam, Samuel, B11

Quan, Julie, A35
Quarterly Journal of the Library of Congress, G130
Quarterly Review of Literature, C153
Quartermain, Peter, H184
Queen's Quarterly, G164
Quest in Modern American Poetry, H176
Quinn, Vincent, G89; H95

Rachewiltz, Mary de, D22; H216
"Rails Gone for Guns," G199
Rajan, B., H54
Randall, Sir Alec, H87
Random House, A11
"Rapunzel, Rapunzel, Let Down Thy Long Hair," F73
Rasula, Jed, F109, 464, 499, 506; G129, 199
Rathaus, Karol, E8
Ratner, Amy, J7
Ratner, Rochelle, F145, 417, 596
Ray, Man, A10b, 26a.iv, 33
Read, Herbert, J28
"Reading for the Couch," F293
"Reading H.D.'s 'Helios and Athene,'" G111
"Reading, Psychoanalysis, Dialectics," I26

"Reading the Feminine Self: H.D./Freud/Psychoanalysis," I51
Reavey, George, B11
"The Recent Contours of the Muse," F336
Reche, Denis, G46
Reck, Michael, H94
"Recovering the Human Equation: H.D.'s 'Hermetic Definition,'" G221
"The Redirected Image: Cinematic Dynamics in the Style of H.D. (Hilda Doolittle)," G143
"The Rediscovery of H.D.," G135
Redon, Odilon, A28b, 31
Reeve, F. D., F372, 393
Reflections on the Word "Image", H109
Réflexions sur la poésie américaine, D8
Regier, W. G., F367
Reid, Coletta, H146
Reinhard, Alice, F438, 471
Reisinger, E., C82
"A Relatively Brief Encounter: Consultations with the Master," F282
"A Relay of Power and of Peace: H.D. and the Spirit of *The Gift*," G198; H241
"Relief from Coziness," F380
Religious Trends in English Poetry, H39
"Re-living," G147
"Remembering H.D.," G255
"Remembering Oneself: the Reputation and Later Poetry of H.D.," G161
"'Remembering Shakespeare Always, but Remembering Him Differently': H.D.'s *By Avon River*," G136
"Re-membering the Mother: A Reading of H.D.'s *Trilogy*," G170; H216, 241
"A Renaissance of Women Writers," F109, 465, 499, 506
Renaux, Sigrid, G262, 265
"(Re)Placing Woman: The Politics and Poetics of Gender in H.D.'s *Helen in Egypt*," G307
Reporter, F260
Repression and Recovery: Modern American Poetry and the Politics of Cultural Memory, 1910–1945, H234
"Re(reading)-Writing the Palimpsest of Myth," G237

Resources for American Literary Study, F447
Responsibilities and Other Poems, C175
"The Resurrection of Hilda Doolittle," G112
"Reticence and the Lyric: The Development of a Personal Classicism among Four Women Poets of the Twentieth Century," I52
Rettallack, Joan, F297, 345, 375, 437, 530
"Return of the Repressed in H.D.'s Madrigal Cycle," H241
"Return of the Vers Libertine," G16
A Return to Pagany, B17; C109
Revell, Peter, H176
"Reveries of a Cataloguer," G189
Review, F601; G167
Review of Contemporary Fiction, F108
A Reviewer's ABC, H65
Revista Letras, G262
Revue Français d'Etudes Américaines, G126, 178
Rexroth, Kenneth, B17; H75, 120
Rheinische Post, F245
Rhein-Neckar Zeitung, F241
Rhythmus, C60
Rich, Adrienne, J14
Richard Aldington: A Biography, H230
Richard Aldington: An Intimate Portrait, H86–87
"Richard Aldington and Marianne Moore," G86
"Richard Aldington in His Last Years," G48
Richard Aldington: Reappraisals, H245
Richards, I. A., H17
Richards, Sue, A38a.iii
Richardson, Dorothy, B7; G250
Richardson, Kenneth, H106
Richardson, Maurice, F271
Richmond News Leader, F319, 355, 381
Richmond Times-Dispatch, F211, 248, 402
Rickword, Edgell, F129
"Rico and Julia: The Hilda Doolittle–D. H. Lawrence Affair Reconsidered," G109
Riddel, Joseph N., G69, 98
Ridge, Lola, F63
Ridgeway, Christopher, H201
Riga, Frank P., F454

Rising Generation, F364
"Rites of Participation," G54, 56
"Ritual," F86
Riverside Press, A9a
"Roads to Tragedy," F139
Robb, Christina, F404
Robbins, Reginald C., E3–4
Robert McAlmon and the Lost Generation—A Self Portrait, H77
Roberts, Warren, H92
Robertson, Andrew, H157
Robeson, Eslanda, A12
Robeson, Paul, A12
Robinson, Alan, H209
Robinson, Edwin Arlington, A11
Robinson, Janice, F109, 297, 326, 345, 375, 437, 457, 459, 465, 499, 506, 518, 530, 585, 588–93, 595, 596, 601; G300, 302–3; H181, 216; I11
Robles, Jamie, A32
Roche, Judith, G245
Rockwell, Kenneth, F214
Rodgers, Martha, F500; G121
Roessel, David, F146; G231, 293
Rogers, Leona, F258
Rogers, W. G., F212, 215
"Ein Roman über D. H. Lawrence," F320
"Romantic Thralldom in H.D.," G99; H241
Romig, Evelyn M., G96
Ronald, Ann, H155
Rood, Karen Lane, H170
"Rose Cut in Rock: Sappho and H.D.'s *Sea Garden*," G195; H241
"The Rose Loved of Lover or the Heroines in the Poems of the 20's by H.D.," H179
"Rosemary for Remembrance from H.D. to Shakespeare," F223
Rosenfeld, Paul, B9
Rosenmeier, Rosamond, H168
Rosenthal, M. L., H190
Rosset, Barney, A25a, 26a
Rossum-Guyon, Françoise, H238
Rovit, Earl H., F322, 401; G105
Row, Stephen, A24d, 27a.v, 39b
RSA, Journal of American Studies, G285
Ruihley, Glenn Richard, H141
Rummel, Walter, B1
"Running," G188

Saarbrücker Zeitung, F482
Sackville-West, Vita, F179
The Sacred Wood, H6
"Saffo in America: Hilda Doolittle," G50
Sage, Robert, F80
Sagetrieb, C172, 489, 591, 597; G65, 80, 127, 129, 136, 148, 163, 165, 175, 208–14, 217, 219, 221, 224, 226, 273–74, 276, 282, 284
St. Andrews, B. A., F436
" 'Saint Hilda,' Mr. Pound, and Rilke's Parisian Panther at Pisa," G124
St. James Press, A2a.iii
St. Martin's Press, A2a.iii
St. Louis Post-Dispatch, F531
Salisbury, Stephan, J9
Salmon, J. C., I1
Salt and Bitter and Good, H139
Sampson, David, E10
San Francisco Chronicle, F225, 313, 326
San Francisco Jung Institute Library Journal, F298
San Francisco Review of Books, J21
San Jose Studies, G123, 215, 218, 222–23, 225
Sandoz, Paul, F44
Sandrof, Ivan, F390
Sapir, Edward, F54
"Sapphistries," G150
"Sara Teasdale's Prize," G12
Sardello, Robert, H243
Sarton, May, A6a.iv; H216
Satherwaite, Alfred, G84
Saturday Review, F14, 67, 336
Saturday Review Gallery, G28
Saturday Review of Literature, A13; C64, 68; F40, 63, 75, 94, 115, 185, 200, 219, 316; G18, 28
Saturday Review of Politics, Literature, Science, and Art, F31
Scalapino, Leslie, G147
"Scarlet Experience: H.D.'s *Hymen*," G219
Schaffner, John, A35; E15
Schaffner, Perdita, A4, 10b, 16b, 17a.ii, 26a.iv, vi, 34, 35, 39; E15; G81, 188; H169, 177, 182, 191, 216, 241
Scharnhorst, Gary, F449
Schattenhofer, Monika, F476
Schaum, Melita, G271

Schede, M., C71
Schmickl, Gerald, F481
Schmidt, G., G227
Schmidt, Judith, A25a.iii, iv, 26a
Schmitz, Alexander, F478
Schoeck, R. J., G248
Scholastic, G25
"Schöne Frau Hilda Doolittle's 'Hermione,' " F472
Schorer, Mark, F169
Schöuer Leben/Kurv, F481
"Schreiben heilt die Seele über Hilda Doolittle—H.D.," H217
Schröter, Michael, D13
Schulman, Grace, G76
Schultz, Robert, G131
Schultz, Stephen Paul, I30
Schumann, Kuno, H210
Schupham, Peter, F395
"Scientific Lyricism: A Study of H.D.'s Modernist Writing," I16
Scobey, Katherine, G146
Scoggan, John, G78; I23
Scotsman [Edinburgh], F153, 176
Scott, Bonnie Kime, B20, H240
Scott, Winfield Townley, A26a.iii; F209, 318
The Second American Caravan, B9
"The Second Chapter," F18
See, Carolyn, F445
Seed, David, F332, 470, 503
Seed, C110
Seeds of Recognition, G134
Segal, Charles, H235
Seidman, Barbara Ann, I24
Seiffert, Marjorie Allen, F45
"Selected Letters from H.D. to F. S. Flint: A Commentary on the Imagist Period," G68
Sélincourt, Basil de, F130
Selver, Paul, H71
Sergeant, Howard, H56
Sewanee Review, F163; G22, 34
Sexchanges, H231
"Sexual Linguistics," G162
Seymour, William Keyne, B6
Shakespeare Head Press, A10a
Shakespeare's Sisters: Feminist Essays on Women Poets, G94; H161
Shakespeare's World, F224

Shanks, E., F67
"The Shape of Poetry 1910–1920: Convention, Reform, and Revolution," I33
Shapiro, Daniel, I33
Sharber, Kate Trimble, F213, 253
Sharpe, Pat, F583
"Shattering Silences," F536
Shattuck, Roger, H73, 75
Shaw, Marion, F527
Shay, Frank, B2c
" 'She Herself Is the Writing': Language and Sexual Identity in H.D.," H206
Shikina, Seiji, I37
" 'Shock Knit within Terror': Living through World War II," G181
Shoedsack, Ernest B., C93
A Short History of American Poetry, H134
Short History of Italian Art, C83
Shucard, Alan, H236
Shugar, Dana, G284
Sicherman, Barbara, H168
"Sie war Ezra Pound's Dryade," F482
Siegel, Carol Roberta, I42
Sievert, Heather Rosario, G97; I35
Siggins, Clara M., F285
Signets: Reading H.D., H241
Signs: Journal of Women in Culture and Society, G128, 139, 150
Silber, Mark, A24c.i
Silverstein, Louis, G189, 206, 233, 249, 297; H241
Simon & Schuster, A7
Sinclair, May, B7; F20, 65; G7
Sirocco, C96
Sisson, C. H., G83; H156
Sitwell, Edith, B7; G30
Sitwell, Osbert, A20, 31; F149
Sixty American Poets, 1896–1944, H49
Skelton, Robin, F309
Skepticisms, H2
"The Skipper's Guide," F136
Small Press, F91
Small Press Book Review, F605
Smith, Martha Nell, G242
Smith, Paul, G157, 190; H192, 226
Smith, Penny, G263
Smith, Raymond V., F371
Smoller, Sanford J., H142

Smyers, Virginia, G177, 232, 287; H221
Soho Weekly News, F417
"Some Anticipations of Imagism," H90
Some Contemporary Poet, H7
Some Imagist Poets, A2; B3; F549–53
"Some Recent Verse," F31
"Something for a Biography," G33
Sonntagsblatt, F240
Soucasna literatura spojenych statu— odzvoleni presidenta Wilsona po velkou hospodarskou krisi, H27
Sound and Form in Modern Poetry: A Study of Prosody from Thomas Hardy to Robert Lowell, H82
South Atlantic Quarterly, G42, 152
Southern Humanities Review, F589
Southern Review, C161; F371, 569; G53, 105, 125, 166, 280, 306
Southern Review: Literary and Interdisciplinary Essays, G237
Spaeth, J. Duncan, F221
"Spear-Shaft and Cyclamen-Flower," F23
Spectator, F21, 32, 97, 116, 133, 275, 391
"The Spell of the Luxor Bee," G222
Sphere, A4a, 5; C50
Spicher, Julia, G202
Spiller, Robert E., H81
Spingler, Andrea, D14
"Spiritual Realism in H.D.," F538
Spoo, Robert, G289
Springfield [Mass.] Sunday Republican, F22
Springfield [Mass.] Republican, F262, 266
"Staccato," F44
Stagberg, Norman C., H17, 46
Stages of Greek Religion, C76
" 'Stamping a Tiny Foot against God': Some American Women Poets between the Two Wars," G130
Stand Magazine, F107, 275, 370, 396, 525
Stanford, Derek, F521
"Staring at the Pacific and Swimming in It," H216
Stauffer, Donald Barlow, H134
Stead, C. K., H83

Stealing the Language: The Emergence of Women's Poetry in America, H218
Steele, Joy Cogdell, I15
Stein, Gertrude, B7; G250
"Stein, Richardson, and H.D.," G250
Stephen Austin and Sons, Ltd., A23
Stevens, Wallace, A2a.iii
Stilwell, Robert, F340
Stimpson, Catherine R., G272
Stock, Noel, H111
Stone, Irving, C119
stone country, F436
Stonier, G. W., F173
Stony Brook, G49, 59, 65
Storm, Marion, F72
Storr, Anthony, F282
The Story of American Literature, H25
The Story of Our Literature, H11
Stoyva, Johanna, F533
"A Strange Little Tribute of Poet to the Bard of Avon," F226
Stratton, Don, J17
Strausbaugh, John, F288
Strean, Herbert S., H171
"The Stretched Meter of an Antique Song," F560
Stromberg, Kyra, F477, 480, 482
Studi Americani, G50
Studies in Mystical Literature, G145
Studies in the Literary Imagination, G98
"A Study of H.D.: Her Life and Work," I19
Stumpf, Ron, J10
Stuttaford, Genevieve, F507
Stuttgarter Zeitung, F239, 472
Style, G88
"Style in H.D.'s Novels," G72; H228
"Submission to Male Supremacy Sacrifices Poet's Humanity," F353
Sulfur, F109, 464, 499, 506, 602; G154
Sullivan, Shirley, F354
Sullivan, William, H236
Sumac, G58
Sunday Independent [Ashland, Ky.], F290, 532
Sunday Referee, F129
Sunday Royal Gazette [Hamilton, Bermuda], F215
Sunday Star-Ledger [Newark, N.J.], F405
"Survivals," F382

"Survivors of the Blitz," F188
Sutton, Walter, G208
Svendsen, Kester, F230
Swann, Thomas Burnett, F572, 573, 574; H78
Swensen, May, F341
Swenson, Tree, A37
Sword, Helen, G275
SZ [Süddeutsche Zeitung], F477

Tagesauzeigo, F438, 471
Taggard, Genevieve, A11
"A Tale of a Jar," F203
"A Talented Poet Unlucky at Love," F578
"Talk Straight as the Greek," F365
Tanner, Wesley B., A15b, 29
Tart, Alison, F442, 486
Die TAT, F243
Tate, Allen, H49
Taupin, René, H22
"Tausend Exemplare," F246
T.B.L.W., F134
"Teetering between Friends and Lovers," F452
Tel Quel, G46
"A Tempermental Imagist Poet," F17
Temple, Frédéric-Jacques, H86–87
Temple, Robert, F331
"Temple Music," F24
"Tendencies in American Poetry," F554
Tendencies in Modern American Poetry, F554; H1
Terrell, C. F., J17
Texas Quarterly, G48
Textual Practice, G279
"Their Own Editors," F557
"The Thematic Development in the Poetry of H.D.," I22
"Theme and Imagery in the Poetry of Hilda Doolittle," I5
"Theme and Meaning in the Poetry of H.D.," I4
"Themes for Bronze," F123
"Theorem, Poem, Biography," F82
Theweleit, Klaus, H227
Thiebaux, Marcelle, F544
"The Thieves of Language: Women Poets and Revisionist Mythmaking," G128

"This Fascinating Genius Called H.D.," G122
"This H.D. Should Just R.I.P.," F448
This Modern Poetry, H30
This Quarter, A9; C69; F566
"The Thistle and the Serpent," H178
Thomas, Macklin, G32
Thorns of a Rose: Amy Lowell Reconsidered, H141
"Those Queer Greeks," F135
"Thought and Vision," F27
Thought and Vision: A Critical Reading of H.D.'s Poetry, H224
"The Three Ages of Poetry," F129
"Three Imagist Poets," G9
"Three Late Poems by H.D.," F346
"Three Misfits," F288
Thurley, Geoffrey, H150
Thus to Revisit: Some Reminiscences, H8
Tietjens, Eunice, G26
Tillman, Nathaniel, F237
Time, J31
"Time and American Autobiography: Four Twentieth Century Writers," I15
Time and Tide, F135, 158
"Time in a Room: H.D.'s *Bid Me to Live*," G285
Times [London], F102, 152, 177, 467; J28
Times Literary Supplement, C128; F1, 5, 11, 13, 16, 33, 98, 105, 114, 131, 150, 171, 196, 233, 272, 296, 306, 323, 330, 344, 387, 469, 502, 518, 570, 595
Tinker, Carol, C163
"To Anthea," A26
"To Preserve a Living Tradition," G39
"To the Wilderness," G10
Tod, Margaret, F124
Toll, Seymour, F600
Tomlinson, Charles, F324
Toronto Globe and Mail, F413
"Tradition, Identity, Desire: H.D.'s Revisionist Strategies in *By Avon River*, *Winter Love*, and *Hermetic Definition*," I49
Tradition and Change: Studies in Contemporary Literature, H4
"Tradition and the Female Talent," H215

Tradition in the Making of Modern Poetry, H56
Transatlantic, A5
Transatlantic Review, C62
transition, C89; F80
"Translation and Transposition," H73
Travis, S., G226
The Trend of Modern Poetry, H26
"*Tribute to Freud* and the H.D. Myth," H228
"Tribute to H.D.," J14
"*Trilogy* and the *Four Quartets*: Contrapuntal Visions of Spiritual Quest," G261
"*Trilogy* and *The Pisan Cantos*: The Shock of War," G208
Triquarterly, G57
Troy, William, F85, 139
Trueblood, Charles K., F89
"Truth, Dare, Slush, or Promise," F515
The Truth of Poetry: Tensions in Modern Poetry from Baudelaire to the 1960s, H104
Trying to Understand What It Means to Be a Feminist: Essays on Women Writers, F596
Tuatara, F363
Tulsa Studies in Women's Literature, G183, 278
Turksib, C106
"Turtle and Mock Turtle," F36; H98
Turtle Island Foundation, A32
Twenties: Actes du GRENA, H179
Twentieth Century Authors, H47
Twentieth Century Literature, G84, 244, 275
Twentieth Century Writing: A Reader's Guide to Contemporary Literature, H106
20th-Century Poetry, H194
Twentieth-Century English Literature, H84
Twin City Sentinel, F313
Two Cities, C148
"Two Englands," F324
Two Englishwomen in Rome, C121
"Two Notes: I. On H.D.; II. On Imagism," G7
"Two Poems for H.D.," G269
"Two Poetic Moods," F306

General Index of Titles and Names / 227

Two Songs for Voice and Piano, E2
"Two Ways of Spelling It Out: An Archetypal-Feminist Reading of H.D.'s *Trilogy* and Adrienne Rich's *Sources*," G306

Über den tod von Albert Steffen, Béla Bartok, H.D., H154
Ulrich, Hans, H202–3, 210
"Eine Unangepasste," F438, 471
Understanding Poetry, H35
Unger, Barbara, F539
"'Unhelpful Hymen': Marianne Moore and Hilda Doolittle," G87
"Uniqueness with a Note on Vers Libre," F16
"Unity in H.D.'s *War Trilogy*," G72
"Unless a Bomb Falls . . . ," A35; H182
The Unspeakable Mother: Forbidden Discourse in Jean Rhys and H.D., H233
Untermeyer, Jean Starr, C117; H88
Untermeyer, Louis, A6a.i, iv, 11; F15, 40; G16, 18; H3, 12, 17, 40, 107
"Unveiling H.D.," F533
Urtecho, Jose Coronel, D37
Urzidil, Johannes, D11

Valley News Dispatch [Tarentum, Pa.], F406, 455
Van Doren, Mark, A8a.ii; F26, 74, 87
Van Gerven, Claudia, I34
Vanacker, Sabine, G250
Vauxhall, John, F141
Venturi, Adolfo, C83
Venus in Scorpio, C123
Verga, Giovanni, C74
"Vers-Libre in Full Bloom: A Note on the Prosody of Andre Spire: II," G21
"Vertical Verse," F113
Victory in Limbo: Imagism, 1908–1917, H138
Vidal, Amparo Rodriguez, D32
Videntes e sonâmbules: Coletanea de poemas norte-americanos, D29
Vines, Sherard, H20
Virago Collectors Cards, J19
Virago Press, A26a.vi, 34a.iii, 35

Virginia Quarterly Review, C142; F60, 170, 195, 204, 368, 496, 524
"Virginity and Erotic Liminality: H.D.'s *Hippolytus Temporizes*," G281
Vocadlo, Otaka, H27
Vogue, F265
Voices, F44, 124, 237, 560, 562
Von Hopkins bis Dylan Thomas: Englische Gedichte und deutsche Prosaübertragungen, D18
Voring, Georg von der, D17
Votivtavlor: Tolknihgar, D40
"The Voyage In," F104

Waggoner, Hyatt H., H102, 211
Wagner, Charles, F208
Wagner, Linda W., F447, 460; G70; H237
Wagner, R., C82
Wagner-Martin, Linda, F545, 606
Wake, C120, 128
Walkup, Kathy, A32
Wallace, Emily, C1; G85, 173, 207; H193
Wallace Stevens Journal: A Publication of the Wallace Stevens Society, G271
Walpole, Hugh, B12
Walsh, John, A9b, 10b.i, 18b, 26a.iv; G264; H216
Walston, Charles, C85
Walton, Eda Lou, F122
"Wandlungers in der Naturkonzeption in der amerikanischen Lyrik des 20. Jahrhunderts," H202
The War of the Words, H225
Ward, A. C., H84, 113, 143
Warner, Rex, F335
Warren, Robert Penn, H35, 124
Washington [D.C.] Blade, F542
Washington [D.C.] Post, F282, 514, 535, 579; J30
Washington [D.C.] Times, F490
Wasserman, Rosanne, I38
Waterman, Cary, F581
Watts, Emily Stipes, H151
Watts, Harold H., G34; H59, 194
Waugh, Arthur, H4
WCW & Others, H207; G156
We Are Voyagers, Discoverers: H.D.'s Trilogy *and Modern Religious Poetry*, H244

We Moderns, H42
"We Speak As We Can," F32
Weatherhead, A. Kingsley, G72; H96, 228
"A Weaving at the Zollbrücke in Zürich," H216
Weinstein, Norman, F427
Weirick, Bruce, H13
Die weiten Horizonte / The Vast Horizons: Amerikanische Lyrik 1638 bis 1980, D19
Die Welt, F478
Wescott, Glenway, F12
Western Morning News [Plymouth], F174
"What Are Poets Saying?" F354
"What Do Women (Poets) Want?: Marianne Moore and H.D. as Poetic Ancestresses," G172
"What Is Not Said: A Study in Textual Inversion," G279
"What's in a Box?: Psychoanalytic Concept and Literary Technique in H.D.," H216
What the Poem Means: Summaries of 1,000 Poems, H108
"'What Words Say': Three Women Poets Reading H.D.," G258
Whitall, James, H31
Whitby Gazette, F183
White, Eric Walter, B18; H149
"White Lightning," F85
Whitman, Alden, F580
Whitman, C117
"Who Buried H.D.? A Poet, Her Critics, and Her Place in 'The Literary Tradition,'" G79; H228
Wide Angle, G132
Wilhelm, James J., G149
Wilkerson, David J., G304
Wilkinson, Marguerite, H5
Will, Frederick, F574; H78
William Carlos Williams: A New World Naked, H174
William Carlos Williams Newsletter, G85
Williams, Ellen, H152
Williams, Grace, E5
Williams, Henry L., G298
Williams, Oscar, F162
Williams, William Carlos, B7, 9; F50; G33; H57

"Williams and H.D., or Sour Grapes," G244
"Williams, Pound, H.D.: A Modern Triangle," G156; H207
Williams-Ellis, A., F21, 32
Wilner, Paul, F412
Wilson, James Southall, F60
Wilson Bulletin for Librarians, G23
"Wind in the Garden: A Reading of H.D.'s *Sea Garden*," G202
Wingbeat, J18
Winks, Robin W., H222
Winter, Helmut, F475
Winters, Ivor, H51
"With a Little Song," F558
Without Flaw, F59
Witte, Sarah E., G273
Wolfe, Ann F., F261
Wolle, Francis, H123
Woman + Woman: Attitudes toward Lesbianism, H132
"'Woman Is Perfect': H.D.'s Debate with Freud," G113
"The Woman Poet and Her Muse: Sources and Images of Female Creativity in the Poetry of H.D., Louise Bogan, May Sarton, and Adrienne Rich," I21
"Woman Poet Writes of Lover, Ezra Pound," F406
"Women as Poets," F26
Women of the Left Bank, F145, 608; H212
"Women the Inventors," G76
"The Women Writers: 1986 Calendar," J23
"Women's Freud(e): H.D.'s *Tribute to Freud* & Gladys Schmitt's *Sonnets for an Analyst*," G137
Women's Review, G176
Women's Review of Books, F520
Women's Studies, G90, 103–4, 110, 157, 191
"Woof and Heave and Surge and Wave and Flow," H216
Worcester [Mass.] Evening Gazette, F390
"A World-Famous Poet Remembered at Home," J7
World Literature Today, F294, 426, 461, 522, 546
Wortsman, Harold, A24c.iii

"Wounded Woman: H.D.'s Post-Imagist Writing," H192
W.P.M., F165
Wright, F. A., C72
Wright, Patrick Stephen, I16
"Write, Write, or Die: The Goddess Muse of H.D.," H213
Writing beyond the Ending, H204
"The Writing Cure: Transference and Resistance in a Dialogic Analysis," G247
Writing for Their Lives: The Modernist Women, 1910–1940, H221
Writing like a Woman, G144; H189
"Writing on the Wall—With Freud," F279
Wylie, Elinor, A11

Yale Review, C141, 165; F47, 169, 192, 202
Yalom, Marilyn, G125, 139
Yeats, William Butler, C175
"A Young American Poet," G4
"Young Ezra Pound through H.D.'s Eyes," F414
"Youthful Days and Costly Hours," H193

Zajdel, Melody M., G175, 191; H170; I17
Zaturenska, Marya, H50
Zigal, Thomas, G156; H207
Zilboorg, Caroline, G268–69, 276, 288; H245
Zinnes, Harriet, F373
Zonë, G199
Zürich Samstag, F320
Zwei amerikanische Dichterinnen: Emily Dickinson und Hilda Doolittle, G91